FRANCE AND BRITAIN 1940–1994:
THE LONG SEPARATION

FRANCE AND BRITAIN 1940–1994:

The Long Separation

P. M. H. Bell

*To Caroline Cracraft,
With warm good wishes
from the author, on the
occasion of the Kemper
Lecture.   St. Louis, 19 March 1999.*

Philip Bell

Longman
London and New York

Addison Wesley Longman Limited
Edinburgh Gate, Harlow
Essex CM2O 2JE, England
and Associated Companies throughout the World

*Published in the United States of America
by Addison Wesley Longman Inc., New York*

First published 1997

ISBN 0 582 289203 PPR
ISBN 0 582 289211 CSD

British Library Cataloguing-in-Publication Data

A catalogue record for this book is
available from the British Library

Library of Congress Cataloging-in-Publication Data

Bell, P. M. H. (Philip Michael Hett), 1930–
    France and Britain 1940–1994: the long separation / P.M.H. Bell.
    p. cm.
    Includes bibliographical references and index.
    ISBN 0-582-28920-3
    1. Great Britain— Foreign relations—1945– 2. Great Britain—
Foreign relations—1936–1945. 3. World War, 1939–1945—Diplomatic
history. 4. Great Britain—Foreign relations—France. 5. France—
Foreign relations—Great Britain. 6. France—Foreign
relations—1940–1945. 7. France—Foreign relations—1945–
I. Title.
DA589.8.B45 1997
327.41044—dc20   96-28654
                                                                          CIP

Set by 7 in 10/12 Bembo
Produced by Longman Singapore Publishers (Pte) Ltd.
Printed in Singapore

Contents

Contents

Preface and Acknowledgements

This book completes the story of Franco-British relations and views across the Channel in the twentieth century, begun in *France and Britain 1900–1940: Entente and Estrangement*. It starts with the painful separation between the two countries in the summer of 1940, and comes up to the opening of the Channel Tunnel in 1994. The writing has been a labour of love, and I hope that this book will appeal to all those in Britain who hold France high in their affection, as well as to those whose work leads them to make a study of relations between the two countries. (The two categories doubtless overlap a good deal.)

For a second time, I am happy to acknowledge, with warm gratitude, the many obligations I have incurred. I owe a great debt to those friends who have read drafts, with keen eyes and careful judgement: David Dutton, John Lukacs, Ralph White and Charles Williams. The University of Liverpool allowed me a year's study leave to work on this book; the British Academy and the Association for the Study of Modern and Contemporary France awarded me research grants, for which I am most grateful. I have learned much from conversations with participants in the events described in this book, and I am particularly grateful to the following for allowing me to take up their time and learn from their experience: Charles Bremner, Francis Cammaerts, Jean-Louis Crémieux-Brilhac, Sir Nicholas Henderson, Pierre Maillard, Maurice Schumann, Jean-Marie Soutou, Hugh Verity.

Much of the research, reading and writing was carried out during long residence in Paris. I was made most welcome by French historians, and learned much in seminars and even more from conversation.

From a lifetime of work on this subject, there is much archival research behind this book; but by its nature it is primarily a work of synthesis. My main intellectual debts are to those who have worked in the field before me, and I gladly offer my recognition in the bibliographical essay. It is inevitable that the texture of the work grows thinner as we approach very recent times, when the archives are not yet open and perspectives are foreshortened; but there are already pioneers even on the newest paths. Footnotes are used to give sources for quotations and statistics, and sometimes to refer to differing views of complicated issues. Quotations from French sources have been translated, in nearly every case by my wife, who has indeed shared all the toils and delights of this book from start to finish.

Two points relating to style and presentation deserve particular mention. One is a matter of nomenclature. France and the French are relatively straightforward words, which may be used with little fear of misunderstanding. Britain, on the other hand, is a short-hand expression, to denote the state whose proper title is the United Kingdom of Great Britain and Northern Ireland; and British describes a nationality within which the English, Scots, Welsh and Northern Irish have retained distinct identities. The French often refer simply to 'Angleterre' and 'les Anglais', even when they mean Britain and the British; and in translating quotations I have followed the practice of the French writers concerned. For my own part, I have tried to refer always to Britain, and to Franco-British relations, whenever that is proper, reserving England and Anglo-French relations for their own precise meanings.

The other matter is the use of initials and abbreviations. We live in an age where abbreviations proliferate: NATO, EEC, CAP, EMU, and so on. Their purpose is usually the admirable one of securing brevity, but they can also lead to obscurity, partly because they pass so quickly out of fashion. (Who except a few specialists now remembers what FRITALUX stood for? It might well have been a cooking oil or a washing powder.) Therefore, except in a few very well-known cases (e.g. NATO for the North Atlantic Treaty Organisation, EEC for the European Economic Community), I have written out names in full, using abbreviations only in close proximity to the full versions.

P. M. H. Bell
Paris and Kew
1994–96

Introduction

France and Britain 1900–1940: Entente and Estrangement examined relations between the two countries in the first part of the twentieth century.[1] That book ended with the German victory in France in June 1940, the French armistice, and the British determination to fight on. At that point, the two countries had gone from the *Entente cordiale* earlier in the century to a profound estrangement. It remained to be seen how permanent that estrangement would prove to be. The present book takes up the story at the end of June 1940, and brings it to the opening of the Channel Tunnel in 1994. As before, the main thread is the political relationship between France and Britain, interwoven with military and economic sub-plots, and combined with discussion of the images which the two countries have formed of one another over the years. This last strand – views across the Channel – is less prominent than in the earlier book, at least in part because it seems that Franco-British relations did not fully recover from the estrangement of 1940, when France and Britain took such radically different courses.

The story thus begins with the impact of the Second World War, whose effects had still to work themselves out even half a century later. The extraordinary relationship between Churchill and de Gaulle, with its strange combination of friendship and hostility, anger and respect, has left an enduring mark on the history of their two countries. De Gaulle was right to claim later that by his decision to fight on in 1940, and by his very presence at the side of the British, he saved the *Entente cordiale*. Equally, Churchill's long-standing affection for France was if anything deepened by the events of the war. Even he

1. P.M.H. Bell, *France and Britain 1900–1940: Entente and Estrangement* (London, 1996).

1

can seldom have been more moved than when he and de Gaulle walked down the Champs Elysées together on 11 November 1944. Yet the two great statesmen often quarrelled as though they were scarcely grown up, and Britain and France sometimes adopted completely opposite policies – most obviously in Syria and the Lebanon.

The wider impact of the war was similarly ambiguous. In France the Vichy regime and the various attempts at collaboration with Germany breathed new life into the Anglophobia inherited from the past. Yet many Frenchmen (and women for that matter) developed an immense admiration for the British stand against Germany, and by the end of the war there was a fund of goodwill in France towards the British people that lasted for many years. Among those 'happy few', both British and French, who worked closely together in dangerous flights to and from France, or in Resistance networks, bonds were forged of a peculiar intensity which was probably impossible except in the extreme circumstances of clandestine warfare. The atmosphere in Normandy in 1994, during the commemoration of the D-Day landings, showed that this goodwill, at different levels, was far from exhausted after 50 years. By a quirk of human nature, it co-existed in France with an ashamed resentment of the fact that Britain had held out when France surrendered. That sentiment too was enduring, and signs of it – though not often displayed – were still present in 1994.

The British too nursed contradictory feelings about France. During the German occupation of France from 1940 to 1944, British Francophiles had the sensation that a light had gone out of the world and that they were excluded from their second homeland. For some, indeed, this was literally true, because in 1940 Britons long resident in France were forced to flee, and an intimate bond between the two countries was broken. With the Liberation, the Francophiles rediscovered France with a sense of excitement and exhilaration which still shines out even from the printed page. Those who shared such emotions were few in number, but they were prominent on the radio and in the press, where Denis Brogan, Darsie Gillie and others presented a remarkably sympathetic view of France during all the vicissitudes of defeat, occupation and liberation. In the country as a whole, however, different sentiments prevailed. There was a strong feeling that France had let Britain down in 1940. The secret of de Gaulle's popularity in Britain during the war lay in the simple fact that he stood firm when others yielded; but de Gaulle was the exception. The British felt that the French as a whole had been found wanting in the great hour of trial. Later, in 1944–45, many of the British (including some of the troops involved) had a sense that the French were not sufficiently grateful for their liberation, a sentiment which easily found justification because the French (led by de Gaulle himself) began at once to nurture the myth that they had liberated themselves. This was bound to jar on British susceptibilities, and it has continued to do so.

French and British thus regarded one another with a mixture of admiration, affection and resentment. The war ended amid a confusion of emotions, and there were no simple views of each other.

After the war, cultural and personal links between the two countries resumed, though in different ways from those in earlier times. The old patrician elite of British Francophiles found life hard in the straitened circumstances of post-war Britain, and villas on the Riviera tended to be far out of reach. For everyone, tight controls on foreign exchange made visits to France difficult and residence almost impossible, except on official or commercial business. Even so, the British love of France was not dead, but only dormant. The lure of the sunshine of the south, and the *douceur de vivre* to be found almost everywhere, remained strong. In the 1970s and 1980s a fresh spring of admiration for France began to flow, and a new movement of British settlement in France began. The new migrants came from a far wider social range than their predecessors. They bought houses, not in Nice or Cannes, but in the countryside and small towns in Normandy, the Dordogne and the hinterland of Provence. The appeal of a move to a new life was well caught in Peter Mayle's books, *A Year in Provence* and *Toujours Provence*, whose immense success grew out of the new wave of settlement and then encouraged its continuation.

At the same time, British interest in French culture and politics remained keen. French writers set fashions in the novel. French cinema enjoyed a vast prestige. The problems of the Fourth Republic were discussed with sympathetic understanding, and the success of the Fifth analysed with a touch of bafflement and envy – how *did* the French manage to do it? Interest in France never flagged among British intellectuals, academics and journalists.

Opinion in France took a different course. There was little by way of a reverse flow of settlement. London constantly attracted thousands of French people, to work or learn English (or both); but there were very few French purchasers of houses in the countryside or small towns. A French best-seller on the lines of Peter Mayle (*Une année à Yorkshire*, perhaps) is hard to imagine. This is partly a matter of the weather – or at least of French beliefs about the British weather. It is also because, in French eyes, Britain is dwarfed by the vast size and influence of the United States, and the two tend to be lumped together as 'les Anglo-Saxons'. The pull of America, through popular culture of all kinds, is enormous. French politicians and intellectuals tend to deplore it; most of the French public welcome it, as cinema attendances and sales in record shops testify. Either way, British culture and ways of life tend to be swamped by the American versions, and sometimes suffer from an anti-American backlash. At the same time, the former serious-minded French interest in Britain, exemplified earlier in the century by Bardoux, Siegfried and Bourdan, has diminished. As François Crouzet (who is one of the exceptions to this trend) has pointed out, it would be difficult to find in France the enthusiasm and the numbers which sustain two strong British academic associations for the study of French history and contemporary affairs.

It is interesting to compare this state of affairs with the development of French relations with Germany. Since the early 1960s French governments have worked assiduously to promote cultural links with Germany. Educational programmes, student exchanges, cultural events and governmental co-operation of all kinds sometimes have an air of force-feeding, but have none the less produced a genuine growth of Franco-German contacts and goodwill. The contrast with British methods is striking. The British who fall under the spell of France, buy a house there and settle down, act as individuals, on their own impulse. Everything is spontaneous and undirected. French links with Germany, on the other hand, are very largely organised by governments or other official agencies, and there seems to be little spontaneous German settlement in France. Yet in many ways 'le couple France–Allemagne' flourishes, while France and Britain have somehow drifted apart. A mention of 'le couple France–Angleterre' at a party in Paris was greeted by a French wit with the comment 'A couple who don't sleep together!'

From time to time there have been hopes that this gap might be bridged by technological co-operation – the couple may not sleep together, but they can work together to build the Concorde supersonic plane or the Channel Tunnel. Concorde was a remarkable technical achievement; it is still flying, but has never made money and has had no successor. It remains to be seen whether the Tunnel will fulfil either the hopes or the fears which were so freely attached to it. 'England is no longer an island' was the theme of much French comment when the Tunnel opened. The British tended to feel much the same, though many of them were unhappy about it. But will what is essentially only an unusual railway line really transform attitudes and relations between the two countries and peoples? It seems very doubtful.

In political relations, there was perhaps at the end of the Second World War a real opportunity to give fresh substance to the *Entente cordiale*. Indeed, in 1947 a Franco-British treaty was signed at Dunkirk. But little came of this opportunity, insofar as it really existed. From 1950 onwards, relations between France and Britain were increasingly dominated by the issue of European integration, which became a cause of recurrent friction between the two countries. The Schuman Plan of 1950 for a European Coal and Steel Community was a French initiative, rejected by Britain – though in circumstances where the French virtually invited rejection. Thereafter, France pursued a policy of European integration with skill and success, not least in securing French advantages within the new structures. In the process, the French forged a new partnership with Germany, which has been one of the marvels of the late twentieth century.

Britain too had a European policy, but one based on alliances and co-operation between governments, not on integration. British policy was also very much Atlanticist in outlook, placing great emphasis on the North Atlantic alliance with the USA against the Soviet Union, and not on Europe as a possible 'third force' between the United States and the USSR. Not until 1961 did the British change at least a part of their mind and apply to join the European Economic Community. In that very phrase there lay a landmark in British relations with France. To make an application implied the possibility of rejection, and no-one doubted that the power of decision lay with France, and above all with General de Gaulle. For many a long year, since the end of the First World War at least, the British had thought of themselves as the senior partner in any dealings with France. The events of the Second World War had confirmed them in that belief. Now suddenly the position was reversed. It was open to de Gaulle to treat the British not so much as applicants as supplicants, and he rejected their approaches with a severity which bordered on the brutal. He did so twice, in 1963 and 1967, in a drastic reversal of roles between the two countries.

In principle, this 'European' bone of contention between Britain and France might have been removed in the early 1970s. Britain applied once more to join the EEC, this time successfully, with the support of President Pompidou of France. Membership took effect from 1 January 1974. The terms of entry were later revised, on the request of Harold Wilson; and in 1975 the British people were consulted by referendum as to whether the country should remain a member or not. The result showed a two-thirds majority in favour, though only two-thirds of the electorate voted. But in practice the friction between Britain and France continued. The British people were only doubtful converts to the European idea, and Britain was often the odd man out in the EEC, particularly on matters involving supranationalism and loss of sovereignty.

It is a sign of the importance of France in British eyes that British opinion has seen relations with the European Community largely in terms of relations with France. France has dominated the British horizon, sometimes with grievous effects. Friction between the two countries was for several years concentrated and heightened, rather than diminished, through their common membership of the EEC. They quarrelled about contributions to the Community budget; about moves towards greater integration, notably the European Monetary System; and about comparatively minor economic matters like the export of British lamb to France. (French farmers burning lorry-loads of British lamb made spectacular television pictures and big headlines in Britain.) It was as though France and Britain, after being actors on the world stage earlier in the century, now found themselves backstage at a local theatre. Their quarrels seemed worse for being confined in a small space. These quarrels loomed larger for Britain than for France, because the French outlook was not dominated by relations with Britain but with Germany. For them, the Franco–German axis lay at the centre of European affairs.

These changes in relations between France and Britain have been accompanied by another transformation, difficult to delineate with precision but far-reaching in its significance. At some stage in the late 1950s and early 1960s, the spirit of self-confidence crossed the Channel, leaving Britain and settling in France. The 1960s saw a *malaise* and loss of confidence in Britain, which reached its nadir among the disasters of the 1970s, and persisted into the 1990s with the widespread questioning of British institutions. In France, the return of General de Gaulle to power in 1958 and a prolonged period of economic growth restored self-confidence. The recovery was not complete. Memories of 1940 and the years of occupation have not been entirely exorcised. The French economy faltered after its long boom. Large-scale immigration from North Africa brought serious problems which have not been resolved. But for some 30 years, from the 1960s to the 1980s, the French displayed a faith in their country, culture and way of life which was stronger than any such faith in Britain. This contrast became clear in the views taken in one country of the other. French commentators, when interested in Britain at all, concentrated on analysing British decline and its causes. (One writer actually thought it time to conduct an autopsy on England.[2]) British observers of France, on the other hand, were concerned to enquire how the French had managed to do so much better than the British. Why were French standards of living higher? Why did the French high-speed trains work while the British versions did not? Why was Paris clean and London dirty? Such questions had not been asked earlier in the century, and they were symptomatic of the new contrast in self-confidence.

In these various ways the signs of a long separation became apparent. Relations between Britain and France have become largely a one-sided affair. The British remain highly conscious of France – the nearest foreign country, a frequent destination for holidays, and a favourite place to live. Europe, whether as a geographical expression or in the political sense of the European Community (or Union), usually means first and foremost France. The French, on the other hand, regard Britain as only one of a number of neighbouring countries, and by no means the most important – a role which they allot to Germany. For the British, France still looms large, as an object of love or dislike. For the French, Britain has moved to the periphery of their vision compared to the situation in the first half of the century. Their relationship shows a thinning of the close texture of interdependence, even intimacy, of earlier years.

This will not always be so, and may not even be the case for very long. Situations change, sometimes with startling rapidity, and the kaleidoscope of relations between France and Britain may be shaken up again at any time. What does not change is geography, which will not permit the two countries to separate from one another, however much they may be estranged from time to time. History too has bound them together, and there is no sign that history has come to an end. Relations between the two countries and their peoples make a fascinating study. We may never be able to end it in the manner of old-fashioned fairy stories, 'and they lived happily ever after'; but neither will any separation, however long, prove permanent. This book looks at one episode in a liaison which has sometimes proved dangerous, but never dull.

2. François David, *Autopsie de l'Angleterre* (Paris, 1976). As in the case of Mark Twain's death, the reports proved exaggerated.

CHAPTER 1

The Parting of the Ways, 1940

On 3 September 1939 Britain and France declared war on Germany, and for the second time in a quarter of a century became comrades in arms against the same enemy. This time, their unity was reinforced by the sense of being the champions of parliamentary democracy against the rising tide of Nazi totalitarianism. For several months there was very little military activity in western Europe, where the two systems of fortifications (the French Maginot Line and the German Siegfried Line) stood facing one another. During this uneasy lull of the phoney war, the British and French set themselves to recreate the machinery of co-operation which they had developed slowly and painfully during the previous war of 1914–18. A Supreme War Council was soon convened, and met regularly, so that the two Prime Ministers were in frequent consultation. Arrangements for economic co-operation were rapidly made, and a system for joint purchasing in the United States was resumed, with Jean Monnet resuming the guiding role he had first played as a young man in 1917. On 28 March 1940 the two governments issued a joint declaration that they would make no separate armistice or peace with the enemy, and that they would continue their co-operation after peace was made. In the spring of 1940 there was much discussion, between governments and in the press of both countries, as to how this co-operation should be fostered and organised, and there was talk of seeking some form of 'union' between Britain and France. The two countries would thus form a solid block to guarantee the peace and security of Europe when the war was over.

To all appearances the alliance was in good working order, and relations between the two countries cordial. There were naturally some difficulties. The French found the build-up of the British

Expeditionary Force (BEF) in France painfully slow – starting with four divisions in October 1939, it reached only ten by the beginning of May 1940. The British for their part were anxious about the state of French politics. Daladier's government, which had taken France into the war, fell in March 1940, and was replaced by a ministry headed by Paul Reynaud, which in the Chamber of Deputies secured a majority of only one vote over its opponents and those who abstained. The British also feared the strength of opinion in the French parliament in favour of a negotiated peace. But despite such difficulties, the alliance worked well during the calm of the eight-month phoney war, from September 1939 to April 1940.

THE DEFEAT OF FRANCE: ARMISTICE

That calm was shattered by a storm of utterly unexpected ferocity. On 10 May the Germans opened a great offensive in the west, invading the Netherlands, Belgium and France. On 20 May the German armoured spearheads reached Abbeville, near the mouth of the river Somme; the next day they stood on the Channel coast. To the north of this thrust, a large French army, the BEF and the Belgian Army were cut off from the main body of the French forces to the south. There followed the evacuation from Dunkirk, which the British regarded as a miraculous escape but which was none the less a tremendous military defeat. The French, who provided the rearguard for the evacuation and resented the fact that the British got away first, did not regard the operation as any sort of miracle.

The Dunkirk evacuation ended in the early hours of 4 June. On the 5th, sustaining a remarkable pace and momentum, the Germans resumed their offensive against the rest of the French Army and the remaining fragment of the BEF, now consisting of only two divisions. For a few days the French sustained the battle with greater intensity than before, suffering heavy casualties. (It is still not generally recognised in Britain that during the short campaign of 1940 the French Army sustained about 100,000 dead, representing a much higher weekly average than that suffered at Verdun in 1916; though of course the ordeal of Verdun went on far longer.) But by 9–10 June the Germans had breached the French defences on the rivers Somme and Aisne, and in the next few days co-ordinated resistance by the French forces came to an end. The Germans advanced with

9

astonishing speed, fanning out westwards into Brittany and southwards to the Loire and beyond.[1]

On 12 June General Weygand, the French Commander-in-Chief, formally told the French Cabinet that the government should seek an armistice. For the next few days the French government pursued an agonised discussion on whether to ask for an armistice or to carry on the war from outside France, probably from French North Africa. On 15 June they agreed to ascertain German terms, in principle on the grounds that these would certainly prove unacceptable and then the government could pursue the struggle from North Africa with the assurance of public support. Accepting that there was an agreement with Britain not to make a separate armistice, the French government asked British permission to seek terms. On 16 June the British War Cabinet at first agreed, on condition that the French fleet was at once moved to British ports. They then followed this by making an extra-ordinary offer of union between Britain and France, which, the proposal declared, 'shall no longer be two nations, but one Franco-British Union'.[2] This proposal was welcomed by Reynaud, the French Premier, but brushed aside as unwelcome or irrelevant by his Cabinet colleagues. One minister said that the British were trying to turn France into a Dominion – a phrase which was to produce a strange echo when Guy Mollet sought to revive the proposal in 1956. Meanwhile, the earlier British condition about the French fleet sailing to British ports (which revealed the central British anxiety in the matter of an armistice) was lost in the confusion. The British government intended only to suspend their previous message when the offer of union was made; the Ambassador at Bordeaux (where the French government then was) used the word 'cancel'.

During the evening of 16 June Reynaud resigned as Premier, and the President of the Republic asked Marshal Pétain to form a government, which he did with remarkable speed – it is said that he pulled a list of ministers out of his pocket at once. Pétain was then 84 years of age, the only surviving Marshal of France, the victor of

1. For a fuller discussion of the battle of France and its effects on relations between France and Britain, see P.M.H. Bell, *France and Britain 1900–1940: Entente and Estrangement* (London, 1996). The French military casualties of about 100,000 killed were sustained in just over six weeks, from 10 May to 24 June 1940, an average of about 16,600 per week. In the seven months of the German offensive at Verdun (Feb.–Aug. 1916), which is universally recognised to have comprised some of the grimmest fighting of the First World War, the French dead numbered about 315,000, or some 12–13,000 per week on average. Of course the circumstances were very different, but the comparison remains striking.

2. On the offer of union, see P.M.H. Bell, *A Certain Eventuality: Britain and the Fall of France* (Farnborough, 1979), pp. 72–6; the text is printed on pp. 304–5.

Verdun in 1916, and perhaps above all the commander who was generally acknowledged to have been sparing of the lives of his men during the First World War. His prestige was high, and was shortly to become enormous as he emerged as a father-figure and protector for a nation in defeat. Meanwhile, there was no doubt in anyone's mind that he had been appointed Premier to ask for an armistice. Straight away, at half-past midnight on the morning of 17 June, the new Foreign Minister, Paul Baudouin, met the Spanish Ambassador and asked him to transmit to Germany a request for terms for an armistice and for peace. There was no longer any question of requesting British permission for this step; and at 1 a.m. Baudouin simply told the British Ambassador what he had done.

There was a long delay before Hitler in person received the French armistice delegation on 21 June at Rethondes, in the same clearing in the Forest of Compiègne where the armistice had been signed in November 1918. The German terms were severe, but from the French point of view not disastrous. The Germans demanded the occupation of nearly two-thirds of France, including Paris and all the Channel and Atlantic coasts. The French Army was to be reduced to 100,000 men, with a level of armaments to be decided by Germany. The fleet (about which the British were so anxious) was to be demobilised and disarmed under German or Italian supervision at the peacetime stations of the various warships concerned. The Germans undertook not to use the French warships for their own purposes. All factories, ports, shipyards and means of communication in the occupied zone of France were to be handed over to the Germans in their existing state. The costs of the occupation (which were left unspecified) were to be met by the French government. All German prisoners of war in French hands were to be released at once, but French prisoners of war were to remain in captivity until the conclusion of peace. Taken together, these provisions gave the Germans both an economic and a human hold over France. The French government was to hand over on demand any German nationals on its territory – a clause aimed at Jews and anti-Nazis who had taken refuge in France in earlier years. The French delegation made a few counter-proposals, which were rejected; and on 22 June, on the instructions of his government, General Huntziger signed the armistice agreement. An armistice with Italy, on similar lines but involving only a very small Italian zone of occupation, was signed on 24 June. Both armistices came into force at 12.35 a.m. on 25 June.

Until the actual signature of the Franco-German armistice and the receipt of news about its terms, the British government was in a state

11

of uncertainty about events in France. They continued to hope that all or part of the French government would leave Bordeaux for Algiers, and there continue the war. They therefore hesitated to do anything to oppose Pétain's government or undermine its authority. They were thus cautious in their support for General de Gaulle, the former commander of a French armoured division and for a few days a junior minister in Reynaud's government, who flew from Bordeaux on 17 June and arrived in London to continue the war. At first, he received a tepid welcome. On 18 June the Minister of Information, the Francophile Duff Cooper, proposed that de Gaulle should broadcast on the BBC that evening. The War Cabinet, with Chamberlain in the chair in Churchill's absence, refused permission, on the ground that such a broadcast would give offence to the French government at a time when it might still act in accordance with British wishes by going to North Africa. It was only on Churchill's personal intervention that this decision was reversed, and de Gaulle was allowed to make the broadcast which later became famous and was the basis for all his later career. What he said, and its significance, will be examined in the next chapter. At the time, this did not mean that the British government had fundamentally changed its mind. Halifax, the Foreign Secretary, continued to argue that Britain should avoid offending what he called the better elements in Bordeaux. A proposal by de Gaulle for another broadcast on 19 June was turned down by the Foreign Office in favour of a more cautious version, and thereafter he did not broadcast for some days. The British still hoped that the Pétain government, or some of its members, would go to Algiers and rally the fleet and the French Empire to carry on the war. It was only on the evening of 22 June, when the War Cabinet met with a summary of the armistice terms before it and knew that the French had accepted them, that this hope was abandoned. They then concluded that the breaking-point with Pétain's government had come.

The next day, 23 June, Churchill made a broadcast expressing his 'grief and amazement' that the French government had agreed to terms which he described as unacceptable to any government possessing 'freedom, independence and constitutional authority'. The armistice placed France and its Empire in the power of the enemy, and all French resources, including the fleet, would speedily pass into German hands. Churchill promised, despite this, that he would continue to cherish the cause of the French people, and called on all Frenchmen to aid the forces of liberation. This distinction between Pétain's government and the French people was made more emphatic in a government statement, broadcast on the BBC on 24 June, to the effect that the armistice placed the Bordeaux government in complete subjection to the enemy, so that it could no longer be considered as the government of an independent country. On the same day Churchill told the War Cabinet that relations between Britain and the French government 'might well approach very closely to those of two nations at war with each other'.[3] It was a far cry from the close alliance that had prevailed at the beginning of May, little more than six weeks earlier.

THE FRENCH FLEET: MERS-EL-KEBIR

After the armistice was concluded, the key question for both France and Britain was the fate of the French fleet. For France, the fleet was of both symbolic and practical importance. It was the only part of the French armed forces that had survived the defeat intact, and so it symbolised what remained of French pride. Politically, it offered a bargaining counter in future negotiations with Germany, and some defence for the French Empire, stretched vulnerably across the globe. For Britain, it presented an acute danger. The French fleet was a powerful and modern force, which in German hands would tip the balance of sea power and provide cover for a seaborne invasion of England. The British had long contemplated this danger, and could not accept the risk.

The crucial clause in the Franco-German armistice was Article 8, which laid down that French warships were to be demobilised and disarmed at their peacetime stations under German or Italian supervision, according to the port concerned. For two-thirds of the fleet, the ports were Lorient, Brest, Cherbourg or Dunkirk, which were all in the German occupation zone. The French government, and especially Admiral Darlan, Minister of Marine, believed that the Germans would try to seize the warships, but were confident that this could be prevented. Darlan issued strict orders that no commander was to hand over an intact ship to the enemy. Crews were to be prepared to scuttle their ships if the enemy tried to seize them. Darlan himself, Baudouin (the Foreign Minister) and the President of the Republic all sent the British government messages assuring them that in no circumstances would the fleet be allowed to fall into German hands or be used against Britain. These assurances were entirely sincere.

3. Ibid., pp. 102–4.

For some time the British were divided in their views and uncertain as to what to do. The War Cabinet discussed the question on 22 June, after learning the terms of the armistice. Admiral Pound, the First Sea Lord, had visited Bordeaux to talk to Darlan on 18 June, and believed that the French would and could make good their assurances. Churchill declared that in a matter so crucial to British safety they could not afford to rely on the word of Darlan, who might after all be replaced at any moment. Halifax recommended that the British should try all means of persuasion to get the French to place their ships in safety before resorting to force. Churchill agreed, but only on condition that the main point was kept firmly in view: 'in no circumstances must we run the mortal risk of allowing these ships to fall into the hands of the enemy. Rather than that, we should have to fight and sink them'.[4]

On 25 June, after the armistices had come into force, Churchill spoke to the House of Commons. On the terms relating to the French fleet, he said:

> From this text it is clear that the French war vessels under this armistice pass into German and Italian control while fully armed. We note, of course, in the same Article the solemn declaration of the German Government that they have no intention of using them for their own purposes during the war. What is the value of that? Ask half a dozen countries what is the value of such a solemn assurance.[5]

There was no doubt of the answer. Hitler had broken so many promises that there was not the slightest chance the British would believe him. There was no dissent in the House, and the press was unanimous that no risks must be taken. The Labour *Daily Herald* was typical in declaring that if French warships tried to sail to their home ports they must be prevented from doing so. Addressing the Prime Minister, the leader-writer declared that 'in taking action to this end you will have the firmest support of the British people'.[6]

At that time, there were only a few French warships in home waters. All the other ships had sailed to British ports at the time of the request for an armistice, or were in North African ports, at Alexandria in Egypt, or at Dakar in West Africa. The largest single concentration was at Mers-el-Kébir, in Algeria, where there were two modern battle-cruisers (the *Dunkerque* and the *Strasbourg*), two old battleships and several smaller warships. If Article 8 of the armistice was to be

4. Ibid., p. 144.
5. Hansard, *H.C. Deb.*, 5th series, vol. 362, cols 304–5.
6. *Daily Herald*, leading article, 26 June 1940.

14

carried out, the French ships would have to return to their peacetime stations in France. The British problem was how to prevent this. Despite Churchill's stern words in Parliament on 23 June there was still considerable uncertainty among ministers and their advisers as to what to do. It was not until 27 June that Churchill laid down firmly that force would have to be used, and proposed 3 July as the date. Even then doubts persisted. Admiral Somerville, commanding the British force at Gibraltar which would have to deal with the French squadron at Mers-el-Kébir, and Admiral Cunningham at Alexandria, who would have to take action against French warships actually sharing the same harbour, both objected strongly to the proposed operations. They were repelled by the thought of firing on men who until recently had been allies, and Cunningham was also dismayed by the damage which would be caused by a battle inside the port of Alexandria. Both admirals protested, but were firmly overruled. There was a further intervention from France, where the Ministry of Marine was engaged in discussions with the German and Italian Armistice Commissions about the interpretation of the naval terms, and asked the British government to suspend judgement until these talks had been concluded. This had no effect. Churchill told the War Cabinet on 1 July that these conversations could not affect the facts of the situation. The Chiefs of Staff were anxious to end the uncertainty, so that the British warships now watching the various French squadrons could get on with other tasks – of which there were plenty. There was no time to await the results of talks which might be prolonged indefinitely or end unsatisfactorily.

By this time there was no dissent in the War Cabinet. On 1 July the final decisions were taken. Orders were to be sent out on 2 July, and the various operations carried out on the 3rd. On 3 July some 200 French warships and naval auxiliaries were seized in British ports, mostly in Portsmouth and Plymouth. There was almost no fighting, though there was a sharp struggle on board the submarine *Surcouf*, with four killed – one French and three British. It is clear that the French crews, feeling themselves in safe waters, had not maintained the high degree of watchfulness enjoined by their orders from Darlan. At Alexandria, the British and French commanders (Cunningham and Godfroy) both used their own judgement in relation to the instructions from their respective governments. Orders enjoining haste and which might have led to a battle inside the harbour were judiciously ignored, and on 4 July the two admirals reached an agreement by which the French warships discharged their fuel oil and rendered their main armament unserviceable, and in return Cunningham undertook

15

that there would be no attempt to seize the ships by force. This was a triumph for Cunningham's tact in dealing with the French and courage in standing up to Churchill, and for Godfroy's good sense and initiative. It is an episode which deserves to be better remembered than it has been.

At Mers-el-Kébir the outcome was very different. In addition to the two new battle-cruisers and the two battleships there, a strong cruiser squadron lay to the east at Algiers. The British Admiral Somerville commanded two battleships, a battle-cruiser and an aircraft-carrier, so the main forces were evenly matched. Somerville arrived off Mers-el-Kébir in the early morning of 3 July and presented the French commander, Admiral Gensoul, with four choices: (1) to sail to British harbours and continue to fight (i.e. against the Axis); (2) to sail with reduced crews to a British port, from which the crews would be repatriated; (3) to sail with reduced crews to a port in the French West Indies, e.g. Martinique, where the ships would be demilitarised or perhaps entrusted to the United States; (4) to sink their own ships within six hours. If none of these courses was accepted, but the French admiral proposed demilitarisation on the spot, Somerville was authorised to agree, provided that the measures could be carried out within six hours and were sufficient to prevent the ships from being used for a year. Failing any of these, Somerville was ordered to use force to destroy the warships at Mers-el-Kébir.

Throughout the day the British and French commanders negotiated through the British emissary, Captain Holland, a former naval attaché in Paris. It may be that possible chances of success were missed. Gensoul strangely failed to report to his government the full range of choices placed before him, and never explained the possibility of sailing to Martinique. On the British side, the War Cabinet decided not to proceed with the idea of demilitarisation on the spot, which was what Gensoul finally came round to as a way out. However, these were unlikely loopholes. For the French government, any of the options would have meant breaking the armistice terms and so led straight to trouble with the Germans. It seems doubtful whether the British would have wished to detach a strong enough force to escort the French squadron all the way to Martinique. As for demilitarisation on the spot, it was hard to envisage any measures achievable within six hours that would have rendered the ships unusable for a year.

At Mers-el-Kébir, as distinct from Alexandria, there was no time to spare. When the French ships got up steam (a matter of hours) they could use their main armament and put to sea, which would remove the advantage held by the British. Somerville was under orders from

London not to delay, and unlike Cunningham he had no scope for manoeuvre. At 5.54 p.m. (British time; 6.54 for the French) the British ships opened fire, and continued with deadly effect for between ten and fifteen minutes. The battleship *Bretagne* was badly hit, suffered an internal explosion and capsized suddenly, with heavy losses by drowning. The battleship *Provence* and the battle-cruiser *Dunkerque* were badly damaged. On the other hand the battle-cruiser *Strasbourg* (one of the main British targets), together with five destroyers, got clear of the harbour and reached Toulon unscathed. On 6 July British torpedo-bombers from the aircraft-carrier *Ark Royal* carried out another attack on the *Dunkerque*, causing a great explosion on board a vessel lying alongside, inflicting further damage and casualties. In all, the French casualties came to the grim total of 1,297 dead and 351 wounded, with the *Bretagne* alone accounting for over 1,000.[7]

Finally, on 8 July, British naval aircraft attacked the battleship *Richelieu* in harbour at Dakar, inflicting some damage but not enough to prevent her from putting to sea in an emergency. It should also be added that the British seized French merchant vessels amounting to a total of some 450,000 tons – a considerable addition to British shipping resources.[8]

These events caused completely different reactions in Britain and France, at the time and in the years to come. On the British side, the admirals concerned were miserable about their role. Cunningham was scathing about the orders he received from London, and 'interpreted' them with a good deal of latitude. Somerville, who had no such option, wrote to his wife on 4 July that it had been 'an absolutely bloody business to shoot up these Frenchmen, who showed the greatest gallantry. The truth is my heart wasn't in it and you're not allowed a heart in war'. He also commented that it was 'the biggest political blunder of modern times . . . '. He found the attitude of the lower deck quite different, and wrote in a letter of 6 July that 'It doesn't seem to worry the sailors at all as "they never 'ad no use for them French bastards". But to all us Senior Officers it's simply incredible and revolting'.[9]

Churchill reported to the House of Commons on 4 July. In a long speech he emphasised that the naval terms of the French armistice

7. For Mers-el-Kébir and the whole affair of the French fleet, see Arthur J. Marder, *From the Dardanelles to Oran* (London, 1974), Chapter V, pp. 179–288 – the casualty figures are on p. 275; Bell, *A Certain Eventuality*, Chapter 7, pp. 137–64; Hervé Coutau-Bégarie et Claude Huan, *Mers-el-Kébir (1940): La rupture franco-britannique* (Paris, 1994).

8. Coutau-Bégarie et Huan, *Mers-el-Kébir*, p. 160.

9. Marder, *Dardanelles to Oran*, pp. 267–8.

threatened Britain with mortal injury. He paid tribute to the courage of the French sailors, and showed understanding of Gensoul's determination to obey his orders. But he expounded the harsh necessity of what had been done, and added that the action at Mers-el-Kébir should dispose of 'the lies and rumours . . . that we have the slightest intention of entering into negotiations'.[10] MPs received the speech with a remarkable demonstration of support, cheering and waving their order papers; which was all the more noteworthy because up to that time Conservative attitudes towards Churchill had been little more than lukewarm. The press, across the political spectrum, was unanimous in its approval. The *Daily Telegraph* (Conservative) declared that the action was 'a duty which we had no right to shirk'. The *News Chronicle* (Liberal) was ruthless: 'to be weak is to be destroyed'. The *Daily Herald* (Labour) took an elevated tone: 'Every high and honest motive made our Government's decision inescapable.' The general view was that the only alternative to the action taken was to allow the French warships to fall into German hands, which would have amounted to suicide. Most papers tempered their stern approval with expressions of regret at having to fight a former ally, and of sorrow for the loss of French lives. Only the *Daily Mirror* (perhaps closer to the views of Somerville's sailors) wrote that: 'Our hard heart does *not* ache over the decision and the action.' The Ministry of Information's reports on public opinion showed widespread approval of the actions against the French fleet, as being both inevitable in themselves and welcome signs of initiative and a spirit of aggression.[11]

After the war, de Gaulle wrote with distaste in his memoirs of the way the British had gloried in the events of Mers-el-Kébir; and other writers far removed from the General's point of view took the same line. The tone of British comment at the time shows no such tendency, even in the leader columns of the *Daily Mirror*. There was solid, stern and unquestioning support, but no glorying. Quite apart from anything else, there was so much else to think about. Within a few days, the British very largely forgot the whole affair. Attention was concentrated on the threat of invasion, which was thought to be imminent, and then on the aerial Battle of Britain, where real glory was earned by the pilots of Fighter Command. Mers-el-Kébir (which the British tended to call by the easier name of Oran) became merely one half-forgotten episode in a crowded summer. For those who recalled it, it was simply regarded as a desperate measure in desperate

10. Hansard, *H.C. Deb.*, 5th series, vol. 362, cols 1043–51.
11. Bell, *A Certain Eventuality*, p. 159.

times. In historical writing on the events of 1940 the question of the French fleet has received only passing attention, though there have been a few accounts by specialists.

In France, everything was very different. At the time, the funeral ceremonies for those killed at Mers-el-Kébir were solemnly observed. They were photographed for the press and filmed for the news-reels, and made a great impact across the country. The coffins of many of the dead were taken home to Brittany, that cradle of French sailors. The officers of the *Dunkerque* wrote to Admiral Somerville, sending back mementos they had saved from earlier times when they had worked with the Royal Navy, and claiming that the bombardment at Mers-el-Kébir had left an indelible stain on the White Ensign. The whole affair was a gift for propaganda against Britain, and Mers-el-Kébir became a favourite subject for anti-British cartoons. The memory ran deep and long, especially in the French navy. Considerable historical attention has been devoted to the crisis, and particularly to Mers-el-Kébir, of which three studies appeared between 1990 and 1994.[12] The whole episode has proved to be one of those landmarks in relations between France and Britain which is far more prominent from the French side of the Channel than from the British.

In 1956, when French and British forces were in action together during the Suez operation, a French liaison officer heard one of his naval colleagues asking his British opposite number: 'Why did you do it? Why didn't you trust us?' The British naval officer was utterly non-plussed. The Frenchman was talking about Mers-el-Kébir.

Why did the British do it? A good deal of mystery has been created about an essentially simple matter. The times were desperate; invasion seemed imminent; and the British government simply could not afford to risk the Germans seizing control of the French fleet. The British were certain that if the ships were within German reach they would be captured, and if captured they would be used. The German record of speed, efficiency and ruthlessness over the past two or three years was such that the British did not believe that the French would be able to stop them; nor were they inclined to make careful calculations as to how long it might take for the Germans to man the French warships and master their equipment. Churchill's obsession with battle-ships may now seem outdated, but in July 1940, very few battleships in the Channel for a very short time could have been fatal. The

---

12. J-J. Antier, *Le drame de Mers-el-Kébir, 1940* (Paris, 1990); C.V. Rochat, *Pour en savoir plus sur Mers-el-Kébir* (Paris, 1990); Coutau-Bégarie et Huan, *Mers-el-Kébir*. The 50th anniversary of course attracted much attention to the events of 1940.

predominant British motive was thus dire necessity and self-preservation.

There were secondary considerations, of a political and psychological kind. Churchill was anxious to convince the Americans, and above all Franklin Roosevelt, of British determination to fight on; and the French fleet offered a valuable opportunity to do so. On 1 July Roosevelt told the British Ambassador in Washington that American opinion expected the British to seize the French ships rather than let them fall into German hands, and that he himself would do all in his power to promote such an outcome. After the event, the Chairman of the Senate Foreign Relations Committee said that it had been the fear that Britain would *not* act that had undermined American confidence. To convince the Americans of British determination was not the main British motive, but it was a bonus. There was something more. Churchill wished to send to the whole world an unequivocal signal that Britain was as resolute and ruthless as Germany. Mers-el-Kébir was such a signal, to doubters in Britain, to the neutrals, and to the enemy. It was widely received and understood. From Madrid the British Ambassador reported that Spanish opinion had been expecting a quick end to the war, but the attack on the French fleet had brutally destroyed all such hopes. Even in Moscow the action made an impression. Only Hitler, it seemed, did not yet understand. Churchill himself, looking back six months later in January 1941, thought that 'Oran had been the turning-point in our fortunes: it made the world realise that we were in earnest in our intentions to carry on'.[13]

The French on their side were convinced that they were acting rightly. The government, having signed the armistice, had to keep it. Admiral Darlan was unquestionably determined to keep the French fleet out of German hands, though of course more for the sake of France than for that of Britain; and he believed that he had taken all the precautions necessary to do so. The French were therefore sure that they were acting effectively from their own point of view and honourably towards their former ally. Such views have very largely continued to hold good, even among those who supported de Gaulle against Vichy, and among later generations who were not directly involved.

These widely different views, strongly held in each country, carried little weight in the other. Essentially the differences arose from choices made earlier on the fundamental question of war or peace. The British were determined to continue the war, and they followed the logic of

13. Bell, *A Certain Eventuality*, pp. 159–60; Colville diary, 12 Jan. 1941, in John Colville, *The Fringes of Power: Downing Street Diaries 1939–1955* (London, 1985), p. 335.

that decision. The French had decided to end it, and acted accordingly. Each government, by its own lights, acted rightly and out of necessity. The result was a tragic conflict of right against right, which by a strange contrast left the French deeply scarred and the British almost untouched.

The debate has continued, especially in France. At the time, it was not too difficult to draw up a balance-sheet of immediate consequences. The British had seized, sunk or damaged seven out of the nine French capital ships, and secured a number of small warships which would be useful for convoy work. On the other hand the battle-cruiser *Strasbourg* was safe in Toulon, along with a strong force of cruisers and destroyers, manned by crews now bitterly hostile to Britain. The naval balance was thus broadly, but not exclusively, favourable to the British. Politically, there had been some danger that the French government might go to war against Britain in the immediate aftermath of Mers-el-Kébir. Darlan briefly considered making a counter-attack on Somerville's force, intercepting British merchant ships at sea, and sending expeditions against Sierra Leone, the Gambia, or the oilfields of northern Iraq. But political caution and military practicalities prevailed, and all that actually happened was a small bombing raid on Gibraltar on 5 July. Otherwise, the French government confined itself to breaking off diplomatic relations with Britain; and even then they left a diplomatic agent in London. The French also obtained German agreement to the suspension of Article 8 of the armistice, which postponed the movement of French warships to their peacetime stations to be demilitarised. This suspension was never lifted, and so Article 8 became a dead letter. French warships remained where they were, and on a war footing – a dispensation which was in general favourable to the British but on specific occasions – notably at Dakar in September 1940 – worked very much to their disadvantage.

REACTIONS TO SEPARATION

The French armistice of June 1940 and the British determination to fight on set France and Britain on widely divergent courses. Mers-el-Kébir brought them into direct, though limited, conflict with one another. How did opinion in the two countries react to these formidable events? To examine this question we must go back to 17 June and the French request for an armistice.

The first British reactions were remarkably restrained. Churchill set the tone in a short broadcast at 9 p.m. (the peak listening time) on 17 June. 'The news from France is very bad', he began, 'and I grieve for the gallant French people who have fallen into this terrible misfortune. Nothing will alter our feelings towards them, or our faith that the genius of France will rise again. What has happened in France makes no difference to British faith and purpose.' He went on to say that Britain would fight on 'until the curse of Hitler is lifted from the brows of men. We are sure that in the end all will be well'.[14] That was all. This generous and sympathetic lead was widely followed in the press. The *Scotsman*, true to the 'auld alliance', refused to judge France 'in this hour of anguish', and this was typical. Some went further, and acknowledged that Britain bore a share of responsibility for the defeat of France. *The Economist* wrote that 'France has borne the brunt of the military struggle. She has received little help from her neighbour and ally. . . . There can and must be no recrimination'. When the terms of the armistice became known there was a change of tone, but even so the press directed its criticisms towards the Pétain government rather than France or the French people. *The Times* denounced Pétain's government as 'nothing but a puppet of the Nazi regime'. The *Daily Herald*, recalling that Pétain had said he would only accept honourable terms, asked 'If this be honour, what is shame?' The *News Chronicle* declared that 'the Pétain junta' had signed away the fleet, ports and munitions factories 'in cynical disregard of their solemn treaty obligations to a faithful ally . . .'. Accusations of betrayal thus began to emerge, but it was remarkable that they were so muted and took so long to take shape.[15]

These reactions, largely inspired by Churchill's lead, were accompanied by others of a different kind. Among Francophile intellectuals there was an acute sense of loss. A leader-writer for *The Economist* lamented that 'We lose part of ourselves when France's liberties are trampled underfoot'.[16] Raymond Mortimer, novelist and the literary editor of the *New Statesman*, felt as though half of England had fallen into the sea. Denis Brogan, whose affection for France was as deep as his knowledge of her history, wrote that the Pétain government had decided 'to try the daring and despicable experiment of saving all but honour'. But, he continued, there remained France, 'the eternal France, to which we will extend our friendship until the

---

14. W.S. Churchill, *The Second World War*, vol. II, *Their Finest Hour* (London, 1949), p. 191.
15. Bell, *A Certain Eventuality*, pp. 121–2.
16. *The Economist*, 22 June 1940.

day of her resurrection'. And, on another occasion: 'The France of all civilized men is not dead or even captive . . .'[17] Charles Morgan, a novelist whose reputation was then high in both Britain and France (though it is now in eclipse), had just finished a new novel, *The Voyage*, set in France. In a preface dated 23 July 1940 he dedicated the book to two French friends, whom he did not name for fear that they were in the power of the enemy; and he declared his faith in French revival, because 'France is an idea necessary to civilization and will live again when tyranny is spent'.[18]

On the other hand, popular feeling, as depicted in reports to the Ministry of Information, was less deeply moved and less pro-French. There were frequent remarks on the lines of 'At least we have no more allies'; or 'We're better off without the French'; or 'We should have looked after ourselves all along'. The British people, faithful to their sporting metaphors, felt that they were at any rate in the final, and playing at home. But the general feeling was more one of detachment from the French than of anger against them. There was some resentment at being let down, but even that was directed against Pétain's government rather than against the French people – perhaps following the lead given in the press, though people were perfectly capable of making their own minds up when they chose. Then very quickly France fell from the forefront of people's minds, being replaced by the Battle of Britain, air raids and all the business of wartime life.[19] The sense of loss felt by the ardent Francophiles was very real and of long-term importance, but most British people now regarded France simply as a place where German bombers came from and where the German Army was massing for an invasion. The Channel assumed (or, more truly, resumed) its full physical and symbolic importance. Never since the days of Nelson had the British been happier to live on an island. The consequences of that deeply felt instinct on relations between Britain and France were to be long-lived.

One aspect of the French defeat caused particular concern in Britain. How had the collapse come about, and could the same thing happen here? All kinds of military and strategic explanations were put forward, but the favourite explanation was that France had been weakened from within, riven by internal divisions, let down by feeble political leaders, betrayed by Fifth Columnists. The press was almost unanimous in emphasising such interpretations, and Churchill lent

17. D.W. Brogan, 'Il y avait la France' and 'France: 1940', reprinted in *French Personalities and Problems* (London, 1946), pp. 133, 135, 155.
18. Charles Morgan, *The Voyage* (London, 1940), Dedication.
19. Bell, *A Certain Eventuality*, p. 127.

them his authority in a broadcast on Bastille Day, when he spoke of countries which were 'rotted from within before they were smitten from without. How else can you explain what has happened to France?'[20] This sort of explanation was comforting to the British, who believed that they did not suffer from the same sort of decay, and it reinforced impressions already formed in the 1930s, when France had suffered from chronic political instability and social unrest. A picture of French weakness, even rottenness, became firmly embedded in the British mind, where it remained predominant for many years.

Meanwhile, across the Channel, the French people were dazed by the speed of events and the shock of defeat. Their main concern was simply to live from one day to the next. Everyone who could manage it wanted to resume some sort of normal life, and to return to stability after the convulsions of May and June. It was a large part of Pétain's appeal that he offered the reassurance of a father-figure, a point of certainty in a world which had suddenly dissolved. Here, even his great age counted in his favour. The French people also succumbed to an immense passivity and relief at being out of the war. Jean Chauvel wrote that with the armistice the French people entered a state of compulsory neutrality which for a time was universally welcome.[21]

In many ways this was no time to debate the causes of the defeat, and yet it was inevitable that they should be sought. Pétain gave a lead in his early broadcasts, along two main lines: that the French Army had fought with a courage worthy of its traditions but had been crushed by overwhelming numbers and weight of armaments; and that under the regime of the Third Republic the search for pleasure had prevailed, and France was now paying the price of moral decadence. Another explanation of the defeat was speedily added. The British had let France down. They had not fought properly in Flanders; they had headed for the coast and left the French in the lurch at Dunkirk; they had refused to send their fighters to take part in the air battle. Pétain and Weygand had made all these criticisms privately during the battle, and had put them to British representatives directly – for example at the Supreme War Council on 11 June. Now the complaints were set out in public; and in a broadcast on 4 July, immediately after Mers-el-Kébir, the Foreign Minister, Baudouin, also developed a longer-term indictment of British policy towards France. He looked back to 1935, when the British had forced France to alienate Italy

20. Martin Gilbert, *Finest Hour: Winston S. Churchill 1939–1941* (London, 1983), p. 664.
21. Jean Chauvel, *Commentaire*, vol. I, *De Vienne à Alger, 1938–1944* (Paris, 1971), p. 131.

during the Ethiopian crisis, thus sacrificing a valuable ally to no purpose. In 1939 Britain had dragged France into war, but then France had mobilised three million men while the British had sent a mere 200,000 across the Channel. Thus the British had insisted on going to war, but they expected the French to do the fighting. For years, Baudouin concluded, France had followed Britain's lead, to her own detriment. It was time for a change.

Similar reactions emerged in popular opinion, apparently almost by instinct. In Bordeaux at the time of the armistice long-standing Right-wing prejudices against the Jews, the Popular Front and the British sprang up in conversation and in the press. Mers-el-Kébir naturally gave a powerful impulse to anti-British feeling. It was a sign of the times that Béraud's *Faut-il réduire l'Angleterre en esclavage? (Should England be reduced to slavery?)* was reprinted in the immediate aftermath of Mers-el-Kébir. Jean-Louis Crémieux-Brilhac, in his careful study of French opinion in 1940, concluded that it was Mers-el-Kébir rather than the events of the defeat that turned anti-British feeling into a nation-wide sentiment, reinforced rather than created by government propaganda. To condemn the British became a safety-valve for pent-up emotions, which in the circumstances of the time could not be openly directed against the Germans.[22]

For a time the supporters of Britain and the British alliance fell silent. There was no immediate counterpart to the professions of faith in France by the Francophiles in Britain. Yet this silence proved remarkably short-lived. In the 'forbidden zone' in the north, which the Germans cut off from the rest of France, hope for a British victory emerged strongly as early as the summer of 1940. There were several reasons for this. In the north, pro-British sympathies were strong, and so were memories of the previous German occupation in 1914–18. Moreover, the inhabitants could see the Germans preparing to invade England, and did not want them to succeed. In these ways, the Pas de Calais was a special case; but even in Brittany, where the effect of Mers-el-Kébir was particularly strong, a reaction set in before the end of the year. RAF pilots shot down and killed over the province were given proper funerals and flowers were laid on their graves.[23] A

22. For Béraud, see Martyn Cornick, 'Faut-il réduire l'Angleterre en esclavage? A case study of French Anglophobia', *Franco-British Studies*, 14, Autumn 1992, pp. 3–20. Jean-Louis Crémieux-Brilhac, *Les Français de l'An 40*, vol. I, *La guerre oui ou non?* (Paris, 1990), p. 602.
23. Jean-Marie Flonneau, 'L'évolution de l'opinion publique de 1940 à 1944', in J-P. Azéma et François Bédarida, eds, *Le régime de Vichy et les Français* (Paris, 1990), pp. 506–22, and especially pp. 510–11.

reaction against both the passivity at the time of the armistice and the hostility provoked by Mers-el-Kébir was already beginning.

France had suffered a sudden and overwhelming defeat, which struck home to everyone in the country. A tide of some six million refugees spread across the country. In their wake came the German Army, occupying the north and west of the country, marching in a victory parade down the Champs Elysées and settling in every town of the occupied zone. It was a shattering experience, leaving deep wounds. The British, on the contrary, fought on, and 1940 was to become their finest hour. Meanwhile, the war continued. For relations between France and Britain it was to prove a difficult and complicated war.

CHAPTER 2

A Complicated War:
(i) Britain, Vichy and de Gaulle,
1940–1942

From the fall of France in 1940 to the Liberation in 1944, relations between Britain and France assumed an extraordinary aspect. For four years there was no single entity which could be called 'France'. Mainland France was divided between the occupied and unoccupied zones. The German-occupied zone comprised about two-thirds of the country, including the Channel and Atlantic coasts and the city of Paris. The unoccupied zone was commonly called 'Vichy France', because the government under Marshal Pétain was established in the spa town of Vichy, which thus became for a few years the provisional capital of France.[1] Outside France, General de Gaulle launched at the end of June 1940 the movement called Free France, which developed as the war went on and emerged by 1944 as the Provisional Government of France. The French Empire overseas assumed unusual importance, because it was free from German control. At first, with only tiny exceptions, the Empire accepted the authority of Vichy, but as the war went on colonies changed their allegiance to de Gaulle. Relations between Britain and these different entities were complicated.

The first part of the story goes from mid-1940 to the end of 1942. During this period, Britain stood between de Gaulle's Free French movement and Vichy France, maintaining close relations with the first and more tenuous contacts with the second. This complicated and difficult period ended with the Anglo-American landings in French

---

1. The position was in fact more complicated than this outline indicates. Mainland France was divided into five parts: (1) German-occupied; (2) Italian-occupied – a small sector in the south-east; (3) Alsace and Lorraine, where the three departments were annexed by Germany and treated as German territory; (4) a 'forbidden zone' round Calais, under military rule; and (5) the unoccupied zone. There was even a sixth 'special zone' on the border of Lorraine. But for most purposes the simple division between occupied and unoccupied zones will serve.

North Africa in November 1942, which caused the Germans to occupy the whole of France, and effectively finished the life of Vichy as even a semi-independent government.

VICHY FRANCE AND COLLABORATION

The successor to the Third French Republic was the regime set up by Marshal Pétain at Vichy in July 1940. On 10 July the National Assembly voted by a majority of 468 to 80 to grant Pétain full powers to change the constitution. The new regime took the name of *Etat Français*, and adopted the motto of 'Travail, Famille, Patrie' in place of the old Republican trinity of 'Liberté, Egalité, Fraternité'. The government proclaimed its intention of embarking on a national revolution. The precise meaning of this was unclear, but it certainly implied the introduction of an authoritarian form of government, rejecting the ideas of liberal democracy that had long formed a bond between France and Britain.

The sentiments and cast of mind of the principal figures in the Vichy government were hostile to Britain. Pétain had nursed a resentment against the British since 1918, when he believed that the BEF was ready to head for the ports, and that the British had supported Foch against him. In May and June 1940 he was convinced that the British had left France to bear the brunt of the fighting, while coldly pursuing their own safety and their own interests. Laval, who was Vice-Premier in Pétain's government, had stored up his resentment against the way in which the British had treated him in 1935, over the Anglo–German Naval Agreement and the Ethiopian crisis. Weygand, who was Minister of Defence, shared Pétain's views about British betrayal in 1940. Darlan, who was Minister of Marine, had long held that the British conduct of naval negotiations between the wars had been directed at weakening the French fleet. Like Laval, he had resented the Anglo–German Naval Agreement of 1935. Far more seriously, in July 1940 the bombardment of Mers-el-Kébir had provoked him into a fierce hostility to the British. The strongest intellectual influence at Vichy was that of the *Action Française* and its aged leader, Charles Maurras, who had been anti-British since the time of Fashoda. He had long hated England only a little less than Germany, and when he had to be silent about the Germans his whole powers of invective – which were considerable – were concentrated against the British.

Moreover, all the leaders at Vichy confidently expected Britain to be defeated within a very short time. One of Pétain's motives in asking for an armistice had been to make terms before the British did. At the end of June, the Foreign Minister, Baudouin, was convinced that Britain would surrender within a fortnight, and that a government in favour of capitulation was already in waiting. Charles-Roux, the Secretary-General at the Foreign Ministry, recorded that this was the unanimous view of the French government, from top to bottom. Britain was finished. Germany had won the war. Even when, as the summer of 1940 wore on, it appeared that Britain was not finished yet, the fundamental assumption did not change. The Vichy press frequently presented news of the war under the heading 'La guerre anglo-allemande', showing that France was out of the conflict, and inferring that such an uneven contest would not last long. It followed that the future of France would have to be worked out within the new Europe under German control.

This was the basis for the policy of collaboration with Germany adopted by the Vichy government. The word itself came rapidly into use. On 19 July 1940 Laval visited Otto Abetz, the German Ambassador in Paris, and offered 'unreserved collaboration for the benefit of Europe'.[2] He explained at the end of August that he wanted joint Franco-German defence of the French Empire against the British and dissident Frenchmen, and the acceptance of France as an associated power alongside Germany. More important, Pétain repeatedly sought a meeting with Hitler. They eventually met, at the railway station at Montoire, on 24 October 1940. Hitler said that he wanted to associate France with the war against Britain, and Pétain replied that he favoured co-operation in principle, though he could not define its limits. After his return to Vichy, Pétain made a broadcast on 30 October, telling his listeners that he had accepted the principle of collaboration with Germany. The means would have to be worked out in the future, but he emphasised that the collaboration was to be sincere. What he meant was never fully established. What the German Foreign Ministry thought was shown by a draft document, prepared for signature by Hitler and Pétain, providing for French support for Germany in the war. In Pétain's entourage the impression was that the Marshal wanted to improve relations with Germany but to keep France out of war. In the event, Hitler lost interest and nothing happened; but the word 'collaboration' was well and truly launched.

2. Geoffrey Warner, *Pierre Laval and the Eclipse of France* (London, 1968), p. 214.

Vichy renewed its attempts at collaboration on a number of other occasions. On 28 May 1941 Darlan signed, with the German General Warlimont, the Paris Protocols, permitting German aircraft to use French airfields in Syria, German ships to use Bizerta to supply the Afrika Korps, and U-boats to use the naval base at Dakar in West Africa. Little was done to follow up this agreement. Some German aircraft landed in Syria, but their incursion came to a speedy end when the British occupied the country. General Weygand, then Delegate-General in North Africa, objected to German access to Bizerta and Dakar. Above all, the Germans attacked the Soviet Union on 22 June 1941, and set everything else aside.

The attack on the Soviet Union brought to the fore the ideological aspect of collaboration. French fascists in Paris formed the *Légion des Volontaires Français contre le Bolchévisme* (the LVF) to fight on the eastern front, and Pétain's government tried to take this over in 1942. In May 1942 Laval proposed to Ribbentrop (the German Foreign Minister) the idea of 'la relève', by which France would send men to work in German industry in exchange for the release of French prisoners of war. Laval announced this plan in a broadcast on 22 June 1942, using the fatal phrase 'I desire the victory of Germany, for without it Communism will soon be established everywhere in Europe'.[3] The scheme was in effect an offer of help for the German war effort, ostensibly against the Soviets but in fact against anyone – including the British.

These initiatives for collaboration all came from the French side. Their purpose was to establish France in the new German-dominated Europe in such a way as to save something from the wreck of defeat and to gain future advantage. They were inevitably directed against Britain. They accepted the New Order of which Britain was the implacable enemy. If pursued, they would in some cases have led to direct co-operation with the Germans against British forces.

'Vichy' was, and has remained, a short-hand term for a complicated phenomenon. Pétain's personality and prestige were vital to it. The National Revolution never got very far. Foreign policy was improvised by different governments and Foreign Ministers. In the event, no Vichy government actually signed a treaty with Germany or entered the war on the German side. Even so, a fundamental trend in Vichy policy and attitudes was to seek an accommodation with Germany, which implied hostility to Britain.

3. Fred Kupferman, *Laval* (Paris, 1987), p. 337.

DE GAULLE AND THE FREE FRENCH

Pétain and Vichy France stood for collaboration with Germany and the acceptance of German victory. General de Gaulle and the Free French stood for the rejection of defeat and the continuation of the war. De Gaulle took his stand in a broadcast from London on 18 June, which later became famous. He began by saying that France had been defeated by the Germans' tanks, planes and tactics, more than by their numbers. The new government, formed by France's military leaders, had asked to stop the fighting. He went on:

> But has the last word been said? Must hope vanish? Is the defeat final? No!
>
> Believe me, for I know what I am talking about and I tell you that nothing is lost for France. The same means that beat us may one day bring victory.
>
> For France is not alone. She is not alone! She is not alone! She has an immense Empire behind her. She can unite with the British Empire, which commands the sea and which is carrying on with the struggle. Like England, she can make an unlimited use of the vast industries of the United States.
>
> This war is not confined to the unhappy territory of our country. This war has not been decided by the Battle of France. This war is a world-wide war. . . . Today we are struck down by mechanised force; in the future we can conquer by greater mechanised force. The fate of the world lies there.

He called on French soldiers, engineers or armaments workers in Britain to get in contact with him. And he concluded: 'Whatever happens, the flame of French resistance must not and shall not go out.'[4]

The contrast with the line taken by Pétain was complete. The battle of France had not decided the war. France must continue her resistance – that word which was to attain such resonance. France must stand by the British alliance and gain help from the United States. The man who launched this appeal, and who was to play so great a part in relations between France and Britain for the next 30 years, was a professional soldier, 49 years old. He had been an infantry officer in the Great War, was wounded three times, and taken prisoner in March 1916. He escaped five times, but was recaptured each time,

---

4. This follows the English translation (by Patrick O'Brian) in Jean Lacouture, *De Gaulle: The Rebel, 1890–1944* (London, pb edn, 1993), pp. 224–5.

spent long spells in solitary confinement, and read much history and a lot of Shakespeare. The fierce determination to resist, the capacity to endure loneliness, and a great depth of reflective thought, all revealed in this wartime experience, were to be the characteristics of his later life. In the 1930s, he had advocated the creation of a specialised armoured corps, learning some of the arts of politics and gaining the support of Paul Reynaud. When Reynaud became Premier in March 1940 he secured the appointment of de Gaulle as commander of a newly formed armoured division. On 1 June de Gaulle was promoted to Brigadier-General, thus attaining the rank of general which was to become so firmly attached to his name that in later years 'the General' could mean only de Gaulle. On 6 June, Reynaud appointed him Under-Secretary for National Defence, a post which he held only until Reynaud's resignation on the 16th.

During the ten days of his ministerial career, de Gaulle visited London twice, and also attended Reynaud's last two conferences with Churchill. He made a strong impression on the British Prime Minister, which was to be of crucial importance in the next few days. Even so, when de Gaulle made his broadcast on 18 June 1940 he was only the most junior general in the French Army, and a former Under-Secretary who had held office for ten days in a now defunct government. It was not a strong base from which to embark on a great adventure.

De Gaulle's movement made a painfully uncertain start. His radio broadcasts (six in June and another six in July) evoked almost no response. The French Empire remained almost totally loyal to Pétain's government. The British action at Mers-el-Kébir was a disastrous blow to recruitment to the Free French forces, which in mid-August 1940 comprised only 140 officers and 2,100 other ranks. But in the course of the next two years de Gaulle managed to build on these unpromising foundations. In August 1940 the colonies of French Equatorial Africa were won over to the Free French. They were poor, sparsely populated and difficult of access, but they formed a vital territorial base. It was from Chad, in Equatorial Africa, that a tiny force under the then Colonel Leclerc set off on a long march which was to end in Paris, Strasbourg and southern Germany. An attempt in September 1940 to capture the West African port of Dakar ended in humiliating failure, but despite this de Gaulle had secured a firm foothold in Africa.

But Africa was not enough. For some time de Gaulle's movement was virtually cut off from France itself, except for its radio broadcasts on the BBC, which were paradoxically of crucial importance and yet utterly uncertain in their effects. During 1941, through the help of the

British, de Gaulle was able to send agents to France to report on the situation there and on the development of resistance groups. In October 1941 Jean Moulin, who was to prove the key figure linking de Gaulle with the Resistance inside France, arrived in London. He soon embarked on his long and perilous mission to unite the resistance movements in France under de Gaulle's leadership – a mission which culminated in May 1943 with the creation of the National Council of the Resistance, and shortly afterwards led to Moulin's death at the hands of the Gestapo. During 1942 an effective two-way traffic was established between London and France, with Resistance leaders visiting de Gaulle and returning to their *réseaux*. These contacts gave de Gaulle a new authority, and enabled him to emerge as the leader of French resistance to the Germans, within France as well as outside. He was no longer solely dependent either on London or on colonies in Africa. This was later to be crucial.

Meanwhile the Free French established themselves as a fighting force. Their airmen fought with distinction in the Battle of Britain. Their warships took part in the unremitting task of convoy escort in the Atlantic. French troops fought in Syria in 1941 (though unhappily against other Frenchmen), and a Free French Brigade was formed in the British Eighth Army in North Africa. It was this brigade, under General Koenig, which in May–June 1942 fought the battle of Bir Hakeim in the Libyan desert. It was a comparatively small action, in which some 5,500 French troops took part; but it was sternly fought and marked a turning-point in the restoration of the prestige of the French Army. As often in the history of Free France, the symbolic effect was greater than the immediate military results.

De Gaulle also gradually established an organisation which assumed some of the aspects of a government. On 27 October 1940 he issued the Brazzaville Manifesto, declaring that a true French government no longer existed. The body at Vichy which claimed that title was unconstitutional and subject to German control. 'It is therefore necessary', de Gaulle continued, 'that a new authority should assume the task of directing the French effort in the war. Events impose this sacred duty upon me. I shall not fail to carry it out.' He announced the creation of a Council of Defence for the Empire. On 16 November 1940 he founded the Order of Liberation, a striking declaration of confidence in a future event which at the time seemed highly improbable.[5] In September 1941 de Gaulle changed the Council of Defence for the Empire into a French National Committee, whose

5. P.M.H. Bell, *A Certain Eventuality: Britain and the Fall of France* (Farnborough, 1974) pp. 230–1.

members took responsibility for the economy, finance, foreign affairs, and so on. Under the cover-name of a committee there was established the framework of a government.

In the development of his movement, de Gaulle was entirely dependent upon the British. In a moment of exasperation in January 1941 he complained to Passy, the head of the Free French Intelligence services: 'The British yoke had become unbearable. I could not move in any sphere without clashing with the English.'[6] It would have been truer to say that he was unable to move, and the Free French unable to act, without the help of the British, who did not impose a yoke but provided a life support system. The BBC provided the radio service by which de Gaulle and the Free French became known in France. The costs of raising and maintaining the Free French forces were met by Britain – admittedly on condition of repayment by some future French government, but in 1940 that was a very distant prospect indeed. The Free French colonies were protected from the sea by the Royal Navy, and exported their products through British outlets. Contacts between the Free French in London and resistance groups in France were maintained by means of RAF flights and British signals equipment. The French brigade which fought so gallantly at Bir Hakeim was sustained by the supplies and services of the British Army. Behind everything lay the simple fact of British resistance to the Germans, without which the Free French could have done nothing. René Cassin, one of the earliest recruits to de Gaulle, wrote in October 1940: 'If Great Britain did not form an immoveable obstacle to the enemy's designs, there would no longer be a single place in Europe where patriotic Frenchmen could freely express their faith in the restoration of France.'[7]

This close association had powerful positive results on relations between France and Britain. Among those responsible for flights in and out of France there developed bonds which have stood the test of time and developed a particular intensity. Some of the Lysander pilots who made daring landings on rough fields all over France, and the Resistance agents whom they brought back to England, were still in touch 50 years later. Similarly, the companionship of the broadcasting studios, though not of the same kind, often proved long-lasting. Maurice Schumann, the principal broadcaster of 'Les Français parlent aux Français', has remained a friend of Britain and the British through-out his long career. In France, the resistance groups devoted a high proportion of their perilously produced clandestine publications to the

6. J-B. Duroselle, *L'abîme, 1939–1945* (Paris, 1982), p. 332.
7. Henri Michel, *Les courants de pensée de la Résistance* (Paris, 1962), p. 78.

necessity and virtues of the British alliance. Their articles bore eloquent testimony to the importance of the past. One writer insisted that, though the British had burned Joan of Arc, they had seen the error of their ways and now respected her as much as the French did. A Breton wrote that it was necessary to be pro-English even if one was not Anglophile. Another produced an early form of what was to become a classic saying: 'The French detest the English, but they want them to win.' Another version of this was that in France the Anglophiles said 'Let's hope the English win', while the Anglophobes said 'Let's hope those English swine win'.[8] However they chose to put it, the members of the resistance groups knew that they must rely on the British.

Yet because of this inescapable dependence, de Gaulle and the Free French felt bound to behave with the most intransigent independence. Their enemies in France could say, with literal truth, that they were 'in the pay of the English', and therefore they had to display a rigid virtue and incorruptibility. They were accused of betraying the French Empire to the British, or later to the Americans, so they had to show that they were the fiercest possible defenders of every French possession. The result was a constant friction in relations between de Gaulle and the British. De Gaulle described in his memoirs a meeting with Eden in May 1943, when they were saying farewell as de Gaulle left London for Algiers. ' "Do you know", said Mr. Eden pleasantly, "that you have given us more difficulty than all our European allies?" "I have no doubt of it", I replied, smiling too. "France is a great power." '[9] At the time, this was true only in a Gaullian sense; but the more dubious the proposition, the more ardently it had to be maintained.

This political necessity of maintaining a rugged independence was reinforced by the stiffness and angularity of de Gaulle's personality. In large part this was already formed before he arrived in England. He had already reflected on the principles of leadership – 'Distance – self-control – coolness . . . Sudden and rare interventions (like miracles in religions)'.[10] But as leader of Free France he developed another trait of character, acutely divined by Charles Williams in his biography of de Gaulle: the distinction between the symbolic 'General de Gaulle' and the man. ' "General de Gaulle" at that point [the end of June 1940] became the symbol of the legitimacy of the continuing France,

---

8. Clandestine papers quoted in ibid., pp. 132, 134. The story about Anglophiles and Anglophobes appeared in the *New Statesman* as early as 7 Dec. 1940.
9. Lacouture, *De Gaulle: The Rebel*, p. 445.
10. Charles de Gaulle, *Lettres, notes et carnets* (Paris, 1980), vol. II, p. 255. The quotation is from notes for a lecture at the Ecole de Guerre in 1934.

and "I" was there to serve him.' This was no mere trick of style or mode of presentation: 'For good or ill, Charles de Gaulle undoubtedly felt that he was in the same category as Joan of Arc and Clemenceau – a saviour of France.'[11] As he felt, so did he behave; which made him singularly difficult for the British to deal with.

In relations with the British, therefore, the Free French and de Gaulle were at one and the same time the closest and the most difficult of allies. Looking back, the closeness seems more important. The British and Free French shared the same objectives in the defeat of Germany and the restoration of French independence and greatness. The Frenchmen (and women) who spent the war years in London mostly returned to France with a fund of respect and affection for the British that is still not exhausted. At the time, however, the difficulties were such that they often filled the horizon.

CHURCHILL AND DE GAULLE

The British were faced by these two embodiments of France: Pétain's government at Vichy, and de Gaulle's Free French movement on their own doorstep in London. Neither Vichy nor de Gaulle could fill the place held by France from 1914 to June 1940. However great the friction between Britain and France during those years, the British had worked on the basic assumption that, in the event of war with Germany, France would be their principal ally. In 1939 and early 1940 all British planning had rested on that premise. At the end of June 1940 it was no longer true. France could no longer be a major power in the war, and the British had to find a new ally. They were in no doubt where to look: it was to the United States. Churchill set himself, with immense energy and skill, to win the personal friendship of President Roosevelt and the support of the American people. The task proved more difficult than he expected, and it was not until December 1941 that the United States was at war with Germany. In the meantime, Britain had acquired an unexpected ally in the Soviet Union, when Germany attacked that country in June 1941. From the end of 1941 onwards, Britain formed part of a three-power coalition – Churchill's 'Grand Alliance'; and the energies of British diplomacy were directed towards the working of that alliance. France, which had

11. Charles Williams, *The Last Great Frenchman. A Life of General de Gaulle* (London, 1993), p. 350.

for so long been at the centre of British policy, was now on the periphery.

Still, the two embodiments of France were there, and they had to be dealt with. De Gaulle was the nearer of the two, and had the immense merit of being determined to continue the fight, to which Churchill was committed with heart and soul. It was Churchill who insisted that de Gaulle should be allowed to broadcast on 18 June 1940, reversing an earlier decision by the War Cabinet. Churchill secured the issuing of a statement on 28 June recognising de Gaulle as 'the leader of all free Frenchmen, wherever they may be, who rally to him in support of the Allied cause'. It was Churchill again who wrote publicly to de Gaulle on 7 August 1940 undertaking to secure 'the full restoration of the independence and greatness of France'; though in a secret accompanying letter he had to explain that this phrase had 'no precise relation to territorial frontiers'.[12] At the time, this was an act of faith on Churchill's part. No significant French figure, political or military, responded to de Gaulle's radio appeals, until General Catroux, formerly Governor-General of Indo-China, arrived in London in mid-September. It was Churchill's intuitive grasp of de Gaulle's potential, and his personal commitment, that gave the General his start.

Churchill's commitment survived a disaster in the Dakar expedition of September 1940. This first Anglo-Free French venture was aimed at a valuable target. For the British, Dakar offered an excellent base on the convoy route to the Cape of Good Hope; for de Gaulle it presented the opportunity to win over the whole of French West Africa. A large British naval force and a small landing force of Royal Marines and Free French infantry were despatched to Dakar in September 1940, in the hope of an easy victory by over-awing the defenders and gaining the support of elements reported to be favourable to de Gaulle. Nothing of the kind came about. The governor, General Boisson, offered a resolute resistance. The defence was reinforced by the recent arrival of cruisers from Toulon. British warships were damaged in exchanges of gunfire, and by a French submarine attack. An attempted landing by Free French troops was easily repulsed. After three days of desultory fighting (23–25 September) the Anglo-Free French force retired baffled.

This failure attracted a storm of criticism in the British press, and resulted in Churchill having to defend himself in the House of Commons on 8 October. The major responsibility lay with the British, who provided most of the forces and carried out all the planning and

12. Bell, *A Certain Eventuality*, p. 192.

preparations, which had involved long and probably fatal delays. It was the British who had allowed the French cruisers to pass the Straits of Gibraltar *en route* for Dakar. None the less, the temptation to put the blame on the Free French was naturally enormous, and to some extent the British succumbed to it. Notably, the story circulated that lax Free French security had betrayed the destination of the expedition, with officers drinking to 'Dakar' in a Liverpool restaurant and even de Gaulle mentioning his objective while buying tropical kit at Simpson's in Piccadilly. Investigations by the British Security Board showed that failures in British secrecy precautions had been even more glaring, but the idea of Free French carelessness took root and was to affect British policy for the rest of the war. It would have been easy for Churchill to take the same line, to put the blame for failure on the Free French, and use de Gaulle as a scapegoat. He did nothing of the kind. Instead he told the House of Commons:

> I think his [de Gaulle's] judgement has been found extremely sure-footed, and our opinion of him has been enhanced by everything we have seen of his conduct in circumstances of particular and perplexing difficulty. His Majesty's Government have no intention whatever of abandoning the cause of General de Gaulle until it is merged, as merged it will be, in the larger cause of France.[13]

This remarkable display of support was a lifeline for de Gaulle when his fortunes were at their lowest ebb. But in 1941 there began a series of quarrels between Churchill and de Gaulle which tested the links between them to the uttermost, without quite breaking them. The first, and most long-lived, of these disputes concerned the Levant states of Syria and the Lebanon, which in 1919 had been the cause of a bitter quarrel between Lloyd George and Clemenceau. Since 1920, Syria and the Lebanon had been French mandates under the League of Nations. In principle, the French administration was supposed to prepare them for independence; in practice, the French treated them as colonies. In 1940 the two territories accepted the armistice and the authority of the Vichy government. In May 1941, under the Paris Protocols negotiated by Darlan, Vichy permitted German aircraft to use Syrian airfields to fly missions in support of an anti-British rising in Iraq. In June, British, Australian and Free French forces invaded the Levant states, and after some sharp fighting the Vichy commander, General Dentz, asked for an armistice. Negotiations were conducted by the British commander, General Maitland Wilson, with the

13. Hansard, *H.C. Deb.*, 5th series, vol. 365, col. 298.

assistance of General Catroux for the Free French, resulting in an armistice signed at Acre on 14 July. Wilson's main objectives were to get rid of the Vichy French forces as soon as he could, and to secure his own authority over the area. He therefore agreed to send the troops back to France as soon as transport could be found, without giving the Free French any chance to win them over; and the armistice transferred authority over Syria and the Lebanon straight from the Vichy French to the British, without any reference to the Free French at all. Behind this lay a wider political issue. Even before the Syrian campaign, the British authorities in the Middle East had been discussing the need to appeal to Arab opinion by offering early independence to the French mandates. After the campaign, Churchill rapidly took up this idea. He telegraphed to Lyttelton, the British Minister-Resident in the Middle East, on 7 July: 'Our policy is to give the Syrian Arabs independence . . . the Arabs bulk far more largely in our minds than the Free French. . . .' He emphasised that the Arabs must be convinced that 'they have not merely exchanged one set of Frenchmen for another'.[14]

None of this was in the least acceptable to de Gaulle. He wanted his representatives to have every opportunity to rally members of the French forces to his cause. Moreover, it was his fixed policy, for the reasons which we have already seen, to maintain the French Empire in its entirety. It was therefore his intention that Syria and the Lebanon should indeed exchange one set of Frenchmen for another; though that was probably not how he would have put it. De Gaulle adopted a stratagem which was to become almost his trade-mark: he withdrew from the scene, and uttered anathemas from afar. In practice, this meant flying from Cairo to Brazzaville, and denouncing the armistice of Acre on the radio from there. He then returned, and subjected Lyttelton to a tremendous display of temper. For some two hours he poured out a tirade, the gist of which was that unless the armistice was altered to meet his demands he would remove the Free French forces in the Middle East from British command, and effectively bring his alliance with the British to an end. In his memoirs, Lyttelton commented coolly that 'The discussion degenerated into what women call a scene'; but at the time he was badly shaken.[15] The commander of a few thousand French troops, entirely dependent on British support, harangued the representative of the British Empire in his own

14. A.B. Gaunson, *The Anglo-French Clash in Lebanon and Syria, 1940–45* (London, 1987), p. 54.

15. Viscount Chandos (Oliver Lyttelton), *The Memoirs of Lord Chandos* (London, 1962), pp. 247–8.

residence, and got his way. The armistice terms were speedily 'inter-preted' to allow the Free French to seek recruits among the Vichy forces (some 6,000 agreed to join). Lyttelton assured de Gaulle that Britain recognised the historic interests of France in the Levant. In the next few days, in forts where the Union flag had been hoisted, it came down, to be replaced by the Tricolour.

De Gaulle thus won a remarkable success from a position of almost total weakness. But the fundamental political problem remained unresolved. The British, in order to keep the Arabs in the Middle East quiet and to free their hands at a time of acute strategic difficulty, insisted on a guarantee of independence for Syria and the Lebanon. Even de Gaulle was compelled to accept this in principle (it was, after all, the basis of the mandate), but in practice he did everything possible to delay its implementation and to maintain French control. The result was constant friction, as the British tried to press ahead with organising elections, and the French tried to hold them back. To make matters worse, the Levant became the occasion of a terrible personal quarrel between de Gaulle and General Spears. Spears had been Churchill's personal liaison officer with Reynaud in May and June 1940, and had then come to London with de Gaulle. Since then, Churchill had entrusted Spears with the difficult task of liaison with de Gaulle, relying on his deep affection for France and his long experience of working with the French. Spears had accompanied de Gaulle to Dakar, and later to Equatorial Africa and the Middle East. It is clear from his reports to London that Spears saw himself as a mentor rather than simply a liaison officer. (He telegraphed from Equatorial Africa in October 1940: 'previous tendency to assume role of absolute monarch increased but will be dealt with'.[16]) De Gaulle on his side resented what he regarded as British leading strings. Over Syria in the summer of 1941 their relations broke down utterly. By Spears's account, de Gaulle's terrible outburst over the Acre armistice shocked him into a complete loss of faith in France, already undermined by the defeat of 1940 and the treachery of Vichy. However that may be, it is certain that in July–August 1941 Spears became almost instantly an ardent enthusiast for the Arab cause in Syria. There followed some three and a half years of venomous personal quarrel to add to a deep-seated political dispute between Britain and France.

De Gaulle's explosion over the armistice of Acre began to undermine Churchill's loyalty to the General, which had stood so firm at the time of Dakar. Then the next month (August 1941) de Gaulle

---

16. Bell, *A Certain Eventuality*, p. 222.

gave an interview to an American journalist at Brazzaville. The published version, in the *Chicago Daily News* (27 August), represented de Gaulle as saying that Churchill had made a deal with Hitler, using Vichy as a go-between. De Gaulle first denied giving any interview at all, and then disputed the version which was published; but he had clearly said what the correspondent reported, even if perhaps 'off the record'. Churchill was furious. He at once wrote to Eden: 'If de Gaulle's interview with the American press at Brazzaville is authentic he has clearly gone off his head. This would be a very good riddance and will simplify our further course.' On 30 August, three days after the interview was published, Churchill issued a remarkable set of instructions which began '(1) No one is to see General de Gaulle', and ended '(5) No one should see any of General de Gaulle's subordinates either'.[17] When de Gaulle returned to England, he was at first ostracised in accordance with this directive, and then received by Churchill on 12 September.

There ensued a spectacular confrontation. John Colville, who began the thankless task of interpreting, has left a vivid account. He recounts how Churchill began:

> 'General de Gaulle, I have asked you to come here this afternoon.' Churchill stopped and looked fiercely at me. 'Mon Général,' I said, 'je vous ai invité de venir cet après-midi.'
>
> 'I didn't say Mon Général,' interrupted the Prime Minister, 'and I did not say I had invited him.'

Colville struggled against the tide for a while, but was soon dismissed and replaced as interpreter by a Foreign Office official, who soon came out of the room, 'red in the face and protesting that they must be mad'. Then for an hour Colville heard nothing, and began to wonder whether he should go in with some bogus message – 'Perhaps they had strangled each other?' But then the bell rang, and he went in:

> . . . to find the two of them sitting side by side with amiable expressions on their faces. De Gaulle, no doubt for tactical purposes, was smoking one of the Prime Minister's cigars. They were talking French, an exercise Churchill could never resist and one which his audience invariably found fascinating.[18]

So for a time the quarrel was made up, but the basic causes were not removed. Churchill, who was conducting a complex and so far disastrous war, could not abide the arrogant behaviour of de Gaulle, so

17. François Kersaudy, *Churchill and de Gaulle* (London, 1981), p. 151.
18. Ibid., pp. 155, 159.

utterly out of touch with the needs of the time. De Gaulle could not afford, even if he had wished (which he did not), to yield to any British derogation of French independence. Both were prone to anger, though de Gaulle's outbursts were often calculated. Churchill for his part was capable of swinging to the other extreme and vowing that he would never forget that de Gaulle had stood by him in 1940. De Gaulle, at least at that time, showed no such magnanimity.

In December 1941 the Japanese attacked Pearl Harbor, and Hitler chose to seize the opportunity to declare war on the United States. Churchill at once virtually invited himself to Washington to confer with President Roosevelt, in order to ensure that the energies of the United States were concentrated against Germany rather than Japan. In the middle of this crucial conference, on Christmas Eve, a couple of Free French warships commanded by Admiral Muselier, the head of the Free French Navy, took over the islands of St Pierre and Miquelon from the Vichy authorities there. These islands, south of Newfoundland, were inhabited by a few thousand fishermen and their families, whose rights to catch and preserve fish had figured in the *Entente* of 1904. There was a powerful radio transmitter on St Pierre, capable of playing some part in the Battle of the Atlantic, either on the German or the Allied side. Above all, the islands and their people were French, and de Gaulle had set his mind on bringing them over to his side. In the context of the war now raging across the globe, the incident was trivial. Yet the Free French action angered the American Secretary of State, Cordell Hull, who took the view that no territory on the American continent should change hands without the consent of the United States, and invoked the Monroe Doctrine in his support. For Churchill the affair was a potential embarrassment. After all, Muselier had actually sailed from a Canadian port – could the British and Canadians not control this minor ally of theirs?

Fortunately for Churchill, American public opinion took de Gaulle's side. Cordell Hull had rashly referred in public to 'the so-called Free French', and he received sacks of letters addressed to 'the so-called Secretary of State'. Roosevelt, who did not get on with Hull anyway and kept him out of dealings with the British, was more amused than irritated by the affair. In January a compromise was patched up, through Churchill, which allowed the Free French to stay on the islands though using a form of words which pacified the State Department. In itself, the incident was no more than a storm in a teacup, but for Churchill the point was that it happened when it did, right in the middle of a conference where he was trying to fix the strategy and set the tone for the Anglo-American alliance. The Free

French action had endangered these vital matters, and de Gaulle had again shown his utter lack of sense of proportion.

The affair had a sequel. Admiral Muselier had long opposed de Gaulle's conduct of affairs, and had previously tried to displace the General as leader of the Free French. In March 1942, in the aftermath of St Pierre and Miquelon, he tried to secede from de Gaulle's command, taking the Free French fleet with him. He won the support of the First Lord of the Admiralty, A. V. Alexander, and briefly that of the War Cabinet also. But de Gaulle was remarkably astute and resolute in such political in-fighting, and it was Muselier who was compelled to leave the Free French movement, without the fleet following him. The British ministers involved were forced to retreat in some confusion. However, during the crisis de Gaulle was seriously afraid that he might have to resign, or even that he might be arrested. He prepared a 'political testament', to be published in case of necessity – 'If I am led to give up the task I have undertaken, the French nation must know why'.[19] It was a charge of verbal dynamite to be exploded under the British government; but in the event the fuse was not lit.

The British and the Free French were on the same side. Churchill and de Gaulle were united in their determination to fight the war to a victorious conclusion, and they shared the virtues of courage, patriotism and a sense of tradition. But Syria, St Pierre and Miquelon, the Muselier affair, and the clash of two powerful and imperious personalities rendered co-operation extraordinarily difficult.

BRITAIN AND THE VICHY GOVERNMENT

The British and the Vichy government, on the other hand, were on opposite sides. Whatever 'collaboration' meant in principle, in effect it meant helping the Germans to win the war against Britain. The British, fighting for their lives, were bound to use force when they thought it necessary, and did so without much compunction. The result was a number of sharp battles amounting almost to another Anglo-French war to add to those in the past. We have already noted some of these battles: Mers-el-Kébir, Dakar and Syria. In 1942 there was another conflict, this time in Madagascar. The British were afraid that the Japanese, after their triumph at Singapore, would strike across

---

19. Lacouture, *De Gaulle: The Rebel*, pp. 318–19.

the Indian Ocean and seize Madagascar, off the east coast of Africa. In May 1942, therefore, a British expedition occupied Diego Suarez, a harbour and naval station at the northern tip of the island. There followed in the autumn a further campaign in which the British extended their control over the whole island, before handing it over to the Free French.

Thus in four separate conflicts British and French forces fought one another for the first time since Waterloo. The French (and in this connection there was little difference between Vichy and Free French) were convinced that the British intended to take over parts of their Empire. The British had the firm impression that Vichy was keener on fighting them than on fighting the Germans. No formal state of war was declared, but the conflicts were often sharp and casualties numerous. (It has been estimated that the French suffered some 2,000 dead at Dakar, and about 6,500 killed and wounded in Syria.[20])

This was not the whole story of relations between Britain and Vichy France. In 1940 and 1941 the British were anxious to ensure that the French Empire did not fall into Axis hands, or if possible to bring it back into the war on the Allied side. After the failure at Dakar, it was evident that the Free French could not produce these results in the near future, if at all. The British therefore developed a number of contacts with Vichy, mainly through the embassies of the two governments in Madrid. They were willing to offer some relaxation of the economic blockade of unoccupied France and the Vichy colonies (which in any case they did not have enough naval forces to enforce properly), in return for assurances that the Germans would be kept out of the French Empire. No agreement was made, but the British allowed some concessions in the blockade. More positively, the British hoped in the winter of 1940–41 to induce General Weygand, who was then Delegate-General (a combined military–political *supremo*) in French North Africa, to bring Algeria, Tunisia and Morocco back into the war on the British side. Weygand was known to be opposed to collaboration in the style of Laval, and if he would change sides (with his territories) the British were willing to offer military and economic help, and at least to consider recognising his administration. In February 1941 the Foreign Office recommended that if a government were formed in North Africa to resume the war, perhaps under Weygand or Darlan, Britain should at once accord it

---

20. Figures for Dakar in ibid., p. 277; for Syria, see W.S. Churchill, *The Second World War*, vol. III, *The Grand Alliance* (London, 1950), p. 296. The latter figures do not include Free French casualties – the total for British, Australian and Free French together was some 4,600.

full recognition and reaffirm the alliance. Cautious approaches were made to Weygand, but nothing came of them. Weygand himself was reticent, later explaining that he would have welcomed the British if they had arrived with twenty divisions, but not if they came with two.

The British were also willing to consider a deal with Darlan if he brought the French fleet over with him. In November 1941 Darlan made a secret approach to the British, to enquire whether at the end of the war they would refuse to deal with a government of which he was a member. Churchill did not reply to the question as put, but responded instead that if the French fleet at Toulon were to sail to North Africa and resist German attacks, then whoever carried out this action would make a decisive contribution to the Allied cause. 'Such a service', wrote the Prime Minister, 'would entitle the author to an honourable place in the Allied ranks.'[21] Nothing happened on that occasion, but in the autumn of 1942 the question of making some arrangement with Darlan recurred. The British and Americans were preparing to make large-scale landings in French North Africa, and they discussed the possibility of bringing Darlan over to their side. 'Darlan would be a big fish to land if it could be done', said Smuts, the South African Prime Minister, at a meeting with Churchill, Eden and military commanders on 17 October 1942. No-one disputed it.[22] In the event, Darlan was actually in Algiers when the Allied forces began to land on 8 November. Almost at once, the American commander on the spot, General Clark, made an agreement with Darlan (10 November) to secure a cease-fire in Algeria and Morocco. Then on 13 November Clark agreed to accept Darlan as head of the civil administration in North Africa, in return for his co-operation with the Allied forces. These arrangements were elaborated in a wider agreement on 22 November, which effectively accepted Darlan as military and administrative chief in North Africa, and brought him over to the Allied side. At every stage these agreements were ratified by the Allied Supreme Commander, General Eisenhower, and accepted by the British and American governments.

This was the 'Darlan deal' of November 1942, which in a sense was the culmination of earlier British attempts to make contact with Vichy representatives provided they came back into the war. At the time, both Churchill and Roosevelt claimed that it was only a temporary expedient to help the Allied forces in a difficult situation in North

21. R.T. Thomas, *Britain and Vichy. The Dilemma of Anglo-French relations 1940–42* (London, 1979), p. 144.
22. The whole story is set out in Arthur L. Funk, 'Negotiating the Deal with Darlan', *Journal of Contemporary History*, vol. 8, No. 2, April 1973, pp. 94–7.

Africa. But Darlan showed every sign of settling down in the Allied camp as a permanent fixture, which would have raised all sorts of questions about British relations with de Gaulle. Then, on Christmas Eve 1942, Darlan was assassinated, and with his death this strand of British policy which had led towards Vichy came to an abrupt – and certainly a convenient – end.

In Britain, the Darlan deal provoked a widespread outcry in the press, and to a lesser degree in Parliament. Darlan had been a collaborator and a Quisling, and there was a strong feeling that he should not simply be allowed to change sides when it suited him. Moreover, there was a strong public reaction in favour of de Gaulle. The Ministry of Information's Home Intelligence reports noted a general sentiment that de Gaulle had stood by Britain in the dark days of 1940, and the British should stand by him, and not work with someone who had gone over to the Germans. This public reaction was a tribute to the fundamental basis of de Gaulle's position: his determination to continue the war. By his courage he had evoked in response the admiration and loyalty of the British people.

The British government's position in relation to the two embodiments of France, de Gaulle and Vichy, was thus equivocal. For some two and a half years the government had supported de Gaulle, but endured a series of explosive disputes with him. Also for about two years they had entertained hopes that some prominent Vichy leader might come over to the Allied side and resume the war. While Germany was winning, this was a vain hope, but the turn of the tide at the end of 1942 changed the situation, and Darlan was willing to switch to the winning side. Even this late conversion was tactically very useful to the British and Americans, though its long-term results would surely have been difficult and damaging. The British, under the pressures of war, had adopted a dual policy of supporting de Gaulle but at the same time maintaining some contacts with Vichy. At the end of 1942 they might have paid a serious penalty for this duality.

Events worked out otherwise. When the Allied forces landed in North Africa in November 1942, the Germans at once moved into the previously unoccupied zone. The Vichy government remained in existence, but ceased to have any importance. Darlan's death in Algiers brought his extension of the Vichy regime in North Africa to an end. For the remainder of the war, British relations with France were simplified, at least to the extent that the Vichy option was closed. However, what remained – Free France, North Africa, and the French Empire in general – was no simple matter.

CHAPTER 3

A Complicated War: (ii) Britain and de Gaulle, 1943–1944

BRITAIN AND THE FREE FRENCH

The years 1943 and 1944 were ones of Allied victory. Allied armies invaded Italy in 1943 and landed in Normandy in June 1944. By September 1944 France was almost entirely liberated from German occupation. These years also saw crucial developments in the Free French movement, both political and military. The assassination of Darlan had removed one political danger to de Gaulle, but he was at once faced by another. To prepare for the landings in North Africa, the Americans had brought out of France General Giraud, a gallant fighting soldier, much senior to de Gaulle in rank and strongly conservative in his political views. After Darlan's death, Giraud assumed control of the French forces and administration in North Africa, with the support of the Americans. At the Anglo-American conference at Casablanca in January 1943, Roosevelt and Churchill produced a plan for a French Committee, to bring together the Free French with the new elements in North Africa. Giraud was placed in an apparently strong position, as one of the co-presidents of the proposed Committee, and also Commander-in-Chief of all French forces in Africa. De Gaulle was virtually coerced into going to Casablanca, where he was put under heavy pressure to accept these arrangements. He proved indifferent to both threats and blandishments, and the furthest he would go was a brief handshake with Giraud for the benefit of photographers, and a meeting with Giraud which produced a thoroughly uncommunicative communiqué: 'We have seen one another. We have talked.' They agreed that their objective was the liberation of France, to be achieved by the union of all Frenchmen in the war. Giraud objected to a reference to 'democratic principles', but accepted 'human liberties' instead.[1]

At Casablanca, de Gaulle managed to evade the subordination to Giraud which the Americans, and at that time also the British, tried to impose upon him. There followed a long political struggle between the two generals in which de Gaulle emerged successful at all points. Giraud had political prejudices, but little political ability. He later gave his memoirs the title *Un seul but: la victoire*, by which he simply meant military victory over the Germans. In the political in-fighting at Algiers in 1943, de Gaulle ran rings round him. At the end of April 1943 Giraud made a vital concession by giving up his claim to leadership of whatever French organisation was to be set up, and accepting parnership with de Gaulle instead. At the end of May, de Gaulle transferred his headquarters from London to Algiers, where in June a Committee of National Liberation was set up, comprising seven members, with Giraud and de Gaulle as co-presidents. At the time, Churchill greeted this development with delight, telegraphing to Roosevelt that if de Gaulle were now to be violent or unreasonable, he would be in a minority of two against five, or perhaps even isolated. There was at last, he wrote, 'a body with collective authority with which in my opinion we can safely work'.[2] This joy was short-lived. Within weeks de Gaulle had doubled the size of the Committee, and introduced a majority of his own supporters. At the end of July a dispute about the role of the Committee in military affairs was resolved by de Gaulle becoming sole president of the Committee, with Giraud as Commander-in-Chief. But this apparently equal distribution of responsibilities was nullified by the Commander-in-Chief being placed under a Committee of National Defence, whose chairman was de Gaulle. In November 1943 de Gaulle removed Giraud from the Committee of National Liberation altogether. Finally, in April 1944, de Gaulle completed his victory in this internal struggle by assuming command of the armed forces. Giraud vanished from the scene, almost without trace.

While this unequal contest was in progress, de Gaulle tackled the more difficult problem of amalgamating the army of Free France with the army in North Africa, which had owed allegiance to Vichy and Pétain. The two forces were utterly different in character. The Free

1. Jean Lacouture, *De Gaulle: The Rebel, 1890–1944* (London, pb edn, 1993), p. 428. I follow the translation given there, but the opening sentences may be translated in even briefer form: 'We have met. We have talked.'
2. Churchill to Roosevelt, 6 June 1943, in Warren F. Kimball, ed., *Churchill and Roosevelt: the Complete Correspondence* (Princeton, 1984), vol. II, p. 231.

French Army was made up of men who had deliberately, and at no small risk, rejected Vichy. It was independent in spirit, and some of its units had a fine fighting record, sharing the battle honours of the British Eighth Army. The Army in North Africa, on the other hand, had remained loyal to Pétain. It had seen no action for over two years, except to fire briefly on the British and Americans as they landed in November 1942. The Free French were few in number (about 50,000 at the end of 1942); the North African Army mustered about 230,000, with more in reserve.

In principle, de Gaulle always insisted on the total rejection of Vichy, and he regarded collaboration as treason; but in these circumstances he was prepared to compromise. His problem was summed up in the person of General Juin, a divisional commander in the North African Army. Juin had been consistently loyal to Pétain, and in 1941 he had taken part in a mission to Goering led by Benoist-Méchin, a prominent collaborator. But Juin was also one of the best commanders in the French Army, and after he had seen some sharp action against the Germans in Tunisia de Gaulle wrote him a warm letter of congratulation and opened the way to good relations. This was a symbolic reconciliation. In the same way, the amalgamation of the two armies went forward during 1943, painfully but with considerable success. The result was a revived French Army, including Leclerc's famous 2nd Armoured Division, embodying all the spirit of the Free French; Juin's Expeditionary Corps, which fought with distinction in Italy; and de Lattre de Tassigny's *Armée B*, which went ashore with the Americans in Provence in August 1944. In 1943 and 1944 the French Army went back into action, not just in the shape of a gallant brigade as at Bir Hakeim, but as a substantial force.

Free France thus assumed a new political shape in the Committee of National Liberation, and a new military form in a powerful army. De Gaulle, through the agency of Jean Moulin and the National Council of the Resistance, formed early in 1943, forged firm links with the growing Resistance movements within France. There remained the crucial step, towards which de Gaulle always aspired: to become the acknowledged government of France. This depended largely on the British and the Americans, from whom alone external recognition could come; but de Gaulle could do much to promote it. In November 1943 he set up a Consultative Assembly, to exercise some of the functions of a parliament. In January 1944 he nominated *Commissaires de la République* to replace the prefects in France when the country was liberated. This was an act of government, and his instructions to the *Commissaires* made it plain that they were to represent the government to the people. In a speech on 27 March 1944 de Gaulle referred to the Committee of National Liberation as the provisional government of France, though this was not yet a claim which was accepted by the British and Americans.

During this period (1943–early 1944) British relations with the Free French continued in their previous ambiguous state. There were still disputes and explosive quarrels between Churchill and de Gaulle; but at the same time the British maintained a solid support for de Gaulle on a number of crucial issues, and an underlying similarity in long-term interests became increasingly apparent as the war drew to an end.

Among the disputes, the ulcer of the Levant states continued to spread its poison in an unceasing flow. In 1942 the British had tried to press forward with elections in Syria and the Lebanon, while the French sought to delay them. In 1943 the last French opposition was overcome and elections took place, producing nationalist majorities which proceeded to form ministries. In November 1943 the French responded by dissolving the elected assembly in the Lebanon and arresting Lebanese ministers. The British threatened to impose martial law and take matters into their own hands unless the ministers were released. (At this point General Catroux exclaimed that the British ultimatum amounted to another Fashoda, a reference to the Anglo-French clash in the Sudan in 1898 which baffled the new Minister-Resident in the Middle East, who did not know what the Frenchman was talking about! For the French, the past was ever-present.[3]) Spears threw himself into this conflict on the nationalist side, exacerbating the situation to such a degree that finally even Churchill lost patience and insisted on his resignation in December 1944.

The basic issue remained the same. In order to appease Arab opinion, to get on with the war and to secure their position in the Middle East when it was over, the British insisted on the independence of Syria and the Lebanon. De Gaulle, who was determined to defend every part of the French Empire, was totally opposed to independence. The dispute finally came to a head in Spring 1945, with the war in Europe drawing to a close. The French moved reinforcements to Syria, bombarded Damascus, and prepared to impose their control by force. The British then intervened at the end of May in overwhelming strength, surrounded French troops with tanks and guns and threatened to fire upon them unless they withdrew to their encampments. Thus the British brought an effective (if not a legal) end to the French mandate, and imposed their own policy of

3. A.B. Gaunson, *The Anglo-French Clash in Syria and the Lebanon, 1940–45* (London, 1987), p. 136.

independence. De Gaulle, of course, had no belief whatsoever in the British protestations of altruism, holding that the British only sought to expel the French in order to assert their own predominance. The aftermath of this long dispute continued to corrode Franco-British relations well into 1945, and its memories lasted for many years after that.

THE ROOSEVELT FACTOR

Even more important in Anglo-French relations was what may be called for short the 'Roosevelt factor'. By the end of 1942 Roosevelt had conceived a fixed antipathy towards de Gaulle, for reasons which remain unclear. He believed that France was irretrievably weakened by the defeat of 1940, and had forfeited for ever her status as a great power; and he therefore regarded de Gaulle's pretensions to greatness as absurd. Roosevelt's position was often inconsistent. He complained that de Gaulle was a budding dictator, yet he himself continued to recognise Pétain's authoritarian government at Vichy. He claimed that the French people must decide their own form of government, but persistently rejected all evidence that they supported de Gaulle. But his prejudices often threatened serious danger to the French Empire, and perhaps even to France itself. Roosevelt often spoke of detaching parts of the French Empire (for example, Dakar or Indo-China) and putting them under American or Chinese trusteeship. On occasion he even suggested airily that parts of France should be united with Luxembourg and the French-speaking provinces of Belgium to form a new state of Wallonia.

Roosevelt's hostility towards de Gaulle, and towards France in general, put Churchill in an almost impossible position. The American alliance was the lynch-pin of his wartime strategy, and the basis of his hopes for the post-war world. To secure that alliance, he took infinite pains to build up a personal friendship with Roosevelt, which developed into a genuine affection transcending political calculation. He counted on his influence with the President to safeguard British interests at crucial moments. He would allow almost nothing to obstruct the working of the American alliance or cast a shadow on his friendship with Roosevelt. Certainly de Gaulle, with whom his relations were often so difficult, could not be allowed to do so.

Yet Churchill held France in an affection no less than that which he felt for the United States. He had an instinctive and historical sense of the greatness of France which was not far removed from that cherished by de Gaulle himself, and completely opposed to Roosevelt's belief in French decrepitude. Moreover, despite all their quarrels, he understood the reasons for de Gaulle's intransigence and he recognised the greatness which lay beneath the angularity. At Marrakesh in January 1944, after one of his difficult encounters with the General, Churchill said to the British Consul: 'There is no doubt about it! C'est un grand animal!'[4]

Moreover, both Churchill and Eden were convinced that when the war was over France must be restored as a great power. As early as 7 August 1940 Churchill committed the British government 'to secure the full restoration of the independence and greatness of France'.[5] From this he never fundamentally departed; and he was consistently sustained by Eden. Britain needed France as a great power, for practical reasons. After the war, Britain would need a French army to take part in the occupation of Germany, because it was generally assumed that the Americans would not stay long in Europe when the war was over. The French might also be needed – though opinions on this varied greatly – as support against the Soviet Union. Moreover, Churchill regarded the French Empire as a first line of defence for the British Empire, principally against the Americans – he was well aware of Roosevelt's anti-imperialist sentiments. Churchill therefore, out of sentiment but much more out of calculation, fully intended to restore France as a European and an imperial power.

The upshot was that Churchill steered a somewhat erratic course between Roosevelt and de Gaulle, between the United States and France. His policy was by no means one-sided, as was often said later – not least by de Gaulle. It is true that Churchill sometimes clung very closely to the line laid down by Roosevelt, especially when the two were together. In May 1943, when Churchill was in the United States for some three weeks, the President put him under almost daily pressure to break with de Gaulle. At one stage Churchill succumbed, and telegraphed to London proposing that de Gaulle should be 'eliminated as a political force', and that the supply of money to the French National Committee should be cut off as long as de Gaulle was connected with it. But the War Cabinet dissented. Eden wrote in his diary: 'everyone against and very brave about it in his absence'. In fact, Eden, Attlee and Bevin took the lead in setting out the reasons for *not* breaking with de Gaulle: the strength of de Gaulle's position in

4. Martin Gilbert, *Road to Victory: Winston S. Churchill, 1941–1945* (London, 1986), p. 646.
5. P.M.H. Bell, *A Certain Eventuality. Britain and the Fall of France* (Farnborough, 1974), p. 192.

France; the likely reactions in the Resistance movement and the Free French forces (there were sixteen French corvettes on the North Atlantic convoy run); the dangers of interfering in French internal politics. Oliver Harvey commented vehemently in the privacy of his diary: 'We would not break him but make him . . . What fools these Americans are.' Churchill yielded to the opinion of the War Cabinet, and agreed to postpone any action against de Gaulle. Later, on 17 June 1943, Roosevelt tried again, this time by telegram. 'I am fed up with de Gaulle', he wrote (echoing the thoughts of many at different times); and he proposed that he and Churchill should both break with the General. Again, Churchill was at first disposed to agree, but Eden persuaded him to temporise.[6] The crisis passed.

Thus Churchill sometimes hovered on the brink of joining Roosevelt in an attempt to break de Gaulle, but he always drew back. Meanwhile, the general trend of his policy continued to be favourable to de Gaulle, in unspectacular but vital ways.

One of his key interventions was in the affair of the 'Anfa Memorandum', a document approved by Roosevelt but not seen by Churchill during the Casablanca Conference in January 1943. This memorandum purported to recognise on behalf of both the USA and Britain that Giraud had 'the right and duty of preserving all French interests'. This statement was linked with arrangements by the Americans to re-equip the French Army in North Africa, and if pursued seemed likely to ensure Giraud's predominance in North Africa, with de Gaulle as a weak outsider. Macmillan, the British Minister-Resident in Algiers, discovered the document and reported it to Churchill, claiming to take the charitable view that Roosevelt had not realised its true significance. Churchill, without making a fuss about the origins of the memorandum or the failure to consult him about it, simply set himself patiently to amend it in such a way as to render it harmless. The process took some four months, and was not ostentatious, but at the end of it Giraud and de Gaulle were acknowledged as having equal standing in the preserving of French interests.[7] Throughout the prolonged struggle between de Gaulle and Giraud in 1943, Macmillan in Algiers and Eden in London both supported de Gaulle, though in doing so they sometimes had to brave Churchill's wrath when he lost patience with de Gaulle. De Gaulle himself was sufficiently conscious

6. Elisabeth Barker, *Churchill and Eden at War* (London, 1978), pp. 72–3, 78–9; John Harvey, ed., *The War Diaries of Oliver Harvey* (London, 1978), pp. 260–1, entry for 21 May 1943.

7. Arthur L. Funk, 'The Anfa Memorandum: an incident of the Casablanca Conference', *Journal of Modern History*, vol. 26, No. 3, 1954, pp. 246–54.

of the value of Macmillan's help to write him a warm letter of thanks.[8] Eventually, at the end of August 1943 the British government 'recognised' the French National Committee, while the United States would go no further than 'accepting' it – a fine distinction, but marking a real difference between the two governments. In fact, throughout 1943 the British government pursued the aim of setting up a single French political authority to represent all the various territories and forces engaged in the war, while the Americans preferred to deal separately with the different French authorities. There was no doubt that the British policy was in the interests of de Gaulle personally, and was directed towards the restoration of France as a great power.

Another issue which was bedevilled by the Roosevelt–de Gaulle quarrel was that of the kind of administration to be adopted in liberated areas of France when the cross-Channel invasion finally began. Discussion of this question began in mid-1943, a year before the troops went ashore, without any agreement being reached between the Americans, the British and de Gaulle. The Americans, because of Roosevelt's dogged opposition to de Gaulle, refused to accept that the Committee of National Liberation should assume the administration of liberated areas, and proposed instead the imposition of military government, on the lines of the Allied Military Government of Occupied Territories (AMGOT) devised for the occupation of Italy. Eden and the Foreign Office thought that military government would be impractical, because the soldiers would virtually have to co-operate with French administrators of some kind; and also that it would be resented by the French people, who were, after all, to be liberated not occupied. De Gaulle too was utterly opposed to any scheme for military government, which he regarded as an affront to French dignity. He particularly denounced a plan to issue the landing forces with 'military francs', printed by the Allies to allow the troops to pay their way, on the grounds that they would be no better than forged currency. But Roosevelt was adamant, and in this matter Churchill would not even try to persuade him.

THE LIBERATION

These matters were still unresolved when the Allied armies landed in Normandy on 6 June 1944. In practice, events then settled the issue.

8. Alistair Horne, *Macmillan.*, vol. I, *1894–1956* (London, 1988), pp. 185, 187.

In the limited area of the Allied bridgehead, it gradually emerged that the representatives of the Committee of National Liberation (CNL) were well fitted to do the sort of administrative work for which the soldiers had neither the time nor the energy. General Montgomery, commanding the Allied forces, tactfully found an opportunity to meet de Gaulle's *Commissaire de la République* in Bayeux and commend his work. Thus the authority of de Gaulle and his organisation was simply accepted *de facto* in civil affairs. For their part, the farmers and café-owners of Normandy accepted the soldiers' military francs, and then cannily used them to pay the first tax demands which they received after the liberation. De Gaulle's government quietly accepted them, 'forged currency' or not. It was an interesting compromise, even on such a matter of principle.

In July 1944 Roosevelt changed his mind on this question of administration, with a speed which caught the British on the wrong foot. Early that month de Gaulle visited Washington, and was received effusively by the President and Secretary of State, who had previously tried so hard to get rid of him. At a press conference on 11 July, without consulting the British, Roosevelt announced that he was ready to treat the CNL as the *de facto* authority for administering liberated France. The British were left to scramble along behind to do the same, though in fact they had been working with the CNL representatives already. After the liberation of Paris and the obvious establishment of de Gaulle's authority over the whole of France, Roosevelt again moved suddenly, on 23 October, to announce American recognition of the new administration as the Provisonal Government of France. The British were not consulted, and were given hardly any notice, so that they again had to follow suit in undignified haste.

So it turned out that in 1943 the British government, though not always Churchill himself, supported de Gaulle against Giraud, and helped in the creation of the CNL as the sole French authority; but in 1944, on the crucial questions of civil administration and recognition, Churchill committed Britain to an ultimately futile dependence on American policy. In the long run, it was Churchill's dependence on the Americans, and not his long but unobtrusive support for the Free French, which left the deeper mark on de Gaulle's mind. This was largely the result of a dramatic confrontation between the two men just before the Normandy landings.

On 4 June 1944 Churchill received de Gaulle in the train where the Prime Minister had set up his headquarters while waiting for the landings to begin. Churchill was on edge, full of anxiety about this vast and hazardous operation. De Gaulle resented having been kept in the dark about the landings, and still opposed the American plans for military government of liberated territories. Churchill urged de Gaulle to come to terms with the Americans about the administration of France. De Gaulle replied that he did not need Roosevelt's authorisation to establish a government in his own country. At a crucial moment in this confrontation, Churchill said that

> He must tell him [de Gaulle] bluntly that, if after every effort had been exhausted the President [of the United States] was on one side and the French National Committee of Liberation on the other, he, Mr Churchill, would almost certainly side with the President, and that anyhow no quarrel would ever arise between Britain and the United States on account of France . . .

To which de Gaulle replied that 'he quite understood that in case of disagreement between the United States and France, Great Britain would side with the United States'.[9]

That was not precisely what Churchill had said, and it certainly did not represent the whole of his thought on Britain's position between the USA and France. It was disclaimed even at the time by Eden and Ernest Bevin, who between them were to conduct British foreign policy for over a decade to come. But Churchill's words, uttered at a moment of great stress, made a powerful impression on de Gaulle. He recounted the episode vividly in his memoirs, and still referred to it nearly twenty years later, in January 1963, just after he had vetoed British entry into the European Economic Community. Speaking to Alain Peyrefitte, he recalled Churchill's words almost exactly, and concluded: '. . . that has been, in general, English policy since 1942, whether the government was Labour or Tory'.[10]

Not quite three months after the confrontation on 4 June, at the end of August 1944, Paris was liberated from the Germans. This was the result of a week's fighting inside the city by the French Resistance, and the simultaneous entry into the city on 25 August of the French 2nd Armoured Division and the 4th US Infantry Division. The great mass of the Allied armies which made the liberation of Paris possible was of course made up of Americans, British and Canadians. But when de Gaulle spoke at the Hôtel de Ville on the evening of 25 August, he painted a very different picture.

9. PRO, FO 954/9A, record of conversation, 4 June 1944.
10. Alain Peyrefitte, *C'était de Gaulle*, vol. I, '*La France redevient la France*' (Paris, 1994), pp. 370–1.

Paris! Paris outraged! Paris broken! Paris martyred! Paris liberated!
Liberated by herself, liberated by her people with the help of the
armies of France, of the whole of France, of France that is fighting, of
France alone . . .[11]

Later in his speech de Gaulle mentioned 'our dear and admirable
allies', but this passing reference made little impact compared with the
intense emotional repetition of his opening words. De Gaulle wrote in
his memoirs that this was an improvised speech, but it was surely the
product of a long-meditated intention. De Gaulle had to create a myth
which would restore French pride, heal the wounds of the defeat in
1940, and cover the shame of collaboration. His speech at the Hôtel
de Ville therefore struck the thrilling note, so often heard in French
history, of 'la seule France' – France alone. In the context of the time
it was necessary, and in its own way right. But it was not a note
which could find any echo in British hearts. On the contrary, it was
the final act in de Gaulle's display of intransigent independence from
the British (and now of all the 'Anglo-Saxons'), designed to disguise
his fundamental dependence upon them.

It was in a very different spirit that de Gaulle, on 30 October 1944,
invited Churchill to visit Paris. In words which combined grace with
truth, his invitation was addressed to 'Mr Winston Churchill, the great
statesman who, even in the darkest days, never lost faith in France or
in the ultimate victory of the Allies, to which he will have so greatly
contributed'.[12] In reply Churchill proposed dates for his visit which
included 11 November, the first Armistice Day since the Liberation.
De Gaulle was at first alarmed, or perhaps piqued – 'He wants to steal
my 11 November from me', he exclaimed.[13] But he accepted the
dates, and the ceremonies of Armistice Day formed a splendid setting
for an emotional occasion. On the 11th Churchill and de Gaulle laid
wreaths on the tomb of the Unknown Soldier under the Arc de
Triomphe, and then walked together down the Champs Elysées – just
as Churchill had said they would at a time in the war when such a
denouement seemed far from likely. They halted before the statue of
Clemenceau, where de Gaulle had arranged for a military band to play
'Le Père la Victoire', a song composed in 1918 in honour of the
Tiger. 'For you', said de Gaulle in English; and in his memoirs he
commented 'It was only right'. And he remembered how, one

---

11. Jean Lacouture, *De Gaulle*, vol. I, *Le rebelle* (Paris, 1984), p. 833 (English
translation in *De Gaulle: The Rebel*, p. 575).
    12. Ministère des Affaires Etrangères (hereafter abbreviated to MAE), Papiers
Massigli, 217/53.
    13. Jean Chauvel, *Commentaire*, vol. II, *D'Alger à Berne* (Paris, 1972), p. 82.

evening at Chequers, Churchill had sung the old song for him without missing a word. The next day Churchill went to the Hôtel de Ville to receive the freedom of the city. Eden remarked afterwards that 'Not for one moment did Winston stop crying, and he could have filled buckets by the time he received the Freedom of Paris'.[14]

It was a moving and memorable occasion, to which two great men rose with a fitting generosity of spirit – Churchill with utter spontaneity, de Gaulle it appears with a touch of calculation as he demonstrated to his guest the unanimity and order of the people of Paris. If the two previous scenes had signalled the separation of Britain and France, in the British link with the United States and the assertion of 'la seule France', Armistice Day 1944 marked a reconciliation, and seemed to open the way to a renewal of the *Entente*.

Both men sensed this opportunity, but it proved beyond their grasp. After the emotional days in Paris, Churchill accompanied de Gaulle on a visit to the French Army in the field, and on the way back the two statesmen talked privately. De Gaulle, acknowledging that France and Britain would emerge from the war weakened in face of the power of America and Russia, proposed a sort of alliance between them. They would not be able to impose their will, but if they acted together they could act as a block against others. If they acted in accord, he said, 'they will weigh heavily enough in the world's scales so that nothing will be done which they themselves have not consented to or determined'. They would attract support from other countries, and from world opinion, which would distrust the giant powers. It was, coming from de Gaulle, a remarkable proposal. Churchill responded with a frank statement of the fundamentals of his own policy within the Grand Alliance. It was, he said, better to persuade the stronger partners than to pit yourself against them, and that was what he was trying to do. The Americans had immense resources, which Churchill tried to persuade them to use wisely. 'I have formed a close personal tie with Roosevelt. With him I proceed by suggestion in order to influence matters in the right direction.' Russia was a great beast, long starved, and it was not possible to prevent her from eating. Even so, Churchill went on, 'I am trying to restrain Stalin, who, if he has an enormous appetite, also has a great deal of good sense.' He then made an astonishingly far-sighted prediction: 'When it is time to digest, the surfeited Russians will have their difficult problems. Then, perhaps, St. Nicholas can bring back to life the poor children the ogre has put in

14. Gilbert, *Road to Victory*, pp. 1057–61; François Kersaudy, *Churchill and de Gaulle* (London, 1981), pp. 373–87; Charles de Gaulle, *Mémoires de Guerre*, vol. III, *Le Salut* (Paris, 1959), pp. 49–50.

the salting tub.' His own policy was to keep in touch with both. 'Meanwhile, I attend every meeting, yield nothing for nothing, and manage to secure a few dividends.' And he counselled patience to de Gaulle: 'Leave matters in my hands.'[15]

Churchill cloaked his message in fine words about not accepting any breach between Britain and France; and he said he was willing to consider an alliance in principle, but the substance of his reply was unmistakable. He declined de Gaulle's proposal of an Anglo-French combination to act as a block against the USA and the USSR because he was committed to his own independent role within the Grand Alliance, influencing both Roosevelt and Stalin in what he believed to be the right direction. This was a policy which Churchill had followed for the past four years. He doubtless exaggerated his influence on Roosevelt and Stalin, but his claims still had some substance. Only in September 1944 he had conferred with Roosevelt at Quebec, and in October he had visited Stalin in Moscow and struck a deal (the 'percentages agreement') which had secured British interests in Greece. Nor was he entirely wrong to urge de Gaulle to leave matters in his hands. At the Yalta Conference of the Big Three in February 1945, Churchill was to secure for France a zone of occupation in Germany and a permanent seat on the Security Council of the United Nations. Without Churchill's advocacy, France would never have been granted these great assets in the post-war world.

This statement of Churchill's position was more careful, nuanced and accurate than his outburst on 4 June to the effect that Britain would always choose the United States as against France. Churchill refused to give up his links with Roosevelt, and with Stalin too, for an exclusive partnership with de Gaulle; but his intention was not to reject France but to retain his contacts and influence with all three countries. This was a natural, almost an inevitable, position for Britain to adopt after the events of the Second World War since June 1940. It was virtually impossible in November 1944 for Churchill to renounce his standing as one of the Big Three in favour of an alliance with France directed against the Americans and the Russians. It was remarkable that de Gaulle should make the proposal for an exclusive partnership with Britain. It was impossible for Churchill to accept it. There was, in that sense, no going back on the events of 1940.

15. De Gaulle, *Mémoires*, vol. III, pp. 52–3; the translation is taken from *The Complete War Memoirs of General de Gaulle*, translated by Charles Howard (New York, 1984), p. 728.

FRIENDSHIP REDISCOVERED, 1944

Churchill and de Gaulle thus failed to build upon their emotional reunion on Armistice Day 1944. At the same time, the British and French peoples as a whole were fully preoccupied with their own affairs. The British struggled through the last months of a war which many had hoped would end in the autumn of 1944. The French endured a miserable winter, short of food and fuel. Few lifted their eyes from the pressing business of everyday life, the civilians getting through the obstacle course of wartime existence, the soldiers fighting their last campaigns. Yet even so there were some individuals who were restoring old links between the two countries or creating new ones. Perhaps the most intense of these bonds were those between French Resistance agents and their comrades in the Special Operations Executive and the RAF squadrons whose Lysanders and Hudsons flew so frequently between France and England. In 1943 there were no fewer than 133 Lysander and Hudson missions to France; from February to September 1944 there were a further 58. The personal ties thus formed were so strong that they endured, in many cases, for a lifetime. It became customary, at some of the annual meetings which the *amicales* of the former Resistance groups held in later years, to read out not only their own lists of the recently died, but also the names of their British comrades. Those involved, on both sides of the Channel, cherished these links and were to celebrate them with particular warmth fifty years on, during the commemorations held in 1994 and 1995. The numbers involved were very small, but the emotions were intense, and the ties were at once slender yet unbreakable.[16]

These were the warriors, of a particular type, who flourished during the Second World War. There were also a few writers and intellectuals who lifted their eyes from the everyday struggles of life, took stock of their neighbours across the Channel (in both directions), and tried to explain them to their fellow-countrymen.

This was not an entirely new enterprise, even in the war years. Throughout the war, French resistance had been sustained by the

16. See Hugh Verity, *We Landed by Moonlight* (Wilmslow, 1995), pp. 194–209. The whole book is an account of the secret RAF landings in France, written by one of the most experienced, gallant and successful of the pilots involved. I have also had the advantage of a conversation with Francis Cammaerts, a former SOE agent now living in France, who has kept the closest ties with his French comrades. *Gens de la Lune*, the journal of the Amicale des Réseaux 'Action' de la France Combattante, offers many examples of these links across the Channel and the closeness of the old wartime friendships. I am grateful to Group-Captain Verity for allowing me to consult his copies of this journal.

belief that the British would win in the end. As early as December 1940 the novelist Georges Bernanos, a powerful voice among French intellectuals, wrote from his self-chosen exile in Brazil that in the past the French had not taken enough trouble to understand the English. That was a pity, because there was now much to understand and to marvel at. 'Englishmen!' he wrote, 'you are at this moment writing one of the greatest pages in history.'[17] Bernanos's *Lettre aux Anglais* was eventually published in France in 1946, becoming in a sense a letter to the French about the British.

Again in December 1940, one of the early members of the French Resistance, Jacques Debû-Bridel, was also writing about England. 'England stands fast. England will continue to stand fast. She has always, in spite of long setbacks, won the final victory. Such is the gospel of our reviving courage . . . France, the whole of France, has her eyes fixed on the besieged island. Her heart is English. England, the ultimate hope of France.'[18] It was a striking claim, and one rarely heard on French lips. It was also a remarkable tribute to British courage, offered in a dark hour and at no small risk to its author. Nearly four years later, after the Liberation, Debû-Bridel visited Britain and was shown round under the auspices of the Ministry of Information, in order to write a book explaining the British war effort to the French people. His chosen title has now lost much of its force, but was at the time highly evocative. During the German occupation, Jean Hérold-Paquis had ended his regular broadcasts on the collaborationist Radio Paris with the words: 'Londres, comme Carthage, sera détruite' ('London, like Carthage, will be destroyed'). So Debû-Bridel called his book *Carthage n'est pas détruite*. On the contrary, London was very much alive.[19]

Debû-Bridel left his readers in no doubt as to the springs of this endurance. 'If London has held out, it is thanks to the admirable, voluntary discipline of the English people . . .' England was a modern Sparta, organised for war, with its civil defence and Home Guard volunteers, and women engaged in war work. The author was much struck by 'the civic spirit of the English people', which he rather optimistically reported had meant that the black market was almost unknown.[20] He wrote in glowing terms of the Royal Navy, of Spitfire

---

17. Georges Bernanos, *Lettre aux Anglais* (Paris, 1946), quoted in Alexander Werth, *France 1940–1955* (London, 1956), p. xxi.
18. Jacques Debû-Bridel, *Carthage n'est pas détruite* (Paris 1945), p. 9. These passages were written in December 1940, and first published clandestinely under the pseudonym 'Argonne' in 1943.
19. Ibid., pp. 13, 16.
20. Ibid., p. 23.

fighters, and of the bombing offensive against Germany. He also devoted a passage to the RAF raids on France, quoting an Air Force officer who assured him that British aircrews had risked their own lives rather than bomb inaccurately. (This is something which, very movingly, one hears in France to this day.) All this effort and determination had been inspired by one man, Winston Churchill, whose secret, wrote Debû-Bridel, had been to trust the English people.

At the beginning and end of his book, Debû-Bridel struck the note of unity between France and Britain. 'Our two peoples formed, certainly, two different nations, but in spite of everything a single civilisation, more than a thousand years old.' (The phrase used in the original was 'une seule et même civilisation', which has an emphasis which is hard to catch in translation.) The popularity of General de Gaulle in Britain showed the sympathy of the British people for France as a comrade in arms who had suffered a passing misfortune, but was now restored. 'The friendship of our peoples has never seemed to me to be more assured.'[21]

The book was in part a work of propaganda, as the British Ministry of Information intended; but it was more than that. The author had already declared his faith in Britain in the darkest days, and when it was dangerous to do so. His admiration was sincere, and it is worth emphasising the two main themes which sustained that admiration: the character of the British people, with their voluntary discipline and civic spirit; and a sense of unity between Britain and France which was not a matter of institutions but of a shared civilisation.

At much the same time as Debû-Bridel was visiting England, another Frenchman was preparing to publish a much longer and deeper interpretation of the country and its people: Pierre Bourdan's *Perplexités et grandeur de l'Angleterre*.[22] At the time of the armistice in 1940, Bourdan had been in London; and he recalled the atmosphere with something like awe: '. . . a people was passing, within a few hours, from armed indolence to moral heroism . . . and was to take into its care, at the moment when Europe was collapsing, the conscience, the mission, the last hopes of Europe'.[23] The courage of this people, Bourdan added, was inspired by one man, Winston Churchill.

---

21. Ibid., pp. 8, 82–3.
22. Pierre Bourdan (pseudonym of Pierre Maillard), *Perplexités et grandeur de l'Angleterre* (Paris, 1945). The book was written during the war, when the author spent much time in England. He returned to France as a soldier with Leclerc's 2nd Armoured Division in August 1944. See also Pierre Bourdan, *Carnets des jours d'attente, 1940–1944* (Paris, 1945).
23. Bourdan, *Jours d'attente*, p. 16.

Bourdan's massive book, mainly written during the war but drawing also on his experience in the 1930s, was primarily a study of the English character. Strikingly, he argued that the outstanding characteristic of the English mind was not the pragmatism so often noted in France but 'fancy', in the sense of offering free range to the imagination. Alongside such observations he developed two main themes.

The first was the immense strength which England drew from continuity and tradition. English society bore witness to the patient victory of a people over its own unruly instincts. Religion, education and moral strength had inculcated a deep sense of responsibility: 'In fact, English society possesses unwritten legislation, accumulated by tradition, which reaches out infinitely.'[24] This orderly and responsible society had survived the trials of war, despite some weakening of its fabric. Bourdan had seen it at work, both at home in England and among British troops overseas, and he was unstinting though not uncritical in his admiration. He recognised that the virtues of social hierarchy and conformity, which held the structure together, carried with them dangers of snobbery and excessive conservatism. He believed that English society had achieved a remarkable balance between excessive individualism and stifling uniformity, but warned that this equilibrium might not last. But the prevailing tone was one of admiration. Bourdan held that British institutions had preserved a continuity which was almost unique in Europe, not destroyed by war, undermined by enemy occupation, or overthrown by revolution. These institutions were the product of history, the result of successive reforms and accretions. Whatever their faults, they had been strong enough to withstand the ordeals of economic depression, ideological ferment and a great war. The key to this durability, according to Bourdan, lay in both the nature of the institutions and the attitude of the British people towards them. The interaction between people and institutions had produced flexibility as well as continuity – for example, the author noted the moves towards state control during the war, even in a country normally distrustful of the power of the state; and he observed also a shift towards equality in a society accustomed to hierarchy.

This combination of flexibility and stability was crucial. The English themselves, Bourdan thought, were highly conscious of the changes wrought by the war; 'but what especially strikes the foreigner among them is that England has succeeded in retaining its physical and moral

24. Bourdan, *Perplexités*, p. 56.

identity'. This was what made England almost unique in the Europe of the time, and Bourdan had no doubt as to its advantages; he wrote of 'the luxury of continuity'.[25] But he added that this state of affairs implied a dangerous separation from the continent. For four years England had drawn solely on her own intellectual and moral inspiration, untouched by influences from Europe, and much would depend on what happened when that isolation came to an end.

This leads to Bourdan's second great theme: relations between England and Europe. In his *Carnets des jours d'attente*, he wrote that what sustained Britain in 1940 was not only her insular national pride: 'It was a sense of European solidarity which England, an island, had forgotten in times of good fortune and which she rediscovered in the dark days.'[26] He returned to this point in his main work, and added a question. In the summer of 1940, he wrote, 'England was more European than she had ever been, and than she ever has been since, because she identified her own defence with the liberation of Europe'. Britain became, in fact, the champion of Europe. But what course would England follow after the war? 'What reputation will she have, what role will she play in a liberated Europe?'[27] Bourdan noted that the old question as to whether Britain was to be in Europe or not was already emerging in the speeches of politicians, and he argued that it must be answered clearly, not ambiguously. 'To be European with reservations, and to free herself from European responsibilities as soon as other pre-occupations prevail over those of the Continent, would be the surest way to alienate Europe.'[28] Bourdan did not say specifically what he meant by Britain choosing a role in Europe, but he gave a vital clue to his thought. British relations with France, he insisted, went deeper than issues of foreign policy. 'They touch on the fundamental *raison d'être* of England – and indeed on our own – in a civilised world which she has served. These are facts of nature, a nature which is not only geographical and physical but also moral and traditional.'[29] He struck the same note in his *Carnets*, writing that when he and other French soldiers embarked from England for Normandy they knew that they were leaving behind 'one of the last bastions of a civilisation which depends neither on numbers nor on weight, but on the quality and the willpower of men. It was also our own . . .'.[30] This was very close to Debû-Bridel's theme of 'a single

25. Ibid., pp. 379, 405.
26. Bourdan, *Jours d'attente*, p. 66.
27. Bourdan, *Perplexités*, p. 356.
28. Ibid., p. 406.
29. Ibid., p. 427.
30. Bourdan, *Jours d'attente*, p. 199.

civilisation'. Both writers were invoking something deep-rooted and fundamental, a matter of culture and civilisation, not institutions. (It is surely a tragedy that recent debate about 'Europe' is conducted almost entirely in terms of the institutions and intricacies of the European Community, rather than of the cultural identity that Bourdan had in mind.)

The views expressed so eloquently by Bourdan and Debû-Bridel were doubtless held by only a small minority in France. A French historian, writing some fifty years after the Liberation, held that 'For many, the Germans were admired victors before the appearance of the Anglo-Saxons as rivals and liberators'.[31] Even among the French who spent the war years in Britain, or became active members of the Resistance in France, there were many who felt they had to keep their distance from the British and demonstrate their independence – after all, de Gaulle himself set the clearest possible example in that regard. Even so, it was a glowing admiration which shone through the pages of Bourdan's and Debû-Bridel's books. The sense of cultural identity between Britain and France that they conveyed was powerful. There was here an opening on the French side for a new understanding, if it could be exploited.

On the British side, the Francophiles who had felt so bereft when France was defeated and occupied in 1940 were overjoyed at the Liberation. Even in the darkest days they had kept their faith in France. Alexander Werth wrote in 1942 that 'The future of Europe needs . . . a France whose creative genius will once again shine across the world after the years of twilight and darkness'. In September 1942 Charles Morgan published his 'Ode to France', first read to a small gathering of exiled Frenchmen in London:

> Beloved France, despair not,
>   Nothing of thee is ended.
> Into thy sacred hands
>   The Spirit of Man is commended.
> Be one, be only France
>   Though heaven fall.
> If thou but teach Thyself,
>   Thou teachest all.[32]

Even during the occupation, British sympathisers had contrived to keep in touch with French intellectual life. Cyril Connolly published

31. André Martel, *Histoire militaire de la France* (Paris, 1994), vol. 4, p. 246.
32. Alexander Werth, *The Twilight of France* (New York, 1942), p. 314; Charles Morgan, *Ode to France* (London, 1942), p. 5.

some of Aragon's wartime poetry in *Horizon*. Vercors's *Le silence de la mer*, published clandestinely in France by Les Editions du Minuit, was smuggled to England and published there in 1943, with immediate success. In autumn 1944 direct contacts were resumed. In October Charles Morgan visited Paris, and listened to his 'Ode to France' being read aloud at the *Comédie Française*, in the presence of de Gaulle himself, and to fervent applause. (Morgan wrote laconically to a friend that 'An Englishman can't ask much more of life'.[33]) Raymond Mortimer, the literary editor of the *New Statesman*, devoted all his space in the issue of 14 October to a discussion of the first non-clandestine issue of *Les Lettres françaises*, the literary review of the Resistance movements. Similarly, *Time and Tide* (21 October 1944) gave up its book pages to the work of Les Editions du Minuit. Such was the interest of literary editors in resuming contacts with France; and they took it for granted that their readers would be with them.

A few months later, in March 1945, Harold Nicolson (writer, Francophile and Member of Parliament) revisited France for the first time since 1940. Landing at Dieppe, he bent to touch the ground. When the porter asked, 'Monsieur a laissé tomber quelque-chose?', he was quick to reply, 'Non, j'ai retrouvé quelque-chose.' ('Have you dropped something, monsieur?' – 'No, I have recovered something.') This story, which was almost too neat to be true but was none the less significant for that, soon found its way onto French radio, giving much pleasure.[34]

Others, in their own ways, felt much the same. Churchill's emotions when he walked down the Champs Elysées on 11 November 1944 were plain for all to see. Newspaper correspondents were delighted to return to their old haunts. Catherine Gavin, who had felt separation from France as 'not the least of the calamities of World War II', happily returned to share 'the daily life of the brilliant and indestructible French people'.[35] At the time, most of that daily life was hard and dreary; but some of the early reports from Paris were full of the beauty of the city and the sparkle of the autumn fashion shows, and contained a good deal of what has been nicely called the '*Ritzkrieg*' aspect of the Liberation.[36] This brought a hostile reaction in Britain, where the beauties of London had survived less well than those of Paris, and where austerity was the order of the day. There

33. Eiluned Lewis, ed., *Selected Letters of Charles Morgan* (London, 1967), p. 29.
34. James Lees-Milne, *Harold Nicolson* (London, 1981), vol. II, pp. 182–3.
35. Catherine Gavin, *Liberated France* (London, 1955), p. 9.
36. Antony Beevor and Artemis Cooper, *Paris after the Liberation* (London, 1994), p. 79.

was a tendency to assume, as one of the Paris correspondents wrily admitted, 'that the French were *at it again*, guzzling and swilling as in 1940 . . .'.[37]

The champagne moment passed, as such moments do. The French mood, which had at first been so welcoming, turned to one of morosity, suspicion and self-absorption, in which people became 'distrustful of everybody and everything', as Alexander Werth wrote.[38] When C. V. Wedgewood visited Paris in the winter of 1945–46 she noted 'the ranks of frozen cabbages' in the formal surroundings of the Luxembourg Gardens, and observed how dark the churches were without any candles – there were simply none to be found. 'For all the enthusiasm and excitement which renewed contact with French culture has provoked here in England, the frozen fountains have hardly yet begun to thaw.'[39] On the British side, attention turned to finishing off the war and then surviving the peace. The people as a whole simply concentrated on getting through the next day and the next week. For most of them, France might still have been on another planet. Political interest concentrated on the United States and the Soviet Union. France faded from the forefront of the scene, and for practical reasons visits across the Channel were possible only for a very few. For some time, Bourdan's question as to whether Britain was to be part of Europe or not remained unanswered, simply by default. The glowing sense of a single civilisation faded away.

37. Gavin, *Liberated France*, p. 49.
38. Werth, *France 1940–1955*, p. xx.
39. C.V. Wedgwood, 'Return to Paris: Winter 1945', in *History and Hope. The Collected Essays of C. V. Wedgwood* (London, 1987), pp. 464–5. The whole essay (pp. 463–70) is a gem.

CHAPTER 4

The Aftermath of War and the Treaty of Dunkirk, 1945–1947

WEARY VICTORS

Great Britain ended the Second World War in a state of uncertainty and internal contradiction. The country had fought the war in Europe from first to last, and then shared in the victory over Japan. The British were proudly conscious that they had stood alone in 1940, and in 1945 they remained partners in the Grand Alliance, so that Churchill took his place with Stalin, Roosevelt and Truman at the Conferences at Yalta and Potsdam. All this nourished a sense of national self-confidence and achievement. Moreover, virtually no-one doubted that the war had been both necessary and just; and victory had been achieved at a cost that came as a relief after the terrible losses of 1914–18. British dead in the Second World War (including civilians) numbered just over 355,000, with the Commonwealth countries adding another 129,000.[1] Yet at the same time the nation was exhausted. Six years of war had taken their toll on a weary population, whose rations of food had grown ever more spartan. The war effort had absorbed manpower and industrial production. Reserves of gold and foreign currency had been run down. Britain could not afford to pay for the level of imports required to maintain even her straitened standard of living, and was dependent on American assistance. When Lend-lease finished with the end of the war, the only recourse was to ask for loans. The United States advanced a loan of $3,750,000,000, the Canadians another of $1,250,000. Britain had become a poor relation of her trans-Atlantic cousins.

1. Casualty figures, rounded to the nearest thousand, in Martin Gilbert, *The Second World War* (revised edition, London, 1990), p. 746. The total of those killed was less than half that in the war of 1914–18.

At the time, confidence prevailed over exhaustion. The British elected a Labour government in 1945, and embarked on a hopeful new course towards a welfare state. Though austerity was the order of the day, it was seen as the necessary prelude to recovery. The British expected to come through their economic difficulties as they had survived the early disasters of the war. Equally there was no doubt that Britain was still a great power, not of the same stature as the USA or the Soviet Union, but operating at the same level. Britain aspired to maintain this role as a world power by virtue of her special position as the link between three circles: the Commonwealth, the United States and western Europe. In this trinity, the Commonwealth held a special place, for reasons which were both practical and psychological. The Dominions had played a vital role in the war; imperial preference still provided the main framework for British trade; the sterling area was vital for the economy; and the Commonwealth seemed to spread a benign British influence throughout the world.

In 1945, the conclusion seemed to be clear. Britain remained a great power, with worldwide interests and influence. In Europe, she enjoyed the immense prestige conferred by victory and by the continuity of her political life, unbroken by defeat or occupation. In later years, this confidence came to appear illusory. Economic recovery was slow in coming, and failed to achieve the momentum built up in France or Germany. The Commonwealth was to fade away like the Cheshire cat, leaving only a smile behind – and an enigmatic one at that. The prestige of victory proved short-lived. Even the precious stability of British political life came to seem akin to sclerosis. But it was a long time before such doubts set in, and in 1945 the British looked across the Channel from a vantage-point of past achievement and hope for the future.

The position of France was very different. France was indeed one of the victors, and de Lattre had been among the Allied commanders who received the German surrender in 1945. But at a deeper level, as a French writer put it forty years after the end of the war, 'Germany and France had lost the Second World War'.[2] For the Germans this was painfully obvious in the ruins of their cities and the total occupation of their country. The French on the other hand could display the outward trappings of victory, but at bottom, despite the oratory of de Gaulle, they knew that they had been liberated by the American, British and Canadian armies. The revived French Army and

---

2. Joseph Rovan, *France Allemagne. Deux nations, un avenir* (Paris, 1986), p. 133.

the Resistance had played their part, but everyone understood that they alone could never have driven out the Germans.

Worse still, France had suffered the internal wounds of civil war. The *Milice* had fought against the Resistance; the Resistance had been divided within itself. After the Liberation, the purge of collaborators had prolonged the atmosphere of civil strife. Even the big trials, like those of Pétain and Laval, which were meant to clear the air, had left much that was murky. The experience of occupation, collaboration and resistance left France a legacy of division and bitterness which had not completely disappeared even fifty years later. In 1994 Henri Amouroux completed his vast history of France between 1940 and 1945 with a volume entitled *La page n'est pas tournée* – 'The story is not over'.

The physical and economic cost of the war was heavy. The Allies bombed the French railways in 1944, a strategic necessity which left a legacy of dislocation. Food was scarce in the winter of 1944–45, which was exceptionally severe. France had virtually no reserves of gold or foreign currency. In 1946 the franc stood at one-sixth of its 1939 value against the dollar. The cost in lives was also high: approximately 610,000 French dead, including some 360,000 civilians; some estimates put it higher still. This was well above the British total, though less than half the terrible losses of 1914–18.[3]

French institutions, in contrast to those in Britain, had been severely damaged by the war. The collapse of 1940 had dealt a death-blow to the Third Republic. Pétain had set out to replace it by a new *Etat français*, which never achieved coherent form and was utterly discredited by 1944. Resistance groups devoted much time and energy to speculating on a new France, but were inevitably divided as to its form. De Gaulle at least had a clear idea: he wanted a strong presidential Republic, with himself as President, but he failed to win general support for this idea. The result was curious. To all appearances, the last thing anyone wanted was a return to the Third Republic, yet the prolonged labours of two constituent assemblies produced a Fourth Republic which bore an uncanny resemblance to the Third. The French people endorsed the new creation in a referendum, but without enthusiasm: the Yes vote represented 37.7 per cent of the electorate, the Noes 31.1, and the abstentions 31.2.[4]

---

3. Casualty figures in Maurice Larkin, *France since the Popular Front* (Oxford, 1988), p. 118. The figures are difficult: for example, Larkin includes an estimate for casualties among men from Alsace and Lorraine called up into the German Army during the war. André Martel, *Histoire militaire de la France* (Paris, 1994), vol. IV, p. 251, gives an estimate of about 650,000 war dead, including 450,000 civilians.
4. Jean-Pierre Rioux, *The Fourth Republic, 1944–1958* (Cambridge, 1989), p. 106.

The Fourth Republic had none too many friends when it was formally inaugurated in January 1947.

In their economic weakness, and simply to pay for their imports, the French had to do as the British did, and ask for American help. Léon Blum, the Socialist leader, was despatched to Washington in May 1946 on this errand, prompting the piquant headline in the *Wall Street Journal*: 'Karl Marx calls on Santa Claus.'[5] Like many headlines, this was misleading. Blum was no Karl Marx, and the United States was not entirely disposed to play Santa Claus. The Americans were generous in writing off Lend-lease aid which was due to be repaid, in providing loans, and in paying for Canadian agricultural produce to be sent to France. In return, they required the opening of French cinemas to American films; an agreement to end trade quotas and colonial preferences (though with no date fixed); and that the franc should be made convertible within two years. The agreement on films was denounced in France as American cultural imperialism, and the whole package was attacked by the Left as turning France into the vassal of the 'Anglo-Saxons'. Yet in fact the American terms were not severe, and in any case, no-one except the Americans was going to provide the 1,340 locomotives or the 25,750 tractors that France imported from the United States in two years from late 1945 to late 1947.[6]

This Franco-American agreement (the so-called Blum–Byrnes accord) had its effects on French relations with Britain. Not for the first or last time, the British tended to get caught in the backwash of resentment against the 'Anglo-Saxons', even when they had nothing to do with American policy. At a deeper level, the French grew determined to ensure that their dependence on the United States was only temporary. Jean Monnet, who took part in Blum's mission to Washington and was also the head of the central French planning agency (the *Commissariat Général du Plan*), launched in 1946 his slogan 'modernisation or decadence'. France began to choose modernisation. American loans were used to modernise French industry. American locomotives improved the French transport system. Tractors began to change French agriculture. These movements coincided with other changes. In late 1945 the government founded the *Ecole Nationale d'Administration*, and in January 1946 set up the *Commissariat Général du Plan*. The first provided a centre for training an elite of civil servants; the second set a new course for the French economy. It took many years for the consequences of these actions to be worked out, but in the long run the French commitment to modernisation was to change

5. Hubert Bonin, *Histoire économique de la IVe République* (Paris, 1987), p. 124.
6. Ibid., p. 132.

the whole economic balance between France and Britain, and may have been a better bet than the British attempt to build a welfare state on the foundations of an old economy.

At the end of the war there was a strong current of British sympathy towards France. In the Labour government of 1945, Ernest Bevin became Foreign Secretary, in succession to the strongly Francophile Eden. But he continued to show much the same sympathy for France that Eden had done. On 23 November 1945, for example, he spoke movingly in the House of Commons of the significance of French history, culture and civilising influence, which far outweighed the fact that France had been temporarily defeated by an aggressor. 'In the case of France there is a great history', said Bevin, 'and I am convinced that there is a great future.'[7] Attlee, who succeeded Churchill as Prime Minister, had nothing like his predecessor's personal and emotional involvement with France, but he had steadily supported de Gaulle and the Free French during the war, sometimes against Churchill. He had a clear view of the importance of France in post-war Europe which arose from reason, not sentiment.

In France, Britain was represented as Ambassador by Duff Cooper, a former Conservative Cabinet minister and a devoted Francophile. He was a writer (the author of a biography of Talleyrand, among other books), and with his wife Lady Diana he gave the British Embassy in Paris a social and intellectual *éclat* which counted for much in the grim surroundings of post-war Paris. It was a tribute to Cooper's qualities and standing with the French that Bevin allowed him to stay on as Ambassador after the Labour victory in 1945, defending him against criticism on the Labour back benches. Cooper was able to maintain a close, though often difficult, relationship with de Gaulle. He presented French affairs in a favourable light to his government, and pressed the case for a Franco-British alliance strongly – indeed, sometimes beyond the bounds of prudence or the limits of his instructions from London.

But these warm and favourable views of France were counterbalanced by some gloomy British assessments of that country's condition. In January 1946 Duff Cooper had lunch with André Malraux – left-wing intellectual, writer, man of action, and one of de Gaulle's closest associates; and later the same day talked at length with a prominent French businessman. Cooper at once wrote to Oliver Harvey at the Foreign Office to express his alarm that both these visitors, from very different standpoints, foresaw the likelihood of civil

7. Alan Bullock, *Ernest Bevin*, vol. III, *Foreign Secretary* (Oxford, pb edn, 1985), p. 147.

conflict in France in the near future. Harvey passed the letter on to Bevin, who wrote: 'Looks like civil war within a year. Dept. must keep this before them.'[8] The British were particularly anxious about the strength of the Communist Party in France. In February 1946 the Labour Attaché at the Paris Embassy prepared a report on the Communist domination of the *Confédération Général du Travail*, the main trade union organisation. His gloomy analysis was given the unusual prominence of circulation to the Cabinet and the King.[9] With Communist ministers in the government, Bevin complained to the French Foreign Minister, Bidault, that their two countries could not carry on a conversation because there was a third power 'in the cupboard' listening.[10] In March 1946 the British Treasury tried to hurry up French repayments of credits, for fear of the advent of a Communist government which would default on the debt.

The cumulative effect of such views took its toll, even on those who were well disposed towards France. Massigli, the shrewd and well-informed French Ambassador in London, was acutely aware of this pessimistic trend in British opinion. On 5 March 1946 Churchill gave his famous speech at Fulton, Missouri, proclaiming that an iron curtain had fallen across Europe, and appealing for a revived Anglo-American alliance against the Soviet threat. Among the manifold implications of this speech, Massigli saw in Churchill's references to the ruin of Europe and the power of Communist parties on this side of the iron curtain a sign that the old statesman had lost his faith in the resurrection of a democratic Europe and of France. If Churchill, of all men, had lost faith in France it was a grave state of affairs. Not long afterwards, in August 1946, Massigli set out, in a special note for the French Premier, a gloomy analysis of British views of France. In the course of it, he recalled that Bevin had told him recently that he did not know where France was going. The Foreign Secretary had even repeated a question put to him by an MP: 'Are you sure that France is, at bottom, on our side?'[11] It was a disconcerting question.

In France, de Gaulle was Premier until his abrupt resignation in January 1946. His attitude to Britain remained ambiguous and difficult. In an interview for *The Times* (10 September 1945) he declared that there was a community of interest between France and Britain that made it desirable (even necessary) for them to concert their policies,

---

8. PRO, FO 371/59957, Z754/121/17, Cooper to Harvey, 22 Jan. 1946.

9. PRO, FO 371/59958, Z1679/121/17.

10. John Young, *Britain, France and the Unity of Europe, 1945–1951* (Leicester, 1984), p. 37.

11. MAE, Papiers Massigli, 217/53, memorandum by Massigli, 2 Aug. 1946.

and he proposed some form of west European economic grouping round a core made up by the two countries. But he also referred to the obstacles to such an agreement, notably in Germany and the Levant (de Gaulle never let up in his feud with the British over Syria). When de Gaulle left office, the control of French foreign policy passed largely to Georges Bidault, who retained the Foreign Ministry through a number of changing governments. Bidault was a nervy, restless intellectual, with a liking for subtle phrases – almost the complete opposite of Bevin, whom he did not always understand. Bevin for his part sometimes appeared even to have trouble with Bidault's name, rendering it as Biddle, or even on occasion Bidet. He once referred to Bidault in the Commons as 'a dear little man', which was probably meant kindly but gave some offence.[12] Still, in general Bidault was willing to work closely with the British, and in terms of attitude was much more sympathetic to them than de Gaulle had been.

We have seen that British views of France tended to be pessimistic. Massigli's impressions of the British were also sombre. In December 1945 he reported a mood of physical and moral *malaise*, compounded of weariness, disappointment and anxiety. The British had been proud to withstand a siege in their island during the war. Now they were no longer besieged, but instead were shut in because they had nothing to sell and no money to travel abroad. To be thrust in upon themselves, Massigli thought, caused the British to fall back on the 'morose delights of puritanism', typified by Stafford Cripps's exhortations to austerity of life. Massigli thought there was 'a hidden wearing down' of British will-power; though he concluded hopefully that the people's strength of character and 'esprit civique' would pull them through.[13]

French views of Britain were heavily coloured by the fact that they repeatedly had to ask the British for help – never a happy state of affairs for a proud and independent nation. Before the war ended, in March 1945, the British had extended to France a credit of £100 million, later increased to £150 million, to make purchases in the sterling area. By the end of the year this was used up, without the slightest prospect of French exports being able to cover their purchases in the following year. There was nothing for it but to ask the British for more credits, even though it meant being lectured by a Treasury official on the need to devalue the franc and reduce public expenditure.

12. Bullock, *Bevin*, vol. III, p. 82; René Massigli, *Une comédie des erreurs* (Paris, 1978), p. 97.
13. MAE, Papiers Massigli, 217/47, Massigli to Bidault, 22 Dec. 1945.

The French also needed help of a more immediate and material kind. They needed bread to eat and coal to burn. In December 1945 French stocks of wheat and flour were almost exhausted, and the government appealed directly to the British Prime Minister for 100,000 tons of wheat at the beginning of January 1946 and another 200,000 tons by the end of March. The British reply was that their own stocks were low; that the French had been imprudent in their policy on bread rationing; and that Field Marshal Montgomery needed wheat to avoid famine in the British zone of Germany. Finally in February 1946 the Minister of Food simply said he could send nothing to France. In April, the Soviet Union announced that it was sending 500,000 tons of wheat to France, to the great renown of the French Communist Party. On 14 May the French Prime Minister, Félix Gouin, asked Bevin for a loan of 75,000 tons of wheat (to be returned when the harvest came in), saying frankly that he wanted it for political purposes. He wanted to be able to say 'Great Britain bridged the gap', to counteract the popularity being gained by the USSR and the Communists. Bevin sympathised, but he had to refuse, because the government insisted that there was nothing to spare.[14] During the same period, the French government made similar appeals for coal, either from Britain or from the mines in the British zone of Germany. The results were little better, though Bevin was able to allow the export of some coal from the Ruhr from June 1946 until the French elections in November.

The effect of these desperate French appeals for help and the stubborn British negatives was disastrous on both sides. The British gained a fixed impression of French weakness and vulnerability to the Communist threat, and they grumbled repeatedly about French incompetence. (The British were convinced, with much reason, that they knew how to run a rationing system; and they believed the French did not.) They also thought that the French were ungrateful for the help they had received in the form of credits. The French on their side considered that they had precious little to be grateful for, did not like being told how they should run their own affairs, and were affronted that the British could spare wheat to feed Germans when they would send none to France. To the French, the British attitude was a mixture of condescension and hard-heartedness.

14. PRO, FO 371/59976, Z4579/65/17: record of Anglo-French conversations, 14 May 1946; letter by Bevin, 23 May 1945.

MAKING THE TREATY OF DUNKIRK

This atmosphere of gloom and bickering made a sombre background to political relations between Britain and France between 1945 and 1947. It was a curious period, in which each country claimed to want closer relations with the other, but neither did very much about it. In late 1945 the British were prepared to make the running for a formal alliance. In August Bevin told Foreign Office officials that his long-term aim was political, military and economic co-operation in western Europe, based on an Anglo-French alliance. For a time he moved cautiously, because he did not want to offend the Soviets; but by October he had decided that there was no point in worrying about that, and he instructed his officials to prepare a draft treaty. In Paris, Duff Cooper was almost too anxious to promote an alliance. The French were more cautious. Bidault pointed out to Bevin on 10 September that, as good logicians, the French were in favour of the two countries settling their differences first and then making a treaty, while the British seemed to want to conclude a treaty and then let the differences settle themselves. For the next few months the French persisted in this view.

The difficulties separating the two countries were only too obvious, in the Levant, in Germany, and in economic problems. In Syria and the Lebanon the long wartime story of Franco-British conflict reached a climax at the end of May and beginning of June 1945. On 31 May Churchill instructed the British commander in the Middle East, General Paget, to take control of Syria and the Lebanon. On 1 June Paget entered Beirut with a strong force of tanks, proclaimed that the British Army was taking over the maintenance of order, and declared that if the French opened fire his troops would bombard their barracks. De Gaulle briefly contemplated ordering resistance, but thought better of it. He told Duff Cooper on 4 June that 'We are not . . . in a position to open hostilities against you . . . But you have insulted France and betrayed the West. This cannot be forgotten'. Bidault said that the events in the Levant were worse than Fashoda – that old wound still throbbing nearly fifty years on.[15]

The French yielded to superior force, but it remained to be seen how the two countries could get out of the impasse. The two Foreign Ministries worked out a scheme for a joint withdrawal of troops in

15. A.B. Gaunson, *The Anglo-French Clash in Lebanon and Syria, 1940–45* (London, 1987), pp. 177–8; Pierre Gerbet, *Le relèvement 1944–1949* (Paris, 1991), p. 167. It is interesting to note that the author of the Levant chapter, Jacques Dupuy, a former ambassador, implicitly accepts the parallel with Fashoda.

phases, but de Gaulle rejected it. The British, he said, would only go as far as Palestine, which they would never leave, while the French would go to Marseilles. The British could then return to Syria whenever they wanted. Finally, after de Gaulle's resignation, France and Britain both accepted a Security Council resolution on the withdrawal of their forces. In the event, the British left by June 1946, and the French not until April 1947. Contrary to de Gaulle's prediction, the British left Palestine in May 1948, and they never showed any inclination to return to Syria. In this affair, the General's *idées fixes* were completely mistaken.

As for Germany, the French adopted in late 1945 and 1946 a stern occupation policy, aimed at exacting reparations and weakening Germany by cutting off the Ruhr and perhaps also the Rhineland. They were determined to prevent any German economic recovery, on the ground that it would only lead to military resurgence. The British, on the other hand, were less eager to exact reparations (partly because their country had not been occupied or fought over), and they wanted to encourage at least some measure of economic recovery. Otherwise, they would have to feed the population of their occupation zone out of their own resources. In fact, in 1946 the British people had to accept bread rationing, which had not been imposed during the war, in order to release wheat to feed the Germans in the occupation zone. It was not a popular policy, and the government took the view that the sooner the zone began to pay its own way the better. This conflict of policy between France and Britain was sharpened by the developing cold war over Germany in 1946. In June 1946 the Americans proposed an economic merger between their zone and the other western occupation zones. The British accepted, but the French declined. The result was the creation of the Anglo-American 'Bizonia', which became the starting-point of a new West German state. In a speech at Stuttgart on 6 September 1946, the American Secretary of State, James Byrnes, announced a policy of giving the German people responsibility for their own affairs, which was another step towards the restoration of a German government. Again the British agreed, and the French were left in isolation. By the end of the year, Bidault was willing to admit privately that France had no chance of securing its more far-reaching aims, such as the separation of the Ruhr from Germany; but he still could not follow the Americans and British in a policy of reconstructing Germany.

At the same time, Britain, in a tremendous effort to increase exports and improve the balance of payments, sought to sell as much as possible abroad while importing only essentials. They also imposed tight restrictions on foreign exchange, making holidays and residence abroad extremely difficult. The French, for their part, were trying to increase their exports to Britain, which would normally include a high proportion of goods which the British government classed as luxuries or non-essentials – wine, brandy, perfume and *couture* clothing. They also wished to restore the tourist trade to earn foreign currency. In July 1946 Hervé Alphand, the senior official in the Economics Department of the French Foreign Ministry, tried to deal with this problem by asking Britain to accept more French exports as a matter of urgency, and as a long-term solution to consider integrating the French and British economies by removing barriers and controls. The British response was unfavourable. They did not wish to accept more goods from France, and they thought that integration would raise difficulties with the Commonwealth. Bevin told Alphand that the British wanted no Anglo-French Five-Year Plans – they took a pragmatic view of economic affairs.

Despite these differences, Bevin and Bidault agreed on 5 September 1946 to set up a group of experts to discuss the problems. The first meeting was held almost at once (9–16 September), and reached agreement on trade between the two countries covering a host of items – one day's discussions dealt with calf skins, cotton waste, pipes, angora rabbit wool, cider apples and pit-props. The meeting also agreed in principle on the postponement until 1950 of all French repayments on loans made by Britain in 1945. This was formalised in a financial agreement on 3 December, which established the total amount of French debt (at the remarkably precise figure of £99,188,750.1s.4d). Interest was set at half a per cent per annum, and repayment was to be by twelve annual instalments starting on 1 September 1950.[16] This fell far short of the sort of integration the French had proposed, but was a useful and practical set of arrangements.

By the end of 1946 the ground was clearer between Britain and France. The Levant dispute was in the past; France had to face the *fait accompli* of Bizonia in Germany; and the two countries had reached a workable commercial and financial agreement. In October 1946 Bidault broached the idea of an alliance with Bevin, linking it specifically to the idea of a third force in western Europe which could act independently of both Washington and Moscow. But he thought that a treaty would have to wait until a stable government emerged in France, which Bidault hoped would come about after the elections in

16. MAE, Papiers Massigli, 217/57, record of meetings, 9–16 Sept. 1946; text of financial agreement, 3 Dec. 1946, published in London as Cmd. 6988, 1946.

November. These, however, failed to produce the hoped-for stability. The Communists formed the largest single party, closely followed by the Catholic *MRP* (*Mouvement Républicain Populaire*) and well ahead of the Socialists. Yet it was Léon Blum, the Socialist leader, now 74 years old and in poor health, who formed a government in mid–December. He was formally bound to resign on 16 January 1947, when the new constitution of the Fourth Republic was to come into effect. This could scarcely be described as a stable government, and Bevin was inclined to wait for something better before trying for a treaty.

Yet by a strange crab-like scuttle the two governments agreed in less than a month from Blum's taking office to conclude a treaty. The British Ambassador, Duff Cooper, took the initiative on 26 December, asking Blum whether the time had come to conclude the treaty which had been discussed for so long. Blum expressed delight at the idea, but threw in the question of coal supplies for France as a quid pro quo. In reporting to London, Cooper did not like to admit that he had acted off his own bat, and he hinted that it was Blum who had taken the initiative – a piece of sleight of hand that got the discussions off to an awkward start. However, Blum did in fact take up the running, writing to Attlee as one socialist Premier to another, welcoming the prospect of an alliance and reverting to the question of coal. The fate of democracy and socialism in France, he wrote dramatically, turned on France receiving one or two million extra tons of coal per month – only a fraction of British production or that of the Ruhr. He refused to believe that this problem could not be solved, and he was anxious to visit London as soon as possible.

Blum came to London on 13 January 1947, but found the British adamant on the matter of coal. It was a terrible winter, the country was snow-bound and there was no coal to spare; nor would the British allow any increase in exports from the Ruhr for some months yet. But Bevin was very willing to say that he placed great importance on relations with France, that he was keenly aware of the need to control Germany, and that he was ready to make a public announcement of a decision to negotiate a treaty. Blum agreed, even though he did not get his coal. It seems that the British wanted to make a gesture of support to Blum, to strengthen him against Communist pressure; and they found that a treaty was cheaper than coal.[17]

On 14 January 1947 a communiqué was published, to the effect that the two governments were ready to make a treaty. On the 16th Blum resigned, but his successor, Ramadier, pursued the project. The drafting was delayed, mostly by the British. The Foreign Office was

17. See the comment by Gerbet, *Le relèvement*, p. 51.

anxious not to offend the Soviets, and therefore sought to base the text on the treaty of 1942 with the USSR. They thus examined every detail to make sure there were no serious discrepancies between the two treaties. At the same time the British did not want to get into difficulties with the Americans – the Chiefs of Staff advised that the French treaty should be abandoned if it upset the United States. The French, for their part, were irritated that the drafting of some twenty lines of text took nearly six weeks. But the task was eventually completed, and the treaty was signed at Dunkirk on 4 March 1947.

THE SIGNIFICANCE OF THE TREATY OF DUNKIRK

The Treaty of Dunkirk was the only formal treaty of alliance between France and Britain in the twentieth century, and therefore deserves some examination. It comprised four articles. (1) The two governments agreed to consult, and to take appropriate measures, in the event of Germany adopting a policy of aggression, or taking some initiative which made aggression possible. (2) They undertook to assist one another by all means, military and otherwise, in the event of war with Germany. (3) They agreed to consult in the event of Germany failing to carry out the economic obligations imposed upon her. (4) There were to be economic consultations to promote the prosperity and security of both countries.[18] In short, it was an anti-German alliance. The first two articles comprised a precise commitment by Britain which, if made and kept at any time in the 1920s or early 1930s, might well have changed the course of history. In that way it was a backward-looking treaty, and already the threat of a resurgent Germany was fading by comparison with the immediate Soviet danger. Article 4 was rather different, and held out an opportunity for economic co-operation on a wider basis than an anti-German pact.

The treaty was signed at Dunkirk, which was a deliberate allusion to the past. The suggestion came from Bidault, who wanted the alliance between the two countries to be restored at the place where, in French eyes, it had been broken in 1940. The day (4 March) was bitterly cold, with a strong wind off the sea shaking the windows of the Sub-Prefecture where the documents were signed. After the ceremony, Bevin and Bidault went for a supposedly symbolic walk together along the beaches where the evacuation had taken place just

18. MAE, Papiers Massigli, 217/55, for successive drafts of the treaty; Gerbet, *Le relèvement*, pp. 54–5, for the four clauses.

under seven years before. It was no day for a seaside stroll, and it seems that the choice of Dunkirk was a symbolic gesture which did not quite come off.

Massigli, who had worked hard to bring the treaty about, wrote a few days after the signature of the treaty that its main importance was psychological, marking the end of a period of misunderstanding, and that it would achieve more solid significance by stimulating an improvement in Franco-British relations. How might this improvement come about?

During the ten days or so following the signature of the Treaty of Dunkirk, the Foreign Office prepared a long memorandum entitled 'Why it is essential to co-operate with the French'. It opened with a sombre review of Britain's general position, overshadowed by the superior power of the USA and USSR and endangered by their rivalry. Economically, Britain was still barely able to pay for enough imports to maintain even a frugal standard of living. The paper then outlined three main questions which lay ahead. First, could Britain resolve her economic problems without weakening her capacity for independent action? Second, in order to maintain Britain's position as a world power on something like the same level as America and Russia, would she have to pool her political and economic resources with France and the smaller countries of western Europe? Third, what was to be the future of Germany? These questions could not be answered immediately; but meanwhile, without going so far as pooling resources, Britain could at any rate strengthen her own position by improving relations with France.

The treaty was a first step. What were the other bases for co-operation between the two countries? The memorandum set them out:

> . . . we are both geographically equidistant from the two giants, the United States and Russia; we are about the same size; our populations are each dwindling at approximately the same rate; we are both of us too old to feel any impulse towards aggrandisement or expansion; we have roughly the same standards of living; we are heirs to the same culture; we have the same regard to individual freedom; and our social consciousness is developed to about the same point. There are no other two countries of comparable size about which so much could be said. It must too be remembered that in the long run our political interests and objectives are much the same; that in the economic field close co-operation with our nearest neighbour is almost inevitable; and that we are both great colonial powers with many interests in common in that field.

The paper argued that the two countries differed on German policy, but only as to means: they both wanted to ensure that Germany would never again become militarily strong, and that German industrial production was used for the good of Europe as a whole. Finally, the memorandum observed that the French had worked out a five-year modernisation plan, and the two governments should discuss their planning methods. In the future, there might be an even stronger case for economic co-operation if the revival of general world trade proved impossible. Even the idea of a customs union, though remote at present, should not be ruled out.[19]

This is an intriguing document. It contained some strange statements. Geographically, Britain and France are by no means equidistant from the USA and the Soviet Union. The French birth rate had increased during the war, and the population was growing, not dwindling; so, oddly enough, was that of the United Kingdom, and one wonders where the Foreign Office got its figures. The phraseology reveals a sense of weariness – 'we are both of us too old . . .'. The references to culture, standards of living and regard for individual freedom were true enough, but seemed insubstantial as bases for close co-operation. There seemed to be three solid ideas: common colonial interests; economic co-operation, which the authors of the memorandum treated as being almost inevitable; and the far-reaching concept of pooling resources to keep up with the USA and the Soviet Union.

Colonial co-operation seemed a good prospect at the beginning of 1947. Duff Cooper put a strong case for it in January, looking forward to a wide African Union under European guidance which would match the agricultural and mineral resources of the USA and the Soviet Union. Bevin was sympathetic to this idea, and the French government was anxious that the two countries should work together to forestall interference in their colonies by the United Nations. Officials from the two Colonial Ministries met, and discussed the marketing of cocoa, oil-seeds, timber and sisal – sound, practical matters, but without far-reaching consequences. British and French colonies in Africa, even when next to one another, had long been run on completely different lines: on the whole, the British liked to devolve authority onto local chiefs or representative bodies, while the French preferred centralised control. French government officials were suspicious of the liberal tendencies of British policy, which they believed would undermine French rule in Africa – and, some thought,

19. PRO, FO 371/67696, Z3066/940/17, minute by Hoyer-Millar, 15 March 1947, covering FO Memorandum, 'Why it is essential to co-operate with the French'.

was actually designed to do so. A number of meetings between British and French officials took place, but produced little result. Between 1947 and 1950 there were no fewer than twelve colonial conferences on technical co-operation, comprising Britain, France, and usually also Belgium. They dealt with limited subjects like forestry, the tsetse fly, rinderpest, medical problems and nutrition; and also some wider matters, notably education. These subjects were often of crucial importance, yet the conferences tended to remain superficial in their impact, and officials in individual colonies went on their way much as before. On the whole, the British and French usually agreed on the principle of colonial co-operation, but made little progress in applying it.[20]

As for economic matters, Bevin and Bidault had set up a joint committee in September 1946, so that machinery for co-operation was in being. But that was of little avail unless there was a real basis to work on. In practice, the years 1947–48 proved to be the centre of a *mésentente commerciale* between France and Britain.[21] The British, in the grip of the terrible winter of 1947, refused for some time to export any coal at all. In pursuit of a policy of 'austerity', the improvement of their balance of payments, and the prevention of inflation, the British government sought to restrict imports in general and the import of luxury goods in particular. This category, as we have seen before, included important French-produced goods. Thus the British would not sell what the French most wanted to buy, and refused to buy what the French most wanted to sell. At the same time, the British struggled desperately to stave off inflation, while the French were willing to accept inflation in the quest for modernisation. Each government acted sensibly in pursuit of its own priorities – the results were simply incompatible.

There remained the idea of pooling resources with France to maintain an equality with the Americans and the Soviets. From the end of the war to early in 1947 Bevin had thought in terms of a west European bloc, based on close co-operation between Britain and France, not directed against the Americans but as the best means of working with them. This was not far from Massigli's ideas of how the Treaty of Dunkirk should develop. A few days after the treaty was signed, he wrote: 'Between the American giant and the Russian

20. See the detailed treatment of colonial co-operation in John Kent, *The Internationalisation of Colonialism. Britain, France and Black Africa, 1939–1956* (Oxford, 1992), especially pp. 158–62, 202, 209, 333–4.

21. Robert Frank, 'France-Grande-Bretagne: la mésentente commerciale (1945–1958)', *Relations Internationales*, No. 55, 1988, p. 334. The whole article (pp. 323–39) provides a short, clear discussion of the problems of Franco-British commercial relations.

colossus, England is becoming conscious of her European interests, and realises that without close collaboration with France she cannot follow effectively and in the common interest the indispensable policy of the middle way.'[22]

Bidault too cherished the idea of a middle way, or third force, between the two giants. But was a middle way between the United States and the Soviet Union really available for Britain and France in 1947? The next few months after the Treaty of Dunkirk were to show that it was not.

---

22. MAE, Papiers Massigli, 217/55, Massigli to Teitgen, 18 March 1947.

Cold War and the Emergence of 'Europe', 1947–1949

The Treaty of Dunkirk between France and Britain was signed on 4 March 1947. Immediately afterwards Bevin and Bidault made their separate ways to Moscow, where a meeting of the Council of Foreign Ministers (American, Soviet, British and French) was due to open on 10 March – the latest in a series of meetings held since the war to try to work out a European settlement. At this stage, the narrower concerns of Franco-British relations were overtaken, and to some degree overwhelmed, by the strong currents of world and European events.

The world as a whole was facing the obvious breakdown of the former wartime alliance, and the rapid development of the cold war between the United States and the Soviet Union. On 12 March 1947 President Truman of the United States presented to Congress the statement which became known as the Truman Doctrine, offering American help to free peoples facing subjugation or subversion – that is, in effect, against the Soviet Union and communism. Meanwhile, the four Foreign Ministers continued their meetings from 10 March to 24 April; but despite this marathon stint they failed to reach agreement on the German question which was the main item on their agenda. The conference then broke up without agreement, emphasising the collapse of the alliance that had won the war but had manifestly failed to work out a peace settlement.

At the same time, in spring 1947, western Europe was facing a severe economic crisis. The crux was the so-called 'dollar gap' – the inability of Britain, France and other European countries to pay for their imports from the United States. The British were trying to deal with this problem in part by reducing their overseas commitments. In February the government decided to withdraw troops from Greece and cease economic aid to Greece and Turkey. At home a regime of austerity prevailed, and imports were reduced to absolute essentials. In France the crisis took a very sharp form. The winter had been exceptionally cold, the harvest threatened to be poor, and on 1 May the daily bread ration was reduced from 300 grammes to 250 – a particularly grim measure for the French people. Reserves of gold and foreign currency were running out, and it was calculated that in the second half of the year France would only have enough reserves to pay for about half her likely imports.[1]

THE MARSHALL PLAN

Economic collapse seemed imminent, with political upheaval, or even revolution, to follow. Only outside help could save the situation. It was in these circumstances that George C. Marshall, the American Secretary of State, proposed in a speech on 5 June 1947 the scheme which became known as Marshall Aid. In brief, he suggested a large-scale programme of American assistance to Europe (east as well as west), on condition that receiving countries must combine to provide information on their economic situation, and to produce a plan which would co-ordinate American help with their own efforts.

In western Europe, Britain and France held the key to the success of this proposal. The two governments separately welcomed Marshall's speech, and on 10 June Bevin suggested that he should go to Paris to discuss joint action with the French. He met Bidault on 17 June, and they agreed on a common approach. Bevin wanted to prepare quickly a rough statement of European requirements, designed to show what the Europeans could do (and had done) to help themselves. Bidault, for domestic political reasons, wanted to bring the Soviet Union into the discussion at an early stage, and hoped that the three countries (France, Britain and the USSR) would then jointly invite other governments to a conference on the American proposals. Bevin was reluctant to bring in the Soviets in this way, believing that they would only make difficulties; but he recognised that Bidault had difficulties at home, and agreed. They invited Molotov, the Soviet Foreign Minister, to meet them, and talks between the three were arranged for 27 June.

Just before that meeting began, the British tried to secure for themselves a special place in the Marshall proposals, separate from

---

1. Pierre Gerbet, *Le relèvement, 1944–1949* (Paris, 1991), pp. 269–70. There has been some tendency for historians to argue that the crisis was less grave than it appeared at the time. This is easy enough with hindsight, but would have cut little ice in 1947.

France. On 24–26 June the American Under-Secretary of State, Clayton, and the US Ambassador in London, Douglas, met Bevin, Attlee and other British ministers, who sought to persuade them to treat Britain as their partner in helping Europe, and not (in Bevin's phrase) 'lump in' the United Kingdom with the other continental countries. Bevin argued that for Britain to be merely a recipient of aid, rather than a participant in the recovery programme, would sacrifice 'the little bit of dignity we had left'. The Americans firmly rejected these requests, insisting that Britain must be treated like everyone else.[2] The episode was highly revealing. It might well have been damaging, or even fatal, to the American plan and to relations between Britain and France. If the British had succeeded in being treated as a special case, and as partners in the aid programme rather than as recipients, the French would have been much aggrieved, and almost certainly have asked to be accorded similar status. The Marshall Plan would at best have been plagued by an Anglo-French quarrel about their respective rankings, and at worst have foundered in confusion. The Americans, by their insistence, saved their own plan, and Anglo-French relations into the bargain.

The British thus wanted to cling to a pretence of equality with the United States. The French for their part still wanted to avoid offending the Russians, and so forestall trouble with their Communists at home. This too might have wrecked the Marshall Plan, because the Soviets were determined to obstruct it. When the French, British and Soviet Foreign Ministers met in Paris (27 June–2 July 1947), Molotov proposed that the countries requiring aid should simply draw up separate lists of their requirements, rather than co-ordinating their programmes as the Americans required. He also raised a number of questions about Germany which were better avoided if the plan was to go forward. He asked whether the French really wanted to see German resources put into the Marshall Plan instead of into reparations. Did they understand, and accept, that the plan would lead to an increase in German industrial production, with all the dangers that that entailed? The French were indeed worried about all these matters but Bidault and Bevin stuck together, insisting that the American proposals must be discussed as they stood. In particular, they stood by the idea of working out a joint programme, even at the risk of seeing the Russians break up the conference without an agreement.

In the event, Molotov abandoned the conference and went back to Moscow, uttering vague but dire warnings about the consequences if

2. Alan Bullock, *Ernest Bevin*, vol. III, *Foreign Secretary, 1945–1951* (London, pb edn, 1985), pp. 413–15.

the British and French went ahead alone. But go ahead they did. Bevin tactfully proposed that Paris should be the venue for a general conference on the Marshall Plan; the two Foreign Ministers sent out invitations together; and when the conference opened on 12 July Bevin was elected chairman. Sixteen countries attended; the USSR prevented governments in its sphere of influence from doing so. Within five days the conference set up a Committee for European Economic Co-operation, and in two months they prepared a joint plan to submit to the United States. The British and French took the lead in the whole enterprise, and their co-operation made it possible for the Marshall Plan to take shape. In doing so, they took a great step towards the formation of a west European economic bloc; but it was not a 'third force' between the United States and the Soviet Union, as was envisaged after the Treaty of Dunkirk. Instead, it was firmly bound to the United States, and designed to act as the distributor of American aid to its members.

Anglo-French co-operation thus got the Marshall Plan under way. But the French themselves were deeply divided about the aid programme. France received great benefits: some $2,600 million between 1948 and 1951, of which 85 per cent was in gifts and 15 per cent in loans. In 1949 as much as 42 per cent of French imports were paid for by Marshall Aid.[3] Most of this aid was channelled in directions chosen by the French themselves. The French Marshall Aid pro- gramme was adapted from the Monnet Plan already in being for French purposes. The international body set up to supervise Marshall Aid, the Organisation for European Economic Co-operation (OEEC), established its headquarters in Paris, and its first Secretary-General (from 1948 to 1955) was Robert Marjolin, who had been *Commissaire Général Adjoint* of the French Plan, alongside Jean Monnet, and was well placed to direct American assistance to where the French wanted it. There was, of course, a price to be paid. France had to adhere to the General Agreement on Tariffs and Trade (GATT), signed on 30 October 1947, and thus accept some lowering of tariffs and phasing out of quotas. (The French actually contrived to introduce a new, high external tariff in 1948, so that they could later negotiate its reduction under the GATT arrangements.) The French government had to accept American demands that the franc should become a convertible currency at some time in the future. The French also had to accept certain types and amounts of American exports, whether they wanted them or not, and as a result there was much grumbling about 'chewing-gum imperialism'.

---

3. Hubert Bonin, *Histoire économique de la IVe République* (Paris, 1987), p. 153.

There was indeed a powerful campaign against Marshall Aid in France. Rarely can it have appeared more difficult for one country to give money to another. The Communists denounced American aid root and branch, for their own political reasons and those of the Soviet Union. Many who were not Communists complained that France was ceding too much control over her own internal affairs. There was a strong current of neutralist opinion, exemplified by Hubert Beuve-Méry's newspaper *Le Monde*, urging that France should join neither the American nor the Soviet camp, but stand between them and strive to prevent the division of Europe into east and west. The President of the Republic, Vincent Auriol, was closely associated with this view.

These arguments did little to deflect French actions. Some of the French opposed Marshall Aid vehemently. Some welcomed it. Some agonised over the choice. But meanwhile successive governments took the dollars, and on the whole used them to good advantage.

At the time, it was not certain whether the Marshall Plan would prove to be a stimulant for closer Anglo-French relations or a replacement for them. Psychologically, the Marshall Plan tended to work against good relations, because some of the French resentment against the Plan spilt over into antagonism towards the British, through the tendency to lump Americans and British together as 'Anglo-Saxons'. For some time it seemed likely that close practical co-operation would outweigh such sentiments. During the Paris conference on the Marshall proposal in July 1947 the question of a customs union between France and Britain was revived, and the French made specific proposals along these lines in August. The British agreed to set up a committee, which might have meant little or nothing. However, on 22 September Bevin went to Paris to sign the European report on Marshall Aid requirements. During his visit, he called on the French Premier, Paul Ramadier, and launched abruptly into a far-reaching talk about closer understanding, or even some sort of union, between Britain and France. He conjured up a picture of a combined population of 87 millions, backed by the combined resources of two Empires, forming a unit which could match the power of the United States or the Soviet Union. When this meeting ended, Bevin remarked enthusiastically to Duff Cooper (still Ambassador in Paris): 'We've made the union of Britain and France this morning.'[4] They had, of course, done nothing of the sort; but it is interesting that Bevin continued to cherish the aspiration, and that he was still willing to consider some sort of 'third force' to match the two superpowers.

---

4. Bullock, *Bevin*, vol. III, pp. 487–8.

Bidault, the French Foreign Minister, was ready to pursue the idea, and planted an article in *L'Aube* to remind people of the proposal of union in 1940. In London, however, it did not take long for an inter-departmental committee to point out the difficulties: a customs union would conflict with imperial preference, and would be opposed by the Commonwealth. Bevin was not completely deterred, and hankered for some time after the idea of co-operation between the two Empires; but the flurry caused by his meeting with Ramadier came to nothing. Meanwhile, the Marshall Plan went forward, with France and Britain working largely separately within it.

THE BRUSSELS TREATY

For a time the Marshall Plan seemed to provoke more problems than it solved. Communist parties all over western Europe opposed it vehemently, and the strikes and demonstrations held in France were particularly fierce. In November 1947 the Paris–Lille express was derailed by sabotage on the line near Arras, and sixteen passengers were killed. The country was badly shaken. At the same time, the diplomatic cold war was entering its frostiest period. In November–December 1947 the Council of Foreign Ministers of the four former wartime allies met in London for what proved to be the last time. They could agree on nothing, and Marshall brought the conference to an end in failure on 15 December. For some time thereafter the two superpowers virtually ceased to communicate with one another.

In these circumstances, the most urgent problem appeared to be, not the economic recovery of western Europe, but its immediate physical and military security. Bevin believed at the end of 1947 that the Soviet Union was set on the domination of the whole of Europe, either by military force or by Communist subversion. Immediately after the collapse of the Foreign Ministers' meeting in London, he met Bidault and outlined, in urgent tones though with marked lack of precision, a proposal for some sort of federation of western Europe. He did not define what he meant, wanting everything to remain flexible; but he indicated that his proposal comprised economic, political and military matters. The great thing, he insisted, was to act quickly, and to bring in the Americans, who alone had the military strength to resist Russia by force. Massigli, who was present at this conversation, observed that Bidault was irritated by Bevin's vagueness, but still expressed general agreement. The same day, Bevin met

Marshall, and expounded to him an idea for 'a sort of spiritual federation of the West'. Marshall, like Bidault, was somewhat mystified by Bevin's opaque phraseology.[5]

Bevin's language was vague, but the impulse behind it was powerful. He was sure that the Americans must be drawn in to provide military support for western Europe, because no amount of economic aid would stop an invasion by the Red Army; and he was determined to launch some form of Western Union, to reinforce confidence in democracy as the Marshall Plan promised to invigorate the economy. On 8 January 1948 he explained his thinking to the Cabinet in a large-scale review of British policy. He explained the case for 'some form of union in Western Europe, whether of a formal or informal character' – a grouping of west European democratic states, with the backing of the USA and the Dominions, and using all the resources of the European colonial empires. He claimed that the result would be a bloc which would be able to stand on an equal footing with the United States and the Soviet bloc, but he left no doubt that it would be aligned with the Americans. With Cabinet approval, Bevin went on to expound these ideas in a speech to the House of Commons on 22 January. While speaking he departed from his notes to make some stern remarks about the Soviet Union and its 'police state' methods.[6]

This embarrassed Bidault, who for domestic reasons was anxious not to offend the Soviet Union. At the end of December 1947, Bidault had proposed to meet the problem of west European security simply by extending the Treaty of Dunkirk to include Belgium and the Netherlands. Since the Treaty of Dunkirk was directed against Germany, not the Soviet Union, this could be done without giving offence. Again, speaking in the National Assembly on 13 February 1948, he assured his audience that France wished to avoid a breach in Europe, and argued that any pact formed in western Europe should not be directed against unnamed powers (which would in effect mean the Soviet Union) but against Germany. This attitude involved a good deal of pretence, because the division of Europe was already an accomplished fact, and it was far removed from the views of Bevin, who believed that the Soviet threat must be confronted head-on, by military, political and diplomatic means.

For some time Bevin's proposals for western European union made little progress. The proposals themselves were too vague, and the

5. René Massigli, *Une comédie des erreurs* (Paris, 1978), pp. 105–6; Bullock, *Bevin*, vol. III, pp. 498–500.
6. See generally Bullock, *Bevin*, vol. III, pp. 513–20.

differences between British and French attitudes to the Soviet Union were too great. Negotiations for an alliance involving Britain, France, Belgium, the Netherlands and Luxembourg began, but moved very slowly. Then there came like a bomb-shell the Communist take-over in Czechoslovakia (21–25 February 1948). For the west European countries, Czechoslovakia was in a different category from the other states which had previously fallen under Soviet control. It was an established democracy in the heart of Europe. Moreover, it was less than ten years since Hitler's seizure of Czechoslovakia in March 1939 had led almost directly to the outbreak of the Second World War. At once the negotiations for a west European alliance assumed a new urgency. A five-power conference between Britain, France and the Benelux countries opened at Brussels on 4 March, and concluded on the 17th with the signature of the Treaty of Brussels, which bound all its participants to come to the help of any of them if attacked. The treaty made a token reference to Germany, but there was no doubt that the unnamed potential aggressor was the Soviet Union. There was to be a permanent organisation to co-ordinate the policies of the five powers, and a system of joint military commands similar to the Anglo-American commands during the Second World War.

In this new alliance, Britain and France were by far the most important members, and the Brussels Treaty might have brought about a close co-operation between them. Instead, as Maurice Vaïsse has written, the history of the Brussels Pact is that of a long dispute between the French and the British.[7] Their basic attitudes were far apart. The British accepted that there was a risk of war, and were prepared to face it. Indeed, they believed that only a firm stand against Moscow could avert the danger. The French were much more chary. As President Auriol pointed out to Bevin in April 1948, the French people had had enough of warfare; and besides, there was every chance that war with the Soviet Union would mean civil war within France itself. The French government therefore preferred to avoid anything that the Soviets could find provocative. In these circumstances, it was difficult to enunciate a basic policy for the new alliance. It was equally difficult to define a military strategy. Field Marshal Montgomery, the British Chief of Staff, who was appointed Supreme Commander for the Brussels Pact forces, did not believe that the Russians could be stopped short of the Channel, which would condemn France to another invasion and occupation. The French cynically observed that the British were expecting another Dunkirk,

7. Jean Doise and Maurice Vaïsse, *Diplomatie et outil militaire, 1871–1969* (Paris, 1987), p. 408.

only this time it would be planned for. De Lattre de Tassigny, the French general who was appointed to command the land forces of the alliance, naturally preferred a strategy which would protect his own country, and wanted to hold the Russians somewhere to the east of the Rhine. To make matters worse, Montgomery and de Lattre became engaged in a most spectacular quarrel. Sir George Mallaby, who as Secretary to the Military Committee of the Brussels Pact witnessed much of this dispute, later wrote judiciously that: 'It would be a grievous misuse of language to say that relations between the Field Marshal and General de Lattre were not very cordial. In fact their mutual animosity over a considerable period was venomous.' Montgomery's biographer, Nigel Hamilton, wrote that the quarrel was 'one of the *causes célèbres* of its time; an antipathy so great that it poisoned virtually the entire time-span of Western Union'. Part of the trouble was that they were both prima donnas – energetic, vain and self-opinionated to a high degree; and two prima donnas cannot possibly share a stage. They came into immediate conflict on the issue of whether or not de Lattre, as Commander-in-Chief Land Forces, came under the orders of Montgomery or only under his general guidance. (It was ironical that de Lattre played much the same role in relation to Montgomery as Monty himself had done in 1944–45 in relation to Eisenhower as Supreme Commander of the Allied forces in Europe; but this was scarcely a point that Montgomery could be expected to appreciate.) Eventually, it appears that Montgomery became convinced that de Lattre was personally and violently anti-British. 'There burns inside him a deep hatred and suspicion of the British', Montgomery told the Minister of Defence, Shinwell, in May 1950. On the other side, it may well be that de Lattre heard that in January 1948 Montgomery had breezily advised a French general to use 'weedkiller' on some of his colleagues, including specifically de Lattre. It is true that eventually the two prima donnas achieved an emotional, indeed tearful, reconciliation over a dinner at Fontainebleau; but it is doubtful how deep this went. In any case, the damage was done.[8]

Franco-British relations within the Brussels Treaty were therefore, to say the least, difficult. There also arose in 1948–49 three other issues that set Britain and France against one another: the creation of the North Atlantic alliance; the development of a West German state; and the movement for European union.

8. George Mallaby, *From My Level: Unwritten Minutes* (London, 1965), p. 174; Nigel Hamilton, *Monty: The Field Marshal, 1944–1976* (London, 1986), pp. 730–1, 742–3, 765–6. For using 'weedkiller', see Michael Dockrill, 'British Attitudes towards France as a Military Ally', *Diplomacy and Statecraft*, vol. I, No.1, pp. 62–3.

THE NORTH ATLANTIC ALLIANCE

The British were convinced from the start that the five Brussels Treaty powers alone could not ensure the defence of western Europe. Even before the Brussels Pact was signed, Bevin had proposed that there should be three linked security arrangements: the Brussels alliance, an Atlantic treaty with the participation of the USA, and a Mediterranean agreement including Italy. The French too wanted to bring in the Americans. Three times in March and April 1948 the French government sent messages to Washington pressing the case for American support for the Brussels powers. The British and French thus worked in the same direction, though not actually together, in response to the same strategic necessity. They both knew that, if the worst came to the worst, only the Americans could protect them. But they were unable to pursue this common purpose together. The Americans got three-power talks about a defence agreement under way in Washington from 22 March 1948 onwards. The three powers concerned were the USA, Britain and Canada. Bevin tried to get the French invited, but the Americans refused, on the ground that French security could not be trusted. The tragic irony here was that among the British party was the long-standing Soviet agent Donald Maclean, so that (even if the Americans were right about French security) it is hard to see that anything more about the conversations could have been revealed to the Soviets. So the talks went ahead without the French, and speedily reached an American–British–Canadian agreement, set out in the 'Pentagon Paper' of 1 April 1948, envisaging the establishment of a North Atlantic defence treaty.

This was the conception of the North Atlantic treaty, but the period of gestation proved long and difficult. Not until July did conversations begin between the Americans, Canadians and all the Brussels Treaty states; and even then there were all kinds of difficulties. The French, having been excluded from the original discussions, did not know what was going on, and went all out for immediate and specific American help for France. On 24 June the Soviet blockade of Berlin had begun, raising the terrifying prospect of war just around the corner. In August the French insisted that they would only pursue negotiations for a North Atlantic treaty if they were assured of the immediate despatch of American troops and supplies to France, the establishment of an integrated military command, and the inclusion of French officers in the Anglo-American Combined Chiefs of Staff organisation. These demands make an interesting contrast to the later

French rejection of the NATO integrated command, but at the time they were pressed so brusquely that they threatened to wreck the whole negotiation. Sir Nicholas Henderson, a member of the British delegation, has described the methods of Henri Bonnet, the chief French representative, thus:

> He was there to state the French case, the whole of the French case, and nothing but it. This he did with remarkable tenacity and tactlessness from the beginning to the end of the negotiations . . . there were moments when it seemed that Bonnet's importunate behaviour might succeed in breaking everything – but he went on unperturbed.[9]

The heart of the French case lay in two demands: that Italy should be included in the North Atlantic treaty, to protect the Mediterranean flank; and that Algeria, which at that time was legally part of France, should be specifically covered by the treaty. Eventually they gained both points, by means of tough bargaining. For example, they blocked the adhesion of Norway to the treaty in the north until they got their way over Italy in the south. Italy became a signatory to the treaty; and Article 6 stated that 'the Algerian departments of France' were comprised in the area to be protected.

Thus the French negotiating methods paid dividends, but at the cost of a good deal of irritation. The head of the British delegation, Sir Oliver Franks, remarked at one point that he found it difficult to reach agreement 'if a pistol was put at his head. His natural instinct was to react against it . . .'. To which the principal French representative replied that 'his natural reaction was the same, when he was engaged in a negotiation and had the impression of talking to a wall'.[10] At bottom, the British and French negotiators wanted much the same thing, but they managed to cause one another considerable offence by their methods of achieving it.

The final result had ambiguous consequences for relations between Britain and France. They were both founder signatories of the North Atlantic Treaty (4 April 1949). They were for some years its most important European members, and co-operated effectively in all kinds of unspectacular ways, particularly in military affairs. Despite this, the attitudes of the two countries towards the treaty differed markedly. Britain was completely committed to the North Atlantic Alliance. The treaty was negotiated by a Labour government, and fully accepted by the Conservatives; it commanded assent across the political spectrum, except for some dissenters on the far Left. It drew the United States

9. Nicholas Henderson, *The Birth of NATO* (London, 1982), p. 44.
10. Bullock, *Bevin*, vol. III, p. 670.

into the defence of western Europe, and included a Commonwealth member in Canada; it thus fitted precisely into the British idea of the three circles of Europe, USA and Commonwealth. It became, and was to remain for many years, the centre-piece of British foreign policy. Equally, the British armed services became closely integrated in the command structures of the North Atlantic Treaty Organisation (NATO). In France the position was very different. It is true that during the period of negotiations the French government had been eager, almost desperate, to secure American help, and France gained important military advantages from the treaty. But, as with Marshall Aid, help which was needed so badly was almost bound to be resented later. French opinion, unlike British, was deeply divided on the alliance. It was opposed outright by the Communists, and only slightly less vehemently by the current of neutralist opinion which still ran strongly in France. Among intellectuals, the immensely influential figures of Sartre and de Beauvoir opposed the treaty; Raymond Aron supported it, but at the time he carried less weight. Anti-American sentiment was strong; and the establishment of NATO headquarters in Paris (intended as a reassuring gesture towards France) provided a focus for hostility and an excuse for claiming that France was an 'occupied country'. Thus, while French governments held firmly to the North Atlantic Alliance, considerations of internal politics and public opinion meant that they constantly had to look over their shoulders. There was a gap between the demands of foreign policy and strategy and those of internal politics, which made the French less whole-hearted about NATO than were the British. This had its effects on relations between France and Britain, because some of the French anti-American and anti-NATO feeling emerged as resentment of the 'Anglo-Saxons' and dislike of the British as excessively loyal members of the Alliance and slavish supporters of the United States.

FRANCE AND GERMANY: A NEW DEPARTURE

The North Atlantic Treaty of 1949 was firmly, though not explicitly, directed against the Soviet Union. Yet as recently as 1947 there had been no question in most French minds, and probably in most British minds as well, that the main enemy was still Germany. The Treaty of Dunkirk (March 1947) had been explicitly anti-German. Between 1947 and 1949 the German question evolved rapidly, in ways which set Britain and France repeatedly against one another. Already in 1946 the American and British zones of occupation had been merged in the so-called Bizone, from which the French stood out for the next three years, maintaining the separate identity of their own zone. In 1947 the Marshall Plan conference agreed that the western zones of Germany should receive Marshall Aid. In the conditions of the cold war, the Americans were determined to restore economic prosperity and some form of self-government to western Germany as part of the Western side, and the British accepted these objectives. The French policy of exacting reparations and imposing strict controls therefore became impossible. France was gradually compelled to abandon her former German policy, and had to look for a new one.

The crucial changes took place during 1948 and 1949. A long conference on German affairs was held in London from 23 February to 7 June 1948, between the USA, Britain and France, with the Benelux countries as occasional attenders. The Americans and British worked together to secure agreement on the creation of a Federal West German government. The French for their part obtained some safeguards. They had long given up the idea of detaching the Ruhr from the rest of Germany, but they secured agreement in principle on the creation of an international authority to control the production of coal, coke and steel in the Ruhr. The conference also agreed to maintain a long-term military occupation of western Germany by the three Allied powers. When the agreements reached by the London conference were put to the French National Assembly in June 1948, they were endorsed by a majority of only eight votes, reflecting the strong French feeling that the restoration of Germany was moving too far and too fast.

In November 1948 the American and British Commanders-in-Chief in the Bizone handed over the provisional management of the mines and factories of the Ruhr to German managers, leaving the question of their final control to the decision of a future German government. The French objected to this very strongly, and secured some important changes. On 20 November the USA, Britain and France agreed that the question of the ownership of the Ruhr industries should be postponed until the conclusion of a peace treaty with Germany. Since there was no sign whatever of such a treaty, this amounted to indefinite postponement. A further six-power conference (the USA, Britain and France, plus the Benelux countries) set up the International Ruhr Authority previously agreed on in principle, with powers to distribute the production of the Ruhr industries as between exports and domestic consumption. The conference also set up a new Military Security Board, to supervise the demilitarisation of Germany. These precautions did something to reassure the French and maintain a measure of control over Germany. But the fact remained that the Americans, followed by the British, were working to establish a prosperous and vigorous West German state, to which the French remained instinctively opposed.

In the middle of 1948 the Berlin blockade gave a decisive push to events. In June 1948 the Soviet Union imposed a blockade on all land communications between the western zones of Germany and Berlin. The Americans, supported whole-heartedly by the British and more warily by the French, responded by airlifting supplies into Berlin. Both sides stopped short of using force, but for a year (until the Soviet blockade was lifted in May 1949) there was a constant sense of crisis. The division of Germany between east and west was sharpened, and the American determination to set up a West German state was given a decisive impulse. The German Federal Republic came formally into existence in September 1949, with Konrad Adenauer as its first Chancellor. It was far from being a fully sovereign state. An Allied High Commission exercised wide control over economic and foreign policy. German industry was still subject to a programme of dismantling, decided on by the occupying powers. France continued to control the Saar. Above all, the new state was to remain demilitarised. The French government accorded particular prominence and emphasis to this last provision. On 25 July 1949 Robert Schuman, the French Foreign Minister, declared to the National Assembly that Germany had no army and no armaments; she ought not to have any; and she would have none in the future. The Assembly approved this statement whole-heartedly.

The new West German government was by no means content with the restrictions upon its independence, and quickly set about removing several of them; though it left intact the provision on disarmament, which was as sensitive in internal politics as it was abroad. The Federal Government and the three western occupying powers rapidly negotiated the Petersberg Protocol (22 November 1949), which largely ended the programme for dismantling German industry, reduced reparations payments, admitted West Germany to membership of the International Ruhr Authority, and permitted German co-operation in the work of the Military Security Board. The Federal Government was also admitted to membership of the International Monetary Fund and the GATT organisation. The new state thus moved towards greater sovereignty and wider international acceptance. Once again, as with the agreements of June 1948, the French government submitted the new arrangements to the National Assembly, which this time approved them (26 November) by a majority of 78 – a much wider margin.

In this movement towards the recovery of the German economy and the creation of a West German state, the British consistently (though often reluctantly) supported American policy. The 'Anglo-Saxons' thus worked together to erode and ultimately demolish one of the most important aspects of post-war French foreign policy. In 1945–46 the French had set out to achieve a tough settlement of the German question, including heavy reparations, the separation of the Ruhr from the rest of Germany, and the rejection of any strong German government. By the end of 1949 very little remained of these objectives. Reparations had been substantially reduced. The Ruhr was still detached from Germany, but the Germans were now involved in its administration. A West German federal state, with a strong government, had been established. The best that could be said of the new situation (as French diplomats gloomily observed) was that at least Germany was in two parts, so that France faced an immediate neighbour with a population of 45 million rather than 70 million.

THE EUROPEAN MOVEMENT

French post-war policy towards Germany had failed, and a new one had to be found. As early as 14 July 1948 the European section of the French Foreign Ministry recommended that the best course was to seek 'a common Franco-German destiny'.[11] During the next six months, French representatives in Germany, key officials at the Quai d'Orsay, and the Foreign Minister himself, Robert Schuman, all agreed that the best solution to the German problem, and the only one which would offer France real security in the long term, was to bring West Germany within the framework of some form of European union. Thus the German question became intimately linked with the issue of European unity; which was itself another bone of contention between France and Britain.

On 19 September 1946 Winston Churchill made a speech at Zurich which captured the headlines at the time and has remained famous ever since. He appealed for the establishment of 'a kind of United States of Europe', and he made the startling assertion that 'The first step in the re-creation of the European family must be a partnership between France and Germany. In this way only can France recover the moral leadership of Europe. There can be no revival of Europe

11. Raymond Poidevin, *Robert Schuman, homme d'état, 1886–1963* (Paris, 1986), p. 208.

without a spiritually great France and a spiritually great Germany.' France and Germany, he declared, should take the lead in creating the United States of Europe. Britain and the Commonwealth, the United States, and (Churchill still hoped) the Soviet Union would be 'the friends and sponsors of the new Europe'.[12] It was perfectly clear that Churchill was thinking of European unity *without* Britain. The British would lend support and encouragement from outside. None the less, he threw his immense prestige behind the 'European idea', which had been somewhat discredited of recent years through its advocacy by Nazi Germany. Churchill's Zurich speech re-launched that idea on a new and adventurous voyage.

The idea of creating some form of political union in Europe to match its historical and cultural identity was far from new. Aristide Briand had tried to give it shape in 1929–30, and during the Second World War many of the Resistance groups in different countries had opposed the German New Order for Europe with idealistic visions of their own. Churchill's speech struck a responsive chord across western Europe. Under his benevolent, if somewhat detached, sponsorship there developed an international committee linking various organisations advocating European unity, which arranged a vast Congress of Europe at The Hague in May 1948. Churchill agreed to be its Honorary President. Several hundred delegates from sixteen European states attended, along with observers from the United States and Canada. The Congress provided a glittering shop-window for the European idea – or rather ideas, because all shades of opinion from outright federalism to mere co-operation were represented. It made a powerful impression on public opinion, and sowed the seeds for a whole crop of European institutions.

The attitudes of Britain and France to this burgeoning European movement were very different. The British were perfectly prepared to consider schemes for European co-operation, provided that they adopted the methods of agreement and concert between governments, and preferably if they were Atlantic in outlook. For them, the Organisation for European Economic Co-operation was a model set-up. When the OEEC had been created in 1947 to administer the Marshall Plan, the French government had wanted it to have some measure of autonomy in its relations with member governments. The British, on the other hand, insisted on the OEEC being under the control of a Council of Ministers representing all member states and taking decisions unanimously. The British system was adopted, and the

12. Martin Gilbert, *'Never Despair'. Winston S. Churchill, 1945–1965* (London, 1988), pp. 265–6.

OEEC emerged simply as a mechanism for co-operation between governments. This was a formula dear to Bevin's heart. He rightly believed that for the Marshall Plan it worked very well, and he was reluctant to see the principle changed in other circumstances. When the Hague Congress was convened in 1948, the British Labour government declined to send any representatives, partly because it was presided over by the Leader of the Opposition and was thought to work to his advantage, but even more because the Labour Party as a whole distrusted the movement for European union. When he heard of a proposal to set up a Council of Europe, Bevin is reported to have said: 'I don't like it. I don't like it. When you open up that Pandora's box you'll find it full of Trojan horses' – a delightful remark, which has rightly become famous.[13] There lay behind it an instinctive distrust of European talking-shops, and of assemblies which were not responsible to anyone in any sense that Bevin could recognise. These sentiments were widely shared in Britain.

French governments, on the other hand, were eager to promote schemes for European organisations and assemblies, and at least to contemplate measures of integration, rather than simple co-operation between states. On 20 July 1948, shortly after the Hague Congress, Bidault (the French Foreign Minister) proposed at a meeting of the Brussels Pact Consultative Council the creation of a European Assembly, and of an economic and customs union among the five countries of the Pact. The British response was cautious. On earlier occasions, Bevin had himself raised the question of a customs union between Britain and France, but nothing had come of it, and the time seemed past. The British were also unsettled by an indiscreet remark by Bidault in the French National Assembly on 11 June: 'When I speak of Europe, I mean Europe, capital Paris, for it is in Paris that the Sixteen have their capital.'[14] (The Sixteen were the countries participating in the Marshall Plan.) Bidault hastened to play down the significance of this observation, but it was one of those occasions where a significant frame of mind was revealed by an almost stray remark. The French did indeed envisage a Europe with Paris as its 'capital' and with themselves in the leading role. As any Frenchman would remember, that was what Victor Hugo had foretold long ago. And it was, after all, the role which Churchill had foreseen for France in his Zurich speech. The French, in a mood of reviving self-confidence, were recalling from the past a deep-seated sense of mission in Europe.

13. Lord Strang, *At Home and Abroad* (London, 1956), p. 290.
14. Massigli, *Comédie*, p. 115.

Bidault lost office before the end of July 1948, and had no time to develop his proposal for a European Assembly. But his successor, Robert Schuman, at once took up the idea. The Hague Congress had produced a memorandum proposing a European Consultative Council to examine measures to bring about the progressive integration of Europe. Schuman brought this plan to the French Cabinet, which approved it and proposed to the other governments of the Brussels Pact the creation of a European Assembly. Bevin did not like the idea, and opposed any idea of constitution-making for Europe. At the Consultative Council of the Brussels Pact in October 1948 he made a long speech, claiming that he did not see what the French wanted to achieve by their proposal for an assembly: did they want to melt all the countries into one, or set up a sort of European United Nations? Great Britain, he pointed out, was at the centre of a Commonwealth of 400 million people which worked perfectly well on a voluntary basis, without any kind of constitution. To arguments that the Americans were pressing for European union, Bevin replied that he would like to know what the Americans would say to uniting the USA with the countries of Latin America. Rather like Bidault's remark on 'Europe, capital Paris', this was a strikingly revealing comment. Bevin knew perfectly well how the United States regarded Latin America; and he saw British relations with other European countries in much the same light.

However, Bevin eventually accepted the idea of an assembly. On 5 May 1949 an agreement to set up the Council of Europe was signed by the five Brussels Pact countries and five other west European states. Its purpose was defined in general terms as being to achieve a greater unity between its members in order to safeguard their ideals and facilitate their economic and social progress. It was to have no powers of decision, and existed only as a forum of debate about European union. Its seat was fixed at Strasbourg, where its first meeting opened amid great enthusiasm in August 1949. Members were nominated by the various countries concerned. The British delegates were appointed by the government, according to the proportions of the main parties in the House of Commons. The other nine governments allowed their respective parliaments to nominate delegates. In effect, the Council represented a compromise between the British, who did not really want an assembly at all, and the French, who wanted an assembly with some measure of independence and political powers.

The underlying attitudes of Britain and France to this venture were more important than the precise make-up and functions of the Council of Europe. The British outlook was summed up in two papers which Bevin presented to the Cabinet on 27 October 1949. The first argued that Britain must support the Council of Europe, as it now existed, and do nothing to undermine the hopes of solidarity and co-operation it had aroused. The second and more important (which was signed by both Bevin and Cripps, the Chancellor of the Exchequer) dealt with the wider question of the economic unification of western Europe. While accepting that Britain should be prepared to make some sacrifices for this purpose, the document emphasised that 'we should not run risks which would jeopardise our own chances of survival if the attempt to restore Western Europe should fail, and we should not involve ourselves in the economic affairs of Europe *beyond the point at which we could, if we wished, disengage ourselves*'. The paper concluded: 'We must remain, as we always have been in the past, different in character from other European nations and fundamentally incapable of whole-hearted integration with them.'[15] In other words, Britain was an island. This simple fact of geography had been reinforced by the lessons of history, and most recently by the events of 1940, which were fresh in all memories.

French attitudes were very different. French governments had a practical purpose in mind when they urged European union as a means of dealing with the German question. But behind this lay a cast of mind which (like British attitudes) had its origins both in the distant past and in recent events. When Sir Nicholas Henderson was appointed British Ambassador in Paris, his French colleague in Bonn told him that he must always remember two facts: 'firstly, that we had a Revolution, such as you have never had; secondly, that we were defeated in 1940, and you were not. You will find these facts relevant to all your dealings with the French'.[16] This advice, though given in 1975, applied equally at the end of the 1940s. The Revolution, commented Henderson, has constantly inspired the French with a sense of global mission. 'Mission' is a word which recurs frequently in French political parlance, and is closely attached to the European idea. Bidault, while he was Foreign Minister, once declared that 'France is above all a European country. Our mission at present is to make France the champion of European union'.[17] There could be no clearer contrast than that between Bidault's words and those of Bevin's paper for the British Cabinet, with its plain assumption that Britain was *not* a European nation. As for the events of 1940, the French drew from

---

15. Bullock, *Bevin*, vol. III, pp. 733–4. The italics are mine.
16. Nicholas Henderson, *Channels and Tunnels* (London, 1987), pp. 72–3.
17. Pierre Gerbet, *La construction de l'Europe* (Paris, 1983), p. 75.

them a very different lesson from that learned by the British: that their security must be found within Europe.

The cynical might observe that the French sense of mission was usually found to coincide with French interests, just as the British often found that their interests coincided with morality. In this at any rate the two countries were similar. But at this stage of their history they were far apart in their sense of mission and of national identity. France was above all a European country; the British felt that at bottom they were separate from continental Europe. Bidault declared that France was the champion of European union; Bevin and the British Cabinet decided against involvement in European affairs beyond the point at which they could not disengage themselves. In 1949, over something so vague in its purposes as the Council of Europe, these differences did not prove crucial. In later years they were to be very grave.

There has been a strong tendency to see the immediate post-war period as one of lost opportunities in relations between Britain and France and between Britain and Europe. For the only time in the century there was an Anglo-French alliance; but what might have been crucial between the wars proved an anachronism in 1947. The real importance of the alliance was as the basis of the Brussels Treaty, which itself led to the creation of NATO. This was not really a case of a 'lost opportunity': the opportunity was grasped, but it was not an *Anglo-French* opportunity – it was something wider.

Again, it is often said (even in the 1990s) that 'the leadership of Europe' was there for Britain to take in the few years after 1945. Insofar as this meant leadership in creating European institutions, the British had no intention of grasping it – they would only lend support from outside, like a flying buttress. In the very different sense of taking the lead in establishing the political and military security of Europe, they grasped the opportunity with both hands. The result was highly successful, but it had less to do with Europe alone than with the whole Atlantic Alliance. The years 1945–49 were not a time of lost opportunities, but of opportunities which transcended the narrow framework of relations between Britain and France.

CHAPTER 6

Separation: Schuman Plan and After, 1950–1955

On 18 September 1949 the British government devalued the pound by nearly one-third of its exchange rate against the dollar, from $4.03 to the pound to $2.80. They did so under the impulse of dire necessity, with British exports falling rapidly, the balance of payments worsening, and reserves of dollars and gold dwindling at an alarming rate. To achieve devaluation with the least possible damage, two conditions were necessary: the co-operation of the United States, as Britain's principal creditor, and absolute secrecy with regard to everyone else. The British Cabinet reached its decision early in September, and then from 7 to 12 September Bevin and Cripps (the Chancellor of the Exchequer) held talks in Washington to ask for American help, which was willingly provided. At that stage, the French government was told nothing, even though Robert Schuman, the Foreign Minister, was in Washington from 13 to 17 September for political talks with Bevin and Dean Acheson, the American Secretary of State. The French Finance Minister, Maurice Petsche, was also in Washington at the same time, but heard nothing about the devaluation until he was given a few hours' notice of the event during the evening of 17 September. Petsche reacted strongly, saying that it was a brutal decision. Roger Makins, the Foreign Office official who broke the news, reported that Hervé Alphand, the head of the economic department at the Quai d'Orsay, became 'somewhat hysterical'.[1] The reaction in Paris was equally vehement.

The British were genuinely surprised by the French resentment, and pointed out that they had told the French at the same time as members of the Commonwealth (other than the Canadians, who had

1. Alan Bullock, *Ernest Bevin*, vol. III, *Foreign Secretary, 1945–1951* (London, pb edn, 1985), pp. 720–1.

been involved along with the Americans). But the French could point to several occasions when Bevin had emphasised the need for Anglo–French economic co-operation. The joint economic committee set up by Bevin and Bidault in September 1946 was still in existence, but had not been used. Moreover, French interests were very much affected, and indeed damaged, by the British action. The extent of the devaluation of the pound was such that France had to follow suit with the franc. The West German mark was also devalued, which again had consequences for France. The French were understandably aggrieved. The British, on the other hand, were reasonably happy with their handling of an unpalatable business. In October 1949 Bevin and Cripps reported to the Cabinet that the episode had emphasised how much Britain depended on the United States and Canada, as against European countries; and they were pleased with the way they had been able to work with the Americans.

At much the same time as these events, a scheme for economic association between France, Italy and the Benelux countries was approaching fruition. From 1947 to 1949 a project for a Franco-Italian customs union had been under desultory discussion, without making serious progress. Then the French tried to translate this into a wider enterprise, bringing in Belgium, the Netherlands and Luxembourg. In November 1949, two months after the British devaluation, a basis for negotiation was achieved, and by February 1950 a firm proposal was worked out between the various governments. (This was a period when no plan was presentable without a set of initials to describe it. The proposed association was at first called FRITALUX, which seemed absurd, and then renamed FINEBEL, which sounded like a processed cheese.)

Whatever its initials, the project foundered, on two different obstacles. There was widespread opposition within France, from firms and pressure groups alarmed by the prospect of competition from Italy and the Low Countries. Also the British, though technically not involved, disapproved of the scheme, and encouraged resistance by the Dutch and Belgians. By February 1950, even while the final details were being completed, it became clear that the project was politically defunct. The French Foreign Minister, Schuman, who had put a good deal of effort into this design, drew two lessons from it: that it was best not to alert French pressure groups and give them time to mobilise; and that the British were determined to obstruct moves towards European union. From these two lessons he drew a single conclusion: that if any similar manoeuvre were to be attempted in future, there would be a high premium on surprise.

These two events left their mark. The British devaluation emphasised their determination to act alone in emergency, and confirmed their close reliance upon the United States. The failure of the Franco-Italian-Benelux scheme convinced Schuman of the need for shock tactics if France was going to act effectively on projects for European unity.

Did France have the will for such action? The British did not think so. At the beginning of 1950 the Embassy in Paris surveyed the past year and found signs that the French were at last emerging from their long convalescence after the trials of defeat and occupation. There was *joie de vivre* in the air, and in more practical terms a government had managed to remain in office for over a year. However, in London this report drew a dismissive minute from Evelyn Shuckburgh: 'the nation has not yet acquired a will to survive'.[2] This was not just the view of a single official. In February 1950 the Ambassador in Paris, Oliver Harvey, sent home a long analysis of French opposition to the North Atlantic Treaty and to the policy of resisting the Soviets which it represented. This despatch attracted a number of gloomy minutes in the Foreign Office. Strang, the Permanent Under-Secretary, was emphatic: 'The slaughter of the First World War and the occupation during the Second have broken France's spirit. There is no reason to think that she would be more resolute in 1950 than she was in 1939–40. The only thing to do is to go on nursing and encouraging and fortifying.'[3]

There was an opportunity for the British to do some encouraging in March 1950, when President Auriol made a state visit to London – the first of the post-war era. The Speaker of the House of Commons, addressing the President in French, devoted most of his remarks to Auriol's opposition to the armistice in 1940, and Madame Auriol's fine record in the Resistance. In reply, the President too recalled the common struggle against Germany, and wondered why, after making such sacrifices, the two countries had turned so quickly to their own separate and selfish interests. It was sadly apparent that to find common ground the orators had to look back to the war. The visit went well enough at the personal level, without making much impact on relations between the two countries.

These were in a kind of slack water. Britain and France had not come closely together since the Treaty of Dunkirk, but neither had

---

2. PRO, FO 371/89166, WF1011/1, Harvey to McNeill, 3 Jan. 1950; minute by Shuckburgh, 6 Feb. 1950.

3. PRO, FO 371/89185, WF1023/2, Harvey to Bevin, 23 Feb. 1950, and attached minutes.

they moved sharply apart. They were both members of NATO and the Council of Europe, while approaching those two organisations in different ways. They had not achieved economic co-operation, but were not in commercial conflict. The French were exasperated by the British chariness about European unity. The British doubted French commitment to the cold war, and had no faith in French resilience or power. It was during this lull that the Schuman Plan for a European Coal and Steel Community was suddenly revealed.

SCHUMAN PRESENTS HIS PLAN

At 6 p.m. on 9 May 1950 the Foreign Minister of France, Robert Schuman, gave a press conference at the Quai d'Orsay. The circumstances were not overtly dramatic. There were some 200 journalists present, but no-one had arranged for photographs, or for the proceedings to be recorded for the radio. Schuman spoke in a hesitant voice. At one point he turned over two pages at once, which shortened the text but somewhat obscured its meaning. Yet his speech was to prove a momentous event in the history of Europe and of relations between France and Britain. It is worth examining in some detail.

Schuman observed that it was five years, almost to the day, since the German surrender in 1945. Now France was taking the first decisive step in the construction of Europe, and was associating Germany with it. In the past, European unity had not been achieved, and the result had been war. Now, Europe would not be made at a single stroke, but by concrete achievements building up a real solidarity. The key lay in ending the age-old conflict between France and Germany. So Schuman came to his main point.

> To this end the French government proposes immediate action at a limited but decisive point; the French government proposes to place the whole Franco-German production of coal and steel under a common High Authority, in an organisation open to the participation of other European countries. The pooling of coal and steel production will immediately ensure the establishment of common bases for economic development, the first stage in European federation . . .
>
> Thus the fusion of interests which is indispensable to the establishment of an economic community will be simply and swiftly brought about, and the ferment of a wider and deeper community will be produced in nations long set against each other by division and

bloodshed. By pooling basic production, by the institution of a new High Authority whose decisions will be binding on France, Germany and the countries which subscribe to it, this proposition lays the first concrete foundations of a European federation indispensable to the preservation of peace . . .

Schuman went on to explain that the proposed High Authority would, in the shortest possible time, proceed to modernise the industries under its control, remove all customs dues on coal and steel between the participating countries, level out transport costs, and equalise progress in the living conditions of workers in the industries. The Authority would be made up of independent individuals, nominated by governments. Its decisions, Schuman declared, would be binding.[4]

Schuman's speech was above all concerned with relations between France and Germany. The only foreign country mentioned by name, several times over, was Germany. The first step towards ending the long Franco-German conflict was to be the placing of their coal and steel production under the control of a common High Authority; and this was itself to be the first stage of European federation, which was mentioned twice in the passage cited above. The functions of the new High Authority were to go beyond the removal of internal customs barriers, and include some form of social harmonisation, or even levelling, which was implicit in the vague phraseology about equalising progress in living conditions. The aims set out were therefore nothing less than Franco-German reconciliation, the preservation of peace, European federation and social harmonisation. It was a remarkable programme.

Where did these ideas come from? There had been several proposals, dating back to before 1914, for some sort of combination between the coal and steel industries in Germany and France. In that sense the idea of a coal and steel community was far from new, and in early 1950 there were specific economic reasons for reviving it. The French needed a reliable supply of coal and coke, and were anxious to secure this from Germany on a permanent basis. In early 1950 there were indications that the steel industries of western Europe were heading towards over-production, leading to a fall in prices unless something was done to regulate both production and prices collectively. The idea of 'harmonising' coal and steel industries was thus in the air. More important, the new state of West Germany had come into being in 1949, and was already advancing towards full sovereignty. The possibility of German rearmament, repeatedly declared unacceptable by

4. Raymond Poidevin, *Robert Schuman: homme d'état, 1886–1963* (Paris, 1986), pp. 260–2.

France, had been raised by the United States government early in 1950, and was likely to come about at some stage. France needed a new policy towards Germany; and even more a new attitude. As long ago as July 1948 the French Foreign Ministry had been talking of 'a common Franco-German destiny'.[5]

These ideas were given precision and impetus by Jean Monnet and Robert Schuman. Monnet was a shadowy figure, almost the classic case of the *éminence grise*. He had made his name within a very limited circle during the First World War, when as a very young civil servant he played a key role in setting up joint Allied Boards to make purchases of wheat in the United States, and then to control Allied shipping. He had resumed almost exactly the same work in 1939–40, with the Anglo-French Purchasing Board. In June 1940 he was one of the moving spirits behind the offer of union made to France by Churchill's War Cabinet. He himself liked to say that he had worked for so long as an international civil servant that he had become entirely international in outlook. But in fact from 1946 onwards he had devoted his talents to the service of France as the head of the *Commissariat du Plan*. In that post, he had become accustomed to quick and fluid action, operating on the margins of normal political and bureaucratic systems and achieving his ends by unorthodox methods. One of his English admirers, Richard Mayne, has argued that, while not a systematic thinker, he was very good at picking out the next definite step towards a distant aim, itself only dimly discerned. He appears to have had one crucial fixed idea: that only individuals could set a policy in motion, but only institutions could carry it on and ensure its permanence. His actions in 1950 certainly followed this pattern. He proposed a definite step towards a distant aim – European federation; and he insisted that an institution – the High Authority – must be created to give permanence to his policy. Thus the essential elements of the Schuman Plan were conceived by Monnet, a convinced internationalist who was determined that France should take the lead in internationalism.

Robert Schuman was the vital political partner in the project. He was very much a man of the borderlands between France and Germany. His father, a Lorrainer, served in the French Army in 1870, but did not opt for France when the war was over. Schuman grew up in Luxembourg, attended German universities, and then practised law in Metz, a city almost equally divided between French and German populations. Schuman served in the German Army in 1914, though

---

5. See above, p. 99.

for medical reasons only in a non-combatant unit; and he later worked in the German civil administration in Lorraine. In November 1919 he was elected to the French Chamber of Deputies, to represent the Moselle department. He was a devout Catholic, and after the Second World War he joined the Christian Democrats (MRP). He was a modestly successful Minister of Finance in 1946, and became Foreign Minister in July 1948. He had no previous experience of foreign policy, and between the wars he had shown no particular interest in Franco-German reconciliation or European unity. But he was bilingual in French and German; he had lived and worked in both countries; and he was deeply rooted in Catholic European culture – 'the defender of a certain kind of western Christian civilisation'.[6] By the whole experience of his life and the cast of his mind he looked towards the Rhine and Germany. In his dealings with Chancellor Adenauer he spoke and wrote in German; they shared a Catholic faith and culture, and a certain common outlook from the Moselle–Rhine valleys. As against this, he did not visit England before he became Foreign Minister; he understood English without speaking it well; and he had no particular sympathy with Britain or the Atlantic culture. As a minister, he was brisk and practical, often preferring not to consult or even inform the National Assembly about matters of foreign policy, knowing full well the delays and difficulties which might result.

This attitude to parliament meant that he shared some of Monnet's methods in approaching the coal and steel project. Monnet was accustomed to working informally, getting results by avoiding the 'proper channels'. Schuman had learned the virtues of secrecy and speed through his unfortunate experience with the FRITALUX affair. He explained his coal and steel proposal to the Cabinet only during the morning of 9 May, when he was due to give his press conference the same evening. He did not show his colleagues the text of his speech, and it is said that some ministers did not fully understand what they had agreed to until they read the newspapers the following day. The National Assembly was not consulted at all. Like a good military commander, Schuman counted on the advantage of surprise.

There were only two exceptions to this secrecy. One was the American Secretary of State, Acheson, who was in Paris at the time and was told of the proposals in general terms and in the strictest confidence on 8 May. There was more to this communication than courtesy, or even diplomatic calculation. There is evidence that the actual timing of Schuman's initiative was decided by American

6. Poidevin, *Schuman*, p. 423.

pressure, and that Acheson had been insisting that the French should produce something new on German policy quickly.[7] Next, a summary of the proposals and a letter of explanation were conveyed to Adenauer, the West German Chancellor, on the morning of 9 May; and Schuman received his full approval before he addressed the press conference at 6 p.m. Bevin, on the other hand, was only informed during the morning of 9 May that Schuman was going to take an important initiative; and Massigli handed him the text that afternoon, not long before Schuman's press conference and at a time when Bevin was heavily preoccupied. Bevin was infuriated by this treatment, and not much mollified when Acheson later reminded him that it followed very closely the course which the British themselves had adopted at the time of the devaluation of the pound in 1949.

The question naturally arose: did Schuman and Monnet keep the British in the dark in order to exclude them from the Plan, or with the intention of bringing them in once the project was under way? Alan Milward has written that, after their first independent action, the French tried hard to bring the British in, but only on French terms. The French historian Pierre Gerbet has argued that the French did not specifically wish to exclude Britain, but Germany was vital to the plan while Britain was not. This puts the relative importance of the two countries in Schuman's mind in a very clear light. Schuman himself made two statements after the event which leave little doubt as to how he saw the matter. In March 1951 he referred to the need for Europe to unite in a world divided into giant blocs – the United States, the British Empire, and the Soviet bloc. This clearly implied that Europe was separate from the British Empire, and vice versa. In June 1954, in a lecture at Harvard, he said that Britain regarded the Commonwealth as the apple of her eye, and that European integration would have 'at best its benevolent good wishes, never its full support'.[8] By that time, admittedly, three more years had passed, but it seems very likely that his view in 1950 was the same. He did not believe that Britain would adhere to an integrated Europe. Whether Britain was excluded or was bound to exclude herself was a distinction almost without a difference. For Schuman, as both his words and his actions on 9 May made clear, the essence of his Plan lay in relations with Germany, not Britain.

As to Monnet, he had at an earlier stage believed that an integrated

7. François Duchêne, *Jean Monnet. The First Statesman of Interdependence* (London, 1994), p. 190.

8. Pierre Gerbet, *La construction de l'Europe* (Paris, 1983), p. 13; Alan S. Milward, *The Reconstruction of Western Europe, 1945–51* (London, 1984), p. 400; Poidevin, *Schuman*, p. 372.

Europe could be built round a Franco-British core. He had tried this idea out in conversations with Edwin Plowden and other British officials, in March 1949 and again in February 1950, but had received little response. It is likely that he thereafter discounted the British as partners in his European schemes, and decided to go ahead without them. Monnet himself denied this, and went out of his way in his memoirs to stress his close ties with Britain. Massigli, in an account which is far from sympathetic to Monnet, argues that Monnet wanted British co-operation, but only on his own terms and without compromise. He intended, by sheer speed of action, to 'bounce' the British into acceptance of the Schuman Plan, and especially his central idea of a High Authority; and he was accustomed to dealing in France with ministers who were of little substance and did not know their own minds. Bevin had ample substance, knew his own mind, and was not susceptible to being 'bounced'. It is doubtless difficult to discern Monnet's precise intentions with regard to Britain and the Schuman Plan, and it may even be that in a strict sense he did not have any. But actions speak louder than words or thoughts. In practice, like Schuman, Monnet took great care to ensure German participation in the Plan, and very little to secure that of Britain.

THE BRITISH REACTION

The immediate British reaction to the Schuman proposals was coloured by resentment at the way in which they had been presented. A meeting of ministers on 10 May agreed that 'The French Government had behaved extremely badly in springing this proposal on the world' without any attempt at consultation with the British or Americans.[9] Massigli wrote in his memoirs that even if Bevin had been the most modest and accommodating man in the world (which he was not) he could simply not have accepted a proceeding which infringed Britain's dignity as a great power, and trespassed on British rights as one of the occupying powers in Germany. The only surprise was that Bevin kept his anger within bounds. On 10–11 May there were first Anglo-American and later Anglo-Franco-American talks in London, in preparation for a full North Atlantic conference; and Bevin took the view that this was no time for a stand-up fight with the French. British resentment was therefore set aside for a time, but it remained alive.

9. *Documents on British Policy Overseas (DBPO)*, series II, vol. I, No. 3, record of meeting, 10 May 1950.

Despite this resentment, the normal processes of British government were set to work on the issues raised by Schuman's proposals. The Economic Committee of the Cabinet, the Chiefs of Staff, and the Foreign Office all presented reports on the Schuman proposals on 11 May. The Economic Committee was hostile, on the grounds that the Plan would damage the British steel industry and ran counter to British and Commonwealth approaches to commercial questions. The Chiefs of Staff were in favour, because they believed the scheme would strengthen western Europe and make its defence more secure. The Foreign Office found something to be said on both sides: on the one hand the Plan offered a useful means of controlling Germany, but on the other it tended towards a European federation, which Britain could not join.

This advice was inconclusive, and for some time the British government sought to avoid the crucial choice which was presented by Schuman's proposal. Monnet came to London on 14 May, and reiterated the key point in that choice. The British, he insisted, must accept the principle of a supranational High Authority as a necessary pre-condition for any talks about the proposal as a whole. The British government tried to do something quite different. They expressed general approval of Schuman's plan, but would not accept the supranational principle. Attlee told Massigli informally that Britain must be in the Plan from the beginning. Bevin told Paris that the proposals should be followed up without loss of time; Britain wanted to take part in conversations with France and West Germany at once, in order to find out how the scheme would work in detail. But the British constantly insisted that they could not accept in advance the principles set out in Schuman's speech of 9 May. In the French view, this was mere dissembling to conceal British rejection of the core of the scheme. In Schuman's own words: 'In a limited but important area, we wish to arrive at a fusion of sovereignty.'[10] The British did not wish to arrive at any such fusion of sovereignty, and the result was an impasse.

The French pressed for a British decision without delay. On 1 June Schuman put forward some amendments to his proposals, but kept the central issue unchanged. He told the British Ambassador in Paris that he must have a reply by at the latest 8 p.m. the next day. This amounted to a sort of ultimatum – surely the first such demand made by a French government to the British in the twentieth century. It was a remarkable sign of the firmness and self-confidence that characterised French actions during this whole episode.

10. MAE, Papiers Massigli, 217/75, Schuman to Massigli, 7 June 1950.

The British Cabinet met to consider the question on 2 June. It was a thinly-attended meeting. Attlee and Cripps were on holiday. Bevin was in hospital, though he was consulted there. Herbert Morrison took the chair. The Cabinet considered whether to join the French and other governments in declaring that they 'set themselves as an immediate aim the pooling of their coal and steel production and the institution of a new High Authority', whose decisions would be binding. Ministers quickly decided that they could not; indeed, they held that no British government could accept such a commitment without assessing the consequences.[11] The low attendance at this meeting, and the absence of senior ministers, do not appear to have been significant. There is no sign that Attlee, Bevin or Cripps dissented from the decision taken, which coincided with their known views. They made no attempt to alter it later. The meeting, though not fully attended, represented fairly the whole Cabinet's point of view.

The British government thus declined the French proposals. This proved to be a crucial parting of the ways between France and Britain. Six countries, led by France, went ahead to form the European Coal and Steel Community. In 1957 the same six formed the European Economic Community. In both cases Britain remained outside, and the gulf thus fixed proved extremely difficult to bridge. What were the causes of this breach over the Schuman Plan?

The main point on the French side bears repeating. Both Schuman and Monnet insisted that the British must accept the principle of a supranational authority before taking part in any discussions about the Plan. Schuman, dismayed by the earlier British delays with regard to the Council of Europe, and their indirect applying of the brakes to the FRITALUX proposal, believed that no British government would accept a supranational authority. Therefore, if Britain were to take part in a conference without accepting the principle in advance, the result would only be delay, and perhaps even the sabotage of the whole project. There was much justification for this view. Cripps in fact suggested during May that Britain should join in the Schuman Plan at once and then render it harmless from within; and if this were to be the British approach it would indeed have nullified the negotiations.

Poidevin, Schuman's scholarly and sympathetic biographer, concludes that 'Schuman and Monnet could not hope to see their conceptions carried out without putting England provisionally out of the game. Straight away, they tried to close the door to London's

11. Bullock, *Bevin*, vol. III, p. 780.

manoeuvres'.[12] If Schuman really believed that *no* British government would accept a supranational authority, it is hard to see the significance of 'provisionally' – Britain would have to be put out of the game for the foreseeable future. The crucial words in Poidevin's summing up are 'straight away'. The French were determined to act speedily and keep up the momentum of their proposal. That was the point of their near-ultimatum to the British on 1 June. To permit delay would allow opposition to mobilise, perhaps in France, perhaps elsewhere. Schuman could not risk it. He was in a hurry, believing that he had a short-lived opportunity, and one which might not recur. He had to keep up the spurt, and for a few weeks he did so. On 20 June 1950, only six weeks after his press conference on 9 May, Schuman opened a conference of six countries in Paris to work out means to put his proposals into effect.

The central issue for France, as it had been since 1945, was the German question. French Europeanism was an attempt to find a new answer to that old question, which was why Schuman and Monnet both attached such key importance to the concept of the High Authority. The significance with which they endowed it was that of a talisman rather than anything practical. Schuman himself spoke of the tiny fraction of sovereignty that member states would give up, and when the High Authority itself came into being its actions proved to be extremely limited in scope. Yet sometimes there is more meaning in a talisman or a symbol than in any amount of prosaic fact, and who is to say that Schuman was mistaken? Certainly, at the time, all that mattered was that he believed he was right.

British motives and attitudes were quite different. They were not subject to the same urgent impulse to deal with the German question, which for them was important but not crucial. For them, the major foreign policy issue of the day was the cold war, to which the Schuman Plan appeared to have only minor relevance. On one fundamental point they were quite clear: Britain simply could not join any form of European federation, to which Schuman had so carefully referred. A memorandum by a Cabinet committee on guidelines for British policy after the rejection of the Schuman Plan stated firmly: 'It is assumed that it is not the policy of His Majesty's Government to participate in a federal regime in Western Europe or in forms of integration leading to such a system.'[13] This was not an issue in party politics between Labour and Conservatives. It was true that, while in opposition, Churchill had shown himself more sympathetic to the idea

12. Poidevin, *Schuman*, p. 277.
13. *DBPO*, series II, vol. I, No. 144, 10 July 1950.

of European unity than did Labour leaders; but when the Conservatives returned to office in 1951 they followed the same policy as their predecessors. Eden, the Conservative Foreign Secretary, approved a circular to all diplomatic posts: 'We cannot subordinate ourselves or the control of British policy to federal authorities.'[14] For a Labour government, coal and steel (both recently nationalised industries) were particularly sensitive issues. It is reported that Herbert Morrison said, the night before the Cabinet came to its decision on 2 June 1950: 'It's no good, we can't do it, the Durham miners won't wear it.'[15] That was sound Labour Party instinct. But other reasons for opposing federalism were common to both parties and formed part of the common stock of British political thinking and instincts: the Commonwealth and the sterling area; the Atlantic connection with the United States; and the long island story of British history. The refusal of European federation by Britain was taken for granted, and scarcely needed to be explained.

Moreover, the British government was convinced that the Schuman Plan, and the general movement for European unity of which it formed a part, arose essentially from weakness and fear. The main tenor of reporting from the British Embassy in Paris since 1945, endorsed and sometimes amplified in the Foreign Office, was dominated by the impression of French weakness – political, economic, and perhaps above all in terms of morale. In October 1948 Sir Ivone Kirkpatrick, a senior official, later to become Permanent Under-Secretary, prepared a memorandum for Bevin in which he described France as 'the weakest link in the Western chain . . . The Parliamentary regime is discredited . . . the economic situation goes from bad to worse . . . It is difficult to see how this regime can last much longer'.[16] A Foreign Office memorandum, considered and endorsed by Eden in December 1951, concluded that '*The defeat and humiliation suffered by many European countries* has stimulated a desire for closer integration in Western Europe'.[17] More emphatically still, Sir Edmund Hall-Patch, the principal British representative with the OEEC, wrote in his carefully considered final despatch: 'This tendency to partial European federation is not an urge to European brotherhood on a healthy basis. *It is based on uncertainty and fear.*'[18] These two last comments were

14. Ibid., No. 416.
15. B. Donoughue and G.W. Jones, *Herbert Morrison* (London, 1973), p. 481.
16. PRO, FO 371/73105, Z8829/829/G, minute by Kirkpatrick, 8 Oct. 1948.
17. *DBPO*, series II, vol. I, No. 414, memo. by PUS's Committee, 12 Dec. 1951. The italics are mine.
18. Ibid., No. 466, Hall-Patch to Eden, 8 July 1952. The italics are mine.

made after the Schuman Plan, but they reflect the general thinking of the time. Behind them lay the assumption, ever-present if usually unspoken, that Britain's position was very different. Britain had not been defeated or humiliated, and the British had no sense of operating from uncertainty or fear. They stood outside Europe as they had done in 1940, and might have to do again. They were still drawing on the capital of their wartime glory.

Massigli believed that other differences of mentality were also at work. He believed, as many Frenchmen had done before him, that the British were concerned with facts, not with principles. The essence of the French proposal in the Schuman Plan was to require acceptance of the principle of the High Authority before any discussion of how it was to be applied. Massigli commented: 'It is asking something which has no meaning to a British mind. For an Englishman, a principle does not exist of itself; it is defined in and by its application.'[19] There was a further mental gap between Monnet's faith in the expert technocrat, working untrammelled by parliaments or ministers, and the British appeal to common sense and the need for responsibility. Attlee told Massigli that the British could not accept the High Authority unless it were to be responsible, in a constitutional sense. Even if the experts were correct, said Attlee, the people had the right to tell them they were wrong. Nothing could have been further from Monnet's approach, which worked essentially in a tradition which went back to Colbert in the seventeenth century: government by enlightened bureaucracy.

These differences of motive and attitude ran deep. Schuman understood this, writing to Massigli on 7 June 1950 that he was convinced that 'the present development, which *is due to the very character of the British people as well as to their geographical situation*, could not be avoided'.[20] Yet at the same time he genuinely hoped to avoid a serious breach in relations between France and Britain, and thought that means could be found to associate Britain with the Coal and Steel Community after it had been set up. Similarly, the Foreign Office and the British Embassy in Paris thought that discussions could somehow be kept going and serious consequences avoided.

These hopes did not last long. On 12 June 1950 the Executive Committee of the Labour Party published a pamphlet on *European Unity*, drafted by Denis Healey and presented at a press conference by Hugh Dalton, formerly Chancellor of the Exchequer and still a senior

---

19. René Massigli, *Une comédie des erreurs* (Paris, 1978), p. 236; MAE, Papiers Massigli, 217/75, Massigli to MAE, 26 May 1950.

20. Ibid., Schuman to Massigli, 7 June 1950. The italics are mine.

figure in the Labour Party. The pamphlet declared that socialists would only welcome a European economic union if it was based on planning for full employment, social justice and stability: conditions which, it was claimed, existed only in Britain and the Scandinavian countries. Dalton threw in for good measure that Britain would not permit any delegation of sovereignty even if all European governments were socialist. (Which of course they were not: both Schuman and Adenauer were Christian Democrats.) It was of course true that the Executive Committee of the Labour Party was not the British government; but Bevin had initialled the final draft of the pamphlet, and Attlee had been present at the meeting where it was accepted.

The French reaction was violent. Press comment was almost uniformly hostile. An article in *Le Monde* by Maurice Duverger (15 June) declared that: 'now the way is clear. The authors of the Schuman Plan have forced the English to come out into the open'. *L'Année Politique*, under the editorship of André Siegfried, a long-standing friend and sympathetic interpreter of Britain, described Dalton's press conference as 'This blunt repetition of ancient principles'. Such reactions were fairly typical. In private, Monnet commented that the Labour Party pamphlet showed that he was right to think it useless to try to secure British agreement to the Schuman Plan. Even Massigli thought it likely that the pamphlet and its launching were intended to make it impossible for a Labour government to adhere to the Plan at a later date.[21]

The general British attitude was confirmed by a debate in the House of Commons on 27 June 1950. The Conservative Opposition urged that Britain should take part in discussions on the Schuman Plan on the same basis as that adopted by the Dutch, who had accepted the principle of a supranational High Authority but reserved the right to withdraw if the principle proved unworkable. Churchill and Eden both argued that it was dangerous for Britain to remain outside the discussions, leaving the French and Germans to take charge. This appeared to reveal a division of opinion between the parties, but at bottom the debate demonstrated that neither believed there was any question of Britain joining a European federal union. Churchill was categorically opposed to any federal movement limited to Europe. Nearly every speaker rejected the idea of accepting for British coal and steel an authority which was not responsible to any government or parliament. There were no great revelations in this, simply the public confirmation by the House of Commons of a settled attitude of mind.

---

21. *L'Année Politique*, 1950, p. 140; Massigli, *Comédie*, p. 211.

From this there was no appeal. As Schuman wrote to Massigli a few days later, 'one cannot persist in trying to reconcile the irreconcilable'.[22]

It is worth adding that at this stage, when the six founder members of the ECSC were working out the details of their association, the British government did nothing to hinder their deliberations, even though they might well have done so – for example, by publishing the alternative proposals they were preparing, which might have acted as a counter-bid to the Schuman Plan. The main motive for this abstention was doubtless the belief that the Plan was in any case doomed to failure, so that intervention could safely be postponed; but even so the fact deserves to be recalled.[23]

CONSEQUENCES

There was a strange disparity between the broad political consequences of the Schuman Plan and its immediate practical effects, which were very limited. After the initial spurt, progress was slow, and the famous High Authority only began to operate in August 1952, by which time it had been circumscribed by a Council of Ministers with complicated voting arrangements. From 1 January 1953 the Authority levied a small tax on the selling price of coal, iron and steel in the member countries – a function normally exercised only by governments. But no drastic shift of power followed. The Schuman Plan did not achieve uniformity among the coal and steel industries of the Six, but rather 'a patchwork of intergovernment deals'. Italy retained tariffs for some years, and the equalisation of freight charges was not achieved.[24] In 1959 demand for coal diminished as a result of low oil prices, but the French Premier at the time (Michel Debré, the first Premier under de Gaulle's new Fifth Republic) refused to allow the High Authority of the Coal and Steel Community to take decisions which might entail the closure of French coal-mines. Other member states also tried to deal with the problem of falling demand by national, not Community, policies. Meanwhile, in 1954, a *Conseil Permanent d'Association* was created as a liaison body between Britain and the High Authority. Thus the actual role of the High Authority proved in practice to be

22. MAE, Papiers Massigli, 217/75, Schuman to Massigli, 5 July 1950.
23. Milward, *Reconstruction*, pp. 405–6.
24. Patrick McCarthy, 'Condemned to Partnership', in Patrick McCarthy, ed., *France-Germany, 1983–1993* (London, 1993), p. 7.

much smaller than was envisaged in 1950, and British association with it was developed without much difficulty. There was some temptation to ask what all the fuss had been about.

However, in this case the essence did not lie in the details or in practical matters. The Schuman Plan amounted, not to a reversal of *alliances* by France (French security depended too much on the North Atlantic Treaty for that), but to the reversal of *an alliance*. As Monnet's biographer has written, the Schuman Plan marked the French abandonment of 'the safety net of the *entente cordiale* with Britain'; though this was less risky than it looked because the Americans were always there to provide another net.[25] Just over three years after the signature of the Treaty of Dunkirk, an alliance with Britain against Germany, France deliberately chose an association with Germany from which Britain was excluded. Moreover, Monnet was proved right in his belief that men could launch an idea and institutions would perpetuate it. The institutions of the Coal and Steel Community may have done very little in a practical sense, but they formed the framework which later developed into the European Economic Community and so influenced the course of European history and relations between Britain and France. A little over thirty years after the launching of the Plan, a French historian could reflect that it had 'allowed France to seize the initiative and to replace, as leader of Europe, a too-reluctant Great Britain'.[26] The French had struck out, following their own policy and backing their own judgement, and not allowing their new European project to sink or swim according to British decisions. Previously, France's political, and above all psychological, position had been too weak, and Britain's prestige too great, to allow such an initiative to be taken. The Schuman Plan was a sign of a fundamental shift in relations between France and Britain.

It was easier to discern this thirty years later than it was at the time. For some time after mid-1950, Bevin and his officials at the Foreign Office continued to believe that the Schuman Plan would fail, and Britain must be ready to step in with a realistic substitute when it did so. More important, the latter part of 1950 was dominated by events which dwarfed the significance of the Schuman Plan and emphasised Britain's continuing role as a world power, an ally of the United States, and leader of the Commonwealth.

On 24 June 1950 the Korean War began. On the 28th (the day

---

25. The fine but all-important distinction between alliances and an alliance is drawn by Massigli, *Comédie*, p. 187; on the safety net, see Duchêne, *Monnet*, p. 204.
26. Gerbet, *Europe*, p. 101.

after the Commons debate on the Schuman Plan) Attlee announced in Parliament that British forces were to go to the support of the Americans in Korea. At the end of August the period of conscription was extended from eighteen months to two years. British troops were soon joined in Korea by forces from Canada, Australia and New Zealand. Not long afterwards, for the first (and surely the last) time in history a Commonwealth Division was formed. Britain, the Commonwealth and the United States were back in action together, and Britain was acting as a world power. Bevin told Massigli on 31 August: 'We are setting an example for Europe.'[27]

It was an example that France was in no position to follow. Domestic opinion was sharply divided by the Korean War. The Communists took the side of North Korea, and the strong neutralist lobby was in favour of non-intervention. In any case, the French Army was heavily engaged in Indo-China, and had virtually nothing to spare for Korea. Eventually, at the end of October 1950, the French despatched a token battalion, which went into action in January 1951; but that was all. Diplomatically too the French let Britain take the lead. In December 1950 both Britain and France were alarmed that the Americans intended to use atomic bombs in the Korean War, and thus risk a world conflict. French ministers visited London to discuss how to restrain the Americans. But it was Attlee alone who flew to Washington to talk to President Truman; and Schuman told reporters that there was no need for him to go as well, because France and Britain were agreed on essentials. France was ready to let Britain play the hand.

The lesson of these events was clear. The peace of the world, or even of Europe, was not going to be safeguarded by the pooling of west European coal and steel resources, but by armed force in Korea and (perhaps) by British influence on the Americans. In these matters the leadership of western Europe lay with Britain, and the Schuman Plan suddenly seemed less important.

GERMAN REARMAMENT AND THE EUROPEAN DEFENCE COMMUNITY

The Korean War also brought to a head the painful question of German rearmament, which the Americans had been considering for some time. War in a divided Korea might well be followed by war in

27. MAE, Papiers Massigli, 217/47, Massigli to MAE, 2 Sept. 1950.

a divided Germany, for which NATO was manifestly unprepared, with an impressive command structure but not enough troops on the ground. The Americans looked round desperately for soldiers, and inevitably turned towards West Germany. At a NATO meeting on 15 September 1950 the Secretary of State, Acheson, formally proposed the establishment of German forces under NATO command.

This confronted France with an acute dilemma. French governments had asserted repeatedly that they could not accept German rearmament; and it is striking that they did not believe that the Schuman Plan had yet made any real change in the German situation. Yet they were in no position to resist if the Americans really insisted. The French Premier at the time was René Pleven, an ardent advocate of European union; and Schuman was still Foreign Minister. Both were in close touch with Monnet, who argued that the only way out was to transform the disagreeable necessity of complying with American demands for German rearmament into an opportunity for European integration. There was no time to allow Europe to develop slowly: they must make a dash for it. Pleven agreed, and proposed an outline plan for a European Army which would permit a form of German rearmament without creating a German Army. Under the Pleven Plan, there would be a European Army made up of separate national battalions, with no more than one German battalion per division – normally, one-ninth of the total strength. As the details were worked out, this idea of the battalion as the largest national unit had to be abandoned as impractical, and national brigade groups of about 5,000 men were proposed instead.

On this basis, though with innumerable complications, the project emerged as a proposed European Defence Community, with the same six members as the Coal and Steel Community. A treaty to set up this new body was signed in Paris on 27 May 1952 – a monstrous document comprising 129 articles and four extra protocols. The whole proposal by then appeared bizarre in the extreme. If the intention was to bring about German rearmament to counter an immediate Soviet threat, it was absurd to produce after almost two years a treaty so complex as to be barely intelligible, which would itself bring into being after further delay an untried force of dubious military value. It was extraordinary, and a tribute to the momentum of the idea, that six governments signed the treaty, and four parliaments (of Belgium, the Netherlands, Luxembourg and West Germany) ratified it. The Italians waited to see what the French would do.

French policy verged on the schizophrenic. In 1951 Schuman and Pleven plunged further and faster down the federal path. In September

Schuman proposed a common European foreign policy, to be conducted by a federal authority; in October Pleven declared that the enterprise begun with the ECSC and continued with the EDC must now be extended to political affairs. From these proposals emerged the idea of a European Political Community, amounting to a comprehensive scheme for west European federation. Yet on the other hand no French government dared to bring the EDC treaty to the National Assembly for ratification. Opinion on the project was acutely divided, and it was plain that opposition to German rearmament was stronger than enthusiasm for the European idea. Not until two years after the signature of the treaty did Pierre Mendès-France bring the matter to a vote in the Assembly, at the end of August 1954; and then it was in the certain knowledge that it would be defeated. By a majority of 319 to 264 the Assembly postponed discussion of the treaty *sine die*, which amounted to its rejection. The EDC was dead, killed by the very country that had originated it.

This sorry and tortuous tale (whose complications are only hinted at here) had a marked impact on relations between France and Britain. The British position on the EDC proposal remained consistent throughout, even though it was first raised under Attlee's Labour government in 1950 and was concluded during Churchill's administration in 1954. Britain was prepared to consider the proposal for a European Army with a sceptical sympathy, or perhaps a sympathetic scepticism. Attlee, who had been a soldier, doubted whether such an army would work. Churchill memorably remarked that it would produce a military equivalent of sludge. They would certainly not take part in it. Churchill, on a visit to Paris in December 1951, told Schuman that he was opposed to the concept of supranationality, which seemed to him metaphysical; Britain would co-operate with the EDC without being a member of it. He repeated this declaration on a number of occasions, most publicly and formally in the House of Commons on 11 May 1953. Finally, in April 1954 Britain signed an agreement on co-operation with the EDC, laying down procedures for consultation. The British would go no further than this, and consistently maintained the position they had taken up in relation to the Schuman Plan: they would agree to co-operation, but would not accept a supranational authority.

This time events worked out very differently from the case of the Schuman Plan. The British had expected the Schuman Plan to fail, and intended to step in with a realistic scheme of their own; but instead it succeeded, and so the opportunity never arose. The EDC failed, leaving behind it the continuing question of how to accommodate

German rearmament, which had been held up for some four years. This time, the opportunity was there for British intervention, and Eden, the Foreign Secretary, moved with remarkable speed to seize it. Between 11 and 16 September 1954 he visited all the west European capitals, and arranged a conference in London (28 September– 3 October) attended by Britain, the USA, Canada and the six former EDC countries. The problem was how to permit German rearmament, on which the USA still insisted, while providing assurances against the dangerous revival of German military power. Eden's solution was to use the existing machinery of the Brussels and North Atlantic Treaties, and add a new guarantee by Britain for western Europe. Eden proposed that West Germany and Italy should be admitted to the Brussels Treaty, forming a body to be called West European Union, which was to be simply an association of states with no supranational element. At the same time, West Germany was to be admitted to the North Atlantic Treaty, and to establish its own army, but only under an integrated NATO command. Finally, in a dramatic intervention at the London conference on 28 September, Eden undertook that Britain would maintain a force of four divisions on the continent of Europe (principally in Germany), not to be withdrawn without the agreement of a majority of the states signatory to the Brussels Treaty.

This guarantee of a British military presence on the continent was unprecedented. Advocates of European unity observed acidly that Britain was willing to back her own solution to the problems of German rearmament with an undertaking more far-reaching than anything she had offered to the EDC. The British found it perfectly reasonable to support their own proposals, but the architects of the failed EDC resented it. However, Eden's proposals were rapidly supported by Mendès-France, the Premier of France, and by all the other governments concerned. At a conference in Paris in October 1954 it was formally agreed that the restrictions previously imposed on West Germany by the occupation statute should be removed. The Germans could now establish an army up to twelve divisions in strength. West Germany was admitted to NATO, and the new West European Union was formally set up.

What was essentially a NATO solution to the problem of German rearmament was thus worked out inside two months, after the EDC proposals had staggered from one difficulty to another for nearly four years. It was a triumph for Britain, and for Eden personally. By skilful diplomacy, the use of existing treaties and a practical military commitment they had provided a sound working arrangement that made the elaborations of the supranationalists redundant. Eden received the Order of the Garter, just as Austen Chamberlain had after his achievement at Locarno in 1925. The good old days had come again. Britain, from a position outside continental Europe, had stepped in to resolve a crucial Franco-German problem. It appeared that the success of the Schuman Plan might be little more than an interlude, and that the foundations of British policy towards France and western Europe remained sound.

Even at that time, however, the momentum of Franco-German *rapprochement* did not entirely slacken. At the same time as the Paris conference of October 1954 on the German entry to NATO, Mendès-France and Chancellor Adenauer signed a number of Franco-German agreements. One of these provided for an intensification of cultural exchanges, which proved in the long term to be of considerable importance – for example, arrangements for student exchanges between France and Germany became more effective and better financed than those between France and Britain. Another dealt with the status of the Saar, eventually leading to that territory becoming simply a part of West Germany, politically from 1 January 1957 and economically after a further period of transition. This marked the final disappointment of the French hopes of 1945, to separate the Saar from Germany; but it also removed the last territorial point of contention between the two countries.

THE *ENTENTE CORDIALE* AFTER 50 YEARS

The period dominated by the EDC issue was one of continuing British self-confidence. When Churchill returned to office at the general election of October 1951 he at once sought to renew the close relations with the Americans that he had cultivated in wartime. He was also determined to crown his political career, which had been so much concerned with warfare, by becoming a peace-maker. In a speech in the House of Commons on 11 May 1953 he launched the idea of a meeting 'at the summit' between the leaders of the world's great powers; by which he meant (though at first he did not say so) the old wartime Big Three – the USA, the Soviet Union and Great Britain. France would still be excluded from this magic circle, as at the time of Yalta and Potsdam. During the same speech, Churchill went so far as to advise the French to extend their period of military service to two years – a remarkable intervention in French domestic affairs. Even from Churchill, whose reputation in France stood high, the

French felt that this went too far. Churchill seems to have been unperturbed by the wrath he incurred. With advancing years he seems to have felt at liberty to be undiplomatic. Rather over a year later, in August 1954, he met Mendès-France in London, and remarked frankly (in French): 'Votre système parlementaire ne marche pas' – 'Your parliamentary system doesn't work.'[28] In what were to prove the last years of the Fourth Republic, this was fair comment, but from one Prime Minister to another, it was less than tactful.

There were some signs of a changing outlook. Darsie Gillie, that experienced and perceptive observer of French affairs, wrote in May 1954 that although the French, ever since 1940, had lost faith in national action, a number of groups were showing great energy and effectiveness: he picked out the teams of technicians working on the economy, and the bands of European enthusiasts.[29] The Paris Embassy's annual report for 1955 noted the remarkable economic progress achieved during the year, with steady prices and increased purchasing power for the wage-earner. Even so, the report (over the signature of Gladwyn Jebb, who was one of the most distinguished of ambassadors) concluded by referring to 'the general contempt in which France is justly held abroad'. It was clear that 'nearly half the population reject the present political regime, and the other half who acquiesce in it would most certainly not put their hands in their pockets to defend it'.[30] This, of course, was true: at that stage, economic progress went alongside political instability; and the second seemed more important.

In April 1954 there occurred the fiftieth anniversary of the signing of the *Entente cordiale* in 1904. In France, the circumstances were not propitious. The European Defence Community was staggering towards failure. In Indo-China, the battle of Dien Bien Phu had begun, though it had yet to prove a disaster. Despite the gloom, the French press devoted a striking amount of space to the anniversary. *Le Monde* produced a special four-page supplement, including historical surveys, an article by André Maurois (the creator of Colonel Bramble during the First World War) and two contributions by British politicians, Kenneth Younger (formerly a Labour minister at the Foreign Office) and Robert Boothby (a well-known, though highly individual, Conservative backbencher). Both British writers were cautious in their approach. Younger pointed out the differences between French and British policy: in colonial affairs, he thought that France failed to show

28. Jean Chauvel, *Commentaire*, vol. III, *De Berne à Paris* (Paris, 1973), p. 147.
29. *Spectator*, 27 May 1954.
30. PRO, FO 371/124418, WF1011/1, Jebb to Selwyn Lloyd, 20 Jan. 1956.

enough flexibility in Indo-China and North Africa, while in Europe Britain had refused to join the Coal and Steel Community and so stood outside these new developments. Boothby, characteristically robust, declared that disunity between France and Britain was the cause of their weakness. Together, the two countries could have resisted the rearmament of Germany, which had been thrust on them by the Americans; together, they could have made something of the Council of Europe as a forum for co-operation. Instead, the French, by insisting on the creation of supranational authorities, had alienated the British and pushed them out of the main current of European politics. Boothby condemned this outright. In the world as it was, only NATO could ensure the defence of western Europe; other organisations were simply ineffective. As in duty bound, both Younger and Boothby ended their articles by urging co-operation between France and Britain and the forging of a new *Entente cordiale*; but the gist of their contributions was not encouraging.

The principal article in *Le Monde*'s supplement was by Beuve-Méry, the editor (writing, as usual, as 'Sirius'). He began with a catalogue of historical confrontations: Hastings, Crécy, Agincourt, Calais, La Rochelle, Fontenoy, Waterloo, Fashoda and Mers-el-Kébir. In 1914–18 the new bonds of the *Entente* had been sealed in blood, but the effects of centuries of conflict were not easily effaced. Between the wars, Britain had first thought that France was resuming her dominance in Europe, and then had tried to appease Germany at the expense of France and her allies. Now, in the 1950s, the situation was different again. There was talk of the danger of an Asiatic Munich in Indo-China, but that was not the real danger, which lay rather in too great a French subordination to the demands of Anglo-Saxon policy, which Beuve-Méry, in his neutralist mode, thought perilous and provocative. He concluded with a striking, though somewhat obscure, simile: 'This stubborn lion which still wishes to believe in splendid isolation and this garrulous cockerel which can still get drunk on words have still not finally worked out how much they need one another.' He forebore to add his own view on how great that need actually was.[31]

Le Monde took the trouble to print, in a prominent position, all the formal messages that were exchanged between the President of the Republic and the Queen, between the two Premiers (Laniel and Churchill), and between the two Foreign Ministers (Bidault and Eden). It was interesting to see Churchill too referring back to the Hundred

31. *Le Monde*, 9 April 1954.

Years' War, and to Fashoda – which for him was a piece of living history, because he had been with Kitchener at Khartoum, though not at Fashoda itself. There was a report of the debate in the National Assembly, which sent a message of goodwill to the House of Commons; and of a meeting (with a lunch) attended by one of Delcassé's former officials, reported to be the sole surviving witness of the signature of the *Entente*. All the courtesies were properly observed in France. Politically, there was a good deal of emphasis on Britain's role in restraining the Americans from rash actions. For example, a long article in *Combat* concluded that Britain was one of the best guarantors of peace, because the British would not let the Americans drag them into an ideological crusade.[32] The Communist *L'Humanité* paid almost no attention to the anniversary, except to point out that it had been used for differing purposes. Some hoped to use the *Entente* to oppose American pressures; others wanted to exploit it to draw Britain into the European Defence Community, which had been the veiled meaning of Bidault's message to Eden.[33] It was a shrewd comment.

In London, both Houses of Parliament held short debates (interrupting the discussion of the Budget) before passing resolutions to mark the anniversary. In the Commons, the resolution was moved by Maurice Edelman (Labour), the Chairman of the Franco-British Parliamentary Committee, and seconded by Sir Douglas Savory (Conservative), formerly Professor of French at Belfast University, who read in French part of one of Edward VII's speeches in Paris during his visit in 1903. Eden, Attlee and Clement Davies (leader of the Liberal Party) all spoke warmly of the *Entente*, as did Jenny Lee for the Labour Left; so the tradition of cross-party support was well maintained. Comment in the serious press, however, raised many doubts as to the current significance of the *Entente*. A long article in *The Times* reflected that 'In 1954 the difficulties of the *Entente* still revolve round the extent to which it is proper and possible for Britain to be continentally involved'. The Channel, public opinion, and commitments to the Commonwealth and the rest of the world still exercised a restraining influence, which the French found myopic.[34] In the *Daily Telegraph*, the French journalist 'Pertinax' wondered whether the roots of the *Entente* were not being severed. France had embarked, in the Coal and Steel Community, on an experiment in the fusion of sovereignty. If this succeeded, a 'Little Europe' would come into being, which would

32. Ibid., 9, 10 April 1954; *Combat*, 8 April.
33. *L'Humanité*, 9 April 1954.
34. *The Times*, 8 April 1954.

eventually be dominated by Germany. This was an unhappy prospect; yet Britain was obsessively determined to keep out of such ventures.[35] The *Manchester Guardian* observed in a leading article that an 'honest celebration' of the anniversary would have to recall both the success of the *Entente* in war and its failure between the wars. The writer recalled the offer of union in 1940, and wondered whether in 1990, 'when Britain and France and some other countries have found that Europe has become too small to be cemented by mere alliances', that offer might be warmly remembered.[36] *The Economist* was cautiously optimistic, observing that Britain was now committed several times over to the defence of western Europe, including France; which had not been the case in 1914.[37] Neither the *Spectator* nor the *New Statesman* mentioned the anniversary; nor did the *Scotsman*, despite the auld alliance. The British press, indeed, seemed to take the occasion less seriously than the French.

After fifty years, the partners in the *Entente* looked back with understanding, behaved in the present with a proper courtesy, but looked forward with some uncertainty and apprehension. In particular, the question of European organisation, raised so pointedly by the Schuman Plan in 1950, was widely reckoned to be a bone of contention.

35. *Daily Telegraph*, 8 April 1954.
36. *Manchester Guardian*, 8 April 1954.
37. *The Economist*, 10 April 1954.

The Suez Crisis, 1956, and a Strange Offer of Union

In 1956 the *Entente* came suddenly to life. British and French ministers worked together in clandestine accord. The armed forces of the two countries set up a joint command and prepared a combined operation in the utmost secrecy. British and French troops went into action together. The occasion of these events is famous in twentieth-century history as the Suez crisis. The story is a tangled one, and has been told repeatedly, amid much agonising and controversy. Through this maze we must follow the single thread of relations between Britain and France, on which the crisis had profound effects. The two countries, at first drawn more closely together than for many years, were eventually driven apart by their very different reactions to the Suez affair.

THE MIDDLE EAST AND ALGERIA

At first sight, Egypt and the Middle East seemed an unlikely area for Franco-British co-operation. In the nineteenth century the two countries had been rivals in Egypt, and as recently as the Second World War they had fallen into bitter conflict over Syria and the Lebanon. Since 1945, British policy in the area had been directed towards securing oil supplies from the area, keeping Soviet influence out, and generally retaining the Middle East as a crucial element in Britain's position as a world power. British diplomacy had been active in setting up the Baghdad Pact (April 1955), which was designed both as a defensive alliance against the Soviet Union and as a means of preserving British influence in the area. During 1955, British policy was directed towards the consolidation of the Baghdad Pact, and towards a highly secret project (code-named 'Alpha') to attempt a settlement of the Arab–Israeli conflict. Anthony Eden, who was Foreign Secretary until he took over from Churchill as Prime Minister in April 1955, continued to take the lead in Middle East policies.

The British worked on the Baghdad Pact and project 'Alpha' in co-operation with the United States, but to the exclusion of France. Ever since 1945 the British had sought to conduct their affairs in the Middle East separately from the French, on the ground that the latter were hopelessly unpopular with the Arabs. The opening of the Algerian War in 1954 increased that unpopularity. The French took no part in the Baghdad Pact, and indeed actively opposed it. They were excluded from the secret attempts to resolve the Arab–Israeli conflict. When the Egyptian government proposed to build a high dam at Aswan to control the flow of the Nile, the United States and Britain took part in financing the project, but France was kept out. Eden himself tended to regard the French as the enemies of British policy, and he privately referred to them as being 'obstructive', or even 'double-crossing'.[1]

This was not favourable ground for the revival of the *Entente*. However, there were also powerful forces at work to diminish the estrangement between Britain and France. They were both old imperial powers, facing a common problem of nationalist pressure on their empires. For some time they had pursued different policies. The French fought a long and costly war from 1945 to 1954 to preserve their position in Indo-China, but had to admit defeat after the fall of Dien Bien Phu in May 1954. In North Africa, France conceded independence to Morocco and Tunisia in 1954, rather than face constant conflict with the nationalist movements in those two countries. But almost at once, in November 1954, a large-scale insurrection broke out in Algeria, presenting an acutely difficult problem. In French law, Algeria consisted of three departments of France itself, and had a French population of over a million. In principle, a part of the Republic could not simply be abandoned; and in practical politics the *pieds noirs* and their supporters in France could not be disregarded. Successive French governments, starting with that of Mendès-France, committed themselves to the maintenance of French Algeria, and became involved in a guerrilla war which by early 1956 absorbed about half a million French troops.

The British for their part had followed a different path. They left

---

1. Keith Kyle, 'Britain and the Crisis, 1955–1956', in William Roger Louis and Roger Owen, eds, *Suez 1956. The Crisis and its Consequences* (Oxford, 1989), p. 111.

India in 1947, avoiding by a hasty retreat the sort of long conflict waged by the French in Indo-China. As India, Pakistan, and later Ceylon joined the Commonwealth, British governments and political commentators complimented themselves on their sagacity in effecting this transfer of power. But the Middle East presented a more difficult problem. Oil supplies, the trade routes and imperial communications which still depended on the Suez Canal; perhaps above all the imponderable element of prestige and great power status – all combined to make it impossible for the British to abandon their hold on the Middle East entirely. Yet their position was being steadily weakened. In 1948 they abandoned Palestine. In 1951 the Iranian government nationalised the Anglo-Iranian Oil Company. In 1954 the British garrison left the Suez Canal Zone, under a treaty with Egypt which technically allowed them to return in time of international crisis. In 1955 Colonel Nasser emerged as ruler of Egypt and aspirant to the role of leader of Arab nationalism in the Middle East. For some time it was not clear how far Nasser presented a serious threat to British interests. But on 1 March 1956 King Hussein of Jordan dismissed Glubb Pasha, the British commander of the Jordanian Army and the almost legendary embodiment of British influence in the country. The British at once blamed Nasser for this blow to their prestige. Eden already regarded Nasser as a man with wide ambitions, and now thought him a serious danger.

Pressure on the old imperial powers was also mounting in other ways. In 1955 a number of Asian and African states held a conference at Bandung, in Indonesia, which became a focus for the struggle against colonialism. During the same year, the Soviet leaders Khruschev and Bulganin began to bid for influence in the Third World, and made a spectacular visit to India. In the Middle East, using Czechoslovakia as a go-between, the Soviet Union began to supply Egypt with armaments, including modern MiG fighters.

The French and British thus faced common problems. The French were fighting a war in Algeria which they firmly believed they could not afford to lose, but had so far been unable to win. The British were under increasing pressure in the Middle East, and felt that they could yield no more ground there. Both were becoming convinced that the root of their difficulties lay in Egypt and its ruler, Colonel Nasser. The French believed that Egypt was providing crucial material and moral assistance to the Algerian rebels, and that the Algerian War could be won by cutting off that aid at its source. For the British, Nasser seemed to be at the centre of a web of intrigue against them. Nasser also stirred, in both Britain and France, memories of the 1930s, so that a reaction against the appeasement policies of that decade, or against the 'Munich syndrome', assumed a powerful (if somewhat incongruous) significance. As early as January 1956 Eden, on a journey across the Atlantic to see President Eisenhower, compared Nasser to Mussolini – 'his object was to be a Caesar from the Gulf to the Atlantic and to kick us out of it all'.[2] In March 1956 Guy Mollet, the French Premier, visited Eden at Chequers and compared Nasser with Hitler, and his book *The Philosophy of the Revolution* with *Mein Kampf*. Later, Hugh Gaitskell, the leader of the Labour opposition in Britain, also compared Nasser to Hitler. During the Suez crisis itself, Eden from time to time compared the situation with the Rhineland in 1936, and Mollet drew parallels with Munich in 1938. Both were occasions, they claimed, when Hitler's aggressive policies could and should have been resisted. Eden had himself been Foreign Secretary at the time of the German occupation of the Rhineland; Mollet, it appears, felt guilty about his pacifism in 1938. In these ways, an emotional current from the recent past influenced the policy of both leaders.

During the first half of 1956 it was by no means clear that the broad threat to their imperial positions and a similarity of views on Nasser would bring Britain and France together in their Middle Eastern policies. France was on close terms with Israel, as the two struggled against Arab nationalism. The Israelis provided France with intelligence about Arab contacts with Algeria. The French sold Israel tanks and aircraft, notably the Mystère IVA, the best French fighter in service, of which twelve were delivered in April 1956, with sixty more to follow. Mollet, the Socialist Premier, was personally strongly committed to Israel, partly out of sympathy for Israel's socialist experiment, and even more through the effects of the death camps and the Holocaust during the Second World War. The British, on the other hand, rejected any close ties with Israel, and based their policy on co-operation with Arab states. At the turn of the years 1955–56, the British military commanders in the Middle East and the Chiefs of Staff in London were considering the possibility of a war against Israel on the side of Jordan. Britain and France also continued to differ markedly in their attitudes to the United States. The British wanted to work with the Americans, and draw them more closely into Middle East affairs; the French tended to be anti-American.

---

2. Evelyn Shuckburgh, *Descent to Suez. Diaries 1951–56* (London, 1986), p. 327.

THE CRISIS OPENS: MILITARY PLANS

The situation was transformed by events in July 1956. The United States abruptly withdrew its financial support from the Aswan dam project. In retaliation, Nasser announced on 26 July that he was forthwith nationalising the Suez Canal Company, and would use its revenues to build the dam. While he was speaking, and acting on the code-word 'Ferdinand de Lesseps', Egyptian troops occupied the Company's offices. This was a direct challenge, psychological and material, to both France and Britain. The Suez Canal Company had its headquarters in Paris, and the French looked back with pride on the engineering achievement of de Lesseps, whose statue still watched over the waterway. The socialist government of the day might not have been anxious to take up the cause of the capitalists of the Canal Company for its own sake, but the seizure of the Canal offered an opportunity to strike at Nasser and end his support for the Algerian nationalists. Britain was concerned, in that about one-third of the ships using the Canal were British, and a large proportion of British oil imports came by that route. Eden spoke dramatically of Nasser having his fingers on Britain's windpipe. More important, there was a strong sense that the whole prestige of Britain as a great power was under challenge. Macmillan, the Chancellor of the Exchequer and formerly Foreign Secretary, told the American diplomat Robert Murphy on 30 July that Britain could defeat Egypt in six weeks, at a cost of some £400–£500 million which she could not afford, but would pay because otherwise she 'would become another Netherlands'. He was not just talking for effect, to impress the Americans. In the privacy of his diary some days later, Macmillan wrote: '. . . if Nasser "gets away with it", we are done for. The whole Arab world will despise us . . . It may well be the end of British influence and strength for ever'. Lennox-Boyd, the Colonial Secretary, wrote to Eden on 24 August: 'I remain firmly convinced that if Nasser wins or even appears to win we might as well as a government (or even as a country) go out of business . . .'[3] Such feelings were widely held, and explain much of the British government's conduct during the crisis.

The British and French reacted strongly to the nationalisation of the Canal. On 27 July, the day after Nasser's speech, the British Cabinet agreed without dissent that it was prepared to threaten, and if necessary carry out, military action. The Chiefs of Staff warned that it was

---

3. Alistair Horne, *Macmillan*, vol. II, *1957–1986* (London, pb edn, 1991), pp. 397, 408; Lennox-Boyd quoted by Kyle, in Louis and Owen, eds, *Suez*, p. 117.

impossible to mount an immediate attack on Egypt, but were instructed to prepare a plan for military operations as soon as possible. To what end was force to be used? The Cabinet set up an 'Egypt Committee', and on 30 July Eden told this committee that: 'While our ultimate purpose was to place the Canal under international control, our immediate aim was to bring about the downfall of the present Egyptian Government.' (Some six years later, on 16 March 1962, Field Marshal Montgomery was to tell the House of Lords that he had asked Eden 'What is your object?', to which the Prime Minister replied, 'To knock Nasser off his perch.')[4] The methods by which this was to be achieved were left unspecified, but were assumed to include military action. It is certain that Eden believed that force was the best way to achieve both his objectives – to overthrow Nasser and to secure the Canal; but it is not clear that he was absolutely resolved on the use of force, or knew how it was to be exerted or justified. To a considerable extent, British policy came to be concerned with the question of how to justify an attack on Egypt to the British public and to world opinion.

The French reaction was simpler. Guy Mollet's government was sure that its objective was to overthrow Nasser, and thus cut off Egyptian help to the Algerian rebels. From 27 July onwards the government was determined on the use of force; but the General Staff was aware that France did not have either the military means or the political capacity to act alone. The British had valuable bases in Malta and Cyprus, and had more forces to spare because they had no commitment like that of the French Army in Algeria. The Chief of Staff, General Ely, therefore took the view, which he was to maintain consistently, that France could only take military action against Egypt in co-operation with Britain. The French certainly moved quickly to bring Britain into planning military action.

The Minister of Defence, Bourgès-Maunoury, despatched Admiral Nomy, the Chief of Naval Staff, to London on 28 July to convince the British that the French would fight, and that if Britain would not join them they were willing to go ahead in conjunction with the Israelis. (In the event, Nomy judged it prudent to keep the latter part of his instructions to himself, and the issue of co-operation with Israel was not raised until later.) It so happened that 28 July was a Saturday,

4. Robert Rhodes James, *Anthony Eden* (London, 1986), p. 469. Montgomery's speech in House of Lords quoted in J.A. Sellers, 'Military Lessons: The British Perspective', in S.I. Troen and Moshe Shemesh, eds, *The Suez–Sinai Crisis, 1956: Retrospective and Reappraisal* (London, 1990), pp. 17–18. Monty added that he had replied that it was necessary to know what the object was *after* Nasser had been knocked off his perch, because that would determine how the operation was to be carried out.

but the Admiral managed to penetrate the inactivity of an English summer weekend to the extent of seeing the First Sea Lord, Admiral Mountbatten, and the Minister of Defence, Sir Walter Monckton. Nomy assured them both of the full co-operation of the French armed forces in overthrowing Nasser. On 29 July the French Ambassador, Chauvel, saw the Foreign Secretary, Selwyn Lloyd, and told him that the French were willing to go all the way against Nasser, and were even prepared to put their forces under British command if necessary. In the light of the history of the two countries, this was an extraordinary offer, and a striking illustration of the eagerness of the French government to press for military action. There were good military reasons for the proposal. The British had the bases necessary for an operation against Egypt, in Malta and Cyprus. They were familiar with the areas to be attacked, from the long British occupation of Egypt. They would have to provide most of the forces. Politically, the offer demonstrated French enthusiasm for the operation and their confidence in British leadership (doubtless more ostensible than real); if accepted, it would also have the advantage of committing the British to the adventure. Unhappily, it was not long before the French came to think that they had made a mistake in putting their forces under the command of an ally who proved (in French eyes) excessively cautious in military planning and uncertain in political commitment. However, at the time the French followed up their offer to accept British command by providing at once a list of the forces they were willing to make available, even including two divisions to be withdrawn from Algeria.

On 8 August the structure of the joint command was agreed upon. There was a British Commander-in-Chief, General Keightley, with a French deputy, Admiral Barjot. The land force commander was British, General Stockwell, with a French deputy, General Beaufre. Similarly, the naval and air commanders were British, with French deputies. These arrangements were much criticised in retrospect. It was lacking in tact, and perhaps also in wisdom, to allot nothing but deputy posts to French officers. The command system that was set up was extremely complicated, and involved great complexities in the transmission of orders or in effecting any change of plan. General Massu, the French paratroop commander, was to claim in his memoirs that the organisation was so complicated that the intrusion of a grain of sand could bring it to a halt; while the Israelis, he commented, were so flexible that they could carry on through a sandstorm.[5] In fact,

5. Jacques Massu and Henri Le Mire, *Vérité sur Suez* (Paris, 1978), pp. 8, 53.

when the forces actually went into action, some degree of separate national command came into operation, as a practical measure; so that, for example, British and French warships supported their own land forces. Even so, the command structure was indeed cumbersome and generated a good deal of friction. The staffs worked together in London, but the commanders to whom they were responsible were geographically dispersed. Keightley (who was British C-in-C Middle East) was stationed in Cyprus, while his deputy, Barjot, shuttled between Paris, Toulon, Algiers and London.

The military planning was plagued by uncertainties and divided counsels. A key question remained that of the actual purpose of the operation. To overthrow Nasser demanded an advance upon Cairo, and probably the defeat of the Egyptian Army in battle, which meant a landing at Alexandria. To seize control of the Canal, on the other hand, would be more directly achieved by a landing at the northern end of the waterway, at Port Said, followed by an advance to Suez at the southern end. The French were certain in their minds that the object was to remove Nasser. Eden too accepted this, but for political reasons he had to put much stress on securing the Canal.

As to methods, the British staffs thought almost automatically in terms of a Normandy-style landing, with careful preparation and a powerful concentration of forces. In the planning of airborne operations, they were much influenced by the disaster at Arnhem in 1944, and were opposed to any improvised parachute landings which could not be supported rapidly by other troops. They were also wary of the Egyptian air force, known to be equipped with some Soviet aircraft, and therefore insisted on a period of aerial bombardment to establish air supremacy ahead of the landings. The British were also anxious to minimise casualties, both to their own men and among Egyptian civilians. The French took very different views. They wanted speed, in both preparation and action. They were willing to take the risks involved in surprise parachute drops. They were already engaged in a stern and bloody war in Algeria, and were not disposed to worry too much about casualties, whether Egyptian or their own. These differences of approach were to prove a constant source of difficulty; and looking back, a French military historian was to argue that, while the British claimed that their methods were 'slow but sure', in fact they proved to be unsure because they were so slow.[6]

The question of co-operation with the Israelis continued to lurk in the background. The French had few doubts on this matter. They

6. Paul Gaujac, *Suez 1956* (Paris, 1986), p. 54.

believed that the Israelis could provide speedy, efficient and ruthless assistance in a campaign against Egypt. As early as June 1956, before Nasser nationalised the Canal, the French and Israeli defence ministries were discussing joint military action against Egypt. General Dayan, the Israeli Chief of Staff, held talks with French officers in July. The French delivered aircraft and tanks to the Israelis. The British, on the other hand, took a very different line. Well into 1956 they continued to make plans for war *against* Israel on the side of Jordan. At the beginning of August Macmillan recommended to the Egypt Committee of Cabinet a policy of co-operation with Egypt, but was at once reproved by Selwyn Lloyd on the ground that it would wreck British links with Arab states, especially Jordan. Eden dismissed the proposal out of hand. The British government preferred to urge caution and restraint on the Israelis, advising them to keep out of the Suez Canal crisis. The French and British thus adopted almost completely opposite policies towards Israel.

Against this difficult background, a series of military plans was produced. What they all had to take into account were the fixed elements of distances and sailing times. From British ports, the distance to Egypt was some 3,600 miles, which would take fast ships ten days and slow ships 24 days. From Malta, the distance was 1,100 miles; from both Toulon and Algiers, 1,800 miles. However eager the French were for speed, these facts of geography could not be changed. At the end of July and beginning of August, the British staffs, working alone, produced a plan for landings at Port Said, with a feint at Alexandria. Then this was abandoned, on the intervention of General Stockwell, in favour of a landing at Alexandria, preceded by two days of air attacks to dispose of the Egyptian air force. Thus when, on 10 August, General Beaufre arrived in London, he was dismayed to find that the British had already proposed a plan ('without waiting for us'), and then changed it ('without consulting us').[7] There was a further Franco-British difficulty arising out of the code-name for the operation. The British first chose HAMILCAR, and troops painted the letter H on the tops of vehicles, as a recognition sign to friendly aircraft. But someone observed that the French for Hamilcar is Amilcar, so that for them the recognition sign should be A. After this mildly absurd linguistic *contretemps*, the code-name was changed to MUSKETEER. Worse still, the British were acutely nervous about French security, and for a few days French officers were excluded from

7. Distances and sailing times in Sellers, in Troen and Shemesh, eds, *Suez–Sinai Crisis*, p. 22. Beaufre's comments in André Beaufre, *L'expédition de Suez* (Paris, 1967), p. 41.

British planning and were actually misled as to the destination of the expedition.

However, a plan was produced, and accepted on 15 August, setting the date for landings at Alexandria at 15 September. On 25 August, this plan was amended slightly, and D–Day fixed for 17 September. To meet that deadline, transport vessels would have to sail from British ports on 3 September, and a French parachute division leave Algeria for Cyprus on 8 September. The final decision to carry out the operation would have to be taken no later than 10 September. In order to meet this programme, British reservists were called up, and various preparations set in motion by both Britain and France.

POLITICS AND POSTPONEMENT

The details of the military planning thus went forward. But at the same time political difficulties accumulated, particularly in Britain. French domestic opinion, in parliament, the press, and the country at large, was strongly opposed to Nasser. In a debate on 3 August the National Assembly demonstrated strong support for a policy of 'breaking the Arab', with dissent only from the Communists. The heaviest political pressure brought to bear on Mollet was from those who believed that, because he was a Socialist, he was bound to be weak; but in fact the Socialist party gave full backing to a policy of firmness.[8] British opinion, on the other hand, began by being united against Nasser at the end of July, but grew divided during August. Hugh Gaitskell, the leader of the Labour Party, who at first appeared to favour rapid – and by implication military – action, now began to oppose the use of force except with the authority of the United Nations, which came to be the stance taken by most of the Labour Party. Among the government ministers in the inner circle conducting policy towards Egypt, there was a strong sense that force could only be used with broad public support, and during August that support was visibly being eroded.

Eden himself had been – or at least appeared to be – a League of Nations man in the 1930s, and retained many of his old internationalist instincts. He was anxious to convince the British people, the United States, and world opinion at large that he would only use force when negotiation had been tried and found wanting. This led him into a

8. Henri Azeau, *Le piège de Suez* (Paris, 1964), pp. 134–8, 146–51; Denis Lefèbvre, *Guy Mollet. Le mal aimé* (Paris, 1992), pp. 255–6.

trap. At bottom, Eden thought from the start that only force would produce the results he sought, yet he felt bound to pursue a negotiated solution, if only to show that one could not be achieved. These two aspects of his policy worked against one another, with results that were always damaging and ultimately fatal.

In search of a diplomatic solution, a conference of maritime states met in London from 16–23 August to discuss the control of the Canal. This conference produced the idea that the Prime Minister of Australia, Robert Menzies, should lead a mission to Cairo to persuade Nasser to accept some sort of international body to run the Canal. The Egypt Committee of the British Cabinet decided, on 29 August, that D-Day for the landings in Egypt should be postponed from 17 September to the 25th, to await the results of the Menzies mission. This order only reached some of those concerned on 2 September, the day before some of the transports were due to sail from British ports.

Menzies arrived in Egypt on 2 September, and left without success on the 9th. At that stage, the American Secretary of State, John Foster Dulles, proposed the creation of a Suez Canal Users' Association to manage the Canal and draw its revenues, which would put indirect pressure on Egypt. Discussion of this proposal took up several days. Eden felt bound to accept it in order not to break with the United States; the French agreed to it very reluctantly in order not to break with the British. Then, on 14 September, both the British and French governments agreed to refer the question of the Canal and the Users' Association to the Security Council of the United Nations, which began to debate the issues on 5 October.

The British government felt that it could not resort to force while these various negotiations were under way. The French might have done so, but could not act without the British. In the meantime, the date for the landings in Egypt was again postponed, first because of another change of military plan, and then as a result of the international negotiations. On 7 September the British Chiefs of Staff proposed to change the landing point back from Alexandria to Port Said. The military Chief of Staff, General Templer, was much opposed to getting involved in street fighting in Alexandria, which he thought would mean long delays before reaching the Canal, as well as risking heavy civilian casualties. Eden was surprised and dismayed by this proposal, but accepted it. The French General Beaufre reflected bitterly that this change came after the staffs had done a month's work on the previous plan, but Admiral Barjot (the French Deputy C-in-C in the joint command) had always preferred the Port Said option. In any case, the British had taken the initiative for another change of plan, which in turn led to a further postponement of D-Day. The landings were now scheduled for 1 October instead of 25 September – the third postponement since planning began. The British also introduced into the new plan the idea of producing an Egyptian collapse by a combination of air attack and psychological warfare. Attacks on the Egyptian air force to ensure air superiority, which had always been part of the operation, were to be followed by six to ten days of air attack to damage the economy and prevent the movement of troops, accompanied by a propaganda campaign. Only when it was certain that there would be no serious opposition would land forces occupy the Canal Zone. Such ideas moved further and further away from French concepts of a sudden attack and rapid exploitation. By this stage, there had already been three postponements of the date for D-Day, and there was soon to be a fourth. The Suez Canal Users' Association met in London, 19–22 September; and at the same time Eden was considering taking the question to the Security Council. To allow scope for these diplomatic manoeuvres, on 19 September the target date for D-Day was put off from 1 to 8 October.

The French government began to lose patience with these Hamlet-like hesitations. In late September, French ministers turned increasingly towards the Israelis in search of bold and determined action. On 19 September (the date of the fourth postponement of MUSKETEER), the Minister of Defence, Bourgès-Maunoury, met Shimon Peres, the Director-General at the Israeli Ministry of Defence, to discuss the possibility of a joint Franco-Israeli operation to seize the Canal. On 20 September Bourgès-Maunoury's *chef de cabinet*, Abel Thomas, and an officer in the Defence Ministry, Colonel Louis Mangin, flew to Tel Aviv to propose direct French naval and air support for an Israeli attack on the Canal, which might itself coincide with Franco-British military action. On 30 September and 1 October General Dayan, the Israeli Chief of Staff, and Shimon Peres visited Paris and pursued discussions about an attack on Egypt, with or without the British. A French mission visited Israel between 1 and 5 October to work out details. It appears that all these activities were carried out in complete secrecy; which puts British fears about French security in a very dubious light.

On 1 October the British planning staff produced for their French colleagues yet another version of the operation, a 'Winter Plan' which would take account of the shorter daylight hours and worsening weather of the winter months. It was also capable of being held in suspense, in view of the fact that the Security Council was to meet on 5 October, and no-one knew how long its deliberations would last.

This 'Winter Plan' was worked out by 12 October, and was due to come into force on the 21st. This was the fifth postponement of the date for the landings (which had last been set for 8 October).

FRANCE, BRITAIN AND THE ISRAELIS: THE SEVRES CONFERENCE

The French were not content with the Winter Plan, and with what appeared to be the British tendency to postpone the operation indefinitely. They now tried to recover the initiative which they had earlier handed over to the British by unreservedly accepting British military command. On 8 October the French Ministry of Defence instructed Admiral Barjot to study a possible French operation in support of Israel without the British – even though Barjot was still Deputy C-in-C in the Franco-British joint command. Guy Mollet accepted this idea in principle, and General Challe, the Chief of the French Air Staff, was sent to New York on 10 October to inform the Foreign Minister, Pineau, of these developments. However, both Mollet and Pineau were anxious to maintain their co-operation with the British, and to bring them into a combination with Israel if at all possible. In mid-October they made a great effort in this direction. On 14 October General Challe, under instructions from Mollet, visited Eden at Chequers, and put to him the idea of an Israeli attack on Egypt across the Sinai peninsula, after which the French and British would intervene to restore peace and secure the Canal. By Challe's account, Eden listened carefully, and insisted on the necessity of there being a credible Israeli threat to the Canal, but did not commit himself. Selwyn Lloyd, who returned to London from the Security Council meeting in New York on 15 October, at first opposed the scheme, but agreed to accompany Eden to Paris to discuss it. The French were now taking the initiative, and the British were responding, though not entirely unwillingly. Eden was being offered the pretext for military action which had so far been lacking.

Eden and Lloyd went to Paris on 16 October, and there met Mollet and Pineau without the presence of officials or the British Ambassador. What precisely was said is unclear, but the ministers certainly discussed the likelihood of an Israeli attack on Egypt, and agreed on Franco-British intervention in that event. It also appears that Mollet urged the need for speed, and to act in conjunction with the Israelis to strike before the Mediterranean weather worsened and before the American

Presidential elections, due to take place on 6 November. (Mollet presumably calculated that President Eisenhower would not wish to oppose the Israelis, for fear of losing the Jewish vote.) It does not appear that the French revealed the full extent of their contacts with the Israelis, but they secured British agreement to a three-power meeting between France, Britain and Israel.

The French then informed the Israeli government of the main lines of their plan. Israel was to attack Egypt across the Sinai peninsula. Britain and France would then request both Israeli and Egyptian forces to retire from the Canal Zone. Then, if one side (i.e. certainly the Egyptians) refused, a Franco-British force would intervene to protect the Canal and ensure its safe working. The object of the exercise was to provide a justification for Franco-British military intervention, and the French were careful to emphasise to the Israelis that Britain would only act if she could appear as an outside intermediary, using force to restore order.

The French now made all the running. They rapidly arranged the three-power meeting to which the British had agreed. The three French ministers who attended (Mollet, Pineau and Bourgès-Maunoury) had all been members of the wartime Resistance, and the conference which they contrived at Sèvres on 22 October 1956 bore the marks of a clandestine rendezvous. The Israeli representatives (the Prime Minister, Ben-Gurion, General Dayan and Shimon Peres) were conducted in great secrecy to a villa at Sèvres, where they were joined by the French ministers in equal secrecy. The two groups then conferred for most of the day. Selwyn Lloyd, the British Foreign Secretary, did not arrive until the evening. During the war, Lloyd had been an orthodox soldier (rising to the rank of brigadier), unconnected with clandestine operations. He was also a man of straightforward character, and disliked the concealment and deception into which he was drawn. Even so, his very presence at the meeting meant that he became involved in its purpose, which was to confirm the plan for an Israeli attack across Sinai, to be followed by a Franco-British military intervention. Lloyd insisted that the Israeli attack must not be on a small scale, but a real act of war, because otherwise there would be no justification for outside intervention and Britain would appear as an aggressor. The meeting ended about midnight, without a definite agreement, but was to resume later. Meanwhile, Lloyd returned to London to report.

The Foreign Secretary did not return for the resumption of the discussions on 24 October, when the British were represented only by officials. It was therefore Pineau, the French Foreign Minister,

Ben-Gurion, the Israeli Prime Minister, and Sir Patrick Dean, a senior Foreign Office official, who signed the Sèvres Protocol on 24 October. This agreement provided that Israel would launch a large-scale attack on Egypt on 29 October, to reach the Canal the next day. On the 30th the British and French governments would appeal for a cease-fire, and request the Egyptians and Israelis to withdraw their forces ten miles west and east of the Canal respectively. If either refused, the British and French would launch military operations on 31 October. The French and Israelis also concluded another agreement, which they did not even mention to the British, promising the despatch of French Air Force fighters for the air defence of Israel and of two French warships to Israeli ports.[9]

These details of the Sèvres conference and agreement were of crucial importance in relations between France and Britain. The ministers involved took entirely different attitudes to what had taken place. Eden desperately wanted to conceal these events altogether. When the two British officials, Sir Patrick Dean and Sir Donald Logan, returned to London on 24 October with their copy of the Sèvres Protocol, Eden at once sent them back to Paris to try to ensure that all copies of the agreement were retrieved and destroyed. Pineau did not wish to do so; and was able to say that in any case Ben-Gurion had departed with his copy and declined to destroy it. This was the beginning of a crucial divergence. Eden consistently denied the existence of the three-power agreement reached at Sèvres, because for him everything had to fit in with his own version of events. Only the claim to be separating the combatants could provide an adequate justification for British intervention, and also preserve Eden's own high reputation in international affairs. As a British historian has put it, 'He attempted to make his own conduct, and that of anyone he could control, conform to the public explanation.'[10]

At the time, this policy was applied even to the extent of keeping the senior British commanders in ignorance of the three-power plan. General Stockwell, commanding the land forces, soon began to wonder what was happening between the French and the Israelis, and by 26 October he grasped that the French knew more about Israeli plans than he did; but he still had a completely different idea from the French about the degree of urgency demanded by what was going on.

9. English versions of these two documents are printed in Keith Kyle, *Suez* (London, 1991), pp. 565–7. Another English version of the Sèvres Protocol, slightly different in wording, is in James, *Eden*, p. 531. Lefèbvre, *Mollet*, pp. 253–4, prints the copy preserved in Mollet's private papers. Kyle, *Suez*, pp. 316–22, 324–31, gives a detailed account of the Sèvres meetings.

10. Kyle, in Louis and Owen, eds, *Suez*, p. 127.

For example, it was only on 29 October, the same day that the Israelis were due to open their attack in Sinai, that British parachute troops were shifted from operations against EOKA in Cyprus to prepare for a drop at Port Said.

The French commanders, on the other hand, pursued their co-operation with Israel with only the thinnest veil of concealment. French aircraft landed at airfields in Cyprus and quickly flew on in an easterly direction. Three French warships, visible to all and sundry, put into Haifa harbour, ostensibly to refuel. Twenty years later, in 1976, Christian Pineau was the first to give an authoritative account of Sèvres. By that time, the French felt that they had nothing to hide and little to be ashamed of.[11]

THE FIGHTING: SINAI AND THE CANAL ZONE

In the evening of 29 October the Israeli attack began according to plan, with a parachute landing at the Mitla Pass, about 150 miles inside Egyptian territory and well towards the Suez Canal. Other Israeli forces began a rapid drive across the Sinai desert to link up with the paratroops. On 30 October the British and French governments presented notes to both Egypt and Israel, requesting them to cease all military action and withdraw their forces ten miles west and east of the Canal respectively. If within twelve hours one or both governments had not complied with these requests, British and French forces would intervene to secure compliance. The Israeli government accepted this ultimatum; the Egyptians did not. At the Security Council of the United Nations, Britain and France twice used their vetoes against American and Soviet resolutions calling on Israel to withdraw, and requesting all states to refrain from the threat or use of force. In the diplomatic arena, the Franco–British combination was hard at work.

Military co-operation proved more difficult. The French worked closely with the Israelis. French fighters stood by to defend Israeli cities against bombing attacks, but were not called on to do so. At sea, the French warship *Kersaint* captured an Egyptian destroyer during the night of 31 October/1 November. On 1 November the cruiser *Georges Leygues* bombarded Egyptian defences at Rafah, on the Sinai coast, in direct support of an Israeli land attack. The British moved less

11. This passage follows Mordechai Bar-On, 'David Ben-Gurion and the Sèvres Collusion', in ibid., p. 146; for the whole article, see pp. 145–60.

rapidly, and did not co-operate directly with the Israelis. Ben-Gurion expected RAF air attacks on Egypt to begin as soon as the Franco-British ultimatum expired, and was dismayed when nothing happened for most of 31 October. The first RAF raids took place in the evening of the 31st, with others following during the night. British and French aircraft then attacked Egyptian airfields, and effectively removed the Egyptian air force from the battle.

There remained the main operation: the landing at Port Said. The French pressed hard for greater speed. On 1–2 November Pineau, with Generals Ely and Challe, visited London and advocated a rapid parachute drop, to be supported on the ground by the Israelis. The British Chiefs of Staff rejected this, partly because of their reluctance to commit parachute troops too far ahead of the seaborne landings, and partly because they insisted on sticking to the idea of separating the combatants, and avoiding open co-operation with the Israelis. In Cyprus there were desperate consultations, as the French commanders (especially Barjot and Beaufre) tried hard to accelerate the landings, and the British applied the brakes. The Task Force commanders worked out a new plan for parachute drops; but General Stockwell insisted on a proviso about there being 'no effective resistance', which led to heated arguments with the French. On 3 November the new British Minister of Defence, Head, and the Chief of Staff, General Templer, arrived in Cyprus, bearing extraordinary orders that the warships supporting the seaborne landings should not use any guns larger than 4.5-inch calibre; although the French battleship *Richelieu*, armed with 15-inch guns, was with the fleet. (Later, the whole plan for a naval bombardment was cancelled; but the British and French naval commanders on the spot opened fire anyway, making a fine distinction between 'bombardment' and 'gunfire support'.) General Stockwell agreed to launch both the air and seaborne landings on 6 November, four days in advance of the timetable previously agreed upon. Then, on 3 November (five days after the Israeli attack, and three days after the start of air raids), the joint commanders agreed on a plan (nicely called TELESCOPE), by which the parachute landings were brought forward to 5 November, to be followed by the seaborne landings on the 6th.[12]

During this period of delay and confusion, before TELESCOPE was agreed on, Admiral Barjot, the French Deputy C-in-C in the joint

12. For details of these last-minute changes of plan, and disputes between the British and French, see Sellers, in Troen and Shemesh, eds, *Suez–Sinai Crisis*, p. 44; on the naval bombardment, Eric Grove, *From Vanguard to Trident: British Naval Policy since World War II* (London, 1987), pp. 190–1. Cf. Beaufre, *Suez*, p. 129, on these few days in Cyprus.

command, requested General Beaufre to make a hasty study of whether the French could act alone – could they, for example, improvise landings at Port Fuad, on the eastern side of the Mediterranean end of the Canal? Beaufre replied that this could be done, but would be very risky.[13] The point is less whether such an operation was actually feasible, but that the French were prepared to consider it. At the beginning of the crisis the French had jumped precipitately into accepting British command. Now, in desperation and at the last moment, they thought of breaking free from that command and striking out on their own.

It did not come to that. In Paris, Mollet was certain that the French still needed British support, and no independent action was attempted. There remained a long and dangerous gap between the opening of aerial bombardment on 31 October and the first parachute landings, which were not authorised by the British Cabinet, after final agonisings, until the evening of 4 November.

In the morning of 5 November 1956 British paratroops dropped near Port Said, and French at Port Fuad. After a pause overnight, the seaborne landings went in early on 6 November, again with the British at Port Said and the French at Port Fuad. Despite some inevitable confusion, the landings proved a remarkable success. By the afternoon of 6 November British and French forces were well established ashore, and ready to move southwards, with every chance of occupying the whole of the Canal Zone as far as Suez in the next two or three days.

This success proved short-lived. The British government came under extreme pressure, at home and abroad, to halt the operation. At home, opinion in the country was sharply divided, and the House of Commons was in turmoil. From 1 November onwards Eden came under increasing attack in the House, and his explanations about separating the combatants carried less and less conviction. Eden himself was tired and in poor health, and stood up badly to the strain. Abroad, the Soviet Union threatened rocket attacks, and while this was not taken seriously there was a disturbing possibility of intervention by Soviet submarines (known to be in the eastern Mediterranean) or attacks by Soviet bombers on the crowded airfields in Cyprus. On the economic side, there was a run on the pound and an alarming drop in British gold and dollar reserves. Macmillan, the Chancellor of the Exchequer and at first an ardent supporter of the use of force, telephoned Washington on 6 November to ask for American help, to be told firmly that the United States would only support a loan by the

13. Gaujac, *Suez*, pp. 177–8.

International Monetary Fund if there were a cease-fire in Egypt by midnight that very night.[14] Eden himself remained desperately anxious to maintain the credibility of his pretext for the use of force, i.e. to separate the combatants, and knew that this could not be reconciled with continuing the advance along the Canal.

During 6 November Eden gave way to these accumulating pressures. At midday he telephoned Mollet and told him that there must be a cease-fire, proposing 1700 hours that day as the time. Mollet was not perturbed by American financial threats, and was under no domestic pressure. When French ministers (Pineau and Bourgès-Maunoury) had visited London on 5 November they had observed the contrast between their position and that of Eden. The British Prime Minister was harassed and at the end of his tether. They too had passed nights without sleep, but they were sustained by the belief that France was behind them.[15] When Mollet received Eden's call, he strongly opposed an immediate cease-fire. If the troops pressed on, another 48 hours would see them in command of the whole length of the Canal, and Britain and France would be in a position to bargain. But the most Eden would concede was to postpone the time of a cease-fire until midnight (Egyptian time), which in view of the need to communicate with the troops on the ground was probably the earliest that was practical.

The French Cabinet then met to discuss the situation. Several ministers were in favour of pressing on. Bourgès-Maunoury claimed that the French forces, either alone or in conjunction with the Israelis, could reach Suez. Pineau wanted to stall for two or three days, capture the Canal, and then use it as a bargaining counter with the Americans and Russians. Lacoste, the minister responsible for Algeria, argued that to give up now would be to present Nasser with a victory and the Algerian rebels with a boost to their morale. Mollet too would have preferred to go on, but insisted that France could not act alone. They had worked with the British so far, and must now follow them in accepting a cease-fire. The Premier's view eventually prevailed, but the whole discussion revealed much bitterness against the British, who had imposed repeated delays, and were finally giving up when victory was in sight. Reluctantly, the Cabinet agreed that there must be a cease-fire at midnight.

14. Diane B. Kunz, 'The Importance of Having Money: The Economic Diplomacy of the Suez Crisis', in Louis and Owen, eds, *Suez*, pp. 215–32, provides a succinct guide to the problems of sterling and the pressure applied by the Americans.

15. Merry and Serge Bromberger, *Les secrets de l'expédition de Suez* (Paris, 1957), p. 202.

On the ground, the British advance troops reached a point about twenty miles south of Port Said. French units behind them believed that if they had been able to pass through the slow-moving British they could have got further. The fighting came to an end, amid some confusion, at 2 a.m. (local time) on 7 November. For some time, the joint Franco-British staff remained in existence, and even prepared a new plan in case hostilities were renewed, aiming to reach Suez within 24 hours. General Keightley, on the other hand, was uneasy about the difficulties of maintaining his forces' toe-hold in Egypt, among a hostile population. The Allied C-in-C announced publicly on 23 November that his forces would withdraw within the next month. The last troops left on 23 December, the French in daylight because General Beaufre insisted on going openly and with such honour as could be mustered, the British after dark the same evening.

AFTERMATH: REACTIONS AND INTERPRETATIONS

The news of the cease-fire was received very differently in London and Paris. In the British government and Parliament there was general and heart-felt relief. Even ministers who had resolutely supported the military operation had found the strain severe, and were glad it was over. In the French Assembly, by contrast, the news was greeted with amazement and anger. Deputies wanted to know why the Allies had halted when the landings had been accomplished and the seizure of the Canal was within reach. Mollet had to defend himself, not because he had started the assault, but because he had stopped it.

These differences increased in the immediate aftermath of the crisis. In Britain, the immediate public reaction to the Suez expedition was ambiguous. Public opinion polls showed a majority against the operation at the time, but growing support for it soon afterwards. The leader of the Labour opposition, Hugh Gaitskell, preferred to drop the subject rather than try to exploit it; and in a curious way the country itself dropped the subject. Keith Kyle, who was a journalist at the time and later wrote a massive historical study of the events, recalled that: 'After a few brief weeks, the subject of Suez, so intensively, so hectically debated, silently departed. . . . By mutual consent Suez, as a topic of conversation, had become taboo.'[16]

16. Kyle, *Suez*, p. 3.

Behind that silence lay conflicting emotions. Many were ashamed that Britain had been an aggressor, and continued to repeat the old Gladstonian slogan that what was morally wrong could not be politically right. Many others had no sympathy with the Egyptians, and were angry that the attack had been stopped rather than carried through. Collusion with Israel was a thorny topic, on which the facts were known with certainty to very few but suspected by many. It was indeed Eden's efforts to conceal this co-operation that were fatal to him, leading him to make statements in the Commons which he himself knew to be untrue (and he was a bad liar), and which sometimes defied common sense. This display by a man who had previously commanded widespread trust damaged Eden's reputation almost beyond repair.

Interestingly, and in some ways curiously, there was little tendency to blame the French for drawing, or even deceiving, the British into a false position. It is true that Aneurin Bevan, the leader of the Labour Left, asked in the House of Commons on 5 December 1956: 'Did Marianne take John Bull to a secret rendezvous? Did Marianne say to John Bull there was a forest fire going to start and did John Bull not say "we ought to put it out" but Marianne then said "No, let us warm our hands by it, it is a nice fire". Did Marianne deceive John Bull or seduce him?' Vicky, the cartoonist of the *New Statesman*, depicted a seductive France as Eve, offering Eden the apple which led to his downfall.[17] But little was made of this, at the time or later. Eden put no blame on the French in his memoirs. Robert Rhodes James, in his sympathetic biography of Eden, makes only a passing reference to French pressure as one of the factors that pushed the Prime Minister into desperate measures.[18]

In France, the immediate reaction was very different. There was no sense of shame about the operation, and in some ways the government contrived to treat the expedition as a victory. The Air Minister held a parade at Rheims for Air Force personnel who had taken part, conferring decorations and making a speech about the exploits of French airmen. Mollet's government was supported by a vote in the Assembly of 325 to 210 on 7 November, and in a foreign affairs debate on 20 December Mollet stuck to his guns about the analogy between Nasser and Hitler. The main motive for the French action, he claimed, had not been Algeria but the memory of Munich. In the 1930s the weakness of the democracies had allowed Hitler to advance

17. Bevan, quoted in Hugh Thomas, *The Suez Affair* (Pelican edn, 1970), p. 85; the Vicky cartoon appears on the front cover of the same book.
18. James, *Eden*, p. 531.

unopposed; and now Nasser was trying the same tactics as Hitler. Mollet quoted Léon Blum, who had said in 1946 that the only certain way to avoid the Second World War would have been early pre-ventive action against Hitler. And yet, Mollet continued, if a French statesman had taken military action against Hitler in the 1930s he might well have been regarded as an aggressor. Who would have known that he had prevented a world war?

Similarly, there was no conspiracy of silence in France about co-operation with Israel. In the debate on 20 December, some ministers spoke as though their main concern had been the security of Israel. The Israelis, acting under French protection and using French equipment, had beaten Nasser's army inside four days, which gave the French something to boast about, even if only vicariously. This theme was developed by Merry and Serge Bromberger, journalist brothers who produced at high speed an account of the expedition, putting the views of the Ministry of Defence.[19] The Brombergers told their readers proudly of the French jet fighters that had beaten Nasser's MiGs, and of the French warships that had fought alongside the Egyptian navy. They described the Israeli Ambassador calling on Guy Mollet to thank him for saving Israel. They claimed that within the defeat of Suez there had been a victory, and said that France had helped David against Goliath.

The British Ambassador in Paris, Gladwyn Jebb, in his annual report describing 1956, noted a mood of defiance and self-confidence in France. In an extraordinary year, everything had gone wrong, and yet at the end of it there was a sense that France had 'somehow found herself'. The main reason for this lay in the Suez expedition. 'France was conscious, for the first time since the war, of being virtually united. This very fact produced a strange exhilaration.' The French had rallied round their armed forces, in an act of simple patriotism. For the failure of the operation, they tended to blame the Americans (rather than the British). They were happy that the attack on Egypt had at least irked Foster Dulles – 'a childish but powerful sentiment', Jebb commented.[20]

With the passage of time, the Suez crisis has left a very different mark on the historiography and the general historical consciousness of Britain and France. In Britain, it became something of an obsession among historians and journalists, partly in an attempt to disentangle events (especially the issue of collusion with Israel), and partly because

19. Merry and Serge Bromberger, *Secrets*.
20. PRO, FO 371/130625, WF1011/1, Jebb to Selwyn Lloyd, 21 Jan. 1957.

Suez came to be seen as a turning-point in post-war history. Alistair Horne, in his biography of Macmillan, wrote that the British people went to bed one night believing that they belonged to a first-class power, and the next morning 'woke up to the reality of relegation to the second division'.[21] This probably overdramatised the effects as felt at the time, but is representative of many retrospective comments. All biographers of Eden must see Suez as a lion in their path, the ruin of their subject's reputation and the greatest single question they have to discuss.

In France, the perspective has been very different. It is a simple but revealing point of comparison that Mollet's only serious biographer devotes a mere twenty pages out of over 500 to the Suez crisis, which is certainly not treated as a great débâcle or as the shipwreck of Mollet's career.[22] French generals who were involved in the operation wrote about it later with a vigour and amplitude in marked contrast to the silence of their British colleagues. They also formed an exception to the tendency to avoid blaming the British. General Beaufre declared that it was 'a campaign in which French resolution was dominated by the British government's indecisiveness'. The result had been 'a short but brilliant military success leading to a total political failure'.[23] General Massu (who during the fighting had, as usual, led his parachutists from the front) breezily condemned 'the faintheartedness of the British command', and thought the main cause of failure lay in the cumbersome organisation devised by the British.[24] Another French officer deplored the excessive sensitivity of British politicians. The cloak-and-dagger aspects of the dealings with the Israelis, he wrote, had been necessary 'so as not to shock the half-closed eyelids of the English and Americans with too bright a light . . .'.[25] Most of these shafts were well directed. One of the few British military historians of the expedition has pointed out that the operation was postponed five times, always by the British. 'We lacked a sense of urgency and willingness to take risks', was his reasonable conclusion.[26] French soldiers, in fact, long continued to hanker after the victory of which they thought they had been deprived; though they were less keen to ask whether, in the circumstances of the time, they could have exploited such a victory.

21. Horne, *Macmillan*, vol. II, p. 2.
22. Lefèbvre, *Mollet*: see pp. 245–64 for Suez.
23. Beaufre, *Suez*, p. 7.
24. Massu and Le Mire, *Vérité*, p. 8.
25. Lucien Robineau, 'Les porte-à-faux de l'Affaire de Suez', *Revue Historique des Armées*, No. 165, Dec. 1986, p. 44.
26. Sellers, in Troen and Shemes, eds, *Suez–Sinai Crisis*, pp. 49, 51.

The French were less affected by Suez than the British largely because for them the truly traumatic event of those years was the Algerian War, in which Suez was merely an episode. It was symptomatic that, after the Suez expedition, Massu's parachutists went straight back from Egypt into a far fiercer battle in Algiers. Even more important, the French came through the crisis psychologically unscathed, believing that they themselves had done well and had been let down by the British, and even more by the Americans. Some even managed to convince themselves that the operation had achieved something. In January 1966 Guy Mollet appeared on French television (in the series 'Face-à-Face') and told his interviewers that the operation had secured one positive result: 'the survival of Israel'.[27] In 1978 Abel Thomas, who had been Bourgès-Maunoury's *chef de cabinet* in 1956, developed this claim at length in a book entitled *Comment Israel fut sauvé*, asserting that the Suez expedition had saved the Israelis from another genocide. Thomas concluded his book with an even greater claim: 'France played in this affair her role of "guardian of the Rights of Man and of Liberty".'[28] The French often claim a special status as defenders of the Rights of Man; but the Egyptians might well have taken a different view. Among the British, Eden tried hard to produce comparable claims and justification for his actions, but most participants preferred to draw a veil over what they regarded as both a defeat and a blunder.

The French were also able to brush aside the Suez crisis because it coincided with new developments in European integration. In late 1956 negotiations to set up the European Economic Community (made up of the same six states as the Coal and Steel Community) were well advanced.[29] It so happened that on 6 November, at the very moment when Eden telephoned to say that there must be an immediate cease-fire in Egypt, Mollet and Pineau were in conference with Chancellor Adenauer and the West German Foreign Minister on matters relating to the EEC. Adenauer had already remarked that the Americans were beginning to think that only they and the Russians counted in the world. When Mollet returned to the room after taking Eden's call, Adenauer said that France, England and Germany would never again be great powers like the USA and the Soviet Union. The only way for them to play a decisive role in the world was by uniting to 'build Europe'. (By one account he went further and said, 'Europe

27. Lefèbvre, *Mollet*, p. 264, cf pp. 431–3.
28. Abel Thomas, *Comment Israel fut sauvé. Les secrets de l'expédition de Suez* (Paris, 1978), p. 277.
29. The formation of the EEC is discussed in Chapter 8.

154

will be your revenge'.)[30] The coincidence could not have been better contrived by a dramatist, and even in a play the scene might well be deemed implausible. But there it was, and to add piquancy it was witnessed by the British Ambassador, Gladwyn Jebb, who chanced to meet Adenauer at the Matignon while Mollet was talking to Eden. In his memoirs, Jebb reflected on the significance of Adenauer's presence: 'From now on it must be obvious that the French would turn more and more towards the Western Germans. The days of the *Entente* based on British leadership were over.'[31]

At the time, Jebb emphasised to the Foreign Office that Suez had confirmed the faith of the French 'Europeans', and had won over many doubters. Europe provided a new vision, which recent French history had sadly lacked. 'Where there is no vision the people perish', as Jebb reminded his readers in London. 'That is why the conception of a western Europe in which France can play a real and leading part is so important.'[32]

GUY MOLLET AND A STRANGE OFFER OF UNION

The remarkable restoration of French self-confidence that accompanied the Suez crisis, and the momentum that was imparted to the process of European integration, were observed by British representatives in Paris and reported to the British government. But their impact was diminished, and the vision of these changes obscured, as a result of a simultaneous episode that forms one of the curiosities of relations between France and Britain.

On 10 September 1956 Mollet visited London for a meeting with Eden about the Suez crisis. During their conversations, the French Premier said that he was so strongly in favour of close relations between their two countries that he wished to revive the proposal of union made by Churchill in June 1940. What lay behind this astonishing suggestion is not clear. It was not a new departure for Mollet, who had made the same suggestion in the National Assembly on 25 November 1949, when he was not in office. His home town was Arras, where there was a strong tradition of pro–British opinion. Paul-Marie de la Gorce has written that both England and Eden

---

30. Lefèbvre, *Mollet*, p. 274; Christian Pineau, *Suez 1956* (Paris, 1976), p. 191.
31. Lord Gladwyn, *The Memoirs of Lord Gladwyn* (London, 1972), p. 285.
32. PRO, FO 371/130625, WF1011/1, Jebb to Selwyn Lloyd, 21 Jan. 1957.

personally exerted a sort of fascination upon him.[33] There was perhaps also a measure of calculation, in that Mollet wanted to wean the British from their dependence on the Americans and tie them firmly into the Egyptian enterprise. He was certainly more aware than the British of the progress being achieved in the EEC negotiations, and was anxious to draw Britain into the European association. He even told Eden that he hoped to see Britain lead the movement towards European unity.

Whatever Mollet's motives, his remarkable intervention impelled the British government, even in the midst of its other preoccupations, to make a rapid survey of its views of France. Eden set up a group of ministers to discuss Mollet's proposal, and the Treasury and Foreign Office were asked to comment. Their responses were revealing.

The Treasury observed that French productivity, national income and standard of living were considerably lower than those in the United Kingdom. The French economy suffered from 'a sluggishness and unresponsiveness to change, to technical progress, and to the needs of large-scale organisation, leading to low productivity and great waste of manpower in agriculture and a large part of industry'. France also showed a chronic tendency towards inflation. French goods were often priced out of foreign markets, leading to recurrent balance of payments crises. French economic life still contained a deep-rooted dependence on protectionism, which only a great upheaval in opinion would change. At that stage in the analysis, a different view appeared (doubtless inserted originally by another writer). The French had put much well-directed investment into basic industries and services; they had recently achieved rapid growth in industrial production; and they had developed advanced technology in motor cars, aircraft and atomic energy. There might thus be forces at work that could refute France's critics in the next ten or fifteen years. This latter assessment was to prove well justified; but despite this intervention the report's conclusion was that Britain would find no economic advantages, and considerable disadvantages, in a union with France. 'Our economy is not strong enough to carry the French . . . and there are no potential economic gains to warrant the attempt.'[34] This followed the conventional wisdom of the day, and took insufficient note of the changes that were under way in the French economy.

The report from the Foreign Office bestowed a brief and condescending glance on the potential advantages of a union with

33. Paul-Marie de la Gorce, *Naissance de la France Moderne*, vol. II, *Apogée et mort de la IV République* (Paris, 1979), p. 367.
34. PRO, PREM 11/1352, Memorandum by Treasury, 22 Sept. 1956.

France. A positive British response would 'encourage and stiffen the French', and might help to remedy 'the weakness and ineffectiveness of France'. But then the negatives piled up. A Franco-British union would not be a natural one, nor would it be popular in either country. It would require a great effort on the part of Britain to make it work, at the expense of British relations with the United States, the Commonwealth, and even European countries other than France. It would upset the Germans, the Scandinavians and the Benelux countries. The report concluded that the arguments against union were decisive, but that something positive should be offered by way of response. The government might propose the setting up of a joint standing committee of junior ministers, or arrange a royal visit to France. Or they might reveal to Mollet the conception of a free trade area in western Europe on which the Cabinet was then working, code-named 'Plan G'.[35]

The group of ministers adopted the main lines of the Foreign Office memorandum as the basis for its own report to the Cabinet, which explained that Britain needed different associations for different purposes (for example, the Commonwealth, NATO, and the OEEC), and therefore a union with France alone would be inappropriate. The free trade area proposals were not yet at a stage where they could be disclosed; and the only encouragement that might be offered in reply to Mollet was a suggestion for closer co-ordination of policy and a royal visit. The Cabinet adopted these conclusions on 26 September.

That was not the end of the matter. Eden went to Paris to see Mollet on 27 September, to find that the French Premier was unwilling to take 'No' for an answer. Mollet insisted that France and Britain must draw closer together, and said that he himself would have liked to join the Commonwealth, on the terms suggested by Churchill in 1940. This imprecise remark was taken by Eden as meaning that France actually wished to join the Commonwealth, and the Prime Minister started another round of discussions in London.

The Secretary to the Cabinet (Sir Norman Brook) prepared a paper opposing the introduction of a foreign country into the Commonwealth (which was then usually still called the British Commonwealth) and arguing that the entry of France would bring in 'a dangerous element of political and economic instability'.[36] Then the existing group of ministers, now with Eden himself in the chair, convened on 1 October to discuss the question. The record of the meeting conveys a remarkable, almost surrealist, impression to a modern reader. Eden

---

35. Ibid., Memorandum by Foreign Office, 22 Sept. 1956.
36. Ibid., Memorandum by Secretary to the Cabinet, 29 Sept. 1956.

declared that if France entered the Commonwealth it would be necessary to bring in Belgium and the Netherlands at the same time; which would create problems if, for example, Germany and Italy wanted to join as well. This elicited general agreement that association with the Commonwealth could not be offered to France alone. Some ministers thought that the entry of France, along with Belgium, the Netherlands and perhaps Norway would be a natural development. On the economic side, the prevailing view was that it would be against British interests to be linked to 'one of the weaker economic systems in Europe', which was how France was regarded. The vision Eden conjured up, and his colleagues seem calmly to have accepted, of various European countries virtually queuing up to join the Commonwealth now almost defies belief; but it is a salutary reminder of the assumptions of the time.[37]

The underlying view of France that ran through all these discussions was a familiar one. The dominant themes were economic weakness (though with some qualifications), political instability at home, and ineffectiveness in foreign policy. These had been the staple ingredients in British views of France since the end of the Second World War, and in some respects from earlier times. The basic assumption was that France was still operating from weakness. The corollary, usually unspoken but none the less significant for that, was that Britain still held a position of strength.

These strange discussions about union with France, or France joining the Commonwealth, took place some five or six weeks before the landings in Egypt. The shock of Suez lay just around the corner. When it came, France was to ride the shock-waves with more confidence and *élan* than Britain. Yet in the British official mind there seems to have been no sense that the flame of self-confidence and vigour was about to cross the Channel, or had perhaps already done so.

37. Ibid., Record of meeting, 1 Oct. 1956. Ministers present were: Eden, Butler, Home, Sandys, Kilmuir, Lennox-Boyd and Nutting.

CHAPTER 8

A New France Confronts an Uncertain Britain, 1957–1960

The Suez adventure, whose failure was highly public, and the strange affair of Guy Mollet and the proposal of union, which remained in a decent obscurity, brought 1956 to a febrile and unhappy end. Relations between France and Britain were difficult, and the two countries' views of one another were in a state of flux. Then, in the next four years, a new pattern emerged. Between 1957 and 1960 Franco-British relations were transformed by three sets of events: the creation of the European Economic Community by the Treaty of Rome in 1957; the return to power in France of General de Gaulle in 1958; and the emergence of France as a nuclear power, with the first explosion of a French atomic bomb in February 1960.

THE EUROPEAN ECONOMIC COMMUNITY

The creation of the European Economic Community (EEC) was unexpected even by the advocates of European integration. In 1954, with the collapse of the European Defence Community, the impulse towards European union (at any rate on a federal basis) seemed to have ebbed away. But during 1955 the idea showed signs of renewed life. Jean Monnet and his friends were still active behind the scenes, and there were ardent integrationists in the Benelux countries. In May 1955 the Benelux governments sent to the other three governments of the ECSC a set of proposals: to extend the existing common market in coal and steel to other sectors of the economy; to amalgamate, over a period of time, all the economies of the Six; and to harmonise their social policies. The governments of the Six called a conference at

Messina in June 1955 to discuss these proposals, and they invited Britain to attend. The British government declined the invitation, adhering to its consistent policy of refusing any form of supranational organisation.

The Messina Conference agreed within two days (1–2 June) on the principle of setting up two new European entities: an Economic Community, and an Atomic Energy Community (Euratom). The Conference set up a committee, under the chairmanship of Spaak (the Belgian Foreign Minister), to work out the details of these proposals, and again invited Britain to join in the committee's deliberations. This time the British accepted; but they sent as their representative only an official from the Board of Trade, with instructions to exercise caution. The Spaak committee pressed steadily on with its work, and in a year's time put a series of recommendations to a conference of Foreign Ministers of the Six at Venice in June 1956. The ministers adopted the committee's main proposals: to set up a European Economic Community, comprising a supranational authority, an Assembly and a Council of Ministers on the lines of the Coal and Steel Community; to bring about a progressive reduction of tariffs on trade between the Six; and to establish a common external tariff on trade outside the Six. The British government declined to accept these proposals, objecting particularly to those concerning a supranational body and a common external tariff. At that stage, Britain effectively ceased to take part in these proceedings.

The Six went ahead. They negotiated treaties to establish Euratom and the EEC, which were signed in Rome on 25 March 1957. Technically, both were Treaties of Rome, but in practice the EEC agreement has come to be known as 'the Treaty of Rome'. It loomed large in relations between France and Britain for many years to come.

The preamble expressed the intention of seeking 'an ever closer union' between the peoples of its signatory states (France, West Germany, Italy, Belgium, the Netherlands and Luxembourg). This phrase, which embodied the central aspiration of the treaty-makers, was left undefined. The text of the treaty, which was long and complicated, provided for the abolition, over a period of time, of all customs duties and other trade barriers between the member states. A common external tariff on imports from countries outside the Community was to be introduced. There was to be free circulation of goods, services, capital and persons within the EEC, and the social welfare policies of the member states were to be harmonised so as to prevent unfair competition. There was to be a common agricultural policy, based on principles which will be outlined later. The member states were to hand over to the Community the power to conclude treaties with other countries, or with international organisations, dealing with matters over which the Community exercised control. In practice, this meant external commercial policy, so that (to take an important example) the EEC as a whole would negotiate with the GATT organisation.

To attain these objectives, the treaty set up four Community institutions, based on the precedent of the Coal and Steel Community. These were: a Council of Ministers, to decide on policy; a Commission, to carry out decisions made by the Council and make recommendations on policy; an Assembly, for purposes of consultation only; and a Court of Justice. The function of the Court was to rule on cases arising from the interpretation of the Treaty of Rome, or from disputes between member states. In 1964 a test case established that, in the event of a conflict between EEC law and national law, the former took precedence. The Court thus attained a position of great authority over the member states, and took a central role in securing an important purpose of the treaty, which required that the application of Community law should not vary from one member state to another. Uniformity in matters controlled by the treaty was vital, because differences would undermine the whole object of integration and harmonisation.[1]

It became common practice in Britain to refer to this new organisation as 'the Common Market', but this was a misnomer. A common market might mean simply a customs union, within which goods could circulate freely between the member states. The Treaty of Rome went much further than that, by introducing a common external tariff, a common agricultural policy, harmonisation of social policies, and a Court whose rulings prevailed over national law. These provisions created something more than a common market; yet it was also something less than a super-state, because only limited powers were delegated by the member states to the Community's institutions. The result was an ungainly creation, of a type not previously known except in the precedent of the ECSC. What it would become in the future no-one knew. The phrase 'ever closer union' remained enigmatic. In these matters lay the seeds of much later difficulty between Britain and France. The frequent use of the term 'Common Market' meant that the British did not face up to the full implications of what the EEC was and might become. The French, as in earlier

---

1. A useful guide to the Treaty of Rome and the institutions it set up may be found in William Nicoll and Trevor C. Salmon, *Understanding the New European Community* (London, 1994), especially pp. 15–20, 59–99.

years, were on the other hand fully prepared to use the language, and up to a point follow the logic, of integration.

French attitudes towards this new Community were at first uncertain. The French economy had long been protected against foreign competition by tariffs, quotas and other measures. French exporters were assured of a safe market in the Empire – as late as 1958, the French sugar-refining industry sold 85.5 per cent of its production to the Empire, and the clothing industry 79 per cent. It was true that this market was limited, in that even the richest French colony could not match the purchasing power of west European countries; but it had the merit of being safe. Equally, the French could buy from their Empire, often cheaply and always paying in their own currency, which helped the balance of payments. The French were naturally chary of abandoning these advantages and safety-nets. Car manufacturers, for example, were afraid of competition from the Germans. Italian refrigerators were known to be cheaper than their French counterparts. In the countryside, the modernisation of French agriculture was only at an early stage, and farmers did not want to open the door to further imports from Europe, which were already large. As for agricultural exports, a serious French economist was prepared to argue as late as 1957 that North Africa, not Europe, offered the best opportunities.[2]

This state of doubt and pessimism meant that France could only accept the EEC if it promised reasonable prospects of security for French manufacturers and advantages for French farmers. The Treaty of Rome met those conditions. Manufacturers were offered the partial security of the common external tariff. They would be exposed to competition within the Six, but protected from outside; so that, for example, French car manufacturers would have to compete with the Germans, but would have the common external tariff as shelter from the Japanese. Again, the harmonisation of social policies meant that the costs of social security payments would be equalised to prevent 'unfair' competition within the Six. French farmers, for their part, were offered the incentives of the principles of a Common Agricultural Policy (CAP), which were outlined in the Treaty of Rome. The objects of the CAP were defined thus: to improve the productivity of agriculture; to secure a fair standard of living for the farming population; to stabilise markets for agricultural produce; to guarantee the availability of food supplies for the Community; and to secure reasonable food prices for consumers. These principles contained some difficulties: attaining fair (or perhaps good) incomes for farmers and a

2. The figures and the general appreciation in this paragraph are taken from Hubert Bonin, *Histoire économique de la IV République* (Paris, 1987), pp. 362, 367–9, 384–5.

secure food supply within the EEC were likely to result in high (rather than reasonable) prices for consumers. The practical details needed to translate these principles and objectives into a policy were left for the future; but meanwhile the treaty held out the clear prospect of advantage for farmers.

These vital reassurances and advantages for French industrialists and farmers could not have been offered within a simple free trade area, where individual states would retain their freedom to regulate their own trade outside the area. In a free trade area, for example, Germany could continue to buy foodstuffs in the cheaper markets of the USA or Canada rather than from the Six. Again, without harmonisation, French social charges would be a handicap as against other countries within the Six. The EEC removed these dangers. France would emerge, over a period, from her existing state of protectionism and face competition within the Six; but she would do so under the shield of the EEC's external tariff and internal regulations. Nothing less would suffice to allay French anxieties.

Economic issues formed only part of the story. The political considerations were also weighty. For France, Germany dominated the horizon. The EEC, like the Coal and Steel Community before it, offered security against a future German danger by enfolding Germany within a new kind of European integration. This course appeared all the more attractive after the Suez crisis of 1956 had demonstrated the frailty of the old *Entente* with Britain, and the need for independence as against the superpowers of the USA and USSR, which had behaved in 1956 as though they ruled the world. The Soviets brandished their rockets; the Americans relied on their dollars; but the result was much the same. To 'build Europe' offered the French a way out of their weakness.

These arguments of *Realpolitik* ran alongside the advocacy of the convinced federalists, guided by Jean Monnet's Committee of Action for the United States of Europe. True federalists may well have been few, but there was a widespread and deep-seated French sense of mission to lead Europe, drawing strength from a historical continuity running from Charlemagne, by way of the crusades, to Louis XIV, and then (under different banners) to the Revolution, the Rights of Man, and Napoleon. This sense of mission was doubtless the least tangible of French motives for promoting the EEC, but it was not the least important.

The case for the EEC in French eyes thus assumed considerable strength. Even so, when Guy Mollet presented the EEC and Euratom treaties to the National Assembly in January 1957 he was still conscious of the defeat of the European Defence Community in 1954. He and the Foreign Minister, Pineau, argued an earnest, and on the whole cautious, case, with little emphasis on the supranational element involved in the EEC. One of their strongest arguments was that the only alternative for France was isolation. (It is interesting to recall that all this was happening only a few months after the proposal of union with Britain – though of course this was never mentioned.) The debate, though long, did not arouse the same passions as that on the EDC – partly doubtless through weariness, partly as a result of the Suez crisis, and partly because the EEC did not touch the same nerves as the French Army and German rearmament. The vote took place on 22 January: 322 for the treaties, 207 against, with 30 abstentions. Those in favour included the Socialists and the Catholic MRP; those against included all the 143 Communist deputies and some Radicals, including Mendès-France. It was a comfortable margin, without being over-whelming.[3] The decision once made, the European commitment of France entered a new phase. The treaties came into effect at the beginning of January 1958.

DE GAULLE AND THE NEW FRANCE

In May 1958 the Fourth French Republic, which had never appeared absolutely secure, finally collapsed, unable to cope with the Algerian war and the threats of a military *coup* which arose from it. In a desperate hour, the President of the Republic called on General de Gaulle to form a government. The result – though it was by no means a foregone conclusion – was the establishment of a new constitution, with a strong Presidency which de Gaulle had every intention of holding himself. The constitution was overwhelmingly approved by a referendum at the end of September, and the Fifth Republic came into being. More important, a new France emerged.

By a long and dangerous process, requiring a high degree of skill, ruthlessness and courage, de Gaulle extricated France from the costly and divisive war in Algeria. (The courage involved was not least physical, as de Gaulle faced a series of assassination attempts.) The agreements finally reached at Evian in 1962 registered, for all practical purposes, the defeat of France; and yet paradoxically they opened the way for de Gaulle to reassert the status of France as a great power, in which he had never lost faith.

3. *L'Année Politique*, 1957, p. 288.

To that end, de Gaulle was fortunate to inherit from the Fourth Republic a powerful economic growth, which had often been masked by the regime's political instability. Between 1950 and 1958 the French rate of economic growth had been much faster than that in Britain, though slower than that in West Germany. In those nine years, the gross national product of France rose by 42 per cent, that of the United Kingdom by 19 per cent, that of West Germany by 79 per cent.[4] As with all percentages of this kind, much depends on the base-line; but there was no doubt that the French economy was in the process of transformation before de Gaulle returned to power in 1958. In this case, he was able to take the credit and reap the advantages of work done by others. With regard to the currency, however, he took a difficult and politically dangerous decision, introducing at the end of 1958 a new 'heavy' franc, equal to 100 old francs. The shock of the change was severe, but the result was salutary, giving France a 'respectable' currency, which could be measured against the dollar, pound or mark without adding a string of noughts.

In foreign policy, de Gaulle pursued with renewed vigour the policy of co-operation with Germany within a European framework which had been begun by Schuman in 1950. He invited Chancellor Adenauer to Colombey-les-deux-Eglises on 14 September 1958 for a studiedly informal (but in fact carefully prepared) meeting, whose success at the personal level was followed up by consistent diplomatic efforts. As for the European framework and the newly-established EEC, de Gaulle adopted a policy of pragmatism. As a devoted patriot, he was entirely opposed to supranationalism or any yielding of French sovereignty; but after coming to power he declared loftily that France had signed the Treaty of Rome and would abide by its terms. What he meant in practical terms was that he was perfectly willing to go ahead with the development of the EEC in accordance with his own ideas. The phrase which embodied his approach so well, 'L'Europe des patries', was in fact used by Michel Debré, but it is perfectly fair to attach it to the General. There was of course no doubt in de Gaulle's mind that in 'l'Europe des patries' France should take the lead. There was more to it even than that. In August 1962 he was to say in private: '. . . if France sets out to become the leader of the Six, which is within our grasp, she will be able to use that position like the lever of Archimedes . . . Europe is the means for France to become again what she has not been since Waterloo: the first in the world'.[5]

---

4. Bonin, *Histoire économique*, p. 294.
5. Alain Peyrefitte, *C'était de Gaulle*, vol. I, *'La France redevient la France'* (Paris, 1994), pp. 158–9.

To be first in the world, or at any rate among the first in the world – that was a truly Gaullian aspiration. One of the General's first moves in foreign policy was to write to President Eisenhower on 17 September 1958 proposing the establishment of a three-power directorate, made up of the United States, France and Great Britain, to take decisions on world problems, including even the use of nuclear weapons, other than in case of immediate self-defence. Eisenhower declined this extraordinary proposal, which even de Gaulle may well not have taken entirely seriously. But de Gaulle continued to pursue a policy of asserting French independence from the United States, first loosening the integration of French forces within the NATO command structure, and finally withdrawing France from NATO as an organisation in 1966. He insisted that NATO headquarters be removed from Paris; though he carefully did not withdraw France from the North Atlantic Treaty itself.

The infallible sign of an independent great power on the world stage was the possession of nuclear weapons. The aspiration to be a nuclear power did not spring from de Gaulle, but went back to the Fourth Republic. In some respects it went even further back. It was on 17 June 1940, when Pétain's government had just asked for an armistice with Germany, that two French atomic physicists took ship to England, armed with their knowledge and 26 containers of heavy water, an important ingredient for making an atomic bomb. In the course of the war, French scientists made a significant contribution to the atomic bomb programme; but the Anglo-American agreement at Quebec in August 1943 forbade any disclosure of information on atomic matters to a third power, except by mutual consent. In practice this ruled out any transmission of information to the French.

Immediately after the war the French began work on their own atomic programme. In 1945 de Gaulle set up the *Commissariat à l'Energie Atomique* to pursue research on atomic energy. In 1952 Félix Gaillard, the minister responsible for atomic energy, began a five-year programme for civilian projects, mainly atomic power stations, and secured funding from the National Assembly. Military purposes were not specifically envisaged in this programme, but neither were they ruled out; and the Assembly rejected an amendment which would have excluded them. The option of developing atomic weapons was thus kept open, and step by step French governments moved down that path. In December 1954 Mendès-France, then Premier, ordered that studies should be undertaken to prepare for the construction of an atomic bomb and an atomic-powered submarine; though he reserved the final decision as to whether to act on these studies until later. In

May 1955, under Edgar Faure's government, funds were specifically provided for the military use of atomic energy. For a time it seemed that Guy Mollet's government might reverse this decision, in favour of joining a European Atomic Community which would renounce military uses. But in July 1956 Mollet ruled that the French capacity to build atomic weapons should be developed alongside membership of Euratom. Later that year the events of the Suez crisis confirmed him in the belief that France must have its own atomic bomb. No later government departed from this view. In April 1958 Félix Gaillard, then Premier, ordered preparations to be made to test an atomic weapon in the Sahara in 1960.

When de Gaulle returned to power in 1958, he therefore found France already embarked on a military atomic programme. The General followed it up, adding his own style, a new impulse, greater resources, and a different strategic aim. His predecessors had seen a French atomic bomb as strengthening the country's position within NATO. De Gaulle saw it as the instrument of an independent policy, outside NATO. In a speech at the *Ecole Militaire* on 3 November 1959 de Gaulle attacked the NATO principle of integrated commands, and declared that the defence of France must be French. He announced that France was to create a *force de frappe*, armed with atomic weapons and capable of operating against targets anywhere in the world. In February 1960 the first French atomic bomb was successfully tested in the Sahara. France became one of the atomic powers, claiming parity with Britain and (in principle though not in weight of fire-power) with the United States and the Soviet Union.

For de Gaulle, France was always in essence a great power. As he wrote in the famous first page of his *Mémoires de Guerre*, 'In my understanding, France cannot be France without greatness'.[6] He acted in accordance with that belief, and the French people for the most part responded to his lead, and were prepared to see themselves as *la grande nation* which they had temporarily ceased to be after the disaster of 1940. Under de Gaulle's leadership the troubles and uncertainties of the Fourth Republic were left behind. Couve de Murville was to write proudly in his memoirs that he was Foreign Minister for precisely ten years (1 June 1958–31 May 1968). During that time he pursued 'a policy which was truly that of France'.[7]

6. Charles de Gaulle, *Mémoires de Guerre*, vol. I, *L'Appel* (Paris, 1954), p. 1.
7. M. Couve de Murville, *Une politique étrangère* (Paris, 1971), pp. 9, 12.

BRITAIN, THE EEC AND DE GAULLE

The British were confronted by these new phenomena of the EEC and de Gaulle's France, and for some time did not know what to make of them. The EEC in particular was something which they felt ought not to have happened. The British government regarded the Messina Conference of 1955 with indifference, and did not even trouble to attend. The common assumption was that this new venture would go the same way as the European Defence Community had done in 1954. During 1956 events began to undermine this comfortable supposition. The proposals for a new Community went ahead steadily, and the British began to regard them with dismay. They did not want to join the EEC, for all the reasons that had prevailed in earlier cases; yet they did not want to be excluded. To be outside the EEC's common external tariff would damage British exports to the member states, and political exclusion might also prove dangerous. The British answer to this dilemma was to try to change the nature of the organisation that was evolving before them. In the latter part of 1956 the British government produced a scheme for a free trade area comprising all the European members of the Organisation for European Economic Co-operation (a total of sixteen countries). Its arrangements should be confined to industrial products, excluding agriculture and foodstuffs. This offered Britain two important advantages. A simple free trade area would permit member states to retain control over their own tariffs with regard to non-members, and so allow Britain to maintain Commonwealth preferences. The exclusion of agricultural products would remove the danger of high food prices which was implicit in the proposed principles of the EEC's Common Agricultural Policy.

By an unhappy coincidence of timing, these proposals were worked out during the spectacular events of the Suez crisis. The government's scheme was presented to the House of Commons in November 1956, and was heavily overshadowed by the aftermath of Suez and the uncertainty surrounding Eden's political future. In December Selwyn Lloyd, the Foreign Secretary, expounded the proposals at a meeting of the North Atlantic Council. He first made a gesture towards the European idea by suggesting the creation of a new European Assembly to absorb the different European institutions that were proliferating in bewildering variety. He then put forward the British plan for a sixteen-nation free trade area which would cover virtually the whole of western Europe.

It was only too plain that these British proposals would remove the very elements of the EEC which were vital to calm French fears and safeguard French interests: the common external tariff and the Common Agricultural Policy. If carried through, the British plan would end by dissolving the EEC in the free trade area 'like a lump of sugar in an English cup of tea', as a French historian has nicely put it.[8] At the end of 1957 and the beginning of 1958, in what proved to be the death throes of the Fourth Republic, French governments preferred to prevaricate rather than force the issue by declaring outright opposition. There ensued therefore a slow and complicated negotiation on the British proposals, which kept the scheme in play while making little substantial headway. Then, towards the end of 1958, with de Gaulle firmly in power, there was an abrupt change. The new French government was ready for what Couve de Murville was to call euphemistically 'a frank and direct discussion'.[9] In other words, the French Foreign Minister, and his master at the Elysée, meant business.

On 6 November 1958 Couve met Selwyn Lloyd and Maudling, the minister who had been conducting the detailed negotiations, and told them bluntly that France could not accept the British proposals for a free trade area which ruled out a common external tariff, excluded agricultural products, and did not aim at ultimate economic union between its members. The British ministers were taken aback. Maudling claimed that the French attitude was unacceptable. Lloyd remarked that this was the most critical stage in relations between the two countries since June 1940, which may have seemed exaggerated at the time but proved to be not far from the mark.

The French lead was at once followed by the other members of the EEC, whose Foreign Ministers publicly endorsed the French stand on 14 November. The British scheme for a large free trade area, matured in 1956 and discussed for two full years, was dead. It was killed by the French, because the British had tried to remove from the EEC the very elements that were vital for French interests. In the abrupt intervention by Couve de Murville the British encountered for the first time the stern methods of the new France.

With the collapse of their plan, the British were left to face the EEC as it took shape with unexpected rapidity. It was an unwelcome prospect, and there was a strong tendency to wish that it would somehow go away. The government cherished a lingering hope that the EEC might yet go the same way as the Defence Community. The

8. Pierre Gerbet, *La construction de l'Europe* (Paris, 1983), p. 239.
9. Couve de Murville, *Politique étrangère*, p. 42.

people probably preferred not to think about the question at all. In 1959 there was a general election, in which Macmillan's Conservative government was returned to office with an increased majority. A careful survey of the campaign, published almost at once, contained only one reference to the 'European Common Market', and that was to observe that the issue was neglected.[10]

The British government's tactical response to the new situation was to press ahead with the idea of a free trade area, but now confined to west European countries other than the Six. This took shape as the European Free Trade Area (EFTA), with seven members: Britain, Norway, Sweden, Denmark, Switzerland, Austria and Portugal. EFTA was established by the Treaty of Stockholm (4 January 1960). By contrast with the Treaty of Rome, the Stockholm Treaty was a simple affair. It provided for the progressive reduction of customs duties on industrial goods in trade between the member states, but excluded agricultural products and fish. It set up no institutions except a small Secretariat with offices in Geneva. There was no supranational element in its working, and all decisions were to be taken by the unanimous agreement of a Council of Ministers made up of representatives from all the member states. The objective of free trade in industrial goods was duly attained by July 1967, and resulted in some increase in commerce between the EFTA countries. But in so far as EFTA was designed to form an effective rival to the EEC, and to help Britain in negotiations with the Community, it was only a modest success.

Confronted by the EEC, the British were left floundering and uncertain. Much the same was true of their relations with the new France of General de Gaulle. The image of the old France was too strongly established to be easily changed. When Gladwyn Jebb took up his appointment as Ambassador in Paris in April 1954 (at the time of the 50th anniversary of the *Entente*), he found the outlook on France in the Foreign Office 'a little tricky'. On the one hand, ever since the Schuman Plan there had been a feeling that the French were inclined to take an individual and unpredictable line; on the other, the Fourth Republic was regarded as 'a weak sister who must be kept on the straight and narrow path of Western solidarity by a firm, purposeful and self-confident Britain' – which was broadly the view that the British had held since 1945. Jebb had an interview with Churchill, at which he gathered that his main function was 'to go out and, so far as possible, prevent the French from being so tiresome'.[11] While in post,

10. D.E. Butler and Richard Rose, *The British General Election of 1959* (London, 1959), p. 72.
11. Lord Gladwyn, *The Memoirs of Lord Gladwyn* (London, 1972), pp. 268–9.

Jebb wrote in June 1956 a long despatch on the second volume of de Gaulle's war memoirs. He admired the style, but deprecated the General's ungenerous treatment of the British and Americans. Jebb thought that the book provided no support for the view that de Gaulle aspired to become a dictator; but the Ambassador doubted whether he would ever preside over 'any recognisably democratic regime in France'. The Ambassador felt that de Gaulle's time was slipping away, and he might no longer be 'the man of destiny' when one was needed.[12]

Two years later the moment arrived, and de Gaulle proved after all to be the man of destiny. Jebb soon grasped the essential point that the General meant to restore France to her rightful position as a great power – 'That is what his voices tell him and that is what he must implicitly believe'. The Ambassador hoped that de Gaulle could pull it off; but doubted whether it could be done.[13] Such doubts were widely shared in the British press. David Watson has summed up the consensus of opinion: '[Even] when de Gaulle had been invested with legal authority, the prevailing attitude was still that he had little chance of succeeding.' Some commentators thought that de Gaulle would only be a figurehead, acting on behalf of someone else, probably Jacques Soustelle. (Churchill might well have remarked: 'Some figurehead!') Others believed that the ingrained habits and profound conservatism of French society and politics would prevent any real change in the country – a view for which there seemed much justification.[14]

Harold Macmillan was Prime Minister at the time of de Gaulle's return. At the end of 1957 Macmillan had shared the common British belief that France was in a state of almost fatal weakness. 'The French seem in a dazed condition', he wrote in his diary; 'until Algeria is conquered, evacuated or conciliated, they are immobilised'.[15] He had observed de Gaulle at close quarters in North Africa during the Second World War, and knew better than to regard him as a mere figurehead; but he still seems to have underestimated the General. During a visit to Paris at the end of June 1958, Macmillan tried to press the British plan for a west European free trade area by threatening an economic war if France obstructed it. He got a dusty answer, but in November he returned to the attack, sending de Gaulle a letter breathing vague threats of economic reprisals.

12. PRO, FO 371/124450, WF1091/1, Jebb to Selwyn Lloyd, 21 June 1956.
13. PRO, FO 371/145592, WF1011/1, Jebb, Annual Review for 1958, 9 Jan. 1959.
14. David Watson, 'De Gaulle as seen by the British press in 1958', paper given at a conference at Oxford, 1989. See also David Watson, 'De Gaulle vu par la presse britannique en 1958', *Espoir*, no. 76, 1991, pp. 23–36.
15. Alistair Horne, *Macmillan*, vol. II, *1957–1986* (London, 1989), p. 35.

By early 1960 Macmillan had changed his tactics. The explosion of the first French atomic weapon in February 1960 made a strong impression on him; and during a visit to Paris in March the Prime Minister tried out his undoubted powers of charm. He admired the final volume of de Gaulle's war memoirs, which had recently been published, and in return was treated to an unusual display of Gaullian humour. The General remarked how many fallen French rulers had gone to live in England. 'He paused', Macmillan wrote in his account of the conversation, 'and said he would no doubt be welcomed'.[16]

The following month, Macmillan made sure that de Gaulle was indeed welcomed to England, not as an exile but on a state visit (5–8 April 1960). Everything was done to appeal to the General's sense of history and his love of ordered pageantry, and the visit made a deep impression on de Gaulle. Years later, in his *Mémoires d'espoir*, he wrote a glowing account, dwelling particularly on his reception, on the one hand by the crowds and on the other by the Queen and the Royal family. The Queen flattered him by asking his advice on how to fulfil her role, and de Gaulle replied with splendid dignity and tact: 'In the place to which God has called you, be yourself, Madame!' As Jean Lacouture comments so acutely, 'Charles de Gaulle did not like England. He admired her.'

This admiration shone through the General's speech to the two Houses of Parliament at Westminster Hall on 7 April, in a glowing (and somewhat unexpected) tribute to British institutions.

> Sure of yourselves, almost without seeming to be, you obey in liberty a solid and stable regime. So strong with you, in the political sphere, are tradition and loyalty, the rules of the game, that your government is quite naturally endowed with cohesion and duration, that your Parliament has, throughout each legislature, an assured majority, that this government and this majority are granted continuity; in short, that your executive and legislative powers, by definition as it were, are balanced and collaborate with each other . . ..
>
> So, without the minutely detailed texts of a written constitution, but by virtue of an indisputable general consent, you find the means to ensure, on each occasion, the efficient working of democracy, without incurring excessive criticism from the ambitious or the finicky disapproval of purists.
>
> Well! I tell you that this England, which respects a proper order while practising respect for the liberty of all, inspires confidence in France.[17]

16. Ibid., p. 222.
17. Jean Lacouture, *De Gaulle*, vol. III, *Le souverain, 1959–1970* (Paris, 1986), p. 328.

It was nobly spoken, and breathed the same spirit of respectful admiration as Pierre Bourdan's *Perplexités et Grandeur de l'Angleterre* fifteen years before. The tribute arose from de Gaulle's profound historical sense, and came from the heart. Yet it was perfectly possible for the General to admire British institutions and still maintain unaltered his policy towards Great Britain.

Macmillan thus tried in succession threats and blandishments, without getting much nearer to taking de Gaulle's measure or working out how to deal with him. This was to some extent because the Prime Minister's main attention was elsewhere. When Macmillan took over from Eden as Prime Minister in January 1957, he made his first task the restoration of good relations with the United States, which had been badly shaken during the Suez crisis. This took precedence over relations with France. It was a clear pointer to British priorities that Macmillan and Selwyn Lloyd (still Foreign Secretary in the new government) made a one-day visit to Paris on 9 March, to meet Mollet and Pineau, and then conferred for six days (20–25 March) with President Eisenhower in Bermuda. This policy had some success, and relations with the Americans improved beyond most expectations; but at the cost of further friction with the French.

NUCLEAR WEAPONS

The central issue was that of nuclear weapons. The British, like the French but a step ahead, had developed their own atomic and later nuclear bombs. They had to do so largely alone, because in July 1946 the United States Congress passed the McMahon Act, imposing strict limits on the transfer of information about atomic energy to other countries. In January 1947 the then Prime Minister, Attlee, and a small group of ministers decided to build a British atomic bomb, if necessary alone. But the British did not give up hope of restoring the former wartime co-operation with the Americans on atomic matters. In 1948 they secured what was cautiously called a *modus vivendi* with the Americans on atomic matters. In the event, the Americans interpreted this agreement more restrictively than the British had intended, but despite this the British still hoped for a better deal in the future. Meanwhile, under the *modus vivendi*, joint American–British control over passing information to other countries was to be maintained. The upshot was that the British went ahead with their own atomic programme, and exploded their first atomic bomb in October 1952;

and they also pursued further research in order to build a nuclear weapon. But while perforce working alone, they never gave up hope of restoring their links with the Americans, and they considered themselves bound by their obligations to the United States on secrecy and the non-communication of information. At the end of 1954 and early 1955, the French *Commissariat à l'Energie Atomique* approached the British Atomic Energy Authority for assistance in developing an isotope separation plant like that at Capenhurst. British officials and scientists in the Authority were at first sympathetic, but the Americans opposed the idea and it was dropped. The British actually explained the circumstances to the head of the French *Commissariat*, so that the French were left in no doubt that co-operation with them was excluded because it would offend the United States.[18]

In the immediate aftermath of the Suez crisis, both France and Britain drew similar conclusions about their atomic and nuclear weapons. Mollet was completely convinced that France must make her own atomic bomb. The British White Paper on Defence of 1957 concluded that there was no effective method of defence except an independent nuclear deterrent. From this concurrence of views there might have developed a Franco-British co-operation in atomic and nuclear matters, but in fact the British government continued to believe that collaboration with the United States was the best way forward. They were encouraged in this belief because in 1956–57 they actually secured American help in designing HMS *Dreadnought*, the first British nuclear-powered submarine.

Macmillan concentrated much energy on this matter, and achieved a real success during a visit to Washington in October 1957. Eisenhower agreed to request Congress to amend the McMahon Act in a sense favourable to the British, and in return (in February 1958) the British government permitted the Americans to station intermediate-range ballistic missiles in Britain, thus bringing Soviet targets within their reach. In June 1958 Congress amended the McMahon Act so as to allow the United States to transfer information and material relating to nuclear weapons to states that had already made substantial progress in developing nuclear armaments. The criteria defining 'substantial progress' were so drafted as to apply to Britain, but not to France. After these amendments, the British secured various agreements which allowed them privileged access to some

18. Bertrand Goldschmidt, *Les rivalités atomiques, 1939–1966* (Paris, 1967), p. 328. Goldschmidt visited London with Guillaumat (head of the CEA) in February 1955, to discuss this matter with Plowden (head of the AEA) and Cockroft.

aspects of American nuclear science and technology. For example, they secured a motor for their first nuclear submarine, and permission to build others under American licence; and they received supplies of uranium 235 in exchange for plutonium produced by British reactors. The United States also supplied Britain with various parts for nuclear weapons systems, and information about the design of other elements.

The position of France was very different. The amendments to the McMahon Act which opened doors to the British were of no help to the French, but even so de Gaulle was willing to see what the Americans would do for him. In July 1958 the American Secretary of State, Foster Dulles, visited Paris, and de Gaulle explained to him that he intended to develop a French nuclear weapon, with or without American help; but he none the less enquired whether the United States would be prepared to assist him. Dulles replied that help with nuclear weapons themselves was impossible; but he held out the prospect of providing a reactor for a nuclear submarine. A French mission went to Washington in February 1959 to follow up this lead, but found that all the Americans were prepared to offer was the sale of enriched uranium for use, not in a submarine, but in a land-based reactor which might in turn serve as a prototype for a submarine motor. The French claimed that this went back on Dulles's proposal, and were indignant at being misled. There was certainly a marked contrast between the extensive assistance the Americans provided for the British and the tight restrictions they imposed on a deal with the French.

There was also a sharp difference between the British and French approaches to the nuclear weapons that might be stationed on their territory. When American missiles were based in Britain, they were subjected to a form of two-power control, by which the British government held a power of veto over their use, but not the positive authority to order them to be fired. De Gaulle, on the other hand, maintained that any nuclear weapons based in France must come under solely French control. The defence of France, as he said more than once, must be solely in French hands.

The consequences of these developments were far-reaching. Macmillan could claim important successes for his policy of restoring relations with the United States, and the British embarked on a renewed course of nuclear co-operation with the Americans. They could draw direct comparisons with the position of the French, and count their own advantages. De Gaulle, on the other hand, was confirmed in his belief that Britain was irrevocably bound to the United States in nuclear matters, and that she was not prepared to tread the hard and costly road to genuine independence. If this was true of nuclear policy, which de Gaulle regarded as central to national existence, it would certainly be true in other respects.

BERLIN CRISIS AND PARIS SUMMIT, 1958–60

These were the main events between 1957 and 1960 that tended to drive Britain and France apart. There were a number of other episodes which reinforced this tendency. The Algerian war became a constant irritant. In 1957 Tunisia asked for supplies of arms from France, Britain and the United States. The French refused, unless they could be given cast-iron guarantees that nothing would find its way to the Algerian rebels. The British and Americans, on the other hand, despatched a few hundred rifles and a quantity of ammunition, which was little more than a gesture, but quite enough to infuriate the French. The Anglo-Saxons were ganging up against France; an impression that was confirmed when in 1958 the Americans began to vote against France on the Algerian question at the United Nations, and the British followed suit.

This was an irritant. The Berlin question between 1958 and 1960 threatened to be much more dangerous. In November 1958 Khruschev, the Soviet leader, declared that all troops from the wartime allies should leave Berlin within six months. If they did not, the Soviet Union would unilaterally sign a peace treaty with the East German government, and hand over the control of all movements in and out of West Berlin to the East Germans. This raised the possibility of war if the western powers continued to enforce their rights of access to Berlin after the six months were up.

In face of this problem, Macmillan and de Gaulle adopted very different attitudes. Macmillan favoured concessions. Rather than risk using force to impose their right of access to Berlin, he argued, the western powers should accept East German control over the lines of communication. In February 1959 he virtually invited himself to Moscow to seek a diplomatic solution of the crisis in talks with Khruschev. De Gaulle, on the contrary, took a resolutely firm line. There must be no surrender to threats. If the Soviets actually handed over their responsibilities to the East Germans, France would be prepared to join the Americans in using force if necessary to get through to Berlin. For de Gaulle, this reaction was partly a matter of instinct and long-established custom – he had not hesitated to take a strong line with great powers during the Second World War, and had often got away with it. But there was more to it than that. The Berlin crisis was a German matter, and involved French relations with West Germany. Adenauer wanted no concessions to East Germany over Berlin, and de Gaulle was determined to confirm the understanding he had established with the Chancellor at Colombey in September 1958. The two statesmen met on 26 November 1958, and de Gaulle assured Adenauer that France would stand firm about Berlin, even at the risk of war. France was no mere fair-weather friend. Sir Bernard Ledwidge, then a British diplomat in Paris, regards this as the point at which 'Federal Germany replaced Britain as France's principal partner in foreign affairs'.[19]

In the event, the crisis passed. Khrushchev agreed to a meeting of Foreign Ministers at Geneva to discuss Berlin, and when the deadline which he had set arrived, nothing happened. In the whole affair, de Gaulle came out well, standing firmly by the Americans and West Germans, and showing a stronger nerve than Macmillan. The latter, on the other hand, reaped his reward with the British electorate. He gained a reputation as a peace-maker, and was returned to office in the general election of 1959.

As international relations improved, a four-power summit meeting between the USA, the Soviet Union, Britain and France was arranged for May 1960. The venue was to be Paris, with de Gaulle as the host. After the delegations had gathered in Paris, but before the conference formally began, the Soviet government released the news that an American photographic reconnaissance aircraft had been shot down over Soviet territory, and the pilot captured. Such flights were not unknown earlier, and the event in itself was not a startling novelty. In any case, the Soviet Union could easily have suppressed the information had it wished to do so. Instead, Khruschev used the news to break up the conference. In this affair too de Gaulle and Macmillan adopted very different approaches, as they had done during the Berlin crisis. De Gaulle acted with careful restraint, and opposed making any attempt to find concessions to the Soviets in order to salvage the meeting. Macmillan, on the other hand, tried hard to save the conference, partly because he believed in its value, and partly because he had invested a good deal of personal effort and prestige in bringing it about. De Gaulle's private comment on Macmillan's conduct was

---

19. Bernard Ledwidge, 'The Berlin Crisis, 1958–62', paper given at a conference at Oxford, 1989.

scathing: 'Oh, that man was deplorable, he took a snivelling, Munich-style line.'[20]

It was probably an excessively harsh verdict; but there is no doubt that the French stance during the Berlin crisis of 1958–59 and at the Paris summit in 1960 was firmer than the British. De Gaulle was fully prepared to take a strong line, and France under his leadership had achieved a new self-confidence. Macmillan might have learned something about the steely nature of de Gaulle's resolve, and about the solidity of Franco-German relations, which could have offered useful guidance in the decisions and negotiations to come. De Gaulle probably did learn something about the relative strength of his and Macmillan's nerve and will-power.

20. Hervé Alphand, *L'étonnement d'être: Journal, 1939–1973* (Paris, 1977), p. 334, diary entry 21 May 1960.

CHAPTER 9

The General Says No, 1961–1963

BRITAIN TAKES THE PLUNGE

Alistair Horne, in his biography of Harold Macmillan, writes that 'By the end of 1960 Macmillan had committed himself to apply for full membership of the Six. It was perhaps the biggest single decision of his premiership.' It was a decision reached in an uncertain, even a gloomy, frame of mind. In his diary for 9 July 1960 Macmillan wrote:

> Shall we be caught between a hostile (or at least less and less friendly) America and a boastful 'Empire of Charlemagne' – now under French but later bound to come under German control? Is this the real reason for 'joining' the Common Market (if we are acceptable) and for abandoning (a) the Seven (b) British agriculture (c) the Commonwealth? It's a grim choice.[1]

These reflections showed little enthusiasm for the enterprise, and an uneasy premonition of failure. The phrase 'if we are acceptable' was a tell-tale admission of weakness. Macmillan was aware that an application to join the European Economic Community implied the possibility of rejection, and he understood that the decision would lie in the hands of France – which meant General de Gaulle. In January 1961, after bracing himself to take the plunge, Macmillan wrote to President Kennedy of the United States:

> *De Gaulle wants the recognition of France as a Great Power, at least equal to Britain.* He suspects the Anglo-Saxons. So long as the 'Anglo-Saxon' domination continues, he will not treat Britain as European, but as American – junior partner of America, but a partner . . .

1. Alistair Horne, *Macmillan*, vol. II, *1957–1986* (London, pb edn, 1991), p. 256.

And he went on to wonder: 'Can what *we* want and what *de Gaulle* wants be brought into harmony? Is there a basis for a deal?'[2]

To these crucial questions the answers lay primarily, not in his own hands, but in those of de Gaulle. For the first time in the twentieth century, at any rate in peacetime, the success or failure of a vital British policy was to be decided by France.

Macmillan's reasons for attempting to join the EEC, an enterprise so momentous in nature and yet so doubtful of success, are still not wholly clear. A logical case could be made on economic and political grounds. By 1960, the various ministries concerned with economic affairs had come to believe that it would be in Britain's economic interest to join. The European Free Trade Area had proved only a modest success. Trade with the Commonwealth was stagnant, and was expected to decline. The EEC, on the other hand, in the first three years of its existence, had achieved strong economic growth, and American investment was being attracted to the Six rather than to Britain. On balance, it seemed likely that British industry would be stimulated into greater efficiency by competition within the EEC, and that British exporters would find better opportunities within the Common Market than outside it.

Politically, the Commonwealth was becoming steadily more nebulous and less reliable. The Suez crisis had disillusioned many Conservatives with the Commonwealth. The India of Nehru had not fulfilled the extravagant hopes placed upon it. The newly independent members were often non-aligned, or even hostile, in the cold war. South Africa, with its policy of apartheid, was a cause of endless friction. Even the formerly solid friends of the old Commonwealth – Canada, Australia and New Zealand – were becoming more dependent on the USA than on Britain. The change was as yet far from complete. Much remained of former trading patterns. Commonwealth sentiment was still strong in the Labour Party, and among officials accustomed to a particular kind of co-operation. In 1965 a very experienced civil servant wrote in his memoirs: 'I cling to my faith in a Commonwealth mystique.'[3] So did many others. Even so, the old Commonwealth which had stood together in two World Wars was changing rapidly, and the old ties counted for less than before.

British relations with the United States were also in an ambiguous condition. The 'special relationship' had cracked at the time of the Suez expedition, and was in any case largely one-way traffic. The

2. Ibid., p. 285.
3. George Mallaby, *From My Level. Unwritten Minutes* (London, 1965), p. 141.

British valued it highly, the Americans much less so. Despite these difficulties, Macmillan had made great, and partially successful, attempts to get on better terms with the United States. In 1958 he had secured favourable arrangements on nuclear matters from President Eisenhower, and by 1961 he was trying hard to make a good impression on the new President Kennedy. An application to join the EEC fitted in very well with this approach, because the United States had long supported the various moves towards western European integration (mainly in the belief that it would strengthen the countries concerned in their opposition to the Soviet Union). In March 1961 George Ball, a senior official in the State Department (and a long-standing friend of Jean Monnet), told Edward Heath that the United States wanted Britain to enter the EEC. More important, in April Kennedy repeated the message to Macmillan in person. It appeared, in fact, that Britain should join the EEC as a means of strengthening its ties with the United States, not to replace them.

Other factors were also at work. In party-political terms, the 'Supermac' who had won the general election of 1959 had run into difficulties at home, and was looking for a new idea and new impetus for his government. The influence of a new generation of senior civil servants, replacing those whose outlook had been dominated by the Second World War, was also significant. Nora Beloff observed a change of mind, or even of fashion, in the Treasury and the Foreign Office, which she dated precisely between 1959 and 1961. In 1959 it was eccentric to be in favour of British entry into Europe; in 1960 it became 'all right' to do so; by 1961 'you were a stick-in-the-mud if you thought otherwise'.[4] The change may not have been quite so rapid and complete as that, but it was real enough.

A sceptical French observer later wrote that there was another motive for the British conversion, not much mentioned in Britain but in his view decisive. Britain was continuing to follow her centuries-old policy of not allowing Europe to unite against her.[5] As far as Macmillan's instincts were concerned, there was probably something in this; though he would have put it differently. Macmillan had been badly shaken by the collapse of the Paris summit in May 1960, which had demonstrated Britain's powerlessness to influence world events at that level. Yet he still believed, from his upbringing, experience and sheer habit, that Britain was and must remain a world power. If Britain could manage to join the EEC, Macmillan persuaded himself that she

---

4. Nora Beloff, *The General Says No. Britain's Exclusion from Europe* (London, 1963), p. 89.

5. François David, *Autopsie de l'Angleterre* (Paris, 1976), pp. 194–5.

would somehow be able to lead it and use it as a means of extending British influence in the world – not *instead of* the Commonwealth and the special relationship with the United States, but in addition to them. Macmillan thus invested the application to join the EEC with vague but inspiring visions of the future, which in his mind probably counted for more than calculations of economic interests.

The Prime Minister put the case for opening negotiations with the EEC to the House of Commons at the beginning of August 1961. His approach was cautious. Technically, he did not propose to make a formal application to join the Community, but only to ascertain whether suitable terms would be available on which to apply. He placed the main emphasis on the likely economic advantages, adding some references to the opportunities for British leadership in the free world. He avoided questions of sovereignty and the implications of the 'ever closer union' to which the Treaty of Rome referred.[6] This was doubtless good political tactics, but stored up problems for the future. On 3 August the Commons voted by 313 to 5 in favour of opening negotiations.

This was an enormous numerical majority, but a distinctly curious result. The five contrary votes were made up by four left-wing Labour members and one Conservative. Twenty-one Conservatives abstained, as did almost the whole of the Labour Party. These massive abstentions (there were 630 MPs, so 312 did not vote) reflected widespread doubts about the project which were not fully brought out into the open. The Conservative Party responded loyally to the Prime Minister's lead, but the abstentions and the lone opponent represented the tip of an iceberg of doubt – about sovereignty, about the old Commonwealth, and about whether Britain was really 'European'. The Labour Party was mostly opposed to British entry into the EEC, but contained also a minority which was keenly in favour. The party was already bitterly divided on the issue of nuclear weapons, and the leader, Hugh Gaitskell, wanted to avoid another open split if at all possible. Abstention offered at least a temporary escape from trouble.

Gaitskell himself sometimes grew irritated with those who showed strong feelings about the EEC, whether for or against. In 1962 he was to exclaim that the subject was 'a bore and a nuisance and had always been so'.[7] But behind this façade of irritation lurked powerful

6. There is evidence that Macmillan and Heath considered the potential effects on British sovereignty of entry into the EEC, and consulted the Lord Chancellor on constitutional issues. But they did not draw out these issues in public debate. Mark Deavin discusses these issues in a forthcoming Macmillan book, *Macmillan's Hidden Agenda*.

7. Philip Williams, *Hugh Gaitskell* (London, 1979), p. 702.

emotions. As negotiations on British entry proceeded, Gaitskell felt more and more strongly, mostly on the question of independence. In a television broadcast on 21 September 1962 he declared that if the government intended to join a European federation it would mean 'the end of Britain as an independent nation; we become no more than Texas or California in the United States of Europe. It means the end of a thousand years of history; it means the end of the Common-wealth . . .'. A little later he said in private: 'I suppose that I have been all along more emotionally against the Common Market than I realised.'[8] If Gaitskell was slow in articulating his feelings, it is not surprising that others were in the same boat. There was a powerful element of doubt lurking in the background to the British application to join the EEC – or, as the British usually put it, the Common Market. The British themselves sensed this. So did the French.

BRITISH SELF-DOUBT

Doubt was in the air. The British application to join the EEC coincided with a crisis of self-confidence and national identity. It seemed that the self-assurance engendered by the great days of 1940 and victory in the war had suddenly run out. The British became conscious of their poor economic performance in relation to their European neighbours, and their loss of prestige in the world. This phenomenon was by no means universal. Young satirists and leaders of fashion retained their confidence to the point of brashness. Yet even they devoted their energies to undermining existing values and certainties without replacing them with anything more solid than the mini-skirt, the music of the Beatles and an aura of 'permissiveness'. It is hard to divine whether the onset of these changes was simply simultaneous with the decision to apply for membership of the EEC, or whether the two were directly connected. In any case, the new British malaise became the subject of much public discussion – indeed, a tendency towards national self-examination was probably itself a symptom of disease, or at least of hypochondria.

In this mood of self-doubt, British observers looked across the Channel with a new interest, and registered some striking contrasts with their own country. A series of articles in *The Observer* struck a chord of response among its readers and became the starting-point for a collection of essays, edited by Arthur Koestler and disturbingly

8. Ibid., pp. 729, 747.

entitled *Suicide of a Nation?* A number of the contributors made their points by drawing comparisons between Britain and France. Contrary to practically all previous British beliefs, they argued that the French had found out how to run their country efficiently and the British had not. Michael Shanks, an economist, found the contrast between London and Paris 'profoundly depressing and disquieting'. He drew a dismaying comparison between the higher education systems of the two countries. Both the British and the French set out to educate a governing elite; but 'in terms of the needs of modern industry and society the French system works and ours does not'. The French *grandes écoles* (notably the *Ecole Nationale d'Administration* and the *Ecole Polytechnique*), which had no equivalent in Britain, produced civil servants and technocrats who were highly cultured, understood science, economics and the art of administration, and moved easily between the upper echelons of the civil service and industry. The British 'generalist' tradition, in which students read for an Arts degree at Oxford or Cambridge and were then trained as administrators within the civil service, had served very well in the past, but failed to meet contemporary demands. Another writer, highly placed in an international company, claimed that France had become 'the foremost power in Western Europe', despite the grievous handicaps imposed by defeat and occupation during the Second World War, political instability under the Fourth Republic, and the long Algerian war. The secret lay in the fact that, largely because of the political instability, France had virtually of necessity been run by a cadre of top-class administrators, highly trained, often young, and markedly receptive to new ideas.

John Mander, a journalist and assistant editor of the intellectual review *Encounter*, linked these themes to a wider psychological diagnosis. Between 1954 and 1958 (i.e. before de Gaulle returned to power) 'French self-confidence had grown as fast as British confidence had declined'. The French had achieved a firmer grasp of reality. The British had exchanged 'the fact of empire for the fantasy of commonwealth', while the French had been compelled to face realities by the shock of defeat and occupation. The result was that since the war the French, along with other west Europeans, had shown more dynamism than the British. 'Our role was that of old-man-down-on-his-luck; Europe's role that of young-man-on-the-make.'[9]

These were severe comments, and it might be misleading to attach too much significance to a few disenchanted observers. But the sense

9. Arthur Koestler, ed., *Suicide of a Nation?* (London, 1963), pp. 56–9, 176–7, 147–9.

of change and decay was widespread, and has made a profound impression on historians. Kenneth Morgan, in his standard history of Britain since 1945, writes that between about 1961 and 1964 'Britain embarked on a traumatic process of self-examination, self-doubt, and declining morale, a perception of external weakness and internal decay from which it had yet fully to recover in the late 1980s'.[10] The French historian Roland Marx has been equally emphatic, though putting different dates on the phenomenon. Between 1955 and 1961, he writes, 'the tunic was torn, the king appeared more and more naked, thoughtlessness gave way to an increasingly precise self-criticism'.[11] François Bédarida, a Frenchman whose understanding was gained from long residence in England as well as deep historical knowledge, reflected in the mid-1970s that round about 1955–56 the British people passed through a number of drastic changes. They enjoyed the onset of affluence – welcome, yet disorientating. There was a reversal of principles, in which the old nineteenth-century code of morality, half religious and half ethical, gave way to the pursuit of liberty and an atomised individualism, so that the British found themselves adrift without landmarks. This coincided with a loss of national self-confidence, which had been so strong early in the century and been reinforced by the events of 1940. Bédarida attributed this particular change to the shock of the Suez crisis and its sudden revelation of British weakness.[12] Both Marx and Bédarida saw a close connection between these psychological changes and the British application to join the EEC. Bédarida summed it up: 'Little by little the English felt themselves condemned to become Europeans.'[13]

Loss of confidence on one side of the Channel came at the same time as a revival of confidence on the other. France was on the move. Gladwyn Jebb, at the British Embassy in Paris, was struck in 1960 by 'the rather arrogant self-confidence of a new generation of Frenchmen', who were taking over from the generation marked by defeat in war. France, he found, was 'much more confident and combative'.[14]

10. Kenneth O. Morgan, *The People's Peace. British History 1945–1990* (Oxford, pb edn, 1992), p. 197.
11. Roland Marx, *Histoire de l'Angleterre* (Paris, 1993), p. 641.
12. François Bédarida, *La société anglaise du milieu du XIXe siècle à nos jours* (Paris, 2nd edn, 1990), pp. 349–53.
13. Ibid., p. 386.
14. Lord Gladwyn, *The Memoirs of Lord Gladwyn* (London, 1972), pp. 306–7.

THE BRITISH APPLICATION: THE DETAILED NEGOTIATIONS

These psychological considerations have assumed more significance in retrospect than they did at the time. Negotiations for British entry into the EEC got under way in October 1961, and for much of the time assumed the gritty and unexciting form of detailed discussion of commercial terms. The British minister in charge of these negotiations, which took place in Brussels over a period of sixteen months, was Edward Heath. Heath was already 'European' in political orientation, and his maiden speech in the House of Commons had been in favour of British acceptance of the Schuman Plan in 1950. However, his biographer John Campbell believes that as yet he had not developed any profound European convictions: 'It was the job that consolidated his European faith, rather than his faith that recommended him for the job.'[15] At the time, it was certainly a task which required above all an infinite capacity for taking pains.

On 10 October 1961, in the august surroundings of the Quai d'Orsay in Paris, Heath formally expounded the British case to the Council of Ministers of the EEC. He claimed that Britain was prepared to accept the Treaty of Rome, but at once proposed the addition of a number of protocols to that treaty to meet the specific needs of Britain and the Commonwealth. The British requested a long period of transition, of twelve to fifteen years, before the full application of the Common Agricultural Policy in Britain. They also asked, on behalf of Commonwealth countries, for important exceptions to the EEC's common external tariff. They wished for a total of 27 Commonwealth products (including, for example, aluminium, tin and paper) to be exempted from duty; and they requested that Canada, Australia and New Zealand should be assured of 'equivalent outlets' for their agricultural products in the EEC to make up for a diminution in their exports to Britain. These requests closely concerned French interests, and it was from France that the main opposition arose.

In the course of 1961, before the negotiations with Britain began, the EEC countries had been engaged in working out the details of the Common Agricultural Policy, which had only been outlined in the Treaty of Rome. The French government was determined that the CAP must be fully agreed, set up and working before Britain entered the EEC. Otherwise, they were afraid that the whole complicated project might get lost in the changes that would accompany British

15. John Campbell, *Edward Heath: A Biography* (London, 1993), p. 114.

membership. This object was achieved, and on 14 January 1962 the six member states of the EEC agreed on the details of the Common Agricultural Policy.

The CAP was to assume considerable importance in relations between Britain and France in subsequent years. Its details were complicated, but its essence was simple. There was to be a common market for agricultural produce, applied to producers and traders though not to consumers. Producers were to receive a single price for a given commodity – wheat, for example – whether grown in the prairies of the Beauce in France or on a small farm in Germany. These common prices were to be fixed annually, and converted into national currencies by using the so-called 'green' exchange rate, set by the Council of Ministers, which did not always follow the market exchange rates between the various currencies involved. Prices in the shops in the six countries were not identical, as any visitor could see. Another element in the CAP was 'Community preference', making it cheaper for the consumer within the EEC to buy Community produce rather than imports – for example, French wheat rather than Canadian or American. There was to be *'solidarité financière'*, by which agricultural prices were to be maintained at a high level by payments for surplus production and subsidies for exports. Funds for these purposes were to be provided by the *Fonds d'Orientation et de Garantie* (European Agricultural Guidance and Guarantee Fund), financed partly by levies on agricultural products imported into the EEC from outside, and partly by direct payments by member states. The import levies were of course paid mainly by countries which imported large quantities of agricultural produce from outside, notably West Germany. The Germans therefore paid more into the Guidance and Guarantee Fund than they received from it; the French on the other hand received more than they paid in.[16]

These arrangements resulted in high food prices within the EEC. A French historian estimated that in the first ten years of the CAP's operation (1962–71), EEC prices were between 50 and 100 per cent higher than world prices; and a British economist estimated that the average ratio of EEC to world prices over a number of products, 1968–79, varied between 139 and 229.[17] They also led to heavy surplus

16. Jean Chombert de Lauwe, *L'aventure agricole de la France de 1945 à nos jours* (Paris, 1979), pp. 292–9, provides an excellent analysis of the CAP. See also Michael Davenport, 'The Economic Impact of the EEC', in Andrea Boltho, ed., *The European Economy: Growth and Crisis* (Oxford, 1982), pp. 234–6.

17. Chombert de Lauwe, *L'aventure agricole*, p. 300; cf Davenport, in Boltho, ed., *European Economy*, p. 237. The figures present difficulties, because EEC prices form part of world prices, and have an effect upon them.

production, which was purchased and stocked by the EEC. They resulted also in the rapid modernisation of agriculture; stable prices, even if at a high level; and something close to self-sufficiency in foodstuffs within the EEC. France secured considerable advantages, because the important agricultural sector of the French economy was assured of high prices, subsidised by the Guarantee Fund, to which West Germany was the major contributor and from which France was a significant beneficiary. The benefits were by no means confined to France. If income from the CAP was calculated per head of population instead of by country, the Netherlands did particularly well; and small-scale German wheat farmers were able to grow and sell their crops in what would otherwise have been hopeless economic circumstances. Even so, France had a strong interest in the CAP, and insisted on its being firmly established before a possible British entry into the EEC. For many years to come, the CAP was to be a bone of contention between France and Britain.

The provisions of the CAP were agreed on by the Six in January 1962. They began to operate in the course of that year, and were due to be fully applied over periods of time which varied according to the different aspects of the scheme. The British delegation discussing terms of entry to the EEC were dismayed to find new conditions being created even while their negotiations were in progress. The whole principle of the CAP ran counter to existing British practice, which was based on low food prices. Foodstuffs were imported cheaply from Commonwealth countries, and British farmers were subsidised by deficiency payments, which made up the difference between the farmers' high production costs and low market prices. Thus consumers benefited from low food prices, and farmers were subsidised by direct government payments, rather than by the high prices imposed by the CAP. If Britain were to accept the CAP by joining the EEC (and the two now went together), the British government would ultimately save money on deficiency payments, but make a large contribution to the Guarantee Fund. The British consumer would have to pay higher prices for food. The British negotiators sought a long transition period to delay and absorb the effects of these changes.

Meanwhile, the introduction of the CAP imposed immense complications on the negotiations. The British team had to reach separate agreements for each agricultural product and for each Commonwealth country as well as for the United Kingdom, a task which they tackled with immense patience and success. By January 1963, after a year of toil, they had secured agreements on some 2,500 products, with less than 30 still outstanding.[18] It was a remarkable

18. Figures in Campbell, *Heath*, p. 215.

achievement, and a tribute to the skill and persistence of Heath and the British officials. In the detailed economic negotiations, success was very near. But that was only part of the story, and not the main plot.

MACMILLAN AND DE GAULLE

Looking back near the end of his life, Macmillan remarked to his biographer that 'Ted [Heath] was . . . a first-class staff officer, but no army commander'.[19] Using this analogy, Heath pursued the staff work at Brussels during 1962 with great success. What about Macmillan in his role as army commander?

Macmillan knew from the start that British entry into the EEC was a matter between Britain and France, and that de Gaulle would have the decisive word. It is the task of an army commander to read the mind of his opponent, and it is by no means clear that Macmillan divined de Gaulle's policy correctly, or even realised fully that the General was in fact an opponent. In *L'Année Politique* for 1960, Raymond Aron, that shrewdest of political analysts, argued that de Gaulle intended to keep Britain out of the EEC (which she had not yet applied to join) because the General was convinced that the British were so closely bound to the Americans that Europe would have no independent existence if they were allowed to enter. If Aron was right, then Macmillan's whole strategy was doomed to failure before he started. This was a formidable proposition for the 'army commander'. It is plain that in his gloomier moments Macmillan glimpsed the truth, but could not – even dared not – accept it. He knocked at the door, in the hope that eventually de Gaulle would open it. Macmillan went on knocking for over a year, at three separate meetings with the General, in November 1961, June 1962 and finally December 1962.

The two protagonists were very similar in age – de Gaulle was born in 1890, Macmillan in 1894. Both had fought as infantry officers in the Great War. They had met, and got to know one another, in North Africa in 1943 when Macmillan was British Minister-Resident in Algiers, where de Gaulle was struggling to establish his authority in the Committee of National Liberation. Macmillan had supported de Gaulle, who had written him a warm letter of thanks after a particularly difficult passage. Macmillan became Prime Minister in 1957, de Gaulle Premier of France, and then President, in 1958. Both were accomplished actors, though in very different styles. As statesmen,

19. Horne, *Macmillan*, vol. II, p. 243.

Macmillan, behind his unflappable façade, was nervous and sensitive; de Gaulle in his public persona was completely impassive. Macmillan was like a cruiser – fast, manoeuvrable but lightly armed; de Gaulle like a battleship – more ponderous, but heavily gunned. It was to prove an unequal contest.

The two met on 25–26 November 1961 at Macmillan's private house at Birch Grove. Macmillan had invited de Gaulle to England to talk about Britain's application to join the EEC, and the General suggested that they should meet, not at Downing Street or even Chequers, but in completely unofficial surroundings, where they could talk (said de Gaulle) as 'vieux copains' – old friends. There ensued some very plain speaking, though the note was not always friendly. Macmillan pressed for a rapid conclusion of the negotiations for British entry, which had begun in October. The opportunity, he claimed, was favourable but fleeting. De Gaulle, himself and Adenauer were the men of destiny. If they let their chance slip, it would not recur. If the negotiations failed, said Macmillan, 'people would think that the real cause of failure was that the United Kingdom was not wanted in Europe'. Britain might then turn away from Europe, towards the United States and the Commonwealth. Perhaps the British would no longer be prepared to keep troops in Germany. (Macmillan was bold enough at this stage to use a scarcely-veiled threat.) De Gaulle declared himself impressed by Macmillan's profession of faith in Europe, but wondered what sort of Europe it was to be. The British were Europeans, in their own fashion. Canadians, Australians and New Zealanders had been Europeans once. India and African countries, on the other hand, were not European at all. If the EEC countries were to let in the rest of the world, 'they would lose themselves; Europe would be drowned in the Atlantic'.[20]

This was to be de Gaulle's recurrent theme during the whole period of the British application to join the EEC: the entry of Britain, with all her Commonwealth attachments and her links with the United States, would change the Community out of all recognition. This objection was probably fatal, even at the early stage of that first meeting. Charles Williams, de Gaulle's most recent British biographer, argues that at Birch Grove 'The difference between the two men on the future of Europe was set out with complete clarity'.[21] But Macmillan either could not or would not see it. He had staked so much on securing entry to the EEC that he had to find room for

20. Ibid., pp. 314, 317–18.
21. Charles Williams, *The Last Great Frenchman. A Life of General de Gaulle* (London, 1993), p. 419.

hope. When the meeting was over, he mused in his diary about de Gaulle – 'the Emperor of the French', who 'talks of Europe and means France'. He went on:

> The tragedy of it all is that we agree with de Gaulle on almost everything. We like the political Europe (*union des patries* or *union d'états*) that de Gaulle likes. We are anti-federalists; so is he. We are pragmatists in our economic planning; so is he . . . We agree; but his pride, his intense 'vanity' for France – she must dominate – make him half welcome, half repel us, with a strange 'love–hate' complex. Sometimes, when I am with him, I feel I have overcome it. But he goes back to his distrust and dislike, like a dog to his vomit.[22]

Thus, in the privacy of his own reflections, Macmillan grasped something of the depth of de Gaulle's opposition; yet he clung to the hope of a similarity of political views, and to a belief in his own personal influence and powers of persuasion.

In March 1962 de Gaulle's position was strengthened by the conclusion of the Evian agreement with the Algerian nationalists, bringing the long war in Algeria to an end. The agreement was confirmed by the French people in a referendum on 8 April. Also in April, an earlier proposal by de Gaulle for a form of European political union (called the Fouchet Plan, after the name of the chairman of the committee set up to work it out) foundered because the Dutch and Belgians tried to tie its acceptance to the entry of Britain into the EEC. The French refused to accept this condition, which was surely an indication of their position on the EEC negotiations themselves. By May 1962 the British Ambassador in Paris, Sir Pierson Dixon, had concluded that de Gaulle had already decided to reject British entry, and was only waiting for a suitable opportunity. Dixon thought that if the French legislative elections which were due to take place in November went well for de Gaulle, his hands would be free and he would declare his opposition. Macmillan still refused to believe it, arguing that the General, 'torn between emotion and reason', had not made up his mind.[23]

Macmillan therefore determined to try his persuasive powers again, and he asked de Gaulle for another meeting. At the Château de Champs, on 2–3 June 1962, Macmillan deployed once more his European aspirations and convictions. He explained that the Commonwealth no longer possessed its former importance, and agreed

---

22. Horne, *Macmillan*, vol. II, p. 319, quoting Macmillan's diary, 29 Nov. 1961.

23. Ibid., p. 326. For Dixon's views, see PRO, PREM11/3775, Dixon to FO, 23 May 1962.

that Commonwealth preferences in trade must gradually disappear. He emphasised that Britain was ready to accept the common external tariff and the Common Agricultural Policy (though with suitable transitional arrangements). He referred twice, with great seriousness, to the profound change from an older generation brought up in the days of Kipling and the Empire to the youth of the present day, who were ready to look to Europe for a new ideal. (The reference to Kipling made its mark: the French record has Macmillan saying that 'the England of Kipling is dead'.) He claimed that the British people, especially the young and those engaged in business, were ready to join the EEC. The French Ambassador to London, Geoffroy de Courcel, who was present at the conference, claimed that Macmillan went so far as to propose nuclear co-operation between Britain and France in return for British entry into the EEC. Before the meeting, Macmillan and the Foreign Secretary, Douglas-Home, had indeed discussed the possibility of Britain and France being in some way 'European trustees' of nuclear weapons. However, the British record of the meeting at Champs indicates only that Macmillan said that in the event of a Soviet attack on western Europe the United States might hesitate to use its nuclear weapons, and some European deterrent was therefore perhaps necessary. This form of words fell far short of a firm proposal for co-operation; and it appears that there was a serious mis-understanding on this important point.

De Gaulle professed himself impressed by Macmillan's earnestness. He recognised that British views had changed a great deal in the past two or three years. But he returned to his old theme: if Britain joined the EEC, it would become something different. 'Your entry would change everything. We must examine it closely.' And at another point in the discussion: 'Of course, if your membership should prove possible, we will not oppose it. But – one must face facts – it will then be a different Common Market.' De Gaulle also wondered whether France and Britain could really follow a common policy towards the Soviet threat – he recalled that they had differed widely on the Berlin crisis. Could they agree on a policy that did not depend on the Americans? Macmillan assured him that the British did not want to be satellites of the Americans.[24]

The atmosphere of these talks was cordial, and de Gaulle seemed

24. Jean Lacouture, *De Gaulle: The Ruler, 1945–1970* (London, 1992), p. 354; Horne, *Macmillan*, vol. II, p. 328; Alain Peyrefitte, *C'était de Gaulle*, vol. I, 'La France redevient la France' (Paris, 1994), p. 302; Maurice Vaïsse, 'De Gaulle et la première candidature britannique au Marché Commun', *Revue d'Histoire Diplomatique*, 1994, No. 2, pp. 135–7. The British record of the conference is in PRO, PREM11/3775, which also contains minutes on the preceding discussion of nuclear matters.

pleasantly relaxed. Yet the meeting led to no certain result. The respective ambassadors (even Dixon, who was usually pessimistic) thought there had been real progress. Couve de Murville, who usually interpreted de Gaulle's mind correctly, thought that agreement was near. On the other hand, the General had kept returning to his leitmotif, that if Britain entered the EEC everything would be changed; and there was no sign that he wanted to change everything. It was perhaps just possible that a firm British offer of a nuclear partnership, independent of the United States, would have induced him to change his mind; and there has been much speculation as to whether Macmillan offered, or hinted at, some such possibility. Yet in practice there was surely no chance of any such arrangement. The British had no wish to give up their nuclear links with the United States, which Macmillan had carefully built up from 1958 onwards, and which were at that very time approaching a crucial stage. On the French side, de Gaulle was so firmly set on an independent *French* nuclear deterrent (he was wont to insist that the defence of France must be French) that it was virtually impossible for him to accept anything else.

When the meetings at the Château de Champs were over, Macmillan hoped that he had avoided the danger of a French veto, if only for the time being. That was the most that could be said; and even that was probably over-optimistic. Subsequent events were ominous from a British point of view. In July 1962 Couve de Murville blocked the negotiations at Brussels by raising new questions about the export of foodstuffs from Canada, Australia and New Zealand, and about exports of sugar from the British West Indies. No agreement was reached on these matters before the long summer recess began on 5 August. Negotiations were not due to be resumed before the French legislative elections in November. When they took place, those elections returned an Assembly in which the Gaullists and their allies had an absolute majority.

Between July and November 1962 there were two other important developments. First, Franco-German relations, already close, were further strengthened. Adenauer made a state visit to France in July. He and de Gaulle took the salute at a joint parade of French and German troops at Mourmelon; and later the two statesmen attended high mass together in Rheims cathedral. In September de Gaulle reciprocated with a carefully prepared visit to West Germany, during which he reiterated (in excellent, well-coached German) the message that Franco-German co-operation was the basis of the new Europe. *Le couple France-Allemagne* was becoming well established, and it is striking to see the device of formal state visits, which had previously served to develop the *Entente cordiale*, being used to promote the new alignment. There was no sign that Britain would be able to join the two partners in some political equivalent of a *ménage à trois*. Indeed, while he was in France, Adenauer had remarked to de Gaulle that they must not allow Britain to become the arbiter of Europe and play her old game of divide and rule. The second development took place in the United States, where in October 1962 Congress adopted a Trade Expansion Act which offered significant tariff concessions to the states of an enlarged EEC if Britain and other countries were allowed to join the Community. This reinforced the impression that British entry fitted into the 'grand design' of American policy, and that the application to join was an 'Anglo-Saxon' affair.

De Gaulle now had an absolutely secure base in France. He had carefully covered his flank by reinforcing his ties with West Germany. (If by chance he was thinking in terms of a replay of Waterloo, then he had ensured that Blücher had changed sides.) He had good reason to think that the British and Americans were still acting in concert – a view in which he was shortly to be sharply reinforced. Returning to Macmillan's analogy of the army commander, the General was in a strong position, had made sure of his allies, and was sure he could read his opponent's mind. He was ready to deal with the British.

At that stage (the end of 1962 and the beginning of 1963) the EEC negotiations crossed with other events which had long been in the background. The British were involved in two vital sets of negotiations: with de Gaulle on entry to the EEC, and with the Americans on nuclear armaments. These two transactions now became dangerously entangled.

On the issue of nuclear weapons, the British had for some time been considering how to replace their existing bombing aircraft, which were becoming obsolescent. They set out to build a missile, the Blue Streak, but had to abandon the project in 1960. The Americans then agreed to supply them with Skybolt, a missile to be fired from an aircraft, which was in the course of development. But the Skybolt missile too had its difficulties, and after prolonged uncertainty the Americans finally announced its cancellation at a NATO meeting in Paris on 10–11 December 1962. The British were again left looking for a replacement, and asked the United States to supply them with Polaris, submarine-borne, missiles. In principle, this made no difference to the British position in relation to the Americans. The changes would simply be technical and logistical. A British nuclear warhead would be attached to an American-built Polaris missile, to be fired from a submarine, instead of to an American-built Skybolt missile, to be fired from an aircraft. In practice, the impact of the change was considerable. British strategy, and the relations between British services (the RAF and the Navy), were openly shown to be at the mercy of an American technical failure over Skybolt. The British government then had to ask the Americans for help again, this time for Polaris; and at the end of December 1962 they were waiting for an answer from President Kennedy. British dependence on the United States in the crucial matter of nuclear weaponry, which had long existed, was glaringly exposed at the very time when the EEC negotiations were reaching the point of final decision. For de Gaulle, there could have been no clearer demonstration of the essential relationship between Britain and the United States.

It was as these events were coming to a head that Macmillan set out for his third and final meeting with de Gaulle, at the Château de Rambouillet on 15–16 December 1962. It was a strange meeting, beginning with a pheasant shoot – a sign of French devotion to *la chasse*. Macmillan, who was an excellent shot, had a bag of 77 birds. In the conference, it seems that his aim was less sure. The main topics were British entry to the EEC and nuclear weapons. When the meetings were over, Macmillan wrote that he and de Gaulle had agreed on the nuclear question, but that on the European issue the talks had been 'about as bad as they could be'.[25]

On the nuclear issue, this was far too optimistic. Macmillan felt that he had to raise the question, knowing full well that he was about to go to meet Kennedy to ask about Polaris, but not yet being sure of the President's answer. To pass the matter over in silence during the conference with de Gaulle would have been fatal; and yet it was treated in such a way as to result in confusion. De Gaulle emerged from the conversations under the impression that after the failure of Skybolt Britain would embark on co-operation with France on a nuclear deterrent, even if some elements in it had to be bought from the Americans. The British account, on the other hand, presents Macmillan as explaining that he was going to ask Kennedy to supply Britain with Polaris, and making no mention of Franco-British co-operation. It is not clear how such a discrepancy arose. It may have occurred when the two statesmen were talking by themselves, without an interpreter. It may be that de Gaulle heard what he wanted to hear – Alastair Horne writes that 'if de Gaulle misheard at Rambouillet . . . it was almost certainly because he wished to do so . . .'. Jean Lacouture,

25. Horne, *Macmillan*, vol. II, p. 342, quoting Macmillan's diary, 16 Dec. 1962.

the most thorough of de Gaulle's many French biographers, wonders why, if de Gaulle really wanted a Franco-British nuclear deterrent, he did not say so outright.[26] Whatever the truth of these matters, the fact was that Macmillan went off a few days later to meet Kennedy, and secured a deal about Polaris. De Gaulle then claimed that Macmillan had deceived him in the talks at Rambouillet. Thus all that emerged from the conversations about nuclear weapons was a grave misunderstanding and an occasion (which may have been no more than a pretext) for de Gaulle to say that he had been misled.

As to British entry to the EEC, on the other hand, de Gaulle made the position painfully clear. He emphasised to Macmillan that he alone would decide: even if all the other members of the Six wanted British entry, France could still impose a veto. He reverted to his old theme of the profound change which British entry would mean for the EEC. The two points were obviously closely connected in his mind, and he explained that if Britain entered the EEC, to be followed by others, the significance of France within the Community would be diminished. Macmillan pointed out indignantly that this amounted to a fundamental objection in principle to British entry, which should have been raised at the start instead of after a year's intensive negotiation; but he made no impression.

During a particularly difficult passage in the conference, de Gaulle recalled his stormy conversation with Churchill just before D-Day in 1944, saying that Churchill had told him that 'he would always choose Roosevelt rather than de Gaulle and would always choose the larger world rather than Europe'. Macmillan replied that these remarks were made at a particular point in history; and that in any case Britain had stood alone to defend the freedom of Europe. De Gaulle acknowledged this, and said that Britain had never been so European as she was in 1940 – the very point made by Pierre Bourdan in 1944. This apparently extraneous excursion into history was almost certainly very revealing. De Gaulle still resented the passage of arms with Churchill, and still thought that Britain was bound to the United States. Macmillan still remained rightly proud of Britain's wartime record. The past was very much alive at the Château de Rambouillet.

Macmillan returned to London knowing that de Gaulle intended to prevent British entry, yet clinging somehow to a slim hope that he would not finally do so. De Gaulle knew better. He told his ministers on 19 December, three days after the Rambouillet meeting: 'I couldn't give the poor man anything and he looked so sad, so downcast, that I

---

26. Ibid., p. 431; Lacouture, *De Gaulle: The Ruler*, pp. 355–6.

wanted to put my hand on his shoulder and say, as Edith Piaf does in her song, "Ne pleurez pas, milord!"' When had a French statesman last spoken so condescendingly about a British Prime Minister?[27]

On the same day that de Gaulle was talking about Edith Piaf, Macmillan was in Nassau talking to President Kennedy. At this conference (19–21 December 1962) Kennedy agreed that Britain could purchase Polaris missiles, to be fitted with British warheads and carried in British-built submarines. The British Polaris force, when eventually constituted, would normally be under NATO command, but in extreme emergency, when supreme national interests were at stake, control should pass to the British government. The details, worked out later in an agreement signed on 6 April 1963, were favourable to Britain, in that the cost was relatively light and the American missiles would be accompanied by all their supporting equipment. The whole project would take several years to complete. The first British Polaris submarine was in fact commissioned in October 1967, and the four vessels making up the whole force were not completed until December 1969. When the Nassau conference was over, the United States publicly offered to supply France with Polaris missiles, on the same conditions of being placed under NATO command, with provision for withdrawal in grave emergency.

At the end of December 1962, therefore, France faced decisions on two grave matters: the British application to join the EEC, and the American offer of Polaris missiles. On 14 January 1963 de Gaulle publicly rejected both.

THE GENERAL SAYS NO

De Gaulle gave his verdict at a press conference at the Elysée Palace, in the presence of some 500 journalists, and broadcast live on French television. It was one of the most public events in the history of relations between France and Britain. The occasion was so dramatic, and its consequences so momentous, that parts of de Gaulle's statement must be quoted extensively.

> England . . . is insular, maritime, bound by its trade, its markets, its
> food supplies to the most varied and often very distant countries. Her

27. English translation of de Gaulle's remarks, Lacouture, *De Gaulle: The Ruler*, p. 357; cf the slightly different account in Peyrefitte, *C'était de Gaulle*, vol. I, p. 333. On the Rambouillet meeting, Vaïsse, 'La première candidature britannique', pp. 141–5, illuminates several obscure points. The British record of the conference is in PRO, PREM11/4230.

activity is essentially industrial and commercial, not agricultural. She has in all her activities very strong, very individual habits and traditions.

In short, the nature, structure and circumstances peculiar to England are different from those of the other continental countries.

What can be done so that England, in the way that she lives, produces and trades, may be incorporated into the Common Market as it has been conceived and now functions? . . .

It must be admitted that the entry of first Great Britain and then of those other states [the other applicants to the EEC] will completely alter the whole set of adjustments, understandings, compensations and rules which have already been established between the Six, because all these states, like England, have very important individual characteristics. So it is a different Common Market whose construction we ought to envisage, which would be faced with all the problems of economic relations with a host of other states and above all with the United States.

It is predictable that the cohesion of all its members, which would be numerous and very diverse, would not last long and that finally there would appear a colossal Atlantic community dependent upon and dominated by America, which would soon have absorbed the European Community and that is not at all what France wanted to build and is building, which is a specifically European construction.

So, it is possible that one day England may come to transform herself sufficiently to be part of the European Community without restriction or reservation and in preference to anything else, and in that case the Six would open the door to her and France would present no obstacle . . .

If the negotiations in Brussels were not to succeed at present, there would be nothing to prevent an agreement of association being concluded between the European Community and Great Britain.[28]

De Gaulle added that it was very likely that the evolution of Britain, and of the world as a whole, was bringing Britain closer to the continent of Europe. It was a great honour for his friend Harold Macmillan to have discerned this movement of events, and to have taken the first steps along the road which one day would lead Britain to Europe. The General also sweetened the pill a very little with a well-phrased tribute to Britain's wartime record. He concluded by briefly, almost dismissively, rejecting the American offer to supply France with Polaris missiles. France, he declared, would continue to build, and if necessary use, her own nuclear armaments.

In substance, de Gaulle's speech contained nothing surprising. It was

28. Own translation from French original in Jean Lacouture, *De Gaulle*, vol. III, *Le Souverain* (Paris, 1986), p. 337.

possible to predict (as Raymond Aron had predicted in 1960) that de Gaulle intended to keep Britain out of the EEC. During 1961 and 1962 the General's arguments had remained entirely consistent. Geography and history separated Britain from continental Europe. The entry of Britain into the EEC would transform the nature of the Community and diminish the relative weight of France within it. British policy, and especially British defence policy, was inextricably bound up with the United States, while de Gaulle was set on creating an independent French nuclear deterrent. Of all this de Gaulle had made no secret. As early as November 1961 he declared that he would not allow Europe to be drowned in the Atlantic. Moreover, as Maurice Vaïsse has shown, de Gaulle went out of his way to explain his position to various foreign statesmen, though he stopped short of saying that he would reject British entry outright.[29]

De Gaulle thus said nothing new. Equally, it was hard to fault his reasoning. Was Britain in fact ready to commit herself to the EEC in all its aspects? The very fact that Heath and his team at Brussels had negotiated agreements on 2,500 different products showed that Britain required exceptions to the detailed rules. More to the point, Macmillan was still devoted to the 'special relationship' with the United States. Even his decision to apply for membership of the EEC had been influenced by what the Americans wanted. He certainly did not intend to choose Europe as against the USA, but to back both horses at once. In the British public debate, the Labour Party (which might well form the next government) opposed entry, showing that the future of British policy was uncertain.

De Gaulle's logic was surely sound. His timing was carefully judged. By the end of 1962 he was free of the Algerian incubus, had gained a solid majority in the French elections, and had consolidated his links with Adenauer. The Nassau agreement between Kennedy and Macmillan may also have affected the timing, in that it signalled unequivocally that there was no chance of bargaining British entry to the EEC against a Franco-British nuclear partnership – if that was what de Gaulle really wanted. But the cumulative weight of evidence is that de Gaulle was consistently opposed to British entry, and equally devoted to an independent French nuclear force. It is most likely that he merely used the Nassau agreement as a useful theatrical prop in the dramatic performance of his press conference.

The time had come for de Gaulle to unmask his guns. It was the withering verbal broadside which he delivered at his press conference

29. Vaïsse, 'La première candidature britannique', p. 131.

that made such a profound impression. To suggest that Britain might become an associate of the EEC put her on the same level as Greece, or even the former French African colonies. The ostensible compliment to Macmillan's perspicacity in understanding the course of history was in fact to treat the Prime Minister with (as Alistair Horne puts it) 'almost insulting condescension'.[30] This was surely a personal affair as well as a matter of state. De Gaulle had suffered humiliations at the hands of the British during the Second World War, and he now had the chance to turn the tables. Charles Williams, in his biography of de Gaulle, goes further, seeing in the press conference 'the long shadow of Fashoda', that affront to France in 1898, which was well within the General's historical memory.[31] In view of de Gaulle's cast of mind, it is quite possible that the account to be settled went further back still, to Joan of Arc and the Hundred Years' War.

Macmillan, who even after the Rambouillet conference in December 1962 had hoped against hope for a favourable outcome, was badly shaken by de Gaulle's performance. He said to Kennedy on the telephone that same day that the General had 'gone crazy – absolutely crazy'. When Kennedy asked why, Macmillan replied that 'the real simple thing is he wants to be the cock on a small dunghill instead of having two cocks on a larger one'.[32] This was probably not far off the mark, though it hardly amounted to evidence of insanity.

For a few days the British government tried to put a brave face on things, and behaved as though de Gaulle's speech had not killed the British application outright. They hoped that the other five EEC countries, who had supported British entry, might salvage the negotiations at Brussels, which had not formally been wound up. They affected a particular confidence in West German support, and persuaded the Americans to intervene at Bonn on Britain's behalf. This confidence, in so far as it was real, was misplaced. On 22 January, a mere eight days after de Gaulle's press conference, Adenauer and de Gaulle signed in Paris a treaty of co-operation between their two countries. German sympathy for Britain's plight was confined to words. In the last resort, the same was true of the others. Even the Dutch, who had been the keenest advocates of British entry, were not prepared to damage the painstaking work that had been accomplished since the Treaty of Rome in 1957. In any case, whatever the attitude of the other five, the French were perfectly prepared to stand alone. On 29 January it fell to Couve de Murville, the French Foreign

30. Horne, *Macmillan*, vol. II, p. 446.
31. Williams, *Last Great Frenchman*, p. 424.
32. Horne, *Macmillan*, vol. II, p. 446.

Minister, to bring the negotiations at Brussels to an end. The other EEC delegates made sorrowful remarks. Heath spoke emotionally of Britain's commitment to Europe. Couve drily stated the French case, and left it at that.

The British were nonplussed. Macmillan wrote gloomily in his diary on 28 January that 'All our policies at home and abroad are in ruins . . .'.[33] De Gaulle's conduct was deeply resented, especially by those who had worked so hard at the detailed negotiations. The language and manner of the General's rejection was felt as a humiliation. Nora Beloff, in *The General Says No*, opened by asking 'What hit us?'. . . How could we have presented him with such an exposed posterior?'[34] The language was humorous, but the point was serious. De Gaulle's press conference came as a severe shock, which was all the worse because it marked a reversal of the roles to which the British had been accustomed for many a year.

Yet as the indignation subsided, there were signs that the British were relieved rather than dismayed by the substance of de Gaulle's action, whatever they thought of his manner. Public opinion polls were already showing a majority against entry to the EEC before de Gaulle intervened. After the event, Lord Chandos wrote to Lord Avon (the former Anthony Eden) that he felt like a man who had decided that it would be good for his health if he went for a swim in the Serpentine on Christmas Day; but when he arrived, with teeth chattering, he found a notice saying 'Bathing prohibited'.[35] The private correspondence of one member of the House of Lords with another may not usually represent the feeling of the nation, but this probably did so. French historians have noted the element of relief in British reactions. Pierre Gerbet hard-headedly attributed it to fear of high food prices in the EEC, but that certainly underrates the intangible sentiments at work.[36]

De Gaulle's rejection of the British application to the EEC marked a dramatic breach in relations between France and Britain. It had been clear from the start that the fate of the negotiation lay with France. The verdict when finally delivered came with wounding harshness. The British people may have been relieved to be prevented from doing something they did not particularly want to do anyway, but

33. Ibid., p. 447.
34. Beloff, *The General Says No*, p. 7.
35. Quoted in David Dutton, 'Anticipating Maastricht: The Conservative Party and Britain's First Application to join the European Community', *Contemporary Record*, vol. 7, No. 3, p. 537. The whole article is a valuable exposition of the issues.
36. Pierre Gerbet, *La construction de l'Europe* (Paris, 1983), p. 311.

they resented the way de Gaulle had gone about it. Politically, the rejection was gravely damaging to Macmillan's government, which staggered on for a few months, but without conviction. Macmillan had staked all on entry to the EEC, and after his failure he visibly lost his grip. Soon afterwards, his administration foundered miserably in the quagmire of the Profumo–Christine Keeler affair – which incidentally allowed the French to marvel, not for the first or last time, at British attitudes towards the sexual morality of their politicians. But the fatal blow had been delivered not by Profumo but by de Gaulle. Has there been any other occasion when a French ruler has destroyed a British government? If so, it has certainly never been done on television.

Across the Channel, relations between France and Germany grew steadily closer. The Treaty of Paris signed by de Gaulle and Adenauer on 22 January 1963 laid down that there should be regular meetings (twice a year) between the President of the Republic and the Federal Chancellor, and their ministers, to discuss foreign and defence policy, cultural affairs, and education. The most far-reaching clause provided for consultation between the two governments before either reached any important foreign policy decision, so that their actions should correspond as far as possible. If carried through to its logical conclusion, this would have meant the evolution of a joint foreign policy. In the event, the West German Parliament, when ratifying the treaty, added references to the North Atlantic Treaty and relations with the United States which took much of the force out of the original wording. But most of the treaty remained intact, and so did the intentions behind it. Adenauer remarked to Brandt, the German Social Democrat leader, shortly after signing the treaty: 'Look, what is Europe? First and foremost, France and us. And things are going well. If the British make a third, there's no certainty that they'll continue to do so.'[37] The need to prepare two meetings each year (and sometimes three) brought French and German officials constantly together. Cultural and educational exchanges, well organised and liberally financed, produced a network of contacts which in the long run had substantial effects. The Franco-German Youth Office set up under the treaty organised exchanges by some 300,000 French and Germans each year in the early part of its existence; in the first 25 years, the total numbers reached about 5 million.[38] The myriad contacts which were thus nourished may well have produced more results than the somewhat artificial device of a joint foreign policy would have done.

37. Julius W. Friend, *The Linchpin. French-German Relations; 1950–1990* (New York, 1991), p. 39.
38. Ibid., pp. 41–2.

In any case, through constant consultation and the cultivation of common interests, a Franco-German directorate within the EEC developed as the years went by.

De Gaulle's wounding dismissal of Great Britain and his careful promotion of relations with West Germany stood in striking contrast. In the triangle made up by Britain, France and Germany, there was no doubt in 1963 as to which formed the couple and which was the odd man out.

CHAPTER 10

To Join or Not to Join?
Britain, France and the EEC,
1963–1969

DE GAULLE'S DETERMINATION

For some five years after imposing his veto on British entry into the EEC, de Gaulle led France firmly, and sometimes spectacularly, along his chosen routes. French policies were imposed upon the EEC. France withdrew from the integrated command systems of NATO. France pursued its independent path in building and testing nuclear weapons. De Gaulle assumed the role of world statesman, travelling far and wide and speaking as his voices moved him – often more the prophet than the politician. Repeatedly, in these various aspects of his policy, de Gaulle opposed British interests or offended British sentiments.

Within the EEC, the French insisted on the development of the Common Agricultural Policy in ways favourable to themselves. In 1963, West Germany was reluctant to press on with applying the CAP without assurances that the Community would adopt a more liberal policy on external trade in negotiations on the General Agreement on Tariffs and Trade (the GATT). De Gaulle bargained very toughly on this issue, striking a deal which set a lowering of the common external tariff on industrial imports (which suited the Germans) against acceptance of the agricultural policy (which suited the French). Under these arrangements, the CAP was steadily implemented: 1964 saw agreement on common prices for cereals, pig meat, poultry and eggs; 1968 on prices for beef and milk products; 1969 for olive oil; and 1970 for wine and tobacco. These measures offered France, as the principal agricultural producer among the Six, the advantages of a large market protected against imports from outside the Community. From the EEC arrangements in general, all member states benefited.

Between 1958 and 1970, trade within the EEC increased six-fold; trade with outside countries tripled; and the gross national product of the Six together increased by 70 per cent.[1] It was a golden age of prosperity and economic growth.

In 1965–66 France imposed its own concept of the development of the Community as a whole by means of a theatrical display of resolution. According to the Treaty of Rome, a number of issues for which the EEC Council of Ministers was responsible (including, for example, aspects of the Community Budget) were to become subject to majority voting with effect from 1 January 1966. The French government refused to accept these changes, and from June 1965 onwards ceased to attend EEC meetings (except for the Committee on the Common Agricultural Policy, where French representatives continued to appear). This policy of the so-called 'empty chair' (which meant that nothing significant could be done in the Community, because important decisions required unanimous support) was pursued until January 1966, when a meeting of Foreign Ministers in Luxembourg reached a form of agreement. Where the procedures for majority voting applied to questions involving very important national interests, the Council of Ministers should try to reach unanimous decisions within a reasonable time; but it was noted that the French delegation considered that in such cases the discussion should continue until unanimous agreement was in fact reached. This meant that the concept of majority voting was maintained in principle, and so the letter of the Treaty of Rome was observed. On the other hand, the French reserved the right to veto any decision by the Council of Ministers which affected vital French interests; and by implication other states could do the same. This was politely called 'the Luxembourg Compromise', and meant in effect that the French had got their way.[2]

De Gaulle thus used characteristically forceful methods to impose his own concepts upon the EEC. Almost immediately afterwards he acted with equal determination to redefine the position of France within the North Atlantic Treaty. In March 1966 he announced that France intended to withdraw from the Treaty Organisation, and notably the integrated commands, while still adhering to the Treaty and remaining a member of the alliance. The NATO military headquarters, established in Paris, was to move to another country by

1. Pierre Gerbet, *La construction de l'Europe* (Paris, 1983), pp. 256–7.
2. For explanations of the Luxembourg Compromise, see William Nicoll and Trevor C. Salmon, *Understanding the New European Community* (London, 1994), pp. 34–5; Monica Charlot and Jean-Claude Sergeant, *Britain and Europe since 1945* (Paris, 1986), pp. 68–9.

April 1967. The distinction between the Treaty and the Organisation, though plain in de Gaulle's eyes, was not always obvious or acceptable to others, and the Americans were astonished and angered by the French decision.

At the same time, the French continued on their independent path as a nuclear power. France did not adhere to the Test Ban Treaty signed in Moscow in August 1963 by the Soviet Union, the United States and Great Britain. Instead, they went ahead with their own programme of nuclear testing at Muraroa Atoll in the Pacific, where de Gaulle went to watch the first explosion in September 1966.

France thus declared semi-independence from NATO, and from the United States. On the nuclear issue, de Gaulle was prepared to stand against the world. In his world travels, the General followed his own distinctive course, and expressed his own highly individual views. One of his journeys took him to Canada, where in Montreal on 24 July 1967 he cried to a vast crowd: 'Vive le Québec! Vive le Québec libre!' It was an astonishing intervention by a visiting head of state in the affairs of another country, and one which de Gaulle himself would not have tolerated for an instant from a visitor to France.

All these Gaullian actions affected Britain, usually adversely. The development of the EEC was partly against British interests, in that the consolidation of the Common Agricultural Policy moved the Community steadily away from British agricultural policy. But for the British the worst aspect of de Gaulle's policy on the EEC was that he simply ignored them. Lord Gladwyn wrote in a book on *De Gaulle's Europe*, published in 1969, that the General acted as though 'the best way to *faire l'Europe* is to proceed as if she [Britain] were not there'.[3] As to NATO, the British were fully committed to both the Treaty and the integrated command, and thought that the two were too closely bound up to be separated. On nuclear testing, Macmillan regarded the Test Ban Treaty of 1963 as one of the principal achievements of his foreign policy, and both he and his successors were dismayed to see the treaty ignored by the French. De Gaulle's speech in Montreal was primarily an offence against the Canadian government, but it was also an affront to Britain, where links with Canada were still close, and the monarch was Queen of Canada as well as of the United Kingdom. Everywhere it appeared that de Gaulle pursued a policy which was either directly anti-British or at the least indifferent to British susceptibilities.

3. Lord Gladwyn, *De Gaulle's Europe; or why the General Says No* (London, 1969), p. 92.

BRITISH HESITATIONS

At any rate there could be no doubt as to the drive and impetus of French policy. De Gaulle acted with determination and panache, if sometimes with dubious wisdom or discretion. The British, on the other hand, were uncertain and hesitant. In the last year of Macmillan's government, he was almost without a European policy. A Conservative Party official remarked later that joining the EEC was intended to be the government's great stroke, to carry the country forward and enable the party to win the next general election. 'It was Macmillan's ace, and de Gaulle trumped it.'[4] Douglas-Home, Macmillan's successor, had no time to work out a new policy before holding a general election in October 1964. Labour won that election by a narrow margin, and then went to the country again in March 1966, gaining a convincing victory.

The new Prime Minister, Harold Wilson, was uncertain about European policy. The official line of the Labour Party in August 1961 had been to abstain on the issue of a British application to join the EEC. In 1962 Hugh Gaitskell had come out emotionally against joining, but a significant minority of Labour MPs were keenly in favour. The question was always likely to divide the party, and Wilson's instinct was to try to avoid a split. As to his own views, one of his close advisers in later years, Bernard Donoughue, wrote that 'Wilson was always mildly anti-European'. He had no liking for travel on the continent, and always took his holidays in the Scilly Isles. He genuinely liked meat and two veg. and HP sauce. He believed that British parliamentary democracy was the best political system ever invented. He had a real affection for the Commonwealth. Philip Ziegler, his authorised biographer, writes that 'His love for the Commonwealth was romantic and traditional: he relished the idea of Britain at the heart of this great international network; [and] believed that it represented the surest way by which his country could remain among the foremost powers . . .'. His loyalty was particularly to the old white Dominions, but he also believed in the value of Britain's role in Africa and Asia.[5] In the conduct of policy, Wilson sought to maintain close relations with the United States and to continue the

4. D.E. Butler and Anthony King, *The British General Election of 1964* (London, 1965), p. 79.
5. Bernard Donoughue, 'Harold Wilson and the renegotiation of the EEC terms of membership, 1974–5', in Brian Brivati and Harriet Jones, eds, *From Reconstruction to Integration: Britain and Europe since 1945* (Leicester, 1993), p. 204; Philip Ziegler, *Harold Wilson* (London, 1993), p. 219.

British presence east of Suez. He still believed that Britain had a role to play as a world power.

All these preoccupations tended to turn Wilson's attention away from the EEC, but even in his dealings with the Commonwealth and the United States he found himself in difficulties with France. The main question facing him in Africa was that of Southern Rhodesia, which declared independence in 1965. Wilson announced the imposition of oil sanctions against the offending government led by Ian Smith, only to find Rhodesia drawing substantial supplies of oil from the French company Total. Relations with the United States were dominated by the war in Vietnam. The Prime Minister, despite much opposition in his own party and divided opinions in the country, maintained steady support for American policy in Vietnam – though carefully avoiding any intervention by British forces. De Gaulle, on the other hand, vehemently opposed the Americans, and criticised Wilson in private for taking their side.

Wilson thus had no enthusiasm for the EEC, and relations with France on other matters were difficult. The period between the general elections of October 1964 and March 1966 was in any case not one for great initiatives. In the election campaign of March 1966, Edward Heath (now leader of the Conservative Party) declared that he would try again to secure entry to the EEC. Wilson said that Britain should only try again if there was a good chance of success, and if the terms were favourable. 'Given a fair wind, we will negotiate our way into the Common Market, head held high, not crawl in.' He made fun of Heath for 'rolling on his back like a spaniel' at any sign of encouragement from Paris.[6] But he did not commit himself one way or the other.

During 1966 the pressures to try again for entry increased. The Commonwealth link, even though it was precious to Wilson personally and emotionally attractive to Labour because of its multi-racial appeal, was growing ever more tenuous in practical terms. Diplomatic and military cohesion had been in decline for several years, with the advance of neutralism among new Commonwealth countries. In 1965 it was the Soviet Union, not Britain, which intervened to mediate in a war between India and Pakistan, two members of the Commonwealth. British exports to the Commonwealth, which had made up about half the total of exports in 1951, amounted to just under one-third in 1967.[7] The

6. Ben Pimlott, *Harold Wilson* (London, 1992), p. 397.
7. Françoise de la Serre, *La Grande-Bretagne et la Communauté Européenne* (Paris, 1987), pp. 16–17. The whole passage on Wilson's conversion, pp. 16–20, is illuminating.

European Free Trade Area had proved advantageous, but British trade with the EFTA countries still grew less rapidly than with those of the EEC, despite the Community's external tariff. The Confederation of British Industry took the view that British industry needed better access to the markets of the EEC. Psychologically, there was a growing sense of uneasiness and isolation. Even Wedgwood Benn, who both earlier and later was a strong opponent of British entry, felt these doubts. He commented in his diary in January 1965 that defence, rockets, colour television and the Concorde aircraft project all showed that Britain alone could not stay 'in the big League'. The question was, 'do we go in with Europe or do we become an American satellite?' A sense of isolation was weighing upon him, despite his natural Little-Englandism.[8] For a time, Benn became an advocate of entry to the EEC. Paradoxically, the American argument cut both ways. For some, Europe was a refuge from American domination; but as in earlier years, the United States put pressure on Britain to join the EEC. Wilson's determination to maintain good relations with the USA, and his dependence on the Americans to sustain the value of sterling, made him susceptible to American advice.

The problems of sterling in mid-1966 helped to bring the question to a head. A strike by the National Union of Seamen which began in May 1966 caused a run on sterling, and raised the issue of devaluation. On 7 July, the French Premier (Pompidou) and Foreign Minister (Couve de Murville) visited London. In private discussions, Pompidou pointed out that, before the Treaty of Rome came into effect, France had found it necessary to introduce the 'new franc'. Publicly, the French ministers indicated to the press that devaluation of the pound would be necessary if Britain were to enter the EEC. Wilson for his part opposed devaluation, and accepted that support for the pound could only come from the Americans. George Brown, Minister for Economic Affairs, exclaimed, 'We've got to break with America, devalue and go into Europe!'[9] This put the matter too simply for others, who supported devaluation while opposing entry to the EEC. Even so, the sterling crisis which persisted into the autumn, and the balance of payments difficulties which lay behind it, demonstrated that some new solution to Britain's economic problems was needed. Entry to the EEC offered a possible way out.

8. Tony Benn, *Out of the Wilderness: Diaries, 1963–1967* (London, 1987), p. 204.
9. Pimlott, *Wilson*, p. 433.

WILSON TRIES AGAIN

By October 1966 Wilson had made up his mind to try for entry. At a meeting of Cabinet ministers and senior officials at Chequers on 22 October he secured agreement to a plan by which he and George Brown (now Foreign Secretary) would visit the various EEC capitals to sound out the prospects. On 10 November the Prime Minister told the House of Commons that the government would make an approach 'to see whether the conditions exist – or do not exist – for fruitful negotiations . . .'. He said that they had 'the clear intention and determination to enter the EEC if, as we hope, our essential British and Commonwealth interests can be safeguarded. We mean business'.[10] However, he refrained from saying that Britain was actually renewing her application.

Wilson and Brown then set out on their travels. Fundamentally the situation had not changed since January 1963, and everyone knew that the key lay in Paris, with General de Gaulle. The British ministers met de Gaulle on 24 January 1967. The General spoke of the difficulties involved in a British application, but did not specifically declare that he would reject it. Wilson, who as Ben Pimlott has written, 'found it hard to be a half-hearted salesman', embarked on his tour a lukewarm advocate of British entry, but returned 'tolerably hot'.[11] On 30 April the Cabinet, though divided, agreed to make a formal application. On 2 May Wilson told the House of Commons of this decision. On 8 May he explained that this was not a matter involving a European federation: '. . . the federal momentum towards a supranational Europe in which all issues of foreign policy and defence policy, for example, would be settled by majority voting, for the time being at least, has died away'. British opinion, he believed, 'would not contemplate any rapid move to a federal Europe'.[12] This issue was to assume considerable importance in later British dealings with the EEC, and with France.

On 16 May de Gaulle held a press conference in Paris. He raised a number of familiar objections to British entry. Britain was still not a truly European power, and would act as a Trojan horse for the Americans. Sterling's role as a reserve currency would differentiate it from other European currencies. The British economy was not yet strong enough to sustain membership. He set out three possible

10. Hansard, *H.C. Deb.*, 5th series, vol. 735, cols 1539–40.
11. Pimlott, *Wilson*, p. 439.
12. Hansard, *H.C. Deb.*, 5th series, vol. 746, col. 1093.

courses: first, to do away with the EEC in its existing form, and replace it by a new free-trade organisation; second, to create a form of association with the EEC for Britain and other candidates from EFTA; and third, to wait until Britain had achieved the profound changes which were necessary for her to become a member of the EEC as at present constituted. Strictly speaking, he did not declare that he would repeat his veto of January 1963, but effectively he left his position in no doubt.

At this stage, it must be a matter for wonder that Wilson chose to persist. It would admittedly have been hard to withdraw, but the Prime Minister was a skilled political tactician. To press on was to expose Britain, as a sympathetic French historian has put it, to 'the intolerable humiliation of a new French veto'.[13] Wilson went to see de Gaulle in Paris on 18 June (the anniversary of Waterloo, and of the General's broadcast from London in 1940). By Wilson's own account, de Gaulle spent a long time talking about American policy in Vietnam and British support for it. He wondered aloud whether it was possible for Britain to follow any policy except that of the United States. If the British were to separate themselves from the Americans in matters of defence, and of policy throughout the world, then a new situation would arise. The inference seemed obvious: that as long as Britain was tied to the United States, she was not acceptable as a member of the EEC. But Wilson kept his hopes alive. He estimated that de Gaulle would use all the delaying tactics at his command, but ultimately no longer had the strength to keep Britain out; though he acknowledged that this was a dangerous prophecy. He looked forward to a further meeting with de Gaulle, and prepared a present for the occasion. At a lighter moment during their conversations, the two had discussed the ethics of cheating at patience, and Wilson commissioned a special pack of patience cards, embossed with the fleur de lys, to give to the General when they next met.[14]

It appears that this optimism was grounded in the hope that the British case was so strong that no reasonable man could reject it, and that the other five members of the EEC could prevail on de Gaulle to change his mind. The British government indeed adopted a very different position from that taken up in 1961. George Brown set out the British conditions to the EEC Council of Ministers on 4 July 1967. There was no longer any question of requesting substantial changes to the Treaty of Rome. The British government declared itself

13. Roland Marx, *Histoire de l'Angleterre* (Paris, 1993), p. 690.
14. Pimlott, *Wilson*, p. 441; Ziegler, *Wilson*, p. 335. The cards were saved as a present for de Gaulle's 80th birthday, which he did not quite attain.

ready to accept the Common Agricultural Policy, though requesting changes in the way the costs were distributed among member states. Instead of asking for guaranteed outlets in the EEC for a wide range of Commonwealth products, as in 1962, they now requested guarantees only for New Zealand dairy products and West Indian sugar. They no longer sought exemption from the common external tariff for various raw materials imported from Commonwealth countries, but declared their willingness to accept the common tariff as amended by current negotiations on the General Agreement on Tariffs and Trade. (This was the so-called 'Kennedy Round' of negotiations, continuing long after President Kennedy's death.) On behalf of certain Commonwealth countries in Africa and the West Indies, Britain requested only that they should be associated with the EEC on the same terms as those relating to former French colonies in Africa. As to the members of the European Free Trade Area, Britain proposed that states which did not join the EEC should be allowed a year of transitional arrangements to prepare for the change. In his speech presenting these proposals, George Brown also accepted that the EEC was a dynamic and changing organisation, and that it would exercise influence on political and defence matters as well as on economic affairs, thus offering at least a conciliatory gesture towards the political aspirations of the European movement.[15]

On 29 September 1967 the EEC Commission issued a formal statement, accepting that the adhesion of Britain (and three other candidates – Denmark, Ireland and Norway) could be advantageous to the Community, but observing that Britain would need to stabilise its economy, resolve its balance of payments problems, and reassess the international role of sterling. It was painfully clear, from the terms of both the British application and of the Commission's comments, that Britain was negotiating from a position of weakness.

Negotiations began, and while they were in progress the British government was finally compelled to devalue the pound. The French had earlier recommended this step, and it might have been expected to ease the path of negotiation. But the opposite proved true. De Gaulle took devaluation as further proof of British weakness. This time, as distinct from the long delays in 1962, he did not spin things out. At a press conference on 27 November he repeated his criticisms of the British economy, which would need to be much healthier to fit in with EEC rules. He declared that British entry in present conditions

---

15. See the lucid explanation of these complicated matters in Gerbet, *Europe*, pp. 335–6.

would lead to the degeneration of the EEC into a mere free-trade area. Britain would have to undergo a profound change before being ready for membership. Meanwhile, some form of association or commercial agreement might be arranged. The rebuff was less dramatic, and much less startling, than in January 1963, but in many ways worse for Britain for being more condescending. At best, associate status would have put Britain on the same level as Greece or Turkey; at worst, on that of the former French colonies. It was as though an old-fashioned headmaster had delivered a deflating end-of-term report in public: 'Come back when you can do better.'

In his diary near the end of the year 1967 Hervé Alphand, who in earlier times had been compelled to negotiate financial arrangements with patronising British Treasury officials, indulged in some lofty reflections of his own. 'One day, doubtless, if she makes the necessary effort, England will join Europe. She will have to balance her budget, reform her old habits, get her workers to work, relax her ties with the Commonwealth. It is a profound transformation, but each country must make her own sacrifices and no-one else can do it for her.'[16] On the other side of the Channel, several years later, one of Harold Wilson's biographers, Ben Pimlott, wrote sadly of 'the spectacle of the British Prime Minister trailing round Europe with a begging bowl'.[17] The dreary replay of the British attempt to join the EEC, ending with the same public rejection by de Gaulle, was indeed an occasion for gloomy reflections on the state of relations between France and Britain.

For a short time Wilson tried hard not to take 'No' for an answer. He insisted that the British application for membership still stood. He tried to persuade the other five EEC members to put pressure on de Gaulle to change his mind. In January 1968 he sought to isolate the French by proposing discussions between the Five and the four aspirants to EEC membership (Britain, Denmark, Ireland and Norway) on subjects not formally within the remit of the European Community. This made no headway, largely because the Franco-German axis proved solid, and Germany would attempt nothing which might lead to difficulties with France. The Six held firmly together.

In the latter part of 1967 Britain had devalued the pound and been rejected as an applicant to the EEC. In January 1968 the Prime Minister announced that British forces would shortly be withdrawn from Malaysia, Singapore and the Persian Gulf, marking the end of the

16. Hervé Alphand, *L'étonnement d'être: Journal, 1939–1973* (Paris, 1977), p. 494.
17. Pimlott, *Wilson*, p. 443.

military role east of Suez which was the most obvious remnant of the old British Empire, and which Wilson himself had previously claimed to be vital. Shortly after he took office in October 1964 Wilson had declared that 'We are a world power, and a world influence, or we are nothing'.[18] At the beginning of 1968 it was painfully clear that Britain was no longer a world influence, and on Wilson's own reckoning nothing was left as an alternative. It seemed that Britain had found the opposite of the Midas touch, so that everything she touched turned to dross. France, on the other hand, seemed to have achieved economic prosperity, self-confidence, and a prominent role in world affairs. De Gaulle, figuratively as well as literally, stood head and shoulders above those around him.

THE EVENTS OF MAY 1968 IN FRANCE AND THE 'SOAMES AFFAIR'

The events of May 1968 brought a drastic change. Suddenly, in face of a student revolt which no-one understood, the French government was unable to control parts of its own capital. De Gaulle himself was tired, depressed and badly shaken. Unable to respond to events, he vanished for several hours on 29 May, not just from Paris but from the ken of his ministers, taking counsel with General Massu at Baden-Baden – an extraordinary recourse. It is true that de Gaulle then recovered his nerve. He called a general election at the end of June, winning an overwhelming right-wing majority in the Assembly. Calm was apparently restored. But the reality was different. Hervé Alphand, so confident at the end of 1967, was drawing gloomy conclusions as early as 19 May. Everything was at risk: France's position in the world, the value of the franc, the future of the EEC, the shape of French society. 'We are living through a sort of nightmare . . .' He added on the 25th: 'The English are making fun of us and taking their revenge for the arrogance of certain over-confident Frenchmen.'[19] He might well have counted himself among those who had been over-confident, and he was right to think that there were those in Britain who were not sorry to see de Gaulle in trouble. Many of the old British beliefs about French instability and propensity to revolution came back into prominence.

18. Quoted in David Reynolds, *Britannia Overruled: British Policy and World Power in the Twentieth Century* (London, 1991), p. 226.
19. Alphand, *Etonnement*, pp. 504–5.

The damage to France was serious. A part of the Gaullist miracle had been psychological, the effect of de Gaulle's own prestige and national self-confidence. Suddenly the prestige was punctured and the self-confidence lost. De Gaulle himself told ministers on 19 May that they had lost in five days the gains of ten years of 'struggle against idiocy'.[20] Some of the economic gains too were imperilled by increases in wages, which in turn raised production costs. By the autumn of 1968 French exports were in decline and the exchange value of the franc falling. By November, devaluation seemed certain, and even the German government pressed for it. A meeting of Finance Ministers of leading western countries in Bonn on 20–22 November agreed to offer large credits to France, on the assumption of devaluation. In the event, de Gaulle – for whom the exchange value of the franc was a matter of national prestige – refused to devalue. For a time his will prevailed, but the economic problems that had caused the crisis remained, and nine months later his successor had to devalue.

It was in the aftermath of these events that de Gaulle turned towards Britain in what was at least a change of attitude, and perhaps a tentative change of policy. It has entered the history of Franco-British relations under the name of the 'Soames Affair'; though in fact Sir Christopher Soames seems to have done no more than carry out his duties as Ambassador in Paris. The affair presents one of those puzzles which will keep historians fascinated for years and is far from being resolved; but the main events and their effects are clear enough.

On 4 February 1969 President de Gaulle and his wife entertained the Ambassador and Lady Soames *à quatre* at the Elysée. It was an informal affair, and de Gaulle went out of his way to talk to Lady Soames about the history of the *Allée des Cygnes*, and what an excellent place it was for walking dogs. After the ladies left, de Gaulle kept the Ambassador for a long talk about Europe and Franco-British relations. The General said that it might be possible to hold direct and confidential discussions to clear up some of the economic and monetary problems between France and Britain. If that could be done, de Gaulle indicated that he would be willing to consider transforming the EEC (which he had not himself constructed) into a much looser organisation in which Britain and the other three EFTA applicants could find a place. In political and military matters, France, Britain, West Germany and Italy might assume a leading position and co-ordinate their policies. (According to some accounts, de Gaulle

---

20. Charles Williams, *The Last Great Frenchman: A Life of General de Gaulle* (London, 1993), p. 463.

used the word 'directorate' in this connection.) Discussions on these matters would have to include all the parties concerned, but they could begin with direct and secret talks between France and Britain.

It is not clear what exactly de Gaulle had in mind. The idea of loosening up the EEC certainly appears to be a marked departure from his position during the two British applications to join the Community. It is possible to see his approach (as Charles Williams does) as presaging a real change of policy, harking back to his talk with Churchill in November 1944 and the idea of close Franco-British co-operation. Pierre Maillard, on the other hand, with a close knowledge of de Gaulle's mind, especially on relations with Germany, thinks that the President intended no more than to take soundings. But at least the nature of the occasion was utterly different from de Gaulle's earlier diplomacy by press conference – it was an oasis in what had become a distinctly bleak desert of relations between France and Britain.

Soames prepared an account of this conversation, checked it with Bernard Tricot (Secretary-General at the Elysée) and with Michel Debré (the Foreign Minister), and sent it to London. There, it appears that the Foreign Secretary, Michael Stewart, suspected a trap. If the British accepted the idea of confidential discussions, de Gaulle could expose them to the Germans as willing to do a deal with France in secret; if they declined, he could claim that they had turned down a chance to improve Franco-British relations. By some accounts, Harold Wilson at first wished to take up de Gaulle's proposal, but followed instead Stewart's advice to reveal the approach to the Germans. Whatever the truth of this (and it would scarcely be surprising if de Gaulle's behaviour in 1963 and 1967 had left a legacy of distrust), there is no dispute as to what happened next. Wilson was already due to visit Chancellor Kiesinger of West Germany on 11–12 February. On the 12th, in the course of this visit, he gave Kiesinger an account of what de Gaulle had said.

Later on the same day, Soames called on Hervé Alphand, the Secretary-General at the Quai d'Orsay, and told him that the British government found de Gaulle's suggestions very interesting and was ready to discuss them. He added that Wilson had found it necessary to inform Chancellor Kiesinger of the matter. Alphand replied that de Gaulle's original proposal had been for confidential conversations between Britain and France. The reply that France had been expecting had in fact been made to the German Chancellor, and the project had been gravely compromised.

That proved to be a masterly understatement. Within a few days the British Foreign Office gave the press an account of Soames's conversation with de Gaulle (a step which a British diplomat present in Paris at the time has described as 'perhaps without precedent in British history'[21]), accompanied by 'guidance' to the effect that de Gaulle seemed to be considering breaking up both the EEC and NATO. De Gaulle was furious, and Soames found himself denied even an interview with the French Premier.

Taken in its best light, de Gaulle's original conversation on 4 February might have opened the way to friendly and serious contacts between the French and British governments. Adherence to the old-fashioned rules of secret diplomacy as practised at the time when the *Entente* was negotiated in 1902–4 might at least have revealed what was actually intended. Instead, the whole affair ended in a dreadful public quarrel. Jean Lacouture, in his massive biography of de Gaulle, was sure that the British, through Wilson's disclosures to Kiesinger and the Foreign Office briefings to the press, were taking revenge for the snubs administered by the General at his press conferences in January 1963 and November 1967 – 'acts of revenge', wrote Lacouture, 'that only very old families and very old diplomatic services are capable of exacting'. Nicholas Soames, the Ambassador's son, has said publicly that Wilson and the Foreign Office were responsible for a terrible blunder, which led his father to offer to resign. Philip Ziegler, on the other hand, regards the British attitude as entirely justified on grounds of both morality and politics. It was a tangled tale, and more will yet be heard about it. But as to its immediate consequences there was no room for doubt. Relations between French and British governments were in a grievous state. Charles Williams may be left with the umpire's last word. 'It was now clear, once and for all, that relations between the two countries would never improve while the General was in power. The bitterness and suspicion, accumulated over ten years, was too great an obstacle. Better relations would have to await de Gaulle's successor.'[22]

---

21. Bernard Ledwidge, *De Gaulle* (London, 1982), p. 366.
22. This account of the 'Soames Affair' is taken from: Ledwidge, *De Gaulle*, pp. 363–7; Williams, *Last Great Frenchman*, pp. 479–80; Jean Lacouture, *De Gaulle: The Ruler* (London, pb edn, 1993), pp. 474–7; Pierre Maillard, *De Gaulle et l'Allemagne* (Paris, 1990), pp. 259–64; Alphand, *Etonnement*, pp. 517–19; Maurice Couve de Murville, *Une politique étrangère, 1958–1969* (Paris, 1971), pp. 427–9; Ziegler, *Wilson*, pp. 336–7; Charles Powell, 'Entente Cordiale', transcript of BBC broadcast, 22 Sept. 1994, pp. 25–6.

CHAPTER 11

Britain Joins the Club – With Second Thoughts, 1969–1975

POMPIDOU AND HEATH

De Gaulle's successor was Georges Pompidou, who was elected President of the Republic in June 1969. A year later, in June 1970, Wilson too had a successor, when the Conservatives won the general election and Edward Heath became Prime Minister. For a short period, these two were to bring about a marked improvement in relations between France and Britain.

The central issue remained that of British entry to the EEC, which Pompidou was prepared to accept, largely in order to counterbalance the growing influence of West Germany. But he was in no hurry. Any attempt at British entry must follow a further consolidation of the EEC, to strengthen the foundations already laid and to confirm the advantages that France had secured from the Community. Pompidou's policy for the EEC, and therefore indirectly for relations with Britain, took the shape of a three-fold formula: completion, deepening and enlargement.

Completion meant specifically the settlement of the method of financing the Common Agricultural Policy. This task was made both more urgent and more difficult by the French government's action in devaluing the franc by 12.5 per cent on 8 August 1969. This step, narrowly avoided in 1968, was prepared in the utmost secrecy, without consulting other EEC governments. To counteract some of the effects of devaluation on agricultural prices, the French government introduced provisional taxes and subsidies on external trade in agricultural products, designed to cushion French consumers and farmers against the price changes brought about by devaluation. France took these actions quite independently of the EEC, and in reply the West German government first allowed the mark to float, and then (24 October) revalued the currency upwards by 9.29 per cent. They too put a tax on agricultural imports.[1] These sudden changes in exchange rates and taxes disturbed the system of common prices which was basic to the working of the CAP, and endangered the whole structure that had been so carefully built up.

It was therefore particularly urgent for EEC members to arrive at a system for financing the Common Agricultural Policy. A conference at The Hague in December 1969 laid the groundwork, and the details were completed by April 1970. The method adopted was as follows. Imports of agricultural products from outside the EEC were already subject to a levy. Ninety per cent of the proceeds of these levies, together with 1 per cent of Value Added Tax (VAT) raised throughout the EEC, was to be placed in a Community Budget to finance the CAP. These arrangements were to be phased in over a period of eight years, ending in 1978, when the Common Agricultural Policy would be financed from the Community's 'own resources'. This was bound to raise, at some stage, the question of control over the Community Budget. National parliaments were responsible for national contributions, but who was to control the new 'own resources', and their use?

The EEC thus moved towards 'completion' by consolidating the Common Agricultural Policy, which was always an important French interest. There was also some talk of 'deepening', in inconclusive discussions of political co-operation, monetary union and joint projects in technology. The Hague conference also agreed on the possibility of the enlargement of the Community (which meant in practice the admission of Britain), but only on certain conditions laid down by the French. Agreement on financing the CAP was to be reached in advance of any enlargement; this was achieved in April 1970. In negotiations for the admission of other states, the Six were to act together, adopting a common position which could not be changed without the consent of all the members. In principle this gave a veto to each government among the Six. In practice, recent history showed that this veto was most likely to be used by the French.

Thus Pompidou edged towards a position where he might open the door for British entry into the EEC. After two rebuffs, it was not absolutely certain whether Britain would wish to go through it, but the fact remained that both the major political parties had made the attempt – the Conservatives under Macmillan, Labour under Wilson.

1. Pierre Gerbet, *La construction de l'Europe* (Paris, 1983), p. 351; Hervé Alphand, *L'étonnement d'être: Journal, 1939–1973* (Paris, 1977), p. 525.

The weight of arguments and events pressed in that direction, even if there were few enthusiasts for the European cause. The election of June 1970 brought one of those enthusiasts, Edward Heath, into office as Prime Minister. Heath, unlike Wilson, appeared to have no senti-mental ties with the Commonwealth, and he had grown weary of African and Asian politicians lecturing the British about racism. He was also alone among post-war Prime Ministers in showing little interest in the 'special relationship' with the United States. In these rather negative ways, the decks were clear; but there was more to Heath's position than that. His experience in negotiating terms for British entry in 1961–62, though fruitless at the time, had inspired in him a fixed determination to succeed another time. John Campbell, his recent biographer, interprets this resolve as arising essentially from a desire to reassert British leadership in Europe and even the world – Europe was 'an opportunity for Britain to be "great" again'.[2] But his commitment went deeper still, through a European idealism held with a passion remarkable in an apparently cold and aloof personality. Much later, in a debate on the Maastricht Treaty in 1992, Heath was to remark that he could not see why people were afraid of federalism – after all, Britain had originated two of the most successful federations in the world, Canada and Australia.[3] This recognition that he was prepared to see Britain as a sort of Queensland in a federal Europe was not his stated position in 1970, but it may be that the germ of this aspiration was already present.

Strictly speaking, Heath's government did not have to take a fresh decision to apply for entry to the EEC. The previous application, as Wilson and George Brown had always insisted, had never been withdrawn. On the EEC side, the ground for enlargement was being prepared in discussion between the Six in the first half of 1970. The procedure adopted by the Six at the Hague conference, to reach an agreed position before any negotiation with the British, allowed little scope for subsequent flexibility; for who would risk changing an agreement reached after six months of arduous discussion? However, Heath's government opened technical discussions almost at once, in July 1970.

The British team was led by Geoffrey Rippon, who assumed the role that Heath had played with such patience in 1961–62. Alphand, for whom the British could now do almost nothing right, dismissed

---

2. John Campbell, *Edward Heath: A Biography* (London, 1993), pp. 334–5.
3. Speech quoted in ibid., pp. 799–800.

Rippon's opening statement as an attempt to set the price which the Six must pay 'so that these good Englishmen should deign to join us'.[4]

The detailed negotiations dealt with imports of Commonwealth foodstuffs, fishing rights, British contributions to the Community Budget, and the role of sterling as a reserve currency. On foodstuffs, the long lists of 1961–62 had now effectively come down to two: sugar and butter. Britain imported large quantities of cane sugar from the West Indies; France, with a high domestic production of beet sugar, wanted those imports restricted. Britain imported about 400,000 tons of New Zealand butter each year, amounting to 85 per cent of New Zealand butter production, and by coincidence roughly the same tonnage as the excess production of butter in the EEC. The British wanted special arrangements to safeguard New Zealand exports of butter; the French sought to limit the duration of such arrangements. On fish, the Six were in the process of negotiating a Common Fisheries Policy. If Britain were to enter the EEC, British waters would contain an estimated 60 per cent of the EEC total (insofar as such things can be measured); and the Six wanted the quota allocated to British fishermen to amount to no more than 30 per cent of the annual catch.

On the Community Budget, the British delegation opened by proposing a contribution of 3 per cent of the total; France proposed 21 per cent, payable immediately upon entry, with no period of transition. On sterling, the French Finance Minister, Giscard d'Estaing, declared publicly in March 1971 that the maintenance of sterling as a reserve currency would mean that the pound would remain different in character from other EEC currencies, and so present an obstacle to economic and monetary union. The British were prepared to diminish the role of sterling as a reserve currency, and to run down the sterling balances held in London for other countries, but to do so only over a period of time. They tried to keep this complicated question – a matter of prestige as well as finance – out of the negotiations.[5]

These detailed issues kept the negotiators hard at work, and their efforts showed some results. At the beginning of May 1971 the French made concessions on sugar imports in return for a British quid pro quo on farm prices. A compromise was agreed on the British contribution to the Community Budget. This was to start at 8.6 per cent of the total, well below the French proposal of 21 per cent, but rise over five

4. Alphand, *Etonnement*, p. 536.
5. Gerbet, *Europe*, pp. 367–8; Françoise de la Serre, *La Grande-Bretagne et la Communauté Européenne* (Paris, 1987), pp. 58–9; Campbell, *Heath*, pp. 354–5; Michael Spicer, *A Treaty Too Far* (London, 1992), p. 80.

years to 19 per cent, which was very near the French figure. However, as in 1961–62 and 1967, everyone knew that the fate of the British application did not rest with such details, but with France, and specifically with President Pompidou. Heath, who had in 1962 built an elaborate structure of agreements only to see it collapse at the touch of de Gaulle's veto, understood this very well. The centre-piece of his policy, and the heart of his deeply felt personal aspirations, lay in the hands of the French President.

It was generally believed that Pompidou was in favour of British entry. He had been disconcerted by the rise in German influence at the end of the 1960s. Germany had been less affected than France by the disturbances of 1968; German conduct in the currency crisis of November 1968 had been unhelpful; and France now lacked the asset of de Gaulle's massive personality and prestige. Even so, Pompidou was determined that British entry should not damage the existing workings of the EEC, or diminish the advantages that France secured from it. Above all, he needed to be assured that Britain was really committed to joining the Community as it was, and did not want to turn it into something else. As the French frequently put it, in terms which they felt were particularly applicable, the British must accept the rules of the club they were seeking to join.

All therefore depended on a meeting which took place between Pompidou and Heath on 20–21 May 1971. It was characteristic of the current state of relations between France and Britain that Heath had to make the journey, just as Macmillan had travelled to Champs and Rambouillet in 1962. Heath was the applicant, even the petitioner. It was a striking contrast to 1938, when Neville Chamberlain had put up Sir John Simon to cross-examine visiting French ministers, or 1946, when French governments had begged Britain for loans of wheat. The boot was now on the other foot.

Pompidou and Heath scarcely knew one another – they had met briefly on the occasion of the requiem mass for General de Gaulle, but that was all. They had some similarity in background, in that each had risen on merit and hard work – Pompidou the son of primary school teachers, Heath the grammar school boy. In that sense they were products of their time, while de Gaulle and Macmillan had represented an earlier age. But Heath's greatest asset when he went to meet Pompidou was his absolute belief in his mission. Pompidou wanted to be sure that Britain would accept the Treaty of Rome and the European idea. Heath was the man to convince him. Michel Jobert, the Secretary-General at the Elysée, wrote in his memoirs that shortly before the fateful meeting Pompidou asked him what Heath was like, and recalled his reply: 'upright and tenacious, even unshakeable, perfectly calm. And if you are right, he will admit as much'.[6]

The meetings proved a success. The two men talked for an immensely long time – some twelve hours in all over the two days, often with only interpreters present. They settled a number of points at issue in the detailed negotiations. A compromise was reached on New Zealand butter, and passed down to the delegations at Brussels. It was agreed that British sterling balances should be run down gradually, with no date set for ending the role of sterling as a reserve currency. (In the event, this issue settled itself in 1972, when Britain had to let the pound float in relation to other currencies; the abandonment of a fixed exchange rate effectively deprived sterling of its previous standing.) Heath took a vital psychological initiative by agreeing that, in the event of British entry, French should be retained as the working language of the Community. Pompidou attached great importance to this point, as part of the defence of *francophonie* against the advance of English – which on practical grounds had a strong claim to at least equality of status with French.

The two statesmen agreed that decisions within the EEC on matters involving vital national interests should continue to be taken unanimously. In this Pompidou remained the heir of General de Gaulle and stood by the 'Luxembourg compromise'. If Heath had any federalist aspirations at this stage, it was certainly no time to raise them. When he told the Commons about his talks with Pompidou, on 24 May, he reported that they had agreed that 'the identity of national states should be maintained in the framework of the developing Community'; and he added that 'joining the Community does not entail a loss of national identity or an erosion of essential national sovereignty'.[7]

After this agreement at the summit, terms were quickly agreed at Brussels. There could have been no clearer sign that the crux of the whole matter lay in relations between France and Britain. The same continued to be true in later years, and Britain's position within the EEC was seen very largely in terms of Franco-British relations. The presentation of the issues as the European Communities Bill was put to Parliament and passed through all its stages therefore assumes great importance.

The government set out the case for British entry to the EEC in a White Paper published on 6 July 1971. The political advantages were

6. Michel Jobert, *Mémoires d'avenir* (Paris, 1974), p. 184.
7. Hansard, *H.C. Deb.*, 5th series, vol. 818, cols 32–3.

presented in terms of British influence within Europe: to reject entry would be to refuse both the imperial past and the European future, and leave nothing in between. Economically, the White Paper looked forward to British access to the large-scale EEC market, without the handicap of the common external tariff. Since the creation of the Common Market the Six had enjoyed rapid economic growth; Britain had lost this opportunity in the past, and must seize it now. The cost of the British contribution to the Community Budget was estimated at about £100 million in the first year, rising to £200 million in the fifth year, if the structure of the Budget was not modified. Acceptance of the Common Agricultural Policy would bring an annual increase of 2.5 per cent in the cost of food over the transitional period, which was reckoned to amount to an increase of 0.5 per cent per year in the cost of living. There were problems here which were to create difficulties in the future, in that the costs were certain but the benefits speculative, and depended on British capacity to exploit the new position. The benefits also depended on economic circumstances which were of their nature unforeseeable; the White Paper tended to make the hopeful assumption that economic growth would continue unchecked.

A long debate in the House of Commons (21–28 October 1971) dealt mainly with economic issues, but also with the question of sovereignty. Clause II of the European Communities Bill stated that, in relevant matters, in the event of dispute between United Kingdom law and EEC law, the latter should prevail. From the Labour benches, Peter Shore pointed out that Parliament was being asked to accept in advance all kinds of regulations and directives, and also new taxes which would not go to the Treasury but to the European Commission. Enoch Powell quoted the Lord Chancellor, putting this in legal terms: 'the acceptance in advance as part of the law of the United Kingdom of provisions to be made in the future by instruments issued by the Community institutions'. Winding up for the government, Heath said it was right that there should have been discussion of sovereignty. 'I would put it very simply. If sovereignty exists to be used and to be of value, it must be effective . . . In joining we are making a commitment which involves our sovereignty, but we are also gaining an opportunity.' He did not say precisely what that commitment was.[8]

The vote on the First Reading took place on 28 October. The Conservatives were allowed a free vote. Harold Wilson, the Leader of the Opposition, was at first prepared to accept the same arrangement

8. Ibid., vol. 823, cols 1011–22 (Shore); 2186 (Powell); 2210 (Heath).

for Labour MPs, but eventually decided otherwise. The Labour Party therefore operated under a three-line whip instructing its MPs to vote against the Bill. The result was: for the Bill, 356; against, 244; a majority of 112. Superficially, this was a convincing majority, but it concealed much division and uncertainty. Thirty-nine Conservatives voted against (which despite the free vote still meant voting against their own government), and two abstained. Sixty-nine Labour members voted for the Bill, in defiance of the party whip, and 20 abstained.[9] At the Second and Third Readings, and during the scrutiny of the Bill in Committee, a very different pattern of voting emerged. The Prime Minister treated the passage of the Second Reading as a question of confidence, and won by 309–301, with 15 Conservatives voting against the government. There were 104 divisions during the Committee stage, with government majorities on occasion down to 4, 5, 8 and 11. On the Third Reading the vote was 301–284 – a majority of 17. Throughout the passage of the Bill, some Conservatives voted against, and the government majority was only assured by enough Labour members who supported entry to the EEC staying away from the House at crucial times.[10]

Both the major parties were divided on the issue. Only a small number of Conservatives took the extreme step of voting against the government, but they represented the tip of an iceberg of doubt. Labour was grievously divided, with a substantial minority of committed 'Europeans'. Wilson saw his main task as that of keeping the party together. In an interview on the tenth anniversary of his election to the Labour leadership, he 'openly argued that the issue was not Britain and Europe, but the future of Labour'.[11]

These details of British internal politics had considerable long-term effects on relations between Britain and France. It was dangerously easy for observers across the Channel to seize on the impressive majority of 112 on the principle of entry to the EEC. It seems that Pompidou genuinely thought, at least for a time, that the issue was settled. He took the wholly unnecessary step, not adopted in any of the other five member states of the EEC, of calling a referendum on the accession of Britain, in order to emphasise the importance of the event. The outcome was only partly encouraging, in that only 36 per cent of the electorate troubled to vote; though of the votes cast, 68 per cent were in favour.[12] In Britain, behind the symbolic act and the

---

9. Figures taken from Campbell, *Heath*, p. 404.
10. Ibid., pp. 438–40.
11. Ben Pimlott, *Harold Wilson* (London, 1992), pp. 600–1.
12. Figures in Gerbet, *Europe*, p. 375.

majority of 112 there lay the realities of divided parties and single-figure majorities in the House of Commons. In France, the referendum reflected a widespread indifference. On the night of 28 October 1971, when the first vote was taken in the Commons, Harold Macmillan (the first Prime Minister to attempt British entry to the EEC) lit a bonfire on the cliffs above Dover, answered by another fire at Calais. The symbolism was striking but misleading.

THE BRITISH HAVE SECOND THOUGHTS

The treaties providing for the entry of Britain to the EEC (together with Ireland and Denmark) were signed in Brussels on 22 January 1972, and came into force on 1 January 1973. The period of transition, for the phasing in of the new tariff system, the change to the Common Agricultural Policy, and the increase of British contributions to the Community Budget, was set at five years. The early years of this time of adaptation proved disastrous. Britain was struck by an intense economic and political crisis. In 1972 Heath tried for quick economic growth and rapid modernisation of industry to prepare for membership of the EEC. The result was a rise in the rate of inflation, and the floating of the pound in June 1972. There was a miners' strike in 1972, and another in 1973, which drove the government to declare a three-day week throughout industry to save fuel. Heath called an election at the end of February 1974, in which Labour achieved a narrow majority over the Conservatives. Heath's Premiership, which had begun with his success in entering the EEC, thus ended in failure at home. At the same time, disaster struck the whole of western Europe from outside. The outbreak of war between Egypt and Israel in October 1973 caused a sudden quadrupling of the price of oil (from $3 per barrel to $11–12), with severe results on all prices and on the balance of payments of every country dependent on oil imports. The economic effects on France and Britain were disastrous, and were all the worse in Britain because they coincided with the second miners' strike.

It is hard to imagine worse circumstances for the first years of British membership of the EEC. Even at the time of entry the country had shown little enthusiasm, except on the part of Heath himself and a few other committed 'Europeans'. Others had been impelled more by fear of exclusion than conviction of the virtues of membership. Kenneth Morgan has summed up the mood at the time of accession as 'one of wary acceptance, since no obvious alternative could be found'.[13] Amid the calamities of 1973–74 this mood turned actively against the EEC, which tended to be blamed for events for which it was only partially responsible. A public opinion poll taken in February 1974 showed that 54 per cent of respondents thought the EEC was responsible for rising prices, and another 34 per cent thought it was partly responsible; 58 per cent thought that Britain had been wrong to join the EEC.[14]

In France, the reaction to the oil crisis was different. On the domestic front, the country pressed ahead with the development of nuclear power stations, which in the long run diminished dependence on imported energy. Abroad, the French (long accustomed to working within the EEC) tried to develop a European response to the crisis. At the beginning of April 1974 President Pompidou died in office. In May Giscard d'Estaing was elected to succeed him, and proceeded to follow a policy based on commitment to Europe and good relations with Germany. He established a close partnership with Helmut Schmidt, who became Chancellor of West Germany in 1974. He regarded Britain, by comparison, as being of small significance. When Sir Nicholas Henderson became British Ambassador in Paris at the end of 1975, he formed the impression that Giscard believed that 'the age-long competitive struggle between France and the UK was over for good with France the victor'.[15] The period of accord between Heath and Pompidou, which saw British accession to the EEC, lasted no more than four years. In March 1974 Heath left office, never to return; in April Pompidou was dead.

At the beginning of March 1974 Harold Wilson formed a new Labour government. His Cabinet was deeply divided on the question of membership of the EEC, with about half the members on each side. Much the same was true among Labour MPs. Wilson himself wanted to stay in, but above all wanted to keep his party together. He produced, almost by sleight of hand, the idea of asking the EEC for a 'fundamental renegotiation' of the terms of entry, to be followed by a referendum. This proved to be a course which almost the whole party could accept.

13. Kenneth O. Morgan, *The People's Peace: British History, 1945–1990* (Oxford, pb edn, 1992), p. 342.

14. Françoise de la Serre, 'Européenne, mais . . .', in Alfred Grosser, ed., *Les politiques extérieures européennes dans la crise* (Paris, 1976), p. 145.

15. Nicholas Henderson, *Mandarin. The Diaries of an Ambassador, 1969–1982* (London, pb edn, 1995), p. 93.

Strictly speaking, the other members of the EEC could have refused the British request, on the grounds that the treaty of accession made no provision for later amendment. In practice they showed some flexibility, and were willing to make minor changes in order to retain British membership. Negotiations were completed at a European summit meeting at Dublin in March 1975, resulting in changes which were largely cosmetic rather than fundamental. The EEC guaranteed to purchase 1.4 million tons of West Indian sugar per year; and special arrangements for imports of New Zealand butter were to be maintained after the previous terminal date at the end of 1977. On the Common Agricultural Policy, however, where the British sought a change in pricing policy, to meet the needs of the consumer and to diminish surpluses, France opposed any significant change, and the only concession was an undertaking to re-examine the methods of the policy. The British asked for a reduction in their contributions to the Community Budget, to take account of their economic difficulties; and a 'corrective mechanism' was introduced to take account of each member's growth rate, gross national product and contribution to the Budget. Wilson described this as a great improvement; Giscard d'Estaing called it a minor adjustment. In practice, it appears that the three criteria never coincided in the way prescribed, so the mechanism had no effect. Finally, the British requested the creation of a new Regional Fund, from which they hoped to receive more than they contributed. This was accepted, though the resources allocated to the Regional Fund were small compared to those devoted to the Agricultural Fund.

The British government pronounced the renegotiation a success, and put the terms to the House of Commons on 9 April 1975. The vote was 398 votes in favour, 172 against, and 59 abstentions. Within the two main parties, the distribution of votes was curious:

	For	Against	Abstentions
Labour	137	145	33
Conservative	249	8	18

The government thus achieved a large majority in the House, but was supported by only a minority in its own party.[16]

There followed the referendum, held on 5 June 1975. The debate was muted, with the press overwhelmingly pro-EEC, and industry providing financial support for the 'Yes' campaign. The enthusiasts on

16. Figures in de la Serre, *La Grande-Bretagne et la Communauté Européenne*, p. 91.

the 'Yes' side (Heath among the Conservatives, Roy Jenkins on the Labour side) presented their case as that of modernity and progress. The leaders of the 'No' campaign were a heterogeneous collection, ranging from Enoch Powell on the Right to Michael Foot and Wedgwood Benn on the Left. The Prime Minister and the Leader of the Opposition (Margaret Thatcher, who had replaced Heath as leader of the Conservative Party) were on the 'Yes' side, without being among the enthusiasts. In the event, 64.5 per cent of the electorate voted, of whom 67.2 per cent voted Yes and only 32.8 per cent No. In terms of the votes cast, the result was decisive (approximately 17 million to 8 million).[17]

Yet the commitment of the country to the EEC remained curiously half-hearted. Turn-out in the referendum had been lower than at a general election. The Labour government had negotiated the new terms, yet did not receive the support of the majority of its own MPs when the new deal was put to the Commons. Labour was to fight the next three general elections (1979, 1983 and 1987) on a platform hostile to the EEC. Conservative opinion was more divided than the Commons vote of 9 April 1975 indicated. Britain remained half-hearted in its commitment to the EEC. France was unwaveringly European, and was steadily developing its links with West Germany. The new axis of Europe lay between Paris and Bonn.

TECHNOLOGICAL CO-OPERATION: CONCORDE AND THE CHANNEL TUNNEL

In 1967 Dorothy Pickles, an experienced observer of Franco-British relations, ended a book on the subject by speculating on the future of the *Entente*. The best she could suggest as a way forward was the possibility of co-operation in technology, notably in aeronautics, and specifically in the project to build a supersonic airliner – the Concorde.[18] The agreement to build this aircraft was signed between the two governments on 26 November 1962, while the first British application to join the EEC was still under way – though close to foundering. It was a complicated undertaking, based in principle on equality of responsibility between the two countries. It involved four companies: two British and two French. In each country, one

17. On the referendum, see David Butler and Uwe Kitzinger, *The 1975 Referendum* (London, 1976).
18. Dorothy Pickles, *The Uneasy Entente* (London, 1967), pp. 162–4.

company was to build the engines (Bristol Siddeley – later Rolls-Royce – in England, SNECMA in France) and another company the rest of the aircraft (the British Aircraft Corporation in England, Sud-Aviation – later Aérospatiale – in France). This was a cumbersome form of organisation, involving two separate lines of construction and testing, one in Bristol and one in Toulouse, which were difficult to co-ordinate. The French *directeur des essais en vol*, André Turcat, later regretted that there had not been a single centre for construction and testing. Naturally, he thought this should have been at Toulouse, where he thought the British participants would have flourished. 'Far from the mists of the islands . . . the demands of tea-time and knocking-off time vanish in the sun . . .'[19] The remark was humorous in style but serious in intent. The whole enterprise, as well as being divided geographically, involved many clashes of systems and received ideas. To issue a certificate of airworthiness, for example, the British employed pilots of long experience; the French used *polytechniciens* who knew nothing about the practicalities of testing an aircraft, but applied the principles laid down in the relevant decrees. The British part of the operation was much plagued by strikes, and the French had to endure the problem of an aircraft being declared 'black'. The British for their part complained that the French tried to take all the credit. When Wedgwood Benn, as Minister for Technology, went to the Paris Air Show in June 1967 he found the Concorde 'presented as a French plane'. (Rather oddly, it appears to have been Benn himself who proposed to adopt the French spelling for the aircraft's name – Concorde rather than Concord.[20]) When the second Concorde to be built made its trial flights in Africa, one side was painted with French insignia, the other with British; but somehow the French side was always presented to the cameras – as the French test pilot cheerfully admitted.

But despite all the difficulties the enterprise went forward. Late in 1964 the British came near to pulling out in face of rising costs, and the French Minister of Finance (Giscard d'Estaing) also suffered doubts; but de Gaulle insisted on pressing ahead. The two principal test pilots got on well together, and the British pilot, Brian Trubshawe, made a particularly good impression on the French team. The aircraft was always behind schedule, but proved an extraordinary technological success. In a time of much trouble between the two countries, it was in its own way a Franco-British success story. Commercially, it never

19. André Turcat, *Concorde: essais et batailles* (Paris, 1977), p. 315.
20. Tony Benn, *Out of the Wilderness: Diaries, 1963–67* (London, 1987), p. 502; Jad Adams, *Tony Benn* (London, 1992), p. 279.

made the impact expected of it. The confident prediction that in future there would only be two kinds of airline – those with Concorde and those left behind – was well wide of the mark. But it is still flying in the 1990s and (despite an appalling noise level) retains a remarkable prestige.

The other great technological enterprise which might have linked the two countries was the Channel Tunnel. This long-running serial story, dating back to the nineteenth century, was revived soon after the end of the Second World War.[21] In 1947 parliamentary committees were set up in both countries to resume studies of the project, but failed to make much impact on governments which already had too much to do and no resources to spare. In 1954, under the impact of the 'European' ideas of the time, the project was more carefully examined. René Massigli, the French Ambassador in London, submitted detailed reports to his government, estimating the economic advantages to France, and hoping that the Tunnel 'by diminishing the geographical insularity of Great Britain, would also do much to lessen the virulence of the psychological insularity of its inhabitants'.[22]

Nothing happened at that stage, but soon afterwards the Suez crisis produced an unexpected consequence by leaving the Suez Canal Company with capital, energy (and even time) to spare. The Company took a new shape and name as the Banque de Suez, and in the true spirit of Ferdinand de Lesseps looked for new worlds to conquer. The Channel presented the opportunity for a great engineering project, more challenging than the Isthmus of Suez had been a century before; and the Company believed firmly that, in the general context of the French economy, a cross-Channel link would be profitable. In June 1957 the Banque de Suez set up a *Groupe d'études du tunnel sous la Manche*, which in turn formed an association with the already-existing French and British Tunnel Companies holding rights in the project from earlier ventures. Technical and commercial studies were undertaken, and there were long discussions as to the rival merits of a tunnel or a bridge. In February 1964 the French and British governments accepted the concept of a tunnel. On 10 July 1966 the British Prime Minister, Harold Wilson, and the Premier of France, Georges Pompidou, signed an agreement to build the Tunnel; but it was not until November 1973 that this was translated into a treaty between the two governments, with an accompanying agreement between the

21. For the earlier history of the Channel Tunnel project, see P.M.H. Bell, *France and Britain, 1900–1940: Entente and Estrangement* (London, 1996); and Keith Wilson, *Channel Tunnel Visions, 1850–1945* (London, 1995).
22. MAE, Papiers Massigli, 217/54, Massigli to Bidault, 15 April 1954.

governments and the companies involved. This treaty was signed by Pompidou, now President of France, and Edward Heath, who keenly supported the project to reinforce Britain's new membership of the EEC.

During the long delay since 1966, the estimated cost of the Tunnel had risen sharply. The French were still willing to pursue the project, and underwrite a large part of its costs. But in 1973–74 British economic conditions became dire, with the miners' strike and the three-day week. Wilson returned to office as Prime Minister in February 1974, and his government saw the Channel Tunnel Bill through its Second Reading in April. But the projected costs of the Tunnel continued to rise. Government guarantees for loans for the Tunnel looked increasingly dangerous, and the likely scale of public expenditure on rebuilding the railways in south-east England seemed out of proportion to other demands on government funds. After long hesitation, the Cabinet decided to abandon the project. It seems that Wilson had never been happy about it at heart, and one of his advisers wrote later: 'I observed the delight with which he cancelled the then channel tunnel project . . .'[23] The Environment Minister, Anthony Crosland, announced the decision in Parliament on 20 January 1975.

Only the previous month, the French National Assembly had ratified the Tunnel Treaty of 1973. French comments on the British decision were severe, and tended to concentrate on the psychological rather than the economic background – a French historian of the tunnel notes that the press saw it as evidence of 'centuries-old mistrust'. *Le Monde* commented that 'Great Britain is an island and intends to remain so', and other papers took the same line. The British decision was much resented in the Nord–Pas de Calais region, where there had already been much expenditure to prepare for the Tunnel.[24] The cancellation of the Tunnel project occurred at the same time as the final stages of the renegotiation of the terms of British membership of the EEC, and it appears that President Giscard d'Estaing took the two together as indicating that Britain was no more than half-committed to Europe. He was confirmed in his belief that the future of France lay in close relations with Germany. The *Entente cordiale* took very much second place to *le couple France-Allemagne*.

Great technological projects, alas, could divide as well as unite. The latest Channel Tunnel vision had made progress (as did that of 1881)

23. Bernard Donoughue, 'Harold Wilson and the renegotiation of the EEC terms of membership, 1974–5', in Brian Brivati and Harriet Jones, eds, *From Reconstruction to Integration: Britain and Europe since 1945* (Leicester, 1993), p. 204.
24. Bernard Sasso, *Le tunnel sous la Manche* (Paris, 1994), pp. 55–7.

to the extent of digging two large holes in the ground. The British cancellation left those two holes gaping and useless. In the past, the prospects of the Tunnel had often been an indicator of the state of relations between the two countries. By that token, in 1975 the outlook was bleak.

CHAPTER 12

Unhappy Partners, 1975–1990

THE NEW MEMBER

For several years in the 1960s and early 1970s, relations between France and Britain were dominated by the long conflict over British entry to the EEC. Was Britain to join? When a member, could the terms of entry be renegotiated? In 1975 it appeared that these disputes were out of the way, and relations between the two countries would get onto a better footing. In 1978 René Massigli, a long-serving French Ambassador in London and a man with a deep affection for Britain, published his memoirs under the title *Une comédie des erreurs*. He used as his epigraph the final line of Shakespeare's play: 'And now let's go hand in hand, not one before another'. This was more than a charming literary touch. Massigli believed that the issue of Europe had divided France from Britain unnecessarily. They could now come together again and go hand in hand.

Massigli's hopes proved ill-founded. Britain and France were both members of the EEC, and British membership had been confirmed by a referendum. But they were uneasy partners. The two peoples took very different attitudes towards the Community. A set of public opinion poll findings illustrates these attitudes over a period of twelve years, revealing a remarkable consistency. The question was always the same, and of an almost startling simplicity: 'In a general way, do you think that (for your country) the fact of forming part of the European Community (Common Market) is a good thing, a bad thing, or neither good nor bad?'

	Great Britain	**France**
1974–82 (18 polls, average)		
Good thing	33	57
Neither good nor bad	23	28
Bad thing	37	7
No reply	7	8
1983 (2 polls)		
Good thing	32	54
Neither good nor bad	29	30
Bad thing	32	8
No reply	7	8
March–April 1984 (1 poll)		
Good thing	34	62
Neither good nor bad	30	27
Bad thing	30	4
No reply	6	7
March–April 1985 (1 poll)		
Good thing	37	68
Neither good nor bad	28	21
Bad thing	30	6
No reply	5	5
March–April 1986 (1 poll)		
Good thing	37	69
Neither good nor bad	28	21
Bad thing	29	5
No reply	6	5[1]

Even making allowances for the errors which can afflict such investigations, and for the fact that poll results give no indication of the intensity with which opinions are held, these figures tell a clear and consistent story. Positive approval of membership never rose above the high 30s in Britain, but reached the high 60s in France. Disapproval never attained double figures in France, but stood at about 30 in Britain (though declining over the years). French public opinion had accepted the idea of 'Europe', and believed that it was a 'good thing' for France; British public opinion had not.

In this the state of public opinion was similar to the attitudes of governments. French governments, under the Fourth and Fifth Republics and under very different political leaders, were committed to the idea of 'Europe' and to the European Community. They were

1. Françoise de la Serre, *La Grande-Bretagne et la Communauté Européenne* (Paris, 1987), p. 217.

certain that the Community brought economic and political advantages, and that it could be used to advance the greatness of France. President Giscard d'Estaing, during the election campaign for the European Parliament in 1979, said that France would not disappear in Europe, but remain present in the role which all great French leaders had sought, from Charlemagne to Louis XIV and from Napoleon to de Gaulle.[2] A French academic writer observed simply in 1990 that all the Presidents of the Fifth Republic were determined to restore France to her proper rank in Europe and the world: 'Paris is called to assume the leadership of Europe.'[3] British governments, on the other hand, had no clear vision of their role and purpose within the Community. Heath, when achieving British entry, had been determined to make Europe the centre of his foreign policy, and use it as a means of restoring British greatness. But in the event his government suffered one crisis after another, and was in no position to pursue such aims. The Labour government that followed saw Europe in quite a different perspective. Callaghan, as Foreign Secretary, told German ministers in 1974 that in the renegotiation of terms 'The touchstone was what would please the British housewife'.[4] This made excellent political sense at home, but lowered the tone abroad. Successive governments thereafter tended to see membership of the EEC as making the best of a bad job on the lines of Bill Bairnsfather's cartoon during the 1914–18 war – 'If you know a better 'ole, go to it'. British politicians, with a few enthusiastic exceptions, felt that they were in the EEC because they had no better hole to go to. They had no vision of European union beyond commercial advantage, and were usually inexpert at using the sort of rhetoric which might have disguised their position.

If the commercial advantage of British membership of the EEC had proved rapid and striking, following the growth rates enjoyed by member states in the 1960s, British views of the Community might well have been different. In fact, British entry coincided with the international crisis produced by the leap in oil prices at the end of 1973, and with the domestic economic crises of the mid-1970s. It was a time for muddling through rather than rapid growth. Later, in the 1980s, British economic performance was satisfactory, and roughly on a level with that of France. A calculation of changes in the gross

2. Charles Hargrove, *Valéry Giscard d'Estaing vu par un Anglais* (Paris, 1981), p. 198.

3. Françoise de la Serre, in Françoise de la Serre, Jacques Leruez and Helen Wallace, eds, *Les politiques étrangères de la France et de la Grande-Bretagne depuis 1945* (Paris, 1990), p. 132.

4. Nicholas Henderson, *Mandarin. The Diaries of an Ambassador 1962–1982* (London, pb edn, 1995), p. 64.

domestic product of the two countries between 1980 and 1989 showed a mean average growth of 2.2 per cent for the United Kingdom and 2.1 per cent for France.[5] By comparison with the 1960s, when France had surged ahead, this was encouraging for Britain; but as a consequence of EEC membership, it was not dramatic. The direction of British trade changed considerably. In 1973, British imports from the EEC (calculated at the twelve members which it attained in 1986) amounted to 36 per cent of total imports; in 1987, 52 per cent. In 1973, British exports to the EEC (again calculated at twelve members) were 35 per cent of total exports; in 1987, 49 per cent.[6] However, as these figures indicate, British imports from EEC countries exceeded exports to them. In 1988 the British balance of payments with the rest of the EEC was in deficit by £13.5 billion.[7] Thus the principal British concern with EEC membership was economic and commercial; but the economic and commercial case, though strong, was never over-whelming, and a constant drip of argument and doubt continued.

QUARRELS WITHIN THE COMMUNITY: THE BUDGET, AGRICULTURE, AND THE MONETARY SYSTEM

On questions of policy within the EEC, Britain followed an individual line on her contributions to the Community Budget, the Common Agricultural Policy, and the European Monetary System. On all these subjects, the dispute was not specifically with France, because Britain was usually in conflict with all or most of the other members; and yet – as in the question of British entry in the first place – events so turned out that Britain and France appeared to be the main antagonists. Now that they were both inside the Community, their quarrels tended to be concentrated and exacerbated rather than dispersed or mollified.

When Britain entered the EEC on 1 January 1973, the British contribution to the Community Budget was set to start at 8.6 per cent of the total, rising annually to reach 19 per cent after a transitional

5. Christopher Johnson, *The Economy under Mrs Thatcher, 1979–1990* (London, 1991), p. 266.

6. J-M. Jeanneney, *L'économie française depuis 1967* (Paris, 1989), p. 88. The EEC had nine members in 1973. Greece joined on 1 Jan. 1981, Spain and Portugal on 1 Jan. 1987.

7. Douglas Jay, 'The Free Trade Alternative to the EEC', in Brian Brivati and Harriet Jones, eds, *From Reconstruction to Integration: Britain and Europe since 1945* (Leicester, 1993), p. 126.

period of five years. The British soon became unhappy with this arrangement, and as part of the renegotiation of 1974–75 Harold Wilson secured a complicated scheme for reassessment, which unhappily failed to work.[8] The transitional period finished at the end of 1978, and in May 1979 Margaret Thatcher became Prime Minister, determined to reduce the British contribution. Her argument was that Britain was close to becoming the largest net contributor to the Budget, because in addition to the direct contributions just described, she also paid large levies on foodstuffs imported from outside the EEC. Yet Britain's gross domestic product per head of population stood only in seventh place among the EEC members, then nine in number. The British claim was that this discrepancy between contributions and national wealth was inequitable. The other members, with France in the lead, argued that it was Britain's own choice to import large quantities of foodstuffs from (for example) Australia and New Zealand, and therefore pay levies upon them which went to finance the Common Agricultural Policy. This condition had been perfectly well known when Britain joined the EEC, and the British had accepted it. Moreover, these levies were separate from the direct Budget contributions, and should not be lumped together with them. Thatcher paid little attention to these distinctions, or to the Community's 'own resources' which went to finance the CAP. She insisted that she was talking about Britain's contributions in general – 'our money' – and that her task was to defend British interests.

The upshot was a long and hard-fought struggle. Thatcher raised the question of Budget contributions at the first European summit meeting that she attended as Prime Minister in June 1979. During the next year she tried to secure a refund of part of the British payments. The other members made offers in November 1979 and April 1980, which the Prime Minister rejected as inadequate. In May 1980 a meeting of Foreign Ministers produced a better figure, amounting to about two-thirds of the British net contribution, to run for three years. Rather reluctantly, Thatcher accepted this proposal. When the three years were up, the dispute was resumed. At the Stuttgart European summit in June 1983 Thatcher again put the British case, to be opposed by François Mitterrand, the President of France, who claimed that it would be fatal for Europe to accept such profit-and-loss accounting for contributions to the Budget. (This was a good example of Mitterrand's ability to combine European rhetoric with the defence of French interests, and makes an interesting contrast in styles with Thatcher's blunt approach.)

8. See above, p. 228.

The conflict was finally resolved by a compromise at a European summit meeting at Fontainebleau on 25–26 June 1984. The British gave up their effort to secure a link between net contributions to the Budget and national prosperity, or gross domestic product. They also ceased to request a rebate based both on VAT payments to the Community Budget and on levies on imports of foodstuffs from outside the EEC, accepting instead the French insistence that only VAT should count for purposes of a repayment. In return, agreement was reached that Britain should receive a regular repayment of 66 per cent of the difference between British VAT payments *into* the Budget and the sum Britain received *from* the Budget. This level of repayment was to remain effective until changed by unanimous agreement, and could therefore not be altered without British consent. Mitterrand was later to grumble (in 1987) that it had always been understood that the British rebate was to be limited in time, and would diminish; but the agreement itself was silent on such matters. The result of this complicated bargaining was less favourable to Britain than Thatcher had originally hoped. The British failed to secure a link between Budget contributions and gross domestic product. They continued to be heavy net contributors to the Budget, because they paid levies on substantial food imports from outside the EEC, and received little from the payments under the CAP which absorbed most of the Budget. On the other hand, they gained some financial advantage in terms of the regular rebate; and after Fontainebleau France became for the first time a modest net contributor.[9]

This conflict on contributions to the Community Budget became particularly sharp between Britain and France because it threatened to affect the financing of the Common Agricultural Policy, which closely affected French interests. The CAP formed the major element in the Community's expenditure. In 1974–75, as part of the Wilson renegotiation, a Regional Fund had been set up, from which Britain hoped to benefit. In fact, there had been little change in the distribution of funds. In 1987, 66.1 per cent of the expenditure from the Community Budget went to agriculture; 7 per cent to the Social Fund; 6.9 per cent to the Regional Fund; and the remaining 20 per

9. The Budget question may be followed in: P. Favier and M. Martin-Rolland, *La décennie Mitterrand*, vol. I, *Les ruptures, 1981–1984* (Paris, 1990), pp. 363–5, 368–9, 200–2, 204–7; Gabriel Robin, *La diplomatie de Mitterrand, 1981–1985* (Paris, 1985), pp. 212–14; Jeanneney, *Economie française*, pp. 89–90; Margaret Thatcher, *The Downing Street Years* (London, 1993), pp. 78–86, 336–8, 537–45. There are useful summaries in: David Reynolds, *Britannia Overruled: British Policy and World Power in the Twentieth Century* (London, 1991), pp. 264–7; and William Nicoll and Trevor C. Salmon, *Understanding the New European Community* (London, 1994), pp. 44–5, 105–8.

cent to a variety of other purposes. In short, two-thirds was spent on the CAP.[10]

From 1976 onwards, British governments sought to reform the Common Agricultural Policy, on the grounds that it raised food prices to an excessive extent and placed an unnecessary burden on the Community Budget. In 1978–79, the ratio of wheat prices to world prices for soft wheat was 193; for white sugar 276; for beef 199; and for butter 403. There were problems of interpretation in these figures, because EEC prices themselves formed a part of world prices and had an effect upon them; but there was no doubt as to the general relationship between prices. It has been calculated that the average ratio of EEC to world prices for a number of products, over the period from 1968 to 1979, ranged from 139 to 229. The results included not only high prices for the consumer but the production of vast surpluses (butter mountains and wine lakes, in the parlance of the time) which could not be sold and had to be stored, at further expense. In 1978 the largest contributors to the CAP (in order of magnitude) were Italy, Britain and West Germany. The greatest beneficiaries were the Netherlands, Denmark, France and Ireland.[11] Per head of population, the smaller countries gained more than France; but in political terms France had put the greatest effort into setting up the CAP and settling the methods of financing it. Most Frenchmen live in cities, but many of them remain emotionally attached to the soil. Farming pressure groups are highly organised, and their pressure sometimes takes the direct form of rioting in the streets, obstructing motorways or blocking ports. For all these reasons, French governments resisted changes which would reduce the benefits of the CAP for their farmers.

In the mid-1980s serious attempts were made to modify the Common Agricultural Policy. In 1983 quotas were introduced for milk production, with penalties for exceeding them; and later the guaranteed prices for cereals and beef were reduced. These measures had some effect, although as a French economic historian put it, delicately, they 'were only partially effective'. In 1986, the EEC price for wheat was 53 per cent above the world price; for butter 175 per cent; and for sugar 200 per cent.[12]

On the subject of the CAP, British and French interests, and even more sentiments, were opposed. On the one hand, French

10. Jeanneney, *Economie française,* p. 90.
11. R. Davenport, 'The Economic Impact of the EEC', in Andrea Boltho, ed., *The European Economy: Growth and Crisis* (Oxford, 1982), pp. 237, 240–1.
12. Jeanneney, *Economie française,* pp. 95–6.

governments were determined to maintain the main lines of the CAP. In January 1987, Jacques Delors, the President of the European Commission, was trying to persuade Chirac, the French Premier, that they must get away from producing surpluses, diminish stocks, and move towards a more selective pricing policy. Chirac is reported to have replied that the CAP was an essential pillar of Europe: 'It is not worth building Europe if the CAP is destroyed.'[13] In Britain, the CAP evoked very different feelings. For example, Kenneth Morgan wrote, in a book notable for its cautious and measured judgements, that in Britain 'The Common Agricultural Policy was remorselessly unpopular, *as it deserved to be*'.[14] In this unpopularity, occasional television pictures of French farmers burning lorry-loads of British lamb counted for more than the detailed bargaining over farm prices and how to cope with surpluses. It was true that British Foreign Office spokesmen, and sometimes the Foreign Secretary in person, observed plaintively that the press made a fuss when a lorry was burned, but said nothing about the thousands of vehicles which passed quietly through the ports. This was true to the point of being a platitude – unburned lorries never make news. It was also irrelevant, in that outbreaks of violence, though rare, were symptoms of a genuine conflict of emotions and interest.

The Common Agricultural Policy was one of the motives which prompted the EEC to move towards monetary union, which again caused friction between France and Britain. In 1969 the devaluation of the French franc (11.5 per cent down in August) and the revaluation of the German mark (8.5 per cent up in October) imperilled the CAP, with its insistence on uniform prices to the producer. In 1970 an EEC document (the Werner Report) proposed to prevent such fluctuations by moving towards monetary union, and possibly towards a single currency. In fact, in the 1970s an attempt was made to keep certain currencies within set limits, not varying more than 2.25 per cent up or down in relation to one another. This mechanism was commonly known as 'the snake'; and to it was added another, with the even more curious name of 'the snake in the tunnel', attempting to relate these limits imposed on European currencies to the value of the US dollar. Both France and Britain took part in 'the snake', but neither could hold its currency within the defined limits, and by 1976 the scheme had been reduced to a group of four currencies linked to the German mark.

13. Jacques Attali, *Verbatim*, vol. II, *Chronique des années 1986–1988* (Paris, 1995), p. 244.
14. Kenneth O. Morgan, *The People's Peace: British History 1945–1990* (Oxford, pb edn, 1992), p. 340. The italics are mine.

In 1978 the EEC members tried again. At a European summit at Bremen (6–7 July 1978) President Giscard of France and Chancellor Schmidt of Germany proposed a new European Monetary System, based on the same principle as the former 'snake', i.e. that participating currencies should fluctuate no more than 2.25 per cent up or down from a fixed value. The states concerned were to place at the disposal of a European Fund sums amounting to 20 per cent of their gold and dollar reserves, to be used to defend the new parities against speculation. A new unit of account, which might prove to be the prototype of a European currency, was introduced, and had to be given a name. Giscard, in his memoirs, relates that he was conscious that to have a French title might be resented as 'intellectual imperialism', and that he therefore proposed to his colleagues at the European summit that the unit of account should be called – and he spoke in English – 'European Currency Unit'. He observed that the British Prime Minister, Callaghan, seemed pleased by this, and the proposal was accepted. Giscard then added, with a straight face, that the abbreviation, to be used for normal purposes, should simply be the initials, ECU; so that the new unit acquired the same name as a French coin from the Middle Ages, the *écu*. The ECU came into being in March 1979, with a value defined by a grouping (or 'basket') of currencies in different proportions, which might vary from time to time. The German mark started by counting for 33 per cent of the total, and remained the predominant element.

Britain took part in the negotiations which set up the new system, but did not join the Exchange Rate Mechanism (ERM) which bound the participating currencies in a close fixed relationship with one another. For a long time, official British policy was that Britain would enter the system when the circumstances were right. Not until June 1989 did the British Prime Minister, Margaret Thatcher, announce that Britain would join the Exchange Rate Mechanism, though still only after certain conditions had been fulfilled. In October 1990, though the conditions had not yet been met, the British government decided to join, with consequences that must be examined later. Meanwhile, for some twenty years between 1970 and 1990, the various schemes for monetary union went forward primarily through the efforts of Germany and France, and required the French franc to be closely bound to the German mark.[15]

15. For guides to the complexities of the European Monetary System, see: Peter Ludlow, *The Making of the European Monetary System* (London, 1982); Pierre Gerbet, *La construction de l'Europe* (Paris, 1983), pp. 396–402; Jeanneney, *Economie française*, pp. 102–6. For Giscard's story about naming the ECU, Valéry Giscard d'Estaing, *Le pouvoir et la vie* (Paris, 1988), pp. 148–52.

THE FRANCO-GERMAN AXIS

This monetary co-operation was only a part of the close relationship between France and West Germany that dominated the affairs of the EEC, and provided the guiding force in western Europe. On the French side, Robert Schuman had begun to build this partnership in 1950. De Gaulle had consolidated it, as perhaps only he, with his long record of resistance to Germany at other times, could have done. There was a brief period of hesitation when Pompidou grew disturbed at German strength, and wanted Britain in the EEC as a counter-weight to Germany. This hesitation was short-lived. Giscard, who became President of France in 1974, made Europe the centre of his foreign policy, and within Europe placed the main emphasis on Franco-German partnership. In his seven years as President, he held fourteen regular meetings with the Chancellor of West Germany, as was laid down in the Franco-German treaty of 1963. To these he added ten other less formal meetings, and frequent contact by telephone. There was every sign that Giscard and his opposite number, Helmut Schmidt, got on very well at the personal level, and they maintained their friendship even when both were out of office. Curiously, they usually spoke to one another in English, in which both were fluent, because neither had a good enough grasp of the other's language to communicate freely. It was an interesting tribute to the ubiquity of the English language. But there was no question of Giscard allowing the British to become attached to this partnership. Charles Hargrove, for many years the correspondent of *The Times* in Paris, wrote that for Giscard Britain represented the past, and Germany the future.[16]

When François Mitterrand succeeded Giscard in 1981, his first foreign visitor after his election victory was Schmidt. Mitterrand followed this up by inviting Schmidt to his house in the country at Latché in October. In their long conversations, Mitterrand said he wanted to revive Franco-German co-operation. He did not want a Paris–Bonn axis, but saw the need for 'a special, privileged friendship between our two countries'. (His words were 'une amitié privilégiée', which sounds much more refined than 'axis', but could amount to much the same thing.)[17] Later, the French President and Chancellor

16. Hargrove, *Giscard*, p. 198. Cf Samy Cohen and Marie-Claude Smouts, eds, *La politique extérieure de Valéry Giscard d'Estaing* (Paris, 1985), which devotes a chapter to French relations with Germany and makes only occasional references to Britain – a fair reflection of the emphasis of French policy.

17. Jacques Attali, *Verbatim*, vol. I, *Chronique des années 1981–1986* (Paris, 1993), pp. 102–3.

Helmut Kohl built up a close working relationship. At all the European summit meetings, the two had breakfast together at the beginning of the principal day's work. It was at one of these breakfasts that they worked out the terms of a compromise with the British on the Community Budget. At that same meeting Jacques Attali observed with delight that they agreed to nominate Jacques Delors as next President of the European Commission without even mentioning his name – 'A master-piece of dialogue between two allies and two accomplices who had no need to go into details to understand one another ...'.[18] In another mode, in 1986 they went to Verdun together to pay homage to the dead of both armies – a gesture of reconciliation which was embodied in their bowing together, their hands linked. In June 1987, at another breakfast (this time at a meeting of the Seven leading industrialised nations at Venice), Mitterrand spoke of integrating the French and German armies at specific points, and Kohl at once advanced the idea of integrated Franco–German divisions. In January 1988, on the 25th anniversary of the Treaty of Paris in 1963, Mitterrand and Kohl set up a Franco–German Defence Council, to meet twice a year, and to maintain a permanent Secretariat, which was to be based in Paris and be headed by a German general. The creation of a mixed Franco–German Brigade, proposed in 1987, was much delayed, but came about in October 1990. In May 1992 one of the regular meetings between President and Chancellor announced a decision to create a joint Corps, to be made up of two German mechanised brigades, a French armoured division and the Franco–German Brigade – a total of 35,000 men. This was to be a 'Euro-Corps', with contingents from other countries; but in effect it was a Franco–German venture. On 14 July 1994 German tanks from this Corps took part in the Bastille Day parade down the Champs Elysées.

FRANCE AND BRITAIN: AN INCOMPATIBLE COUPLE?

Franco-British relations were far less close. There was a step forward during a state visit by Giscard in June 1976, when it was agreed to hold 'summit meetings' between the President and Prime Minister once a year. But this was only half as many as the regular Franco-

18. Ibid., p. 658.

German meetings; which meant that officials also met less frequently to prepare the sessions. The first Franco-British 'summit' took place at Rambouillet on 11–12 November 1976, in circumstances which were less than favourable for Britain, where the economy was still in difficulties and the pound weak. But the British Ambassador in Paris, Sir Nicholas Henderson, reflected that this state of affairs had some advantages – 'the French want us to be down even if they do not want us to be out'.[19] The visits then went ahead on an annual basis, in each country alternately. They soon produced a regular pattern: of private meetings between President and Prime Minister; a dinner; larger meetings involving various ministers; and a press conference. They proved to have real advantages, for example in discussing nuclear weapons and the Channel Tunnel; but they did not achieve the same degree of continuity and intimacy as the Franco-German meetings, which were not only more frequent but had been going on for thirteen years before the Franco-British 'summits' began.

The individuals involved in these meetings seem to have worked out at least a degree of understanding. Giscard found Callaghan straightforward after the oracular ambiguities of Harold Wilson; but Henderson notes that the President thought Callaghan was 'like a politician of the Fourth Republic', which was a dubious compliment.[20] Margaret Thatcher was a puzzle. She seemed to Giscard to come from another planet, showing none of the subtlety and sophistication he enjoyed in conversation. He complained, after a visit by Thatcher to the Elysée, that when he talked about art or culture she turned the conversation to the weather or the British contribution to the European Budget.[21]

Giscard was confronted by this puzzle for some two years, and was then succeeded in 1981 by François Mitterrand. The new President also found Thatcher lacking in culture and breadth of vision. He remarked that she was 'a little bourgeois ideologist'. During a visit to India in October 1982 he told journalists that Indira Gandhi was 'a cultured woman who has ideas, a world vision, in short quite the opposite of Margaret Thatcher'. Yet he set out to use his charm – he was, after all, an accomplished ladies' man, and a senior official observed that 'he will play the charmer with this lone woman among all the men, the flower which lights up their austere toil'.[22] The success of this tactic is not easy to divine, but it was surely limited.

19. Henderson, *Mandarin*, p. 132.
20. Giscard d'Estaing, *Pouvoir et vie*, p. 148; Henderson, *Mandarin*, p. 133.
21. Hargrove, *Giscard*, p. 200.
22. Favier and Martin-Rolland, *Décennie Mitterrand*, vol. I, pp. 364, 325 n.3.

Mitterrand himself remarked after their first meeting that Margaret Thatcher had 'the eyes of Stalin and the voice of Marilyn Monroe'.[23] It was at best an ambiguous compliment, for few admired Marilyn Monroe for her voice. Mitterrand was not pleased to find that Thatcher's policies were more successful than his own in 1981–82. After his election as President, he launched a socialist adventure and a programme of nationalisations, but by late 1982 had to accept failure and turn to a policy of economic rigour and balanced budgets. He remarked testily to the Premier, Mauroy: 'I did not call on you to follow the policies of Mme Thatcher'; but that, or something like it, was what he had to do. By the end of the year, Mitterrand observed: 'It is Reagan and Thatcher who are winning.'[24] It was a mournful admission.

There is no sign that Thatcher was overawed by the French Presidents. When Giscard remarked on the portraits of Nelson and Wellington which greeted him at 10 Downing Street, Thatcher replied that after all she had to look at Napoleon in the Elysée. (In her memoirs she adds tartly that the comparison was not exact: Napoleon lost!) There was a bracing exchange between the Prime Minister and President Mitterrand during a quiet luncheon at Marly in January 1984. Mitterrand complained that the English press were making too much fuss about lorry drivers being taken hostage at Boulogne – they brought the Duke of Wellington into everything; to which Thatcher replied that French peasants wanted all their markets guaranteed, however great the surpluses they produced. It is clear that they could both give as good as they got. During the celebrations of the 200th anniversary of the French Revolution, Thatcher observed in an interview for *Le Monde* that the Revolution had been 'a Utopian attempt to overthrow a traditional order – one with many imperfections, certainly – in the name of abstract ideas, formulated by vain intellectuals, which lapsed, not by chance but through weakness and wickedness, into purges, mass murder and war'. This was a robust contribution to the French debate on their own history, but not universally welcome, not least among intellectuals, who command a particular place of honour in French life.[25]

In her memoirs, Thatcher sketches on the whole a favourable portrait of Mitterrand, and also of Jacques Chirac – 'oddly enough I

23. Attali, *Verbatim*, vol. I, p. 90. This version of Mitterrand's remark seems better attested than the more commonly found 'the eyes of Caligula and the mouth of Marilyn Monroe'; though both may be true.

24. Favier and Martin-Rolland, *Décennie Mitterrand*, vol. I, pp. 439, 451.

25. Thatcher, *Downing Street Years*, pp. 24, 753; Attali, *Verbatim*, vol I, p. 575.

liked both of them'. But she slips the knife in gently by remarking that she found Chirac easier to deal with than Mitterrand, 'because his public actions bore a greater similarity to his privately expressed views'. Not that Chirac escapes unscathed. During one meeting, Thatcher recalled, 'I advised him not to threaten me . . .' It would indeed have been an unprofitable exercise.[26]

A sort of wary respect seems to have been achieved on both sides. There were certainly subjects (notably the Falklands War and nuclear weapons) where Thatcher and Mitterrand stood together.[27] But all the time 'Europe' stood between them. Mitterrand followed the consistent French policy of building Europe on the foundation of Franco-German partnership. It was a Europe which was to be protectionist against the rest of the world, and interventionist (or *dirigiste*) in its own internal affairs. It was also increasingly integrationist in its aims, aspiring towards common policies in foreign policy and defence, as well as in economic affairs. This was very different from Thatcher's view of Europe. She was happy to go forward to a single market within the EEC, which was in principle set up by the Single European Act signed in 1986, and seems genuinely to have believed that this opened the way to 'a free enterprise *Europe des patries*'. Instead, she found the Community moving increasingly towards centralisation and intervention. She was conscious that a Franco-German bloc (which the French hoped to guide 'by superior Gallic intelligence') was setting the course for the EEC, and she could do little to impede it. No-one could accuse Margaret Thatcher of defeatism, but even she wrote that the best she could manage against France and Germany was 'a strategic retreat in the face of majorities I could not block'.[28] Yet she fought stern rearguard actions, so that Mitterrand exclaimed in June 1988: 'She rejects everything!'[29]

THE FALKLANDS WAR

The fact that France and Britain were both members of the EEC, far from improving their relations with one another, created new causes of friction between them. Yet life continued outside the EEC, and some unexpected occasions for co-operation occurred. The Falklands War of

26. Thatcher, *Downing Street Years*, pp. 730, 735.
27. See below, pp. 248–51.
28. Thatcher, *Downing Street Years*, pp. 61, 558–9, 728.
29. Attali, *Verbatim*, vol. II, p. 37.

1982 brought a remarkable display of unity. On 2 April 1982 Argentinian troops occupied the British possession of the Falkland Islands, in the South Atlantic. Margaret Thatcher swiftly decided to send an expedition to eject the invaders, a bold and extremely dangerous enterprise which had to be mounted across 7,000 miles of ocean and in the teeth of land-based Argentinian air power.

In this adventure the importance of France was two-fold: diplomatic and military. Diplomatically, it would have been easy for France (a permanent member of the Security Council of the United Nations) to embarrass Britain by opposing (or merely impeding) a resolution demanding the immediate and unconditional withdrawal of Argentinian forces. There was some temptation to do this. The French Foreign Minister, Claude Cheysson, wanted to support Argentina, on the grounds that the invasion was an act of anti-colonial liberation and that the whole of the Third World would support the Argentinians. But Mitterrand ruled this out at once, telling Cheysson: 'We are the allies of the English, not of the Argentine.' On 3 April Mitterrand telephoned the Prime Minister to assure her of French support, which was at once forthcoming in the Security Council and was maintained throughout the crisis.[30]

Militarily, France supplied armaments to the Argentine and other South American countries. The French Minister of Defence, Charles Hernu, at once suspended all arms deliveries to Argentina, including the despatch of Exocet missiles, against which British defences were inadequate. At the start of the conflict, the Argentinians possessed eight Exocets, one of which sank HMS *Sheffield*. Even a few more might have been fatal to the British expedition. On Mitterrand's authority the French also held up the delivery of Exocets to Peru, because they believed that the Peruvians would pass them on to Argentina. (This was the occasion for a delicate piece of subterfuge. It was difficult to justify breaking the contract to supply the Exocets to Peru; but somehow the papers that were necessary before they could leave the factory got lost in the thickets of French bureaucracy.) Again, when the British asked for information about the French Mirage and Super-Etandard aircraft being used by the Argentinians, the French Air Force responded at once by flying some of these types to RAF airfields to be examined. Margaret Thatcher wrote in her memoirs that during the Falklands War Mitterrand 'was absolutely staunch'.[31] When the

---

30. Favier and Martin-Rolland, *Décennie Mitterrand*, vol. I, p. 382; Attali, *Verbatim*, vol. I, pp. 200–1; Thatcher, *Downing Street Years*, p. 182.

31. Thatcher, *Downing Street Years*, pp. 226–7; Attali, *Verbatim*, vol. I, p. 201; John Laughland, *The Death of Politics. France under Mitterrand* (London, 1994), p. 228.

former President died in January 1996 she again spoke in glowing terms of his loyalty in the Falklands crisis. Steadfastness in time of trouble ranked high in Mrs Thatcher's esteem, and Mitterrand earned her abiding respect.

It should not be assumed that French actions were simply altruistic. France was sending a signal to anyone it might concern that France would protect her own island possessions in various parts of the world. It may even be that Mitterrand was hoping to bind Britain more closely to Europe – he is said to have promised the British his 'European solidarity'. It is also true that the support of the United States was a good deal more significant than that of France for the British operation. Even so, French assistance went much further than calculations of self-interest alone would have dictated; and the Falklands War was an occasion when the Atlantic triangle of Britain, the USA and France worked together, to great effect.

NUCLEAR WEAPONS AND THE UNITED STATES

Rather surprisingly, nuclear weapons emerged as another point of co-operation between Britain and France, and specifically between Thatcher and Mitterrand. At the beginning of the 1980s the two countries were continuing to follow their established paths, in parallel rather than together. In 1980 Britain agreed to purchase the new American Trident I missile, and in 1982 to buy Trident II. France meanwhile continued to develop her own independent nuclear deterrent. But they also had interests in common. In 1979 the United States and the Soviet Union concluded a Strategic Arms Limitation Treaty (the second of its kind, and usually referred to by its initials as SALT II). The British and French found themselves in a difficulty. To oppose nuclear arms limitation was to appear to oppose peace itself; but to apply principles similar to those in the SALT agreement to the small nuclear forces of Britain and France was likely to cripple them. Later, in 1986, President Reagan of the United States and Mikhail Gorbachev, the leader of the Soviet Union, were willing to discuss a 50 per cent reduction in their strategic nuclear weapons. To reduce the British and French forces by 50 per cent would in practice render them useless – for example, to have two nuclear-armed submarines instead of four would mean that they could not remain at sea and refit. There was even talk, at the failed Reykjavik summit between Reagan and Gorbachev in October 1986, of a 'zero option', doing away with all strategic nuclear weapons. At the same time, Reagan was pursuing his plan for a Strategic Defence Initiative (often called 'Star Wars') which would provide total defence for the United States against nuclear attack. If it proved successful, the Americans might withdraw to the safety of this new fortress, and leave Britain and France exposed. In all this there was much to cause alarm to the British and French governments. When Thatcher and Mitterrand met for their regular annual 'summit' on 20 November 1986, they talked long and anxiously about nuclear weapons. Mitterrand thought that the British might have trouble with the Trident missiles supplied by the Americans, and went so far as to wonder about starting a joint Franco-British nuclear weapon project, on the same lines as the Concorde supersonic aircraft. It does not appear that Thatcher pursued this idea, but she was very clear that Britain and France shared the same objective: not to submit their nuclear forces to limitations laid down by the Americans and Soviets.[32] This remarkable conversation put the value of the annual Franco-British meetings in quite a different perspective, and showed a striking similarity of approach between two apparently contrasting personalities.

The emergency passed without requiring the two leaders to take action, but they had shown their willingness to work together. They also stood together on another nuclear issue of the early 1980s, that of the so-called cruise missiles. The Soviet Union developed medium-range, low-trajectory missiles (the SS-20s) that could reach the whole of western Europe from bases in the USSR or other eastern European countries. The question arose within the North Atlantic alliance as to whether American missiles of the same type (Pershings) should be based in Britain and West Germany. (Under the policy laid down by General de Gaulle, and maintained by his successors, no American-controlled weapons could be based in France.) There was much opposition to accepting the Pershing missiles, from nuclear disarmament movements in both Britain and Germany, and from others who, while not in principle against nuclear weapons, considered that the new missiles would be in some way provocative. Both Thatcher and Mitterand took a firm line. Thatcher accepted Pershings in Britain, and rode out the storm of protest. Mitterrand took the most public occasion open to him, a speech to the West German *Bundestag* on 20 January 1983, to tell his listeners (and of course the rest of the world) that Germany should accept Pershing missiles. The German government did so; the missiles arrived; and none of the dire

32. Attali, *Verbatim*, vol. II, pp. 205–6.

consequences predicted by their opponents ensued. In this crisis, Thatcher acted entirely in character: straightforward, strong-minded, pro-American and anti-Soviet. Mitterrand's character was so Protean that it is hard to say whether he was acting in it or out of it; but he often struck anti-American attitudes, and was sometimes equivocal on nuclear weapons (other than French ones). But at the crux both took the same firm stance, and maintained it. Notably, Mitterrand proved able to tell the Germans that they should do something that France would not do, and to show that French influence was still strong in the Franco-German relationship.

AFRICA AND *FRANCOPHONIE*

There were other occasions of disharmony and outright conflict between France and Britain. France pursued an active policy in Africa, which was at least in its side-effects in rivalry with Britain. The French government zealously promoted the cause of *francophonie* in Africa, which was directly opposed to the influence of the English language. In 1973 Pompidou held the first conference of French African states in Paris. Only seven countries accepted his invitation, but the conferences became annual affairs and grew in stature as well as in numbers of participants. Mitterrand gave them a new title, 'Franco-African summits', and drew in countries which were not former French colonies but where French was spoken – the former Belgian colonies of Zaire, Ruanda and Burundi. He even set out to attract countries from English-speaking Africa – Zimbabwe was invited to the 'summit' meetings, and accepted. Eventually, in 1994, the new South Africa led by Nelson Mandela attended Mitterrand's last Franco-African conference, held at Biarritz. By the end of the 1980s, some 40 African states regularly attended these conferences – a far cry from the seven in 1973.

The principal objective of this formidable effort by France was prestige – to show that France still counted in the world, and that the French language could hold its own against the rising tide of English. It also paid dividends in terms of investment and trade – among other things, in arms. In pursuit of commerce, France showed few if any inhibitions, even in dealing with the old South Africa of apartheid and white supremacy. A French rugby tour of South Africa, scheduled for 1982–83, was cancelled, but the sale of a second French nuclear reactor went ahead. On occasion, France did not hesitate to use force rather than see either its interests or its prestige damaged. In 1983–84 Libyan troops moved into the former French colony of Chad, presumably seeking to extend the influence of the Libyan ruler, Colonel Gadaffi. A small but effective French force (no more than about 3,500 strong) intervened to drive out the Libyans. It was doubtless going too far to claim, as one French journalist did, that France 'can still, with 500 men, change the course of history'; but in fact the Libyan move southwards, whose consequences were unpredictable, was stopped.[33]

These various French actions impinged, directly or indirectly, upon relations with Britain. The French language was in competition with English. French prestige vied with that of Britain. The Franco-African conferences were rivals to the Commonwealth links of the former British colonies in Africa. Even Libya set France and Britain against one another. In April 1986 the United States decided to launch air attacks against Libya in retaliation against Libyan terrorist operations. The British government permitted American bombers to set off on these attacks from bases in Britain. In France, President Mitterrand and the Premier, Chirac, combined to refuse an American request for the aircraft to fly across French territory, forcing them to take a much longer route across the Atlantic. In this affair, all kinds of considerations came into play: French policy towards the Arabs in general; concern over oil supplies; attitudes towards terrorism; and unwillingness to be associated with American 'imperialism'. Whatever the reasons, the contrast with Britain was on this occasion sharp. Margaret Thatcher reflected later in her memoirs that 'the Americans may have started to see who their true friends were'.[34]

In the background, indeed, and despite the problems raised by nuclear arms limitation, the long-standing discord between Britain and France over relations with the United States continued. Margaret Thatcher regarded the United States as Britain's most important ally, and President Reagan as a personal friend. Mitterrand was careful to distance himself from the United States when it suited him to do so, and on the personal level he and Reagan could scarcely begin to understand one another. The genial, apparently simple-minded former film actor, with his homespun talk and his habit of making a political point by means of an anecdote, and the subtle, cultivated Renaissance prince found it hard to meet on common ground. It was a time when the accidents of personal relations helped to strengthen Anglo-

33. See J.F. Bayart, *La politique africaine de François Mitterrand* (Paris, 1984), p. 53.
34. Thatcher, *Downing Street Years*, p. 442.

American relations, and to sharpen the existing difficulties between France and the United States.

THE TUNNEL AT LAST

On balance, the picture of relations between France and Britain in the late 1970s and 1980s showed more dark than light. The issue of European integration was a constant source of friction. France had opted firmly for close relations with Germany as the mainstay of her policy, and regarded Britain as a poor second. Co-operation over the Falklands War and cruise missiles stood out in contrast, but these were only episodes.

Yet other events were also on the move. In these years the long and tortuous story of the Channel Tunnel was reaching its final, positive conclusion. In March 1980 Margaret Thatcher stated that she saw no objection to the construction of a tunnel, provided that all the British finance was privately raised and no government expenditure was involved. The next year, Mitterrand was elected President, and formed a government headed by Pierre Mauroy, who was Mayor of Lille as well as being Premier, and was particularly anxious to pursue the Channel Tunnel project as a means of developing the north-east, where the old industries of coal and steel were in decline. A new and decisive impulse was given to an old and often discarded idea.

At the first Franco-British summit which Mitterrand attended, in London in September 1981, Thatcher raised the question of the Tunnel – a new departure, because in the past the initiatives had usually come from France. It was agreed to set up a committee of experts to study the various possibilities for a fixed link that were then in the field: a bridge, a hybrid of part bridge and part tunnel, a road tunnel or a rail tunnel. In April 1982 the committee recommended the building of a double rail tunnel, but there were still many problems and delays. Thatcher herself favoured a drive-through tunnel, and it appears that Mitterrand too wanted part of the link to be directly available to car and lorry drivers. The question of raising the funds, and the roles of private and public finance, also caused difficulties. Different proposals, prepared in great detail, had to be considered. The final choice of the two governments was in favour of the proposal by the Channel Tunnel/Trans-Manche Group for a rail tunnel, with passenger trains and also trains carrying vehicles. This decision was announced by the President and Prime Minister together, meeting appropriately at Lille on 20 January 1986. This time, over a century after the first excavations for a Channel Tunnel, there was no turning back.

The key to this change lay in Britain. In France, successive individuals, companies and governments had advocated a tunnel, and pursued the project with enthusiasm and technical skill. The obstacles had come from the British side, for various reasons: fear of invasion; commercial opposition from the Channel ports and shipping companies; and above all the psychological block of a treasured insularity. Over the years, different Prime Ministers (Campbell-Bannerman, Asquith, Lloyd George, MacDonald, Wilson) had intervened decisively against the project – the last as recently as 1975. What had changed?

It was perfectly clear to anyone in Britain (and especially in England) that the old psychological impediments had not disappeared. Sir Nicholas Henderson, the chairman of the Channel Tunnel Group whose proposal was accepted, has written an account of the events, which he opens with lines from Shakespeare:

> This precious stone set in the silver sea
> Which serves it in the office of a wall,
> Or as a moat defensive to a house,
> Against the envy of less happier lands.

'John of Gaunt', he writes, 'hovered over all our negotiations'.[35] Not everyone might quote Shakespeare, but the instinct itself was deep-rooted. It was characteristic that the House of Commons showed little enthusiasm when the decision was announced there, simultaneously with the joint statement at Lille. Opponents of the scheme argued that their constituents would be adversely affected. Anti-Europeans were afraid of closer links with the continent. Support for the Tunnel was mainly tacit, though effective. The key change from earlier attempts was that, for the first time in the chequered history of the Tunnel project, there was a British Prime Minister who was strongly in favour of it, and applied all the drive of her formidable personality to see it through.

This seems at first sight slightly surprising. It certainly did not arise from any great enthusiasm for the 'European idea'; though Thatcher was certainly an enthusiast for the Single Market. It appears that the Prime Minister was seized by the zeal for a great engineering project

35. Nicholas Henderson, *Channels and Tunnels. Reflections on Britain and Abroad* (London, 1987), p. 7.

which had previously been shown only by the French. Nothing on the scale of the Tunnel had been attempted in Britain, certainly since the Second World War, and perhaps not since the great age of the railways; and Thatcher hoped that the enterprise would give the whole country a psychological as well as an economic fillip. It may be, too, that she was encouraged in her support for the Tunnel by the fact that some of the trade unions opposed it – it would diminish the power of the dockers and seamen. But whatever the motive, when Thatcher had set her hand to this particular task there was no looking back. Henderson, who knew his way around the corridors of power, had no doubt that the favourable response to the Tunnel by civil servants in Whitehall arose from the Prime Minister's steadfast support for the project.

On 4 May 1990 Thatcher met Mitterrand at Waddesdon Manor for that year's Franco-British summit. She remarked that they were the architects of the Channel Tunnel, and looked forward to them both being present when the tunnelling teams met, which they were due to do later that year, and again at the first passage, scheduled for 1993. Her enthusiasm, it is clear, was still strong.[36] The tunnellers met at the end of November 1990, but Margaret Thatcher was no longer Prime Minister to preside over this success for her vision and determination.

It was often the case, throughout the twentieth century, that the Channel Tunnel project acted as a barometer of Franco-British attitudes and sentiments, and especially of British feelings towards France. If that was still true, then the final triumph of this long-deferred aspiration showed that there was life in the old friendship yet.

36. Jacques Attali, *Verbatim*, vol. III, *Chronique des années 1988–1991* (Paris, 1995), p. 485.

CHAPTER 13

Views Across the Channel, c. 1970–1990

In the first half of the twentieth century, sympathetic French observers looked at the British with admiration and respect. The glorious British defiance of Nazi Germany in 1940 and the stubborn endurance of the later war years evoked eloquent tributes. Even the strong and persistent current of Anglophobia was largely inspired by what was seen as the misuse of British *strength*. In the 1970s and 1980s a new note of dismay, or even alarm, at British *weakness* entered the writings of those Frenchmen who took a serious interest in their northern neighbours. Even the unsympathetic were perturbed by what they saw – as one journalist has put it with a shrewd humour, 'The present follies of Albion make us regret the days of her perfidies'.[1]

There were some who believed that Britain was in terminal decline. In 1976 François David published a book entitled simply *Autopsie de l'Angleterre*. The author had lived in England from 1946 to 1958, and then returned in 1974–76, to find a catastrophic change. 'This book', he wrote, 'is born of a disappointment. Great Britain, as I knew her, no longer exists.'[2] The collapse was on all fronts. Economically, the British had fallen behind their competitors in western Europe, and especially France and West Germany. Politically, there was a decline in the prestige and authority of Parliament, an insidious public denigration of all established institutions, and a weakening of national unity. The law was challenged, even by politicians. In foreign policy, the writer thought that Britain was excessively dependent on the United States, and a no more than half-hearted member of the EEC.

The outlines of this diagnosis were only too obvious as Britain traversed the crisis of the mid-1970s, with the miners' strikes, the

---

1. Jean Châlon, 'Les Anglais ont-ils perdu la tête?', *Figaro*, 4 July 1995.
2. François David, *Autopsie de l'Angleterre* (Paris, 1976), p. 7.

three-day week and rampant inflation. But David pressed his analysis further, arguing that 'the national will has crumbled progressively'. Political commentators proclaimed repeatedly that British society was in deep crisis, but offered no way out. Among the population as a whole, that great quality of 'l'esprit civique', which the French had admired so much in wartime Britain, was in decay. Yet the British remained astonishingly complacent. France and West Germany had been leaving Britain behind economically for fifteen years, but the British people either refused to believe it, clinging to the conviction that their island was still the workshop of the world, or else they preferred to settle for an easy life rather than face the rigours of competition. David found that those who were knowledgeable enough to understand Britain's relative economic decline still claimed that people enjoyed a better quality of life than their European neighbours. They worked more slowly, and for fewer hours. They had better social services. They were more *comfortable*. David was highly sceptical of such arguments. He was particularly scathing about the National Health Service, of which the British were so proud. In his view, the NHS offered little to the patient, who was inadequately cared for by a doctor who could spare only a few minutes' attention and had no direct material interest in a consultation. (In France, patients expected fifteen minutes for a consultation, and then paid on the spot.) It was true that public opinion surveys showed that the British were content with their lot, but David believed that this satisfaction stemmed essentially from ignorance of the actual conditions of life in other west European countries. One day the veil would be lifted, and the awakening would be harsh.[3]

David could see only one hope: that some profound shock, on the scale of the defeat of France in 1940, would bring the British to their senses. This would indeed have been drastic treatment, and not wholly welcome to the patient. In any case, the general trend of David's argument was that the disease had already gone too far. Britain was widely seen as 'the sick man of Europe' (as the Ottoman Empire was often called in the nineteenth century). The title of David's book implied that the patient was already dead, and proposed an autopsy.

This was an extreme view, and proved premature. A few years later another French observer, Philippe Daudy, found scope for optimism. His book, *Les Anglais*, published in 1989, was the first large-scale attempt to explain the English to the French public since Pierre Bourdan's admiring assessment in *Perplexités et grandeur de l'Angleterre* in

3. Ibid., pp. 114–19.

1945. Daudy's first knowledge of England had come from literature – his mother read *The Pickwick Papers* aloud to him when he was a child. During the war, when he was at school, he listened to the BBC. He thus absorbed a deep regard for the old Britain: the self-confidence of the Victorian age, and the understated heroism of the Second World War. He became a journalist, and was long resident in England. When the Franco-British Council was founded in 1972, to promote good relations between the two countries and peoples, Daudy became Director of the French Section, and a zealous missionary for the cause. He sought not only to explain the English to his French readers, but also to convince the French that the English were worth understanding. In doing so, he painted an excessively rosy picture, which has been in many respects falsified by later events; but his book was widely read, and deserves attention.[4]

Daudy produced an intriguing mixture of optimism and doubt. He was conscious of the muddle and uncertainty of the new Britain, but rejoiced to find some of the old virtues surviving. For example, he found the idea of the 'gentleman' in decline, and standards of dress lower than before; but pointed out that the English still summoned up their formality on great occasions. The Lord Mayor of London still travelled in procession. The boys of Eton still wore uniform. The guards at Buckingham Palace were impeccably turned out. Oxford and Cambridge still provided a combination of beauty, tradition and academic achievement to be found nowhere else.

Daudy thought that British public institutions were fundamentally sound. In the City the merchant banks combined flexibility with security, and Lloyds of London preserved its traditional image of utter reliability. (This, alas, was soon belied.) The law commanded general respect: 'Every self-respecting Englishman respects the law even more.' Daudy found a Trotskyist of the Militant Tendency who assured him that he and his fellow-militants would never break the law; and claimed to believe him. In praising the virtues of the Common Law, Daudy became almost more English than the English. The Common Law and the statute of Habeas Corpus, he declared, had done more to protect individual liberty than proclamations of the Rights of Man or the excessive rigidity of the Napoleonic Code. Parliament preserved some of the reality, as well as the appearance, of past glories. It attracted little public interest in normal circumstances, but in a crisis could still focus public opinion and mobilise the country's political resources. Daudy admired the top echelons of the civil service,

4. Philippe Daudy, *Les Anglais* (Paris, 1989). See pp. 12–15, and also the obituary of the author in *The Times*, 17 March 1944.

describing two successive Secretaries to the Cabinet as possessing 'that mysterious gift, that indescribable ease, that *je ne sais quoi*' which marked them out as men of true distinction.[5]

On the role of the monarchy, Daudy took care to point out to his French readers that everyone knows the Queen, but there is no precise definition of sovereignty in the United Kingdom. In France, the constitution declared the people to be sovereign; but Britain has no written constitution. Again, the constitution of the Fifth Republic reserves to the President of the Republic powers to secure the survival of the nation in time of extreme emergency. There is no such provision in 'the majestic silence of the British constitution'; and yet, if in some tremendous crisis Parliament could not meet or elections be held, the monarch could fulfil the same purpose on behalf of the nation. Daudy was also impressed by the status of the Queen as Head of the Commonwealth, a role and an entity which were both undefined – 'the head of this community which a breath of wind could blow away, but which no storm has been able to break'. Daudy rounded off his encomium of the monarchy by referring to the Queen's exemplary family, a beacon for the guidance of others.[6] (This was another case where subsequent events have left Daudy's picture in tatters.)

Daudy admitted some shade in this glowing portrait. He observed the ravages of unemployment and the decay of the inner cities, the alienation of punks and the poverty of youth culture; but he refused to despair over them. He described the decline in formal religious practice, but noted that people had not dispensed with the supernatural. Instead, unusual sects, astrology, and even magic thrived; though he was reluctant to enquire as to where this trend was leading. Daudy even tackled the question of the attitude of the British towards work, with ambiguous results. 'The attitude to work among the British always disconcerts people from the Continent. Neither bowed down by the weight of some inevitable servitude, nor under a sacred obligation, they seem determined to make an effort only through personal choice and in the certainty of being paid.' Elsewhere in western Europe, the Marshall Plan and the Treaty of Rome between them had produced new attitudes towards work, but in Britain old habits remained unchanged. Trade unions continued to demand higher wages, as though they could draw on an inexhaustible well. In turn, employers put up the prices of their goods, and relied on the rest of

---

5. Daudy, *Les Anglais*, p. 377. The two Secretaries to the Cabinet concerned were Sir Robin Butler and Sir Robert Armstrong.

6. Ibid., pp. 392–3.

the world to buy British products (which were assumed to be irreplaceable) as they had always done in the past. But even here Daudy stopped short of an indictment of British complacency, and adopted instead the comfortable conventional wisdom that David had rejected. The British people, wrote Daudy, were less prosperous than the French, but they enjoyed a more pleasant life, resting on 'a traditional kind of social relations, compounded of indifference and goodwill'. The British were willing to opt out of competition with others, and be content with their lot.[7]

Contentment was Daudy's final impression. 'An Englishman may be unhappy with his lot; the English are happy with theirs.' Was there, he asked rhetorically, any Englishman who could conceive of not being English? After all, when the English went to the New World or the Antipodes, they took England with them and planted it there, whether in a green valley or in some bleak desert.[8] Daudy did not believe that the English had lost their confidence. They clung to their insularity, even while the Channel Tunnel was being dug beneath the Straits of Dover. They continued to believe firmly that the true meaning of democracy was unknown outside their own lands; anywhere else, the rule of law was at the mercy of arbitrary government.

'Look here, upon this picture, and on this.' Hamlet's injunction is very apt. David had found a corpse and called for an autopsy. Daudy, basing his faith on the qualities of the old England which he still found in the new, presented a picture of a body politic which had its troubles but was fundamentally sound in health. Most Englishmen at the time would surely have found Daudy's description far too glowing; yet it showed that there remained in France some lingering nostalgia for the old England of green lawns, ancient traditions and the Royal family. What was hard was to fit the two pictures together, even allowing for the fact that Britain changed a good deal between the mid-1970s and the late 1980s.

Another French observer did much to make sense of the problem. François Bédarida lived in England for several years, and as a historian was imbued with a deep sense of the country's past. He finished a learned book on British society since the mid-nineteenth century in 1976, the same year that David's *Autopsie de l'Angleterre* appeared; and he re-issued it, with a new 'Postface' on the most recent years, in 1990, the year after Daudy's book was published. His analysis is more balanced, and goes deeper, than either. In the mid-1970s Bédarida

---

7. Ibid., pp. 136, 201, 213.
8. Ibid., p. 400.

found grounds for cautious optimism. He acknowledged the evidence of British economic decline, which had begun long ago; and of course accepted Britain's descent from world power. But, like Daudy, he took seriously the hope that the British people were now content to work less hard and enjoy a more peaceable life – to walk along a quiet, shady footpath rather than battle with the traffic on the motorway. It was quite conceivable that the British, having set the pattern for industrialisation in the nineteenth century, would now provide a model for a gentler lifestyle, liberated from some of the stresses of modern competition. Prometheus had passed on, and been replaced by Orpheus.[9] As for dire prophecies of collapse, Bédarida recalled that in 1850 Ledru-Rollin had devoted two volumes to a study of *La décadence de l'Angleterre*, only to be confounded by the tremendous energy and achievements of the next half-century. An ancient civilisation does not vanish overnight. England had ceased to be a great power. 'But the English have it in them to remain a great people.'[10]

Bédarida's later reflections, published in 1990, were more sombre. He was struck by the ceaseless self-examination and doubt of the 1970s, culminating in a crisis in which Britain, on the analogy of a car, simply refused to respond to the steering wheel. Economic crises followed one another in rapid succession; the miners' strikes brought political confusion; the so-called 'winter of discontent' ended in a sort of anarchic stagnation.[11] During the 1970s, in fact, Britain became ungovernable – a diagnosis often heard in Britain itself. It was a sad decline from the days when the British themselves were proud of their capacity for self-government, and when their political good sense was regarded as a model by many outside Britain.

Unhappily, the crisis went deeper than politics. Bédarida saw the whole of British society as divided and uncertain, caught in a contradiction between the aspirations of individualism and collective responsibility. He wondered whether the English were heading towards the loss of their national identity, and arrived at some gloomy answers. There was too much unrestrained individualism (whether among 'yuppies' or the 'common man'). A dangerous under-class was developing, of a kind not seen since the Victorian age. Large-scale immigration was having serious effects, partly through sheer numbers

9. François Bédarida, *La société anglaise au milieu du XIXe siècle à nos jours* (Paris, 1976; second edn, Collection Points, 1990; all references are to the second edition), pp. 401–2.

10. Ibid., pp. 410–11.

11. Ibid., p. 417.

in some areas, and partly through the particular character of some immigrant groups. The final result, he thought, was 'a society which is more like an assembly of atoms than an organic whole as it used to be'. Sadly and expressively he quoted Philip Larkin:

> Our children will not know that it is a different country.
> All we can hope to leave them now is money.[12]

Assessments of whether Britain's decline was terminal or reversible depended to some degree on views of the achievements of Margaret Thatcher's governments in the 1980s. French observers were keenly interested in the 'Thatcher phenomenon', and sometimes analysed it with more detachment than did British intellectuals. Jacques Leruez placed Thatcher's policies in the context of post-war British decline, and the reaction against the utter disillusion of the 1970s. Only when Britain was at the lowest ebb could the counter-offensive begin; and Leruez understood that it was directed not only against Labour and the trade unions, but against historic Toryism and the whole consensus that had dominated British politics since 1945. Consensus had come to mean stagnation, which could only be dispelled by the politics of conviction.[13] But did the treatment work? Leruez argued that a salutary shock had been followed by a spectacular recovery on the economic front, but that the cure was not complete. There were structural weaknesses in the economy that were hard to put right – for example, a poorly trained workforce and low public investment in infrastructure. More important, the attempt to create a new atmosphere of vigour and enterprise was only partially successful. Leruez thought that the country as a whole had not risen to this challenge, resulting in a two-speed society in which some forged ahead and others were left behind. The country as a whole was richer, but there were greater inequalities within it.[14]

The issues were not entirely economic. Leruez quoted Thatcher after the Falklands campaign: 'Britain is great again'; and he thought this was a feeling shared by many British people and a good number of foreigners. There was a sense that Britain was under firm leadership, and was no longer the 'sick man of Europe'. Writing after Thatcher's fall in 1990, Leruez summed up: 'Personally, Mme. Thatcher was widely feared, often admired, more rarely loved, both abroad and in Great Britain.' Her departure left a great gap.[15] It was a modestly

12. Ibid., p. 444.
13. Jacques Leruez, *Le phénomène Thatcher* (Brussels, 1991), pp. 13–15.
14. Ibid., pp. 159–62, 185–9, 295.
15. Ibid., p. 298.

favourable verdict on eleven years of government, and seemed to offer some hope for the country as a whole.

In these French discussions of the British condition there was little that the British were not saying about themselves, though in different ways and with varying emphases. The facts of relative economic decline compared with France and West Germany in the 1960s and 1970s were not in dispute, but they were open to widely differing interpretations. Did the decline matter? Some argued that it did not, because it was better to dwell in a peaceful backwater, away from the stress of competition and overwork. Moreover, much depended on comparisons that most people did not make. Sir Nicholas Henderson wrote in his valedictory despatch on leaving the British Embassy in Paris in March 1979 that 'You only have to move about Western Europe nowadays to realize how poor and unproud the British have become in relation to their neighbours'.[16] The appearance of British towns and the state of British railways compared to those in France and other countries made this perfectly obvious. This was certainly true; but most British people did not move about western Europe at all, and when they did they rarely stayed long enough for these comparisons to strike home. The British people as a whole were probably less influenced by comparisons with their French neighbours than might have been expected.

This was not the result of any lack of information. British observers, well-informed and usually sympathetic, wrote ardently and prolifically about France, and reached a wide readership. The 'new France' of the Fifth Republic was the subject of solid and immensely detailed books by John Ardagh, which were constantly kept up to date.[17] Theodore Zeldin, an eminent historian of France, combined deep knowledge with flair in a survey of *The French*.[18] Christopher Sinclair-Stevenson wrote a book presenting a personal, and highly sympathetic, view of France and the French.[19] These were only the outstanding contributions to a stream of explanation and comment. The British showed every sign of being interested in France. What did they see?

16. Henderson's valedictory despatch, 31 March 1979, on 'Britain's Decline: Its Causes and Consequences', reprinted in Nicholas Henderson, *Channels and Tunnels. Reflections on Britain and Abroad* (London, 1987), pp. 143–58; the quotation is from p. 145.

17. John Ardagh, *The New French Revolution. A Social and Economic Survey of France, 1945–1967* (London, 1968); *The New France. De Gaulle and After* (London, Penguin edn, 1970); *France Today* (London, 1987; Penguin edn, 1988).

18. Theodore Zeldin, *The French* (London, 1983).

19. Christopher Sinclair-Stevenson, *That Sweet Enemy. A Personal View of France and the French* (London, 1987).

John Ardagh's books presented a serious, efficient and dynamic society. He hammered home statistics about economic growth, and described living standards and lifestyles well above those in Britain. Taking the three countries of Britain, France and West Germany, up to about 1960 Britain had been the richest, but in the 1980s was the poorest. By then, Germany was the wealthiest, but France too was doing well. The British, wrote Ardagh, looked at the new France with a mixture of envy and admiration. 'How have those damned French managed it?' they wanted to know.[20] It would have been more accurate to write that 'some of the British' wanted to know; but in any case Ardagh set out to tell them. He advanced two main answers: technical and administrative quality, and the revival of self-confidence and ambition.

The success of French administration sprang from the *grandes écoles*, and especially the *Ecole Nationale d'Administration*, founded at the end of the Second World War as the great training ground for French civil servants, managers and politicians. Selection for the ENA was rigorous, and the training it provided was intensive and highly specialised. The School's graduates were usually destined for the highest posts in government, industry, banking and commerce. But there was more to it than that. Theodore Zeldin acutely observed that the ENA 'has given the routine business of training civil servants the aura of an organised conspiracy'. The *énarques*, as the former students at the ENA were (and are) called, all knew one another and kept in touch. Zeldin found that the mayor of Josselin, a medium-sized town in Brittany, was the 14th Duc de Rohan. He was also an *énarque*, and when he needed something really important for his town he could simply ring up Jacques Chirac, another *énarque* who at the time was Premier of France.[21] British observers were not entirely sure what to make of all this. The natural comparison was with the 'old boy network' in Britain; but for many the 'old boy network' was a stifling anachronism and not to be admired. Again, the *Ecole Nationale d'Administration*, like the whole French system of *grandes écoles*, relied on ruthless selection on academic merit and the cultivation of an intellectual elite. The general trend of thought in Britain, in the educational establishment and in society as a whole, was by contrast anti-elitist. Moreover, the new French aristocracy of intellect was largely the preserve of the privileged classes, who had the wealth and standing to send their children to the best schools in order to gain entrance to the *grandes écoles*. Careers were indeed open to talent, but talent tended to be

20. Ardagh, *France Today*, p. 28.
21. Zeldin, *The French*, pp. 164–5.

nurtured in a particular way and in particular social groups. The British who were aware of the system often deplored the encouragement of what was a social as well as an intellectual caste. And yet the system worked, and some British observers admired its products. The topmost echelons of French administration and business displayed a remarkable efficiency and sophistication, and meshed together with the EEC bureaucracy in Brussels with a skill that the British found difficult to match.

The new psychology of France, springing from a reborn self-confidence and zest, was less easy to pin down. John Ardagh noted, as did any frequent visitor to France, how the atmosphere of the country changed from the late 1950s onwards. The French themselves changed, casting off their backward ways, responding to 'the thrill of the modern world', and taking avidly to all the marvels of technology.[22] Yet they contrived to embrace modernity while retaining their historic pride in the glory of France. Their sense of *la gloire* went back to Louis XIV and beyond, and took many forms. It remained military – is there another European country that has a military parade like that down the Champs Elysées on 14 July? It was strongly cultural, as displayed in the new *Musée d'Orsay*, the vast extensions to the Louvre, and the ambitious if wayward enterprise of the Opera House at Bastille. It was also technological, so that the TGV passenger train, the *Ariane* rocket or a nuclear power station all became sources of French pride.

This was a crucial matter. French pride had been badly shaken by the defeat of 1940 and the ambiguities (and the shame) of collaboration. The turning-point in leaving these events behind and recovering self-confidence was the return of de Gaulle in 1958. De Gaulle set out at once on a course of resolute independence and ambitious patriotism, and he was followed both by the French people and by his successors as President, whatever their political colour. In 1986, under the socialist President Mitterrand, French agents sank the Greenpeace vessel *Rainbow Warrior* in Auckland harbour, and the French government effectively shrugged off the whole affair. Mitterrand himself told Chancellor Kohl that he had expected to be asked to say that he had taken no part in the plan, but instead people told him he had done well; Charles Hernu, the Defence Minister, had never been so popular. A British writer summed up the French attitude briskly: 'If a boat is blown up in Auckland, *tant pis.*'[23] The episode is worth recalling, because it displayed an attitude of mind that

22. Ardagh, *France Today*, p. 17.
23. Jacques Attali, *Verbatim*, vol. II, *Chronique des années 1986–1988* (Paris, 1995), p. 98; Sinclair-Stevenson, *Sweet Enemy*, p. 184.

the British now find hard to understand – a willingness to stand against the world, even if by legal and moral standards France was in the wrong.

The roots of such attitudes ran deep. Sinclair-Stevenson wrote in his book *Sweet Enemies* that 'The French are grumblers, but on one point they are united: France is, for all her faults, the best, most civilised, most beautiful country in the world'. Rather strangely, he chose to call this sentiment chauvinism; but even so he stressed its virtues. 'Chauvinism is alive and well in France . . . It would be absurd and damaging if it did not exist at all. The arts and sciences flourish best in an atmosphere of self-confidence; economic and social improvements are not likely to materialise when a nation has lost her own spirit.'[24] 'Chauvinism' is surely not the best word – patriotism would be better. But whichever word is chosen, the verdict stands.

In all this, contrasts with Britain were painfully obvious. The French were self-confident and proud of *la patrie*. The British were riven with self-doubt and often denigrated their own country. The same was true in simple material ways. The Paris *métro* worked better than the London underground: the one 'clean, attractive and easily comprehensible', the other 'filthy, dangerous and baffling'.[25] John Ardagh, relating the wretched story of Manufrance, a French workers' co-operative which struggled vainly to keep going in the 1970s, was appalled when he visited the firm: 'semi-derelict nineteenth-century workshops, obsolete machinery, worse than anything I'd seen, *even in Britain*'.[26] That single phrase, 'even in Britain', almost thrown away, is highly significant.

Efficiency, self-confidence and dynamism – these were the characteristics of France as seen by most British observers in the 1970s and 1980s. But there were doubters. On the one hand there were those Britons who kept their eyes resolutely closed, and chose to regard France as a country where the people were slightly comic and the drains did not work. More seriously, there were a few who kept their eyes very much open and had grave doubts about the new France. John Laughland, writing from a vantage-point within one of the *grandes écoles* in Paris, published a series of sceptical articles in the *Spectator*, and then a book entitled *The Death of Politics*. His purpose was 'to crawl inside the political system of France to see whether the grass is really so much greener on the other side of the Channel'.[27]

24. Sinclair-Stevenson, *Sweet Enemy*, p. 188.
25. Ibid., pp. 24–5.
26. Ardagh, *France Today*, p. 62. The italics are mine.
27. John Laughland, *The Death of Politics. France under Mitterrand* (London, 1994); see especially p. xxiii.

British admirers of France had come to think that the grass was *always* greener. They marvelled at the TGV, the high-speed passenger train, with its smooth running and excellent time-keeping, and compared it with the miserable British attempts to produce a similar train, which never quite worked. They admired the engineers and technologists who produced such results, and jumped to the conclusion that 'government by administrators is better than government by parliament' – which did not necessarily follow.[28] Laughland was resolutely unimpressed by French politics, as distinct from administration. The political parties were all of recent creation, and represented primarily the personal ambitions of their creators – Mitterrand, Chirac, Giscard d'Estaing – without the corporate loyalties, strength and longevity of the principal British parties. British admirers of France erred in taking for granted, or even disparaging, the value of their own parliamentary institutions, which were the strongest in Europe, and over-praising the virtues of French bureaucracy.[29]

There were other notes of doubt. There were cracks and failings in the new France. In France, intellectuals and culture are of vital importance – Theodore Zeldin rightly observed that 'France has in a way been created as much by intellectuals as by kings and armies conquering territory'. Yet he also thought that in the early 1980s French intellectuals had lost much of their confidence.[30] John Ardagh, so full of admiration for many French achievements, drew similarly gloomy conclusions at the end of a vast survey of French culture in the 1980s. Paris intellectual life, he thought, was made up of 'dazzle and frenzy more than substance'. He could find no masterpieces in any of the art forms; instead, the staple fare was second-rate, 'beautifully gift-wrapped'.[31] There was a terrible emptiness at the heart of French life.

There was another sign of French uncertainty in their anxiety, amounting sometimes to an obsession, with the danger to the French language from the spread of English, or rather of American English. In 1964 René Etiemble published what became a famous book, *Parlez-vous franglais?*, whose title launched a new word in both the French and English languages. Etiemble's subject was the invasion of the French language by English and American words and phrases. His tone was partly humorous and partly ominous – he wrote of the 'enslavement' of France to the Anglo-Saxons, and claimed that the

28. Ibid., p. 266.
29. Ibid., p. 267.
30. Zeldin, *The French*, p. 398.
31. Ardagh, *France Today*, pp. 593, 628.

French language was among the corpses left by the Second World War.[32] But whatever the tone, the intention was never less than utterly serious. Since then, French governments have tried on a number of occasions to use legislation to check the advance of English in France. They have also worked unceasingly to promote *francophonie* in the world at large. In 1986 Mitterrand held the first world conference of *francophonie* at Versailles, amid the grandeur bequeathed by Louis XIV, during whose reign French had been the language of all civilised men. The second such conference was held at Quebec in 1987, when 37 countries were represented by 43 different delegations and sixteen heads of state (including Mitterrand himself) and twelve heads of government attended.[33] Queen Elizabeth II, as Queen of Canada, sent a message of welcome at the opening of the conference. These were the show-pieces of *francophonie*. Behind the scenes, the effort was unremitting. Mitterrand wrote in his *Réflexions*, published in 1986, that he regularly reviewed statistics relating to the place occupied by the French language in foreign schools and universities; and he wished France to cease participating in international institutions which professed to treat French as an official language but did not in practice use it as such.[34]

To many 'Anglo-Saxons' this obsession with the defence of the French language seemed to show a profound self-doubt. If the French language and French culture needed this sort of protection, there must be something amiss. Was French self-confidence only a thin covering over a morass of self-doubt? Sometimes (and this was even worse from the point of view of French self-esteem) the British regarded the cumbrous mechanisms for the defence of the French language as 'high comedy bordering on farce'.[35] In some ways this was true. The debates among French intellectuals about the threat to French culture presented by the opening of the Euro-Disney theme park outside Paris were sometimes astonishing. To describe Euro-Disney as a 'cultural Chernobyl' would have been comical if it had not been so seriously meant. For the debates *were* serious, and revealed more doubt than confidence in the French mind.

The British picture of France was thus, naturally enough, a mixture of light and shade. There was admiration for the achievements of the new France, and even some envy of the French elites and French pride, tempered by doubts as to the durability of those achievements

---

32. René Etiemble, *Parlez-vous franglais?* (Paris, 1964), p. 231.
33. Attali, *Verbatim*, vol. II, p. 381.
34. François Mitterrand, *Réflexions* (Paris, 1986), pp. 17–18.
35. Sinclair-Stevenson, *Sweet Enemy*, pp. 153–5.

and the depth of the self-confidence. But there was a different aspect of British interest in France which showed no signs of doubt. In the 1970s and 1980s the British found a renewed delight in taking holidays in France, and in buying houses there, usually as second homes but sometimes as permanent residences. This movement was largely to the south, to the Dordogne and Provence, where the immense success of Peter Mayle's books, *A Year in Provence* and *Toujours Provence*, was both a sign of the interest that already existed and an impulse to a new flood of purchasers.[36] But the British have also moved back to Normandy, where their predecessors had settled in the nineteenth century and stayed until the German invasion of 1940 drove them out. The new migration came from a wider range of British society than that of the nineteenth century, and it produced a flurry of new activities. There were books on living in France, and guides to French property law. Estate agents specialising in French properties flourished. In 1987 British residents in France began to produce their own newspaper, *The News*, which distressed the logical French mind by appearing at irregular intervals, but showed great staying-power – by September–October 1994 it had reached its 66th issue. The contents were sometimes very English (news of cricket matches in the Dordogne), but also showed a serious concern with French affairs – explanations of changes in French taxation, and guidance on how to deal with the event of death in France. The French often claim that the British are insular (British reluctance to accept the Channel Tunnel has over the years produced a crop of such assertions); yet in fact large numbers of British people commit themselves to living in France, with all the problems as well as the delights that that involves. By the end of the 1980s, British interest in and affection for France at this personal level was probably deeper and more vigorous than at any time since the nineteenth century; and certainly more widely spread.

Views across the Channel in the early 1990s were varied and sometimes contradictory. British people flooded in tens of thousands to France, often on holiday, sometimes to live there. Yet some of them made little contact with the country and its people beyond enjoying the sunshine, the food and the wine. There was a sharp division between those who continued to feel complacent about British superiority and those who used French examples to castigate British faults, whether in administration or technology. In France, the sense of

---

36. Peter Mayle, *A Year in Provence* (London, 1989); *Toujours Provence* (London, 1991). Both were reprinted several times, and *A Year in Provence* became the basis of a television series.

self-confidence and superiority that was so strong in the de Gaulle years and through into the 1970s and 1980s showed some cracks, as the Mitterrand Presidency came to an end amid political and financial scandals, and disturbing reminders of the years of occupation and collaboration. France also suffered the effects of economic depression, worsened by the government's determination to maintain a strong franc and pursue the goal of a single European currency – the thorny aspect of the European vision. In the early 1990s, for the first time for many years, the economic indicators were more favourable in Britain than in France. It has often been the case that the French and British look at one another in order to make comments on themselves. About 1990 those comments, on both sides, were less dogmatic than in recent years.

CHAPTER 14

A New Europe and Some Old Memories, 1989–1994

Between the closing months of 1989 and the end of 1991 the face of Europe was changed beyond recognition. The Berlin Wall came down. Germany was suddenly reunited, and the old East Germany was absorbed into the Federal Republic. The Soviet Union collapsed, and split up into a patchwork of new states, often at loggerheads with one another. Communist governments disappeared all over eastern Europe, and communism as a doctrine became largely discredited. It was a transformation so vast, rapid and unexpected as to beggar belief, and to tax all the resources of statesmanship.

At much the same time, between 1989 and 1992, the states of the European Economic Community were trying to take the next steps towards that 'ever closer union' referred to, though not defined, in the Treaty of Rome of 1957. In April 1989 a committee chaired by Jacques Delors, the President of the European Commission, proposed steps towards economic and monetary union within the Community (the word 'Economic' was being dropped at this stage). After several conferences, the Treaty of Maastricht on European Union was signed on 7 February 1992. This treaty created the European Union, and laid down that a common currency should be introduced by 1999. (It is more accurate to use the term 'a single currency' – in French 'une monnaie unique' – since what was proposed was the eventual substitution of a single new currency for existing national currencies.) The treaty also envisaged that common foreign and security policies should be introduced; and that there should be various common social policies. Thus while one part of Europe, in the east, was dissolving into an assortment of new nation states, the governments of the European Community were trying to create some form of union which, if pursued to its conclusion, would either replace or at least subsume the nation state.

France and Britain were thus plunged into the uncertainties of a new Europe, through the collapse of communism in the east and a leap forward in European union in the west. They had to look forward, with a mixture of fear and hope. Shortly afterwards, in 1994, they were both also impelled to look back. That year saw the 90th anniversary of the *Entente cordiale*, which stirred some reflections on the past, and also the 50th anniversary of the Normandy landings and the Liberation, which released waves of memories and emotions. Thus, within a very few years, the two countries had to think about their relations with one another, in terms of power politics and European integration, and also through the remembrance of things past. Then, also in 1994, the dream (or to some the nightmare) of the Channel Tunnel finally came true. It was a year for taking stock.

THE UNIFICATION OF GERMANY

The unification of Germany came with tremendous speed at the end of 1989. Before it came about, both Margaret Thatcher, the British Prime Minister, and François Mitterrand, the President of France, were dismayed at the prospect. Their underlying attitudes were in some ways different, in that Mitterrand showed every sign of preferring stability rather than liberty in eastern Europe, while Thatcher was prepared to go the other way. A crucial example concerned Poland. In December 1985 Mitterrand received the Communist ruler, General Jaruzelski, in Paris, offering a gesture of support for the man who had introduced martial law in Poland. When Thatcher went to Poland in December 1988 she insisted on going to see the opposition leader, Lech Walesa, in Danzig, and ostentatiously went to mass with him.[1] But Germany seemed likely to bring them together. Thatcher has written in her memoirs that she does not believe in collective guilt, but she does believe in national character; and since unification 'Germany has veered unpredictably between aggression and self-doubt'.[2] She therefore wanted to slow down – assuming that it was impossible to prevent – the process of German unification, and realised that this might best be achieved by Franco–British co-operation. As early as 1 September 1989, at a Franco–British summit meeting at Chequers, she argued that German unification was on the way.

1. John Laughland, *The Death of Politics. France under Mitterrand* (London, 1994), p. 245. Laughland uses the barbed phrase 'Mitterrand-Metternich', p. 247.
2. Margaret Thatcher, *The Downing Street Years* (London, 1993), p. 791.

Gorbachev, the Soviet leader, was too weak to prevent it, and Chancellor Kohl of West Germany positively wanted it – though he did not say so. At that stage, Mitterrand appeared confident that unification was impossible. Gorbachev would not allow a united Germany to join NATO; and the United States would not allow West Germany to leave the Atlantic Alliance. Therefore it would be best for France and Britain to say that unification would come when the German people wanted it, remaining secure in the knowledge that the two superpowers would prevent it.[3] Not until the end of October did Mitterrand begin to sense that Kohl was not telling him everything he either knew or intended on the subject of unification.

On 9 November 1989 the Berlin Wall came down, and events built up a new pace and momentum. On 28 November Kohl took the initiative, addressing the *Bundestag* with a ten-point plan for the reunification of Germany. The Chancellor had previously written to Mitterrand on other matters, saying nothing about these crucial proposals. When Mitterrand heard of the speech, he burst out: 'But he told me nothing! Nothing! I will never forget this!' But he still reiterated that Gorbachev would never allow it. 'I don't need to oppose it, the Soviets will do it for me.'[4] The European Council of the twelve members of the EEC met at Strasbourg on 8–9 December, under French chairmanship. Conducting the official business, Mitterrand insisted that issues of social policy, economic and monetary union, and the television and film industries ('l'Europe audiovisuelle') should remain the business of the meeting. The question of German unification was relegated to discussion outside the formal sessions. If the European Community was really a significant entity, aspiring towards a common foreign policy, this was a curious way of proceeding.

Outside the formal sessions at Strasbourg, Mitterrand and Thatcher had two private meetings to discuss Germany. Thatcher produced maps of Europe on the eve of the Second World War and in 1945, showing the drastic changes in German frontiers between those two periods. She feared that Germany would want to regain Silesia, Pomerania, East Prussia and the Sudetenland – fears which Mitterrand shared, observing in private conversation that Kohl was talking about the unity of the German people, which might include Germans in Polish Silesia and the Sudetenland. Thatcher held that existing frontiers must be respected, and unification postponed. Later, when East

3. Jacques Attali, *Verbatim*, vol. III, *Chronique des années 1988–1991* (Paris, 1995), p. 297.

4. Ibid., p. 350.

Germany had practised democracy for some fifteen years, they could talk about unification. Both leaders agreed that their two countries should draw closer together in face of the new German danger. Mitterrand said: 'We must establish special relations between France and Great Britain, as in 1913 and 1938.' (As a pair of dates, these had an ominous ring.) Thatcher records him as saying that 'at moments of great danger in the past France had always established special relations with Britain and he felt that such a time had come again. We must draw together and stay in touch'. She felt that they both had the will to 'check the German juggernaut', even though they had not discovered how to do it.[5]

For a brief moment the Prime Minister and President spoke in language that would have been understood before 1914 or 1939 – the old language of an *Entente* against Germany. But they went no further. In January 1990 Mitterrand visited East Germany, and despite his private anxieties said in public that he was not among those who wanted to put the brakes on the movement towards unification. On 20 January he again met Thatcher, this time in Paris. The Prime Minister had prepared papers on strengthening Franco-British relations. The two leaders again rehearsed their anxieties, and talked of the need to slow down the move towards unification; but neither of them knew how to do it.[6]

Nothing came of these discussions. On 15 February 1990 Kohl visited Mitterrand and dined at the Elysée. Mitterrand talked about German frontiers, and the necessity of maintaining the Oder–Neisse line between Germany and Poland. He also remarked that in future there would be 75 million Germans and 56 million Frenchmen. Kohl assured him that frontiers would be respected. For him, Franco-German co-operation was the only thing that mattered; and if Germany was united, then the bonds between the two countries would be all the more important.[7] This presumably gave Mitterrand the reassurances he was seeking. The frontier between Germany and Poland was specifically reaffirmed by a new treaty in November 1990. More important, the Franco-German partnership regained its solidarity. As Thatcher reflected in her memoirs, for Mitterrand to challenge Germany on the unification issue 'would have required abandoning the Franco-German axis on which he had been relying . . .'. He was fundamentally unwilling 'to change the direction of his whole foreign policy'. This showed a realistic grasp of the situation. As long ago as

5. Ibid., pp. 368–71; Thatcher, *Downing Street Years*, pp. 796–7.
6. Attali, *Verbatim*, vol. III, pp. 400–1; Thatcher, *Downing Street Years*, pp. 797–8.
7. Attali, *Verbatim*, vol. III, pp. 427–8.

April 1969, de Gaulle had told Maurice Schumann that no French foreign policy could be conceived which was not based on the irreversible nature of Franco-German reconciliation.[8] France was entirely committed to the European Community. After 1990, that Community would include a larger, and ultimately more powerful, Germany; but it was still through co-operation with Germany that France could remain a joint manager of the EC. It was true that German unification raised difficult questions. Would the new Germany still need France as a partner? How would France fare in a Europe where Germany was more powerful than before? But there was no sign that Britain, in terms of economics, politics or common outlook, would make a better partner for France. She would certainly not help France to maintain her leading position in a European Community to which Britain herself was only half-heartedly committed. France persisted in the policy of partnership with Germany. It is hard to think that there was any other choice available.

EUROPE MOVES ON: THE TREATY OF MAASTRICHT

The Franco-German partnership thus survived the crisis of German unification at the end of 1989 and the beginning of 1990. The existence of the new Germany made it more important than ever for France to consolidate the structures of the European Community, and to secure France's position within them. The years 1989–92 saw a new effort to move the Community forward in the direction of closer union, and towards some form of federalism. In April 1989 a committee chaired by Jacques Delors, the President of the European Commission, recommended that the Community should move, by three stages, to a monetary union, with a single currency managed by a European central bank. In April 1990 Mitterrand and Kohl issued a joint statement supporting these proposals. For nearly two years the members of the Community laboured to produce drafts, until finally, at a European summit meeting held at Maastricht on 9–11 December 1991, agreement was reached on a Treaty on European Union. This Treaty was signed at Maastricht on 7 February 1992. It was a vast and complicated document, consisting of 253 pages in the official text

8. Thatcher, *Downing Street Years*, pp. 791, 798; Jean Lacouture, *De Gaulle*, vol. III, *Le souverain* (Paris, 1986), p. 312.

published by the European Community, and open to differing interpretations.[9]

Despite the treaty's obscurities, there was no doubt that its main purpose was the development of closer union between the member states. The word 'federal' did not appear in the preamble, though it had been used in drafts of the treaty right up to the most recent draft prepared on 11 November 1991. The British government insisted that the word be dropped, ostensibly on the ground that 'federal' had a different significance in Britain from that attached to it on the continent; in practice, it would have been virtually impossible to get a commitment to federalism through Parliament. The preamble therefore referred to 'A new stage in the process of creating an ever closer union among the peoples of Europe', and the treaty set out definite steps towards economic and monetary union. (The words were usually capitalised, and then abbreviated to EMU, giving these serious matters a faintly surrealistic appearance, at any rate to English speakers.) The first stage of this movement was already in progress, with the setting up of an Exchange Rate Mechanism, which renewed the attempt to keep currencies within a band of 2.5 per cent up or down from an agreed exchange rate. The Treaty of Maastricht laid down that the second stage was to begin on 1 January 1994, with the creation of a European Monetary Institute, which was itself to be the precursor of a European central bank. The third stage was to be the introduction of a single currency, to begin by 1 January 1999. However, the treaty also provided that the European Council was to decide, by 31 December 1996, whether the economies of member states met four criteria which would enable them to move to the third stage and accept the single currency. These criteria related to inflation rates, the relative size of government deficits and public debt, fluctuation of exchange rates, and the level of interest rates. Taken together, they were very demanding conditions. At the insistence of the British government, a protocol allowed the United Kingdom to opt out of the third stage if it so chose; and on 21 November 1991 the House of Commons had voted to reserve the right of Parliament to decide at some future date whether or not to accept a single currency.

The treaty also laid down that the European Union and its member states should define and implement a common foreign and security

---

9. A summary of the Treaty of Maastricht may be found in *Keesing's Record of World Events*, vol. 37, 1991, pp. 38657–8. Other summaries appear in William Nicoll and Trevor C. Salmon, *Understanding the New European Community* (London, 1994), pp. 280–95 (with sympathetic commentary), and Michael Spicer, *A Treaty Too Far*, (London, 1992), pp. 119–38 (with critical commentary).

policy, which should include the eventual framing of a common defence policy. The means by which these objectives were to be achieved were left vague. In practice, the main foreign policy issues of 1991 (the Gulf War against Iraq, and the disintegration of Yugoslavia) revealed such deep divisions between the member states of the European Community that it appeared highly unlikely that they could agree on any foreign or military policy.

The treaty also included a large number of provisions dealing with immigration, border controls, political asylum, measures against drug traffic, and judicial co-operation. Another section dealt with cultural affairs. One chapter which had been included in all the drafts of the treaty did not appear in the final document: that dealing with social policy. The British government consistently opposed the inclusion of this section (usually referred to as the Social Chapter), on the grounds that it would interfere excessively in internal affairs and damage the British economy by imposing extra social charges. At the very last moment, in the early hours of 11 December 1991, the other EC governments agreed to remove the whole section on social policy from the treaty, and to accept the Social Chapter as an agreement between eleven states. This left the United Kingdom free to accept or reject individual items of social policy introduced under this agreement, as it thought best.

How far did these matters affect relations between Britain and France, as distinct from Britain and all the other members of the European Community? On the issue of the movement towards federalism, or some form of European super-state, the fundamental positions of the two countries may not have been very far apart. British opposition to such aspirations was open and obvious, and exemplified by the removal of any reference to federalism in the pre-amble to the treaty. The French government did not baulk at the word 'federal', and were much readier than the British to talk the language of Europeanism. They were also prepared to accept a single currency, which was a big step. Yet when Delors, the President of the European Commission, proposed on French television on 23 January 1990 a European federation with a political executive to identify common interests, responsible to the European Parliament as well as to national parliaments, Mitterrand at once exclaimed: 'But it's absurd! What is he up to? No-one in Europe would ever want such a thing! By going to extremes, he will wreck what is actually feasible.'[10] There is no sign that Mitterrand had any desire to hand over French foreign

10. Attali, *Verbatim*, vol. III, p. 401.

policy, or even more defence policy, to some sort of majority voting in Brussels. The French nuclear deterrent remained firmly French.

Again, there proved to be in both countries a considerable degree of opposition to the Treaty of Maastricht. In Britain, the parliamentary proceedings to ratify the treaty were long drawn out, and involved some very close votes. The vote on the principle of the Bill approving the treaty, on 21 May 1992, was 336 in favour and 92 against. This was a majority of 244, but was less impressive than it appeared, because the official line of the Labour opposition was to abstain. (In fact, 61 Labour MPs voted against the Bill, as did 22 Conservatives.) At that point, the Danish people voted against the treaty in a referendum (2 June), and further consideration in the House of Commons was postponed. The subject was reopened on 4 November, when a motion to continue proceedings on the Bill was passed by 319 votes to 316 – a wafer-thin majority of three. Thereafter, the process of ratification was again postponed until the Danes had achieved fresh terms and held another referendum, which this time accepted the treaty. The Third Reading of the Bill approving the treaty was taken on 20 May 1993, when the government secured a majority of 292 votes to 112; the opposition included 41 Conservatives voting against their own government, and 65 Labour members who rejected their party's policy of abstention. When the final stage of ratification was voted on (23 July 1993), the Prime Minister made it a question of confidence in the government, and achieved a majority of 339 votes to 299.[11] The whole process was fraught with difficulties for the government, and divided both main parties. The final majority of 40 votes was comfortable but far from overwhelming. Throughout the long procedure, the government refused requests to hold a referendum, partly on constitutional grounds, and partly doubtless out of fear of defeat.

In France, the Assembly passed the ratification of the Maastricht Treaty by the very large majority of 398–77, with 99 abstentions. Then President Mitterrand called a referendum on the treaty, for which there was no constitutional necessity. In June 1992 public opinion polls showed a majority of two-thirds in favour of the treaty, but in a hard-fought campaign that lead was whittled away. Opposition to the treaty was led by two hard-hitting politicians, Séguin and Pasqua, and the debate revealed greater fears about loss of sovereignty and the influence of a united Germany than had previously been apparent. By the end of August, the opinion polls showed the

11. The votes are set out in *Keesing's Record of World Events*, vol. 38, 1992, pp. 38931, 39205; vol. 39, 1993, pp. 39483, 39574.

two sides to be almost level, and defeat for the treaty (and for President Mitterrand, who had committed himself to it) seemed possible. The vote took place on 20 September. The turn-out was 69.78 per cent, and the result was: Yes, 13,162,992 (51.05 per cent); No, 12,623,582 (48.95 per cent). The 'Yes' majority was thus 539,410 (2.1 per cent). 909,377 votes were declared void.[12] Both the campaign and the vote had shown French opinion on the issue of European integration to be far more divided than had previously appeared. It is true that the referendum campaign had been a complicated affair, and many of the 'No' votes were probably anti-government as much as anti-Maastricht. Even so, it was plain that there were doubts in France about the treaty very similar to those in Britain.

When the voting was over, however, French policy resumed its normal European course. Franco-German relations continued to be close. Mitterrand and Kohl appeared to overcome the friction generated between them at the time of German unification. The Euro-Corps made steady progress, and German troops were invited to take part in the Bastille Day parade on 14 July 1994. In September, Mitterrand gave a series of press interviews to mark the approaching end of his long term as President of the Republic, and went out of his way to reaffirm his commitment to the European idea. Specifically, he took pains to emphasise that the monetary union envisaged in the Maastricht Treaty would in fact come about between 1997 and 1999.[13]

British policy was very different. The British government continued to be the odd man out in Europe. They had rejected the whole Social Chapter which was to have been part of the Maastricht Treaty, and signalled their doubts about monetary union by securing the right to opt out. In the event, British policy on monetary union went into reverse in 1992, not long after the Treaty of Maastricht had been signed and before it had been ratified. Britain had joined the Exchange Rate Mechanism only in October 1990, at a rate of exchange of 2.95 German marks to the pound sterling. According to the rules of the ERM, the pound should not thereafter move more than 2.25 per cent up or down from that rate of exchange. In practice, the rate proved too high. In the summer of 1992 there was heavy speculation against sterling, putting pressure on the British government to devalue. Repeatedly, the government insisted that the position of sterling within the Exchange Rate Mechanism would be defended by all necessary means. The Chancellor of the Exchequer (Norman Lamont) and the Prime Minister (John Major) both affirmed their total

---

12. Figures in ibid., vol. 38, 1992, pp. 39081–2.
13. Mitterrand, interview in *Le Figaro*, 9 Sept. 1994.

commitment to the ERM and rejected devaluation. On 16 September 1992 the government raised interest rates by no less than 5 per cent, but still had to take the pound out of the ERM and allow it to float – that is, in practice, to devalue. Then, within that same extraordinary day, interest rates were reduced by 5 per cent, leaving them where they had been at the start of the day. During the crisis, the German *Bundesbank* at first spent heavily to support both the pound and the Italian lira (which was also in trouble, and was devalued before sterling); but at the crunch the Germans let sterling go. The following year, 1993, during a wave of speculation against the French franc, the German government and the *Bundesbank* stood firm, supported the franc, and maintained the exchange rate between the mark and the franc. The Exchange Rate Mechanism itself broke down at that stage, and a meeting of Finance Ministers (2 August 1993) agreed that currencies should fluctuate within a broad band of 15 per cent rather than the old narrow band of 2.25 per cent; but at least the 'strong franc' was saved.

The most immediately important element in the Maastricht Treaty had been the movement towards monetary union. The British were dubious about this from the start, and made sure that they could opt out if they so wished. France, on the other hand, remained committed to monetary union and the introduction of a single currency according to the timetable laid down in the treaty. The two countries thus pursued divergent policies on this vital European issue.

The two were also at loggerheads over an issue of personalities. In June 1994, at a European summit meeting in Corfu, the British Prime Minister, John Major, insisted on vetoing the nomination of Jean-Luc Dehaene as the next President of the European Commission, in succession to Jacques Delors, even though Dehaene had the support of all the other eleven members of the Community. The reaction of the French press was fierce. In *Le Figaro*, a leading article thundered: 'Once more, de Gaulle was right: England is an island, which all the bridges and tunnels in the world will never succeed in linking to the continent. She should not have been allowed into the Common Market. She should have become an associate.' Others were less stern in language, but the general verdict was that the British veto was another sign of their continuing belief that the European Union should be primarily a free-trade area, with the barest minimum of political integration; and that this was opposed to the French conception of Europe.[14] After Maastricht, as before, the French and British had different ideas of Europe.

14. *Le Figaro*, 27 June 1994; summary of French press in *The Times,* 28 June.

A ROYAL VISIT TO FRANCE, 1992

In June 1992 the Queen and the Duke of Edinburgh made a state visit to France. As in the case of other state visits, it was an occasion for the two countries to be on their best behaviour towards one another, and it is interesting to see what was put on show. It was also an opportunity for the French to take stock of the new condition of Britain, and indeed of the Royal family, which was itself plagued by its own difficulties.

The themes of the visit were varied. It remained obligatory – yet much more than routine, because for many people the emotions were still strong – to evoke the memories of the two World Wars. Pierre Bérégovoy, the Socialist Premier, who was himself of the generation of the Second World War, made a moving speech. 'There are, on French soil, near Verdun or Sainte-Mère Eglise, crosses beneath which lie, side by side, young Britons and young Frenchmen who died for liberty. We do not forget that, Madame.'[15] Another theme, common to many state visits in the past, was that of a shared culture. The French Minister of Culture, Jack Lang ('Union Jack Lang', wrote the humorous weekly *Le Canard enchaîné*), escorted the Queen round the splendid new Musée d'Orsay, converted from the old railway station at the Gare d'Orsay, and one of the best examples of French cultural panache and public devotion to the visual arts. By a happy coincidence, the Queen was also able to visit an exhibition of Henry Moore sculptures displayed in the gardens at the Bagatelle. A third theme, and the principal political emphasis, was that of Britain in Europe. The Queen began her visit by declaring that 'Great Britain has her place at the heart of Europe', repeating a phrase used earlier by her Prime Minister. Later, she made a humorous reference to differences between France and Britain, ending on an optimistic note: 'The indelible imprint which France has made on the Community is not always comfortable for those whose institutions are based on different traditions. The Anglo-Saxon tradition is, in a way, to the Latin tradition what oil is to vinegar. Both are needed to make the sauce; if not, the salad is badly seasoned.'[16] On the French side, a television news presenter described the Queen as 'a sovereign of Europe'.

Much of the French press was enthusiastic in its reporting of the

---

15. *Le Figaro*, 11 June 1992.
16. *Libération*, 10 June 1992; *Le Monde*, 11 June. On both occasions, the Queen spoke in French – impeccably, according to *Libération*'s correspondent.

visit. *Le Monde*, it is true, was brief to the point of dismissiveness; but *La Libération*, a left-wing paper, had a headline 'Chapeau, la Reine!', and described the Queen as a star hit. *Le Figaro* headed its leading article 'Vive la Reine', and reflected on the paradox of a Republican people that became on such an occasion 'more royalist than the Queen'. The popular *Quotidien de Paris* observed that for a President of the Republic 'the official visit of a Queen – especially when she comes from England – is a red-letter day'. François Mitterrand, that socialist monarch, with his eye on history, was making the most of the occasion with galas and dinners – 'You would think yourself back in the days of the Bourbons'. Such remarks were familiar from Royal visits earlier in the century – the intensely Republican President Poincaré had always been pleased to welcome monarchs. But on this occasion there was a new note – humorous, good-natured and familiar. People interviewed on the Champs Elysées remarked sympathetically on the Queen's difficulties with her children. *La Libération* reported remarks to the effect of 'Ah yes, she has no luck with her four children – all those divorces'. A cartoon showed two French women saying to one another: 'It's hard work reigning over 50 million British – and two daughters-in-law!' This current of fellow-feeling for the problems of a mother gave the visit a more personal, down-to-earth aspect than earlier state occasions, which had doubtless been more splendid but also more remote. The British monarchy had come down a peg or two, and the Queen was all the more welcome as a result.[17]

The Queen gave much pleasure in south-western France by extending her tour to Bordeaux, where the English connections were still strong. There above all she was welcomed as representing the old England and its enduring qualities. Yet the visit as a whole reflected the new Britain, with its uncertain identity and its ambiguous role in Europe. The British Embassy rounded off an evening's entertainment during the visit with bagpipes and Scottish country dancing; drawing from a French guest the remark that if the United Kingdom broke up it would be hard to replace such a display.[18] There had been enough French comment in recent years about the disunity of the United Kingdom to give these words a sharp edge. Equally, the Queen (obviously on ministerial advice) made Europe a central theme of her speeches, but it could escape no-one that the phrase 'at the heart of Europe' had a hollow ring. Not for the first time, a state visit revealed much about the relations between France and Britain.

Queen Elizabeth the Queen Mother could always be relied upon,

17. *Le Monde, Libération, Le Figaro, Quotidien de Paris*, all 10 June 1992.
18. *The Times*, 11 June 1992.

from 1938 onwards, to smooth the path of Franco–British relations. In June 1993 she unveiled a statue of General de Gaulle in Carlton Gardens, where the General had established his London headquarters during the Second World War. The impulse to erect the statue, and much of the fund-raising effort, came from Lady Soames, the daughter of de Gaulle's old friend and antagonist Winston Churchill, and the widow of Christopher Soames, at one time Ambassador in Paris and the unhappy participant in the 'Soames affair'. Philippe de Gaulle, the General's son, attended the ceremony. Jean d'Ormesson, writer and member of the Académie Française, took the opportunity to suggest that a statue to Churchill should be erected in Paris to match this British tribute to de Gaulle.[19] That time will surely come. Franco–British relations have their moments of warmth and mutual respect; though it is somehow sad that those moments arise so often from wartime memories.

1994: SOME MEMORIES, AND THE TUNNEL AT LAST

The year 1994 brought a number of occasions for reflection on relations between France and Britain. April saw the 90th anniversary of the signing of the *Entente cordiale* in 1904. In May the Channel Tunnel, so long debated, planned and disputed, was formally opened. In June the wartime Allies marked the 50th anniversary of the Normandy landings in 1944.

Recalling the *Entente* proved an ambiguous exercise, even for sympathetic observers of Franco–British relations. *Le Monde* marked the 90th anniversary with a long article, looking back to the events of 1904, but concluding on the theme of separation between the two countries. As early as 1919 the peace settlement had seen the resurgence of rivalry between them, and in recent years England had succumbed to her old temptation of isolation from Europe, while France had sought reconciliation with Germany. Thus the two countries had turned away from one another, and the *Entente cordiale* seemed no more than a golden but fleeting moment of friendship between two ancient nations, destined to be sisters yet enemies.[20] André Fontaine, formerly editor of *Le Monde*, took up much the same theme in a long article in *The Economist*. Fontaine observed that almost

19. Ibid., 24 June 1993, with a photograph of the statue.
20. *Le Monde*, 10/11 April 1994, article by Laurent Zeccini.

everything combined to make the British and French twin peoples. They were roughly the same size in population; they were close neighbours; they had lost their empires and declined from the status of world powers; they both possessed nuclear weapons. Yet if they were twins, they did not spring from the same egg. Each was, in its own way, insular: Britain because it was physically an island, France because of its cast of mind. Each was sharply conscious of its individuality: 'To affirm one's singularity is, by definition, to cultivate one's differences.' Among those differences, Fontaine drew particular attention to the issue of language, not in the simple sense that the two peoples spoke different languages, but because language formed crucial barriers of resentment on the French side and incomprehension on the British. The French were determined to protect the life of their language, which was spoken by no more than 3 per cent of the world's population, whereas English was well on the way to becoming the global language. Most British people simply had no understanding of the French attitude, which only exasperated the French further. Fontaine concluded with an impassioned appeal to the British and French to stop wrangling about Europe, and 'try to settle on a common answer to this question of what Europe should become'. He saw little hope that such a common answer could be achieved; but without it the two peoples would find that they had only two destinations ahead: either to become residents in a retirement home (but at whose expense?), or to be attendants in a museum for tourists from the West and the Far East. It was a bleak prospect.[21]

Charles Bremner, the perceptive *Times* correspondent in Paris, observed that 1994 saw not only the 90th anniversary of the *Entente cordiale* of 1904 but also the 150th anniversary of the first use of that famous expression in 1844. The trouble was that recent history told heavily against cordial relations between the two countries. In France, the wounds of the Second World War had yet to heal, and the French, to escape from the ignominy of defeat and occupation, had thrown themselves into building a Europe created in their own image. Most of the French political establishment believed that Britain did not really wish to take part in this new Europe, which would have to be achieved against British opposition. But there was something even deeper dividing the two countries. Bremner, like Fontaine, attached crucial importance to language. France was afraid of Anglo-Saxon cultural supremacy – 'French civilisation is being drowned by its ancestral Anglophone rival'. Bremner concluded: 'It may surprise

21. *The Economist*, 30 April 1994, article by André Fontaine.

Britons, inured as they are to decline and a sense of national impotence, but France really does believe that the United Kingdom is on the winning side.'[22] It was a fascinating variation on the theme of self-confidence. In the 1960s and 1970s it seemed that the British had lost their confidence, while the French had rediscovered theirs. By the 1990s, perhaps both were racked by self-doubt.

It was sadly apparent that, on the 90th anniversary of the *Entente*, doubts and problems predominated. It was symptomatic that *The Times*, in a leading article on 9 April 1994, felt obliged to point out, rather than taking it for granted, that 'France is, in fact, the friend, ally and partner of Great Britain, and not her enemy'.

Hard on the heels of the anniversary of the *Entente* came the official opening of the Channel Tunnel. This was the end of an old and tangled story. A historian of the Tunnel counted a total of 138 projects for a fixed link (tunnel or bridge, or combination of the two) since 1802.[23] On 6 May 1994 the deed was formally accomplished. The Queen and President Mitterrand inaugurated the Tunnel, and each visited the other's country for the first time without crossing the sea or taking to the air. The occasion was marked with due ceremony, and yet even these observances showed up some marked differences of view. President Mitterrand's principal speech emphasised that the Tunnel would reinforce the European Union. The Queen, in contrast to her speeches during the state visit in 1992, and undoubtedly following the advice of her ministers, did not mention Europe at all.[24] In an age dominated by television, there was much significance in the contrasted presentation of the event on television in the two countries. In France, the inauguration of the Tunnel occupied one channel (Arte) from 8.30 a.m. to 6.55 p.m., as well as taking up much time on the three main channels, with live coverage for many hours. At Montparnasse railway station an enormous screen displayed the opening of the Tunnel nonstop all day, to large though shifting audiences. On British television, BBC 1 provided half an hour in the morning and an hour (extendable) in the afternoon; otherwise, the Tunnel was merely a news story. There was a vast difference in attitude between the two countries – between governments and news editors, certainly, but also between publics.[25]

The opening of the Tunnel seemed to be a greater event in France than in Britain, probably because the British themselves were still

---

22. *The Times*, 9 April 1994, article by Charles Bremner.
23. Bertrand Lemoine, *Le tunnel sous la Manche* (Paris, 1991), p. 9.
24. *The Times*, 7 May 1994.
25. TV programmes set out in the press in both countries, 6 May 1994.

divided and uneasy in mind. The French press were convinced of the significance of the event. Their headlines left no room for doubt: it was the end of English insularity. England was no longer an island. It seems likely that many of the British shared this view, but they were at the very least equivocal in their welcome for the new state of affairs. The *Guardian* brought out a joint edition on the Tunnel with its left-wing equivalent in France, *La Libération*. The *Guardian's* editor, Peter Preston, predicted that in 50 or 100 years' time the date of the Tunnel's opening would remain engraved on peoples' memories, while that of the Normandy landings in 1944 would merely be an obscure anniversary. In time, both French and British would travel as though their countries were part of the same territory, as the young were already doing. The day marked the start of a new and happy co-operation.[26] It may prove to be so; but were such sentiments widely shared at the time? A French journalist reflected shrewdly on the doubts of the British people about the Tunnel. The British, in relation not just to France but to Europe as a whole, suffered from the Norman habit of saying 'p'tet ben qu'oui – p'tet ben qu'non' ('perhaps yes – perhaps no'). The Tunnel was not likely to change this deep-seated frame of mind.[27] François Bédarida, too, putting events in historical perspective, welcomed the realisation of an age-old dream, but doubted whether it would have much effect on attitudes on either side of the Channel. The rivalries that were so often invoked in the media of both countries were the legacy of history and a part of national identity. Metaphorically, the train of prejudice was still on the rails. Would the TGV actually displace it? It was very doubtful.[28]

Alas, for some time even the TGV failed to run. A publicity campaign had led potential travellers to expect a regular service between London and Paris to follow immediately upon the historic journeys of the Queen and the President of the Republic; but in fact this did not occur until November 1994. When the trains began to run, they moved at high speed over the plains of northern France, but then ambled gently from the coast of Kent to Waterloo. This was a contrast that resulted largely from the facts of geography – it is impossible to lay a straight track across Kent along which a train can move at high speed; but all too often it also appeared symbolic of attitudes in the two countries, and seemed to reflect a contrast between modernity in France and backwardness in Britain. Reviews of the economic effects of the Tunnel by mid-1995 found only limited

26. *Guardian-Libération*, joint edition, 6 May 1994, article by Preston.
27. *Réforme*, 7 May 1994, article by Jean-Pierre Richardot.
28. *Guardian-Libération*, joint edition, 6 May 1994, article by François Bédarida.

developments in Kent and the Pas-de-Calais. In France, it seemed likely that the major benefits would be felt in places up to 100 miles from the coast. On the British side, there was no evidence of changes in attitudes towards France or Europe; and indeed there were signs of an increase in 'Euro-scepticism' at the very time when the Tunnel was opened and brought into operation.[29] The Tunnel had been for nearly two centuries the source of dreams for some and nightmares for others. It may well prove to be simply a stretch of railway line.

The formal opening of the Tunnel was followed within a month by the 50th anniversary of the Normandy landings on 6 June 1944. The Queen once again travelled to France, this time (as was fitting) by sea, along with thousands of ex-servicemen, their families, and other visitors. As an occasion in relations between France and Britain, the commemoration proved ambiguous. Along the coast where the British landings had taken place, and inland at Bayeux and other towns, a warm and generous atmosphere prevailed. The Regional Council of Basse-Normandie produced an excellent newspaper-style publication in English. The Council's President, René Garrec, wrote a moving intro-duction, aimed primarily at those who were too young to remember the events of 1944. The veterans who returned to Normandy were proud to have fought in a just cause, against a terrible regime which had reduced Europe to slavery. 'Together with all the people of Lower Normandy, we shall say to them "Thank you, and welcome to the towns and villages of the province".' These men had come to liberate France.[30] Yet shortly before the anniversary, a French public opinion poll conducted for *Le Figaro* showed that 90 per cent of those questioned thought that the Free French had played a major part in the Liberation. Another poll carried out for *Le Monde* revealed that the respondents believed that the Allies and the French Resistance had taken equal shares in driving the Germans out of France.[31] During the commemorations themselves, an impressionistic survey of French television presentation showed a disproportionate emphasis on the role of those few French commandos who took part in the landings.

French public attitudes showed how successful de Gaulle had been in implanting, at the time of the Liberation of Paris in August 1944, the myth of self-liberation. At the end of August 1994 the liberation of the capital was again celebrated with great ceremony, and with heavy

---

29. Clive Church, 'The Effects of the Channel Tunnel – a provisional balance sheet', *Modern and Contemporary France*, new series, vol. 3, No. 1, 1995, pp. 29–39.

30. Conseil Régional, Basse-Normandie, *50th Anniversary of D-Day: Welcome– Bienvenue* (Caen, 1994).

31. Polls reported in *The Times*, 31 May 1994.

emphasis on the role of Leclerc's 2e Division Blindée and the Paris *résistants*, and very little mention of the American 4th Infantry Division, which had reached the Ile de la Cité at much the same time as Leclerc's troops passed the Porte d'Orleans – not to mention the vast Allied forces which made the liberation of Paris possible at all.[32] This depiction of events responded to a natural and deeply felt French need; but it was bad history, and nourished British feelings that the French were not sufficiently grateful for their liberation.

The commemorations of summer 1994 revived the wartime memories that still formed a close bond between individual British and French participants in the great events of 1944. British ex-servicemen were made warmly welcome as they visited the scenes of battles long ago. Members of the special forces who had worked closely with the French Resistance, and the RAF pilots who had flown hazardous missions to bring Resistance leaders out of France and take them back again, attended affectionate reunions with old comrades. Yet at the same time, among those who were not thus personally involved, the memories of war were divisive. The war itself had, after all, been a time of much agony and conflict in relations between Britain and France, and its memory could only reflect that fact.

The coincidence of these three occasions – the 90th anniversary of the *Entente*, the opening of the Tunnel and the 50th anniversary of D-Day – meant at least that during 1994 the two countries and their peoples could scarcely lose sight of one another. Their past relations and their present contacts were constantly on display. In that respect, 1994 was a distinctive year. Was it also exceptional, perhaps even the last of its kind?

---

32. In a twelve-page supplement to *Le Figaro*, 25 Aug. 1994, the US 4th Infantry Division received one sentence of six lines, on p. 9.

Some Snapshots by Way of a Conclusion

There is, by the nature of things, no conclusion to this story. Britain and France remain two old neighbours, whether friends or enemies. They are separated by narrow seas, and now linked by the Channel Tunnel. They are divided and yet drawn together by memories of the past. Those whom geography and history have bound together will not easily be put asunder; but no-one knows what is going to happen to them next. They are often described as sisters, or cousins – at any rate, members of the same family; and there is indeed a family feeling about their relations with one another. Let us then conclude by looking at a few snapshots from the family album, taken during the past half-dozen years.

In 1975 François Crouzet, a French historian deeply learned in British history and also keenly interested in current relations between the two countries, published an illuminating essay on 'Problems of Communication between Britain and France in the Nineteenth and Twentieth Centuries'. When this article was translated into English in 1990, he took the opportunity to add two postcripts, written in 1985 and 1989 respectively. In 1985 he thought that British entry into the EEC had increased friction between Britain and France, because anti-European sentiment in Britain tended to concentrate upon France, as the nearest and apparently most dominating member of the Community. Moreover, probably for the first time in peacetime, millions of people were directly concerned with relations with France, often in relation to food prices or surpluses. The antagonism was mutual. In Britain, France appeared as 'the profiteer of the Common Market', while in France Britain appeared as 'the filibuster who puts spokes in the wheels of Europe and who only came into the EEC in order to sabotage it'. By 1989 Crouzet felt that these disputes had diminished. British hostility against the European Community had become concentrated against the Brussels bureaucracy. (Though of course that bureaucracy was headed by a Frenchman, Jacques Delors!)

Public opinion polls also showed changes over the same years. A survey commissioned by the Franco-British Council in November 1984 (using a sample of 2,000 respondents in each country) showed that 72 per cent of the French regarded the British as 'sympathique', while 61 per cent of the British found the French 'nice'. In autumn 1988 polls showed a marked change from this situation. In October 1988 a sample of respondents in Britain was asked whether France was 'nice' or not: 29 per cent replied Yes; 17 per cent No; and no fewer than 54 per cent had no opinion. In November 1988, a French sample was asked which country was the best friend of France: 54 per cent replied West Germany; Britain came fourth, after the USA and Belgium, with 21 per cent. Crouzet reflected that if these three polls gave a fair picture, the old love–hate relationship between France and Britain was lapsing into indifference.[1] As far as France was concerned, this view was reinforced by an opinion poll in June 1991, when a sample of French respondents was asked whether they had confidence or lack of confidence in the foreign policies of certain countries. In these confidence stakes, West Germany and the United States came first equal, at 46 per cent confident, 30 per cent not. Remarkably, the Soviet Union (then on the verge of dissolution) came third, and Britain lay fourth, with 28 per cent confident and 48 per cent not.[2]

Some optimists about Franco-British relations tended to put their trust in the attitudes of younger generations, growing up with habits of easy travel and interchange, free from the stereotypes cherished by their elders, and sharing a conscious European identity. The Franco-British Council, which exists to promote and improve relations between the two countries and peoples, shed light on these assumptions at a conference on the teaching of history in France and Britain held in May 1993. The question of history teaching and national identity was well to the fore. Jean-Pierre Rioux, an Inspecteur-général de

1. François Crouzet, 'Problèmes de la communication franco-britannique aux XIXe et XXe siècles', *Revue Historique*, No. 515, juillet–septembre 1975, pp. 105–34, translated in François Crouzet, *Britain Ascendant: Comparative Studies in Franco-British Economic History* (Cambridge, 1990), Chapter 14; this version includes the two Postscripts referred to here.
2. SOFRES poll, June 1991, in SOFRES, *L'état de l'opinion, 1991* (Paris, 1992), p. 279.

l'Education nationale, observed that the teaching of history 'was and remains, in the eyes of the French, something which shapes the national consciousness'. National history, which had been in decline after the shocks of the 'events' of 1968 and the Third World emphasis encouraged in the 1970s, was back in favour as a means of dealing with 'the crises of republican values and the strains on the fabric of society in a time of recession . . .'.[3] Antoine Prost, an eminent French historian of education, quoted President Mitterrand as telling his Cabinet on 31 August 1982: 'A nation which does not teach its own history is a nation which loses its identity.' The speaker emphasised that this was not simply the President's personal view: he was 'expressing an opinion which the French currently hold to be true, one that is almost a platitude'. Prost expressed some reservations about such a view, but finally came somewhere near it: 'It [history] is the tool with which French society has thought about itself . . . by gradually defining, not a political consensus, but the civilised means of living through the conflict [of political values]. In this sense, it is correct to say that it is an essential part of the national identity.'[4]

In marked contrast, a British participant in the conference explained that Britain 'no longer seemed to have any clear consensus about its identity and the extent to which the teaching of history should in any way be used specifically to strengthen or even illuminate it. . .'. There was a school of thought which believed that national identity did not exist, and that any attempt to create one was evil. Others deeply resented this attitude, and wished to resist its influence. Somewhere in the wings was a third view, that the way out of the problem was to subsume British history in a European framework and outlook.[5] This contribution was probably typical of the uncertainties prevailing in history teaching in Britain; and if so there was little in common between the British and French approaches to the question.

The conference also considered surveys of knowledge and attitudes in primary schools. In England, a survey showed that the standard picture of France remained one of frogs' legs, snails and the Eiffel tower (which once charmingly appeared as the Eifful tower); though the children had also noted that the French seemed rich and lived in

---

3. Franco-British Council, *History Teaching in Secondary Schools in France and Britain* (conference held 21–23 May 1993); copy of conclusions and papers kindly communicated by the Director of the British Section of the Council. The quotations are from Jean-Pierre Rioux, 'La place de l'enseignement de l'histoire en France et de l'histoire de la Grande-Bretagne à l'intérieur de cet enseignement'.

4. Ibid., Antoine Prost, 'History Teaching and National Identity in France'.

5. Ibid., 'History Teaching and National Identity in Britain'. The writer remained anonymous.

'posh' houses. Many children had already visited France, and attitudes were in general friendly, reflecting an air of holidays and relaxation. It was also clear that television had a marked influence.[6] A French survey on the same matters was more formal and carefully structured. Its authors observed that primary school children had a strongly pronounced sense of national identity. The children also held some clear historical views, notably that the long rivalries with both England and Germany were over, 'resolved by the restitution to France of her due (Calais, Alsace-Lorraine)'. The words, of course, are those of the reporters, not the children; even so, the juxtaposition of these two widely different examples is striking. On the two World Wars of the twentieth century, the report summed up French children's views as being that the French had been at war with the Germans, and the English had helped them. But, the report went on, 'those times are over and the word "entente" doesn't enter their vocabulary; there is no notion of a common purpose or duty'.[7]

In general, the organisers of the conference concluded, in relation to children at primary schools, that: 'The very absence of any prejudices reflects a certain decline in interest. On both sides of the Channel, the traditional enemy – or at least rival – may have been less benevolent, but gave cause for greater reflection. The pupil no longer has prejudices about the other country; equally, he or she has little perception of the place which it has occupied – and still occupies – in his or her own national destiny ... the pupils arriving in secondary schools have neither mutual prejudices nor any feeling of solidarity or community.'[8] This was not far removed from Crouzet's view that the old love–hate relationship was sliding into a mere indifference.

These snapshots showed members of a family who regarded one another with a listless unconcern, tempered only by holiday contacts or dim historical memories. In May 1994, on the other hand, the British Foreign Office and the French Ministry of Foreign Affairs combined to produce a joint brochure, published in both countries and in both languages, putting relations between the two countries, and their views of one another, in the best possible light. Beautifully produced and imaginatively illustrated, the pamphlet stressed the similarities between the two countries, and bestowed a rose-tinted glance on their long historical relationship, quoting de Gaulle to the

6. Ibid., Robert Guyver, 'What English and Welsh Primary Children know about France and French History at the transition to Secondary School'.
7. Ibid., Report and Recommendations, p. 2.
8. Ibid., Report and Recommendations, pp. 2–3.

effect that France and England had for centuries been the homes and champions of liberty, and Churchill on the French contribution to the glory and culture of Europe. It recalled the comradeship in arms forged in the two World Wars. It observed that military co-operation still flourished, citing the jointly produced Jaguar aircraft and the way in which French and British contingents worked together in Bosnia. There were several pages on commercial and cultural relations, sporting fixtures, student exchanges, town-twinning and co-operation in scientific research. The booklet concluded by emphasising the regularity of high-level political contacts at the annual Franco-British summit meetings, and by claiming that the two countries were allies in the world and partners in Europe.[9] The whole picture was too Panglossian to carry much conviction, and it is hard to conceive that even the brochure's authors really believed in its contents; but it was significant that the two Foreign Ministries (and Ministers) thought the effort worth making. As on the occasion of state visits, it was important that the two governments took the trouble to be on their best behaviour, and to produce the equivalent of a carefully posed family group, gathered on the occasion of an important anniversary.

In September 1994 Sir Charles Powell, for many years an adviser on foreign policy to Margaret Thatcher and then John Major, tried to sum up the state of Franco-British relations in a series of programmes on BBC radio.[10] He found that the British were much more concerned, or even obsessed, with the French than the other way round. 'There was an air of polite puzzlement among the French whom I interviewed as to why the relationship was thought worthy of special attention.' Yet Jacques Attali, formerly a close adviser (and self-appointed Boswell) to President Mitterrand, seemed not at all puzzled, and was indeed absolutely forthright. 'Here in Paris when we look at Europe we look at Germany, when we look at culture we look at Italy, when we look at a movie we look at the United States ... England is something which is not a standard for anything, unfortunately ...'[11] Powell himself observed that a young British diplomat who had been seconded to the Quai d'Orsay for a time had reported at the end of her stay that the French Foreign Ministry paid

9. Foreign and Commonwealth Office, Ministère des Affaires Etrangères, *France/Great Britain: The Entente Cordiale Today; France/Grande-Bretagne: L'Entente cordiale aujourd'hui* (London and Paris, 1994).

10. *Entente Cordiale*, BBC News and Current Affairs programme in four parts, 8–29 Sept. 1994, transcript kindly communicated by Sir Charles Powell; cf. article by Sir Charles Powell under the same title, *Spectator*, 3 Sept. 1994, pp. 8–10.

11. *Entente Cordiale*, transcript, p. 5.

very little attention to Britain, whereas the Foreign Office was constantly concerned about French views. There were good reasons for this. Britain saw France as a great continental power, standing across British routes to Europe, both geographical and political. The French, on the other hand, regarded Germany as the key to European questions and to their own security. Even in matters of language and culture, about which the French were so sensitive, it was the United States, not Britain, that posed the main threat.

Powell found something to put on the positive side. The British and French had combined to achieve what he described as 'the two greatest collaborative achievements of this century – Concorde and the Channel Tunnel'. He believed that the Tunnel would have 'a profound psychological impact' on British attitudes. Already businessmen and commercial companies were proving more successful than politicians in overcoming differences between the two countries – for example, Marks & Spencer had achieved a striking success in Paris. People in general were mingling with one another. Some 9 million people travelled from Britain to or through France each year; 60,000 had bought houses in France. Younger people took Europe for granted, after many exchange visits arranged by schools, towns or individuals.[12]

But Europe remained a crucial problem. Powell quoted Margaret Thatcher declaring at Bruges in 1988 that 'We have not successfully rolled back the frontiers of the state in Britain only to see them reimposed at European level, with a European super-state exercising a new dominance from Brussels'. He contrasted this with Jacques Attali saying that the French had given up their Empire, but 'France didn't give up its ideal of being a universal nation'. Instead, the French people had transferred their ideas of 'universal dominance' to Europe.[13] Powell found these remarks 'disarmingly frank'. 'The leadership of Europe', he observed, 'is the key issue round which the relations of Britain and France will revolve. At present it is exercised by France and Germany. Somehow Britain has to find a way to break into the magic circle' – which would be very difficult.[14]

Powell summed up on a note of optimism and exhortation: '. . . now it is the people who are doing most to show that Britain and France can get on: the shoppers, trippers, students, home-owners and businessmen for whom the ancient rivalries which immobilise the

---

12. Ibid., transcript, p. 36; *Spectator* article, p. 9.
13. *Entente Cordiale*, transcript, p. 29.
14. Ibid., transcript, p. 31; *Spectator* article, p. 10.

governing elites seem irrelevant and out-of-date. It's time for governments to catch up.'[15]

But there was a problem even among the shoppers, trippers, home-owners and businessmen who crossed the Channel in such large numbers. Statistics confirm that there was a large increase in movement across the Channel over the ten years up to 1994; but they also reveal striking differences according to the direction of that movement. From 1984 to 1994, visits to France by residents of the United Kingdom (not including those who simply passed through on the way to another country) more than doubled. Figures for French visits to Britain also rose, but they were at a far lower level. The contrast is best shown by a table:

	1984	1994
Visits to France by UK residents (in thousands)	4,482	9,009
Visits from France to UK (in thousands)	1,632	2,779

These figures show that traffic across the Channel has increased dramatically; but also that the flow is greater from Britain to France rather than vice versa, by a ratio of about three to one. Other figures confirm this picture. British business visits to France rose from 532,000 in 1984 to 1,004,000 in 1994; French business visits to Britain rose from 380,000 to 733,000 for the same years. The average length of stay for British visitors to France fluctuated between 6.3 and 7.7 days; for French visitors to Britain it declined sharply – 8 days in 1984, 7.2 in 1989, 5.3 in 1994.[16] The general picture is clear, and provides further confirmation that the British are more interested in France than the other way about.

These snapshots leave different impressions. The official picture presented by the two Foreign Ministries is too rose-coloured to carry conviction. The concept of growing indifference, of two countries losing their old antagonisms and old friendships in a morass of indifference, has more substance, but leaves too much out of account. The most convincing picture is that of a Britain which retains a keen, and sometimes even profound, interest in France and things French, facing a France where that interest is only very partially reciprocated. It

15. *Spectator* article, p. 10.
16. British Tourist Authority, *Digest of Tourist Statistics*, No. 19, Dec. 1995, pp. 50, 52–3, 58, 22, 30, 40. All figures are taken from the International Passenger Survey. They relate to numbers of visits, not of visitors, and include visits from a day trip to a stay of up to twelve months, but not transits to other countries.

was not always thus, and other snapshots a few years hence may tell a different story.

The Treaty of Dunkirk, an alliance between France and Britain, was signed on 4 March 1947, and was to remain valid for 50 years. It will therefore expire, unless renewed, on 4 March 1997. The occasion will surely provoke some reflection on the state of Franco-British relations. In April 2004 the centenary of the *Entente cordiale* will come round, and such is the tenacity and longevity of that phrase that the event is almost bound to be marked in some way. It is reasonable to enquire how far a basis still exists for either an alliance or an *entente* between the two countries.

For an alliance, it is necessary for the partners to have common – or at least similar – interests; to possess confidence that undertakings to one another will be carried out; and to practise co-operation in practical, day-to-day affairs. It helps to have a strong similarity in political and cultural outlook; though alliances have been known to span some wide differences in that regard. It is vital to have a common enemy, and the Treaty of Dunkirk in 1947 was specifically directed against Germany, which had been the common enemy of France and Britain, on and off, for the past 40 years and more. On this vital criterion, the old alliance is already defunct in spirit. In 1994 a French journalist, after a glowing testimonial to the extent of France's debt to England in the past, wrote that 'Europe was built yesterday and will be strengthened tomorrow by the entente and union between France and Germany'.[17] In present circumstances, that is surely true. If France had to choose between Germany and Britain, it is hard to see any grounds for choosing Britain.

For an *entente*, or understanding, the requirements are less exacting: a similar outlook, compatible interests, and a broad confidence in one another. *Entente cordiale* is the phrase that has stuck to Franco-British relations for many years, and it may well be that there is still some adhesive quality at work. The two countries share a common civilisation; they have a marked similarity of political and cultural outlook; and they have a common history, even if it is a story of conflict as much as friendship. On this basis, much understanding still exists. Hardly any Britons feel that they are in a strange land when they cross the Channel. We are at home, though some of the furniture is different. The same is very likely true of the French who make the reverse journey – even though they are fewer in number. On other matters, problems arise. How far are French and British interests

17. Jean-Pierre Richardot, 'France-Grande-Bretagne, mille ans de mésentente cordiale', *Réforme*, 7 May 1994.

compatible, especially while the issue of European integration looms so large? How much confidence do they have in one another, and when does suspicion or doubt arise? There remains some foundation for an *entente*, but it would take a bold surveyor to define its precise extent and its load-bearing capacity.

History and geography can tell us something. History, from Roman times to the present day, shows that the peoples on the two sides of the Channel have always had contacts with one another, though their intensity and warmth have varied from time to time. Indifference has prevailed on occasion, but has not persisted. Geography determines that when the British look across the Channel, France fills the horizon. When they approach Europe as travellers, it is usually to France that they go first, and in France they often remain. This simple geographical fact has had many consequences in personal, cultural and intellectual concerns. For France, geography is different and produces different consequences. France is partly Mediterranean in character; the pull of the south is strong, even in the simplest sense that there is a constant drain of population towards the *Midi* – and even more who would like to go. France also has a border on the Rhine, and has looked eastwards in a way which long predates the present relationship with Germany. Only part of France looks northwards, and the view across the Channel often has less to offer than the vibrant sunshine of the Mediterranean or the romantic scenery and thriving commerce of the Rhine.

History ties the two countries together, and will not be denied. Geography puts them in very different positions from one another, from which it follows that British concern with France, in friendship or hostility, in admiration or dismay, is usually greater than French concern with Britain. So be it. On the British side of the Channel there will long be many who say 'Vive la France, quand même!', and hope to hear an echo from across the narrow seas.

Bibliographical Essay

The following bibliographical essay is an indication of books which I have found particularly illuminating, and to which the reader may turn for further information, enlightenment and often entertainment. It makes no claim to be exhaustive. The place of publication is London for books in English and Paris for those in French, unless otherwise stated.

GENERAL

The bibliographical essay in P.M.H. Bell, *France and Britain 1900–1940: Entente and Estrangement* (1996) offers guidance to general works on relations between the two countries. The reader in search of an introduction to the subject should start with Richard Faber, *French and English* (1975); Douglas Johnson, François Bédarida and François Crouzet, eds, *Britain and France: Ten Centuries* (Folkestone, 1980); and Robert Gibson, *Best of Enemies: Anglo-French Relations since the Norman Conquest* (1995).

The separate histories of the two countries in the general period of this book are essential background to their relations with one another. For Britain, see the admirable treatment in Kenneth O. Morgan, *The People's Peace. British History 1945–1990* (1990; paperback edn, 1992). It is also useful to see a view from the other side of the Channel in the latter part of Roland Marx, *Histoire de l'Angleterre* (1993). David Reynolds provides a succinct analysis of Britain's position in the world in *Britannia Overruled. British Policy and World Power in the Twentieth*

Century (1991). On France, British readers have been very well served by Maurice Larkin, *France since the Popular Front. Government and People, 1936–1986* (1988), and James F. McMillan, *Twentieth Century France* (1992). For the European context, there is a valuable short guide in John W. Young, *Cold War Europe, 1945–1989: A Political History* (1991); while the development of European integration is described in detail in Pierre Gerbet, *La construction de l'Europe* (1983). The process of decolonisation, shared by both France and Britain, may be followed in R.F. Holland, *European Decolonisation, 1918–1981* (1985). J.D. Hargreaves, *Decolonisation in Africa* (1988) distils the author's immense knowledge and experience into a lucid analysis.

Questions relating to atomic and nuclear weapons have formed a strand in Franco-British relations throughout the period. On the British side, Margaret Gowing's official history, *Independence and Deterrence* (2 vols, 1974) is detailed and indispensable; see also other points of view in Andrew Pierre, *Nuclear Politics. The British Experience with an Independent Strategic Force, 1939–1970* (1972), and Eric Grove, *Vanguard to Trident: British Naval Policy since World War II* (1987). On the French side, André Martel, ed., *Histoire militaire de la France*, vol. IV, *De 1940 à nos jours* (1994) contains sections on atomic and nuclear weapons; Centre des Hautes Etudes de l'Armement, *Histoire de l'armement en France, 1914–1962* (1994) includes valuable papers on the same subject. Accounts by non-French authors may be found in Wilfrid L. Kohl, *French Nuclear Diplomacy* (Princeton, 1971) and Wolf Mendl, *Deterrence and Persuasion. French Nuclear Armament in the Context of National Policy* (1970). Bertrand Goldschmidt, who was in the atomic research team during the Second World War, and then participated in French atomic and nuclear policy as both scientist and administrator, has written a number of books which combine personal experience with detached analysis: *L'aventure atomique* (1962); *Les rivalités atomiques, 1939–1966* (1967); *Le complexe atomique* (1980). Goldschmidt possesses the art of making his difficult subject easily comprehensible to the non-scientific reader.

Another subject which has both brought the two countries together and divided them is the Channel Tunnel. The background is explained in Keith Wilson's vivid and entertaining *Channel Tunnel Visions, 1850–1945: Dreams and Nightmares* (1995). Accounts which bring the story up to recent times include: L. Bonnaud, *Le Tunnel sous la Manche. Deux siècles de passion* (1994); B. Lemoine, *Le Tunnel sous la Manche* (1994); Bernard Sasso and Lyne Cohen-Solal, *Le Tunnel sous la Manche: Chronique d'une passion franco-anglaise* (Lyon, 1987); Bernard Sasso, *Le Tunnel sous la Manche* (1994).

VIEWS ACROSS THE CHANNEL

To observe and report on France has long been a favourite British occupation, and its practitioners have been learned, sympathetic and entertaining. At the end of the Second World War, Denis Brogan gathered a number of his essays into a book, *French Personalities and Problems* (1946), which retains a remarkable freshness. Alexander Werth, who wrote prolifically on France in the 1930s, continued the flow with *France 1940–1955* (1956); *The Strange History of Pierre Mendès-France and the Great Conflict over French North Africa* (1957); and *The de Gaulle Revolution* (1960). Charles Morgan was a strongly Franco-phile novelist and writer, whose *Selected Letters*, edited by Eiluned Lewis (1967) contain some illuminating side-lights. Harold Nicolson was another writer whose attachment to France spanned the period from the 1920s to the 1950s: see James Lees-Milne, *Harold Nicolson* (2 vols, 1980, 1981). The post-war years saw new generations of journalists, academics and other writers, who show every sign of continuing to flourish. Catherine Gavin, *Liberated France* (1955) was a vivid first-hand account. Philip Williams wrote a series of studies of French politics: see, for example, *Wars, Plots and Scandals in Post-War France* (1970) and *Crisis and Compromise: Politics in the Fourth Republic* (1972). Arthur Koestler, ed., *Suicide of a Nation?* (1963) was about the state of Britain, but the contributors frequently chose to illuminate their subject by comparisons with France. Dorothy Pickles, an experienced observer of French affairs, summed up her impressions in *France* (1964), and then added an assessment of Franco-British relations in *The Uneasy Entente* (1967). John Ardagh began a series of books on France with *The New French Revolution. A Social and Economic Survey of France, 1945–1967* (1968); see also *The New France. De Gaulle and After* (1970); *France Today* (1987, frequently reissued). Christopher Sinclair-Stevenson, *That Sweet Enemy. A Personal View of France and the French* (1987) offers more than its modest sub-title promises. Theodore Zeldin, *The French* (1983) succeeds in being both idiosyncratic and encyclopaedic. John Laughland, *The Death of Politics: France under Mitterrand* (1994) provides a sharp antidote to some of the more admiring accounts of contemporary France.

Among French discussions of Britain, Pierre Bourdan (the pseudonym of Pierre Maillaud), *Perplexités et grandeur de l'Angleterre* (1945) stands out as the apogee of French admiration of wartime Britain – detailed, glowing but not uncritical; it should be read in conjunction with the same author's *Carnet des jours d'attente* (1945), which is a brief, informal account of his wartime experiences. Jacques Debû-Bridel, *Carthage n'est pas détruite* (1945) is a lighter work, more propagandist in tone, but full of a genuine regard for British courage and public spirit. The next wave of French discussion of British affairs, after a long gap, was in large part the analysis of decline. François David, *Autopsie de l'Angleterre* (1976) was, as the author writes, the result of disillusionment. Philippe Daudy, *Les Anglais* (1989), translated as *The English* (1991), contrived to see decline through rose-coloured spectacles, and no longer carries conviction. François Bédarida, *La société anglaise du milieu du XIXe siècle à nos jours* (1979; revised edn, with a new section on the period 1975–90, 1990) is thorough, balanced and almost painfully perceptive. François Crouzet, *De la supériorité de l'Angleterre sur la France* (1985), translated as *Britain Ascendent. Comparative Studies in Franco-British Economic History* (1990), deals mainly with the nineteenth century (whence the title), but includes the author's article on 'Problèmes de la communication franco-britannique aux XIXe et XXe siècles'; the translation also includes two recent postscripts to that article. Daniel Depland, *Trafalgar* (1995) is lightweight and humorous journalism, but it is salutary for a British reader to see what sort of impression is left by current events on a by no means unsympathetic observer.

No student of Franco-British relations can ignore the anxiety of the French Establishment about the current status and future prospects of the French language. René Etiemble, *Parlez-vous franglais?* (1964) is the vital starting-point. This question tends to be bound up much more with American cultural influence than with British. On French sentiments towards the United States, see Denis Lacorne, ed., *L'Amérique dans les têtes* (1986), translated as *The Rise and Fall of Anti-Americanism. A century of French perception* (1990).

Two excellent journals are devoted to the current affairs and recent past of the two countries: in Britain, *Modern and Contemporary France*, and in France *La Revue française de civilisation britannique*. Lively and illuminating discussions of different aspects of current relations between the two countries took place in 'Entente Cordiale', a series of four broadcasts on BBC Radio Four in September 1994, and at a conference organised in May 1993 by the Franco-British Council on 'History Teaching in Secondary Schools in France and Britain'. The Franco-British Council, with sections in each country, does much to encourage the two countries and peoples to understand one another.

THE SECOND WORLD WAR

On the events of 1940, the defeat of France and the parting of the ways between France and Britain, the essential book on the French side is Jean-Louis Cremieux-Brilhac, *Les Français de l'an 40* (2 vols, 1990), which is the best analysis of the whole context of the French defeat. The British reaction to the defeat is described in P.M.H. Bell, *A Certain Eventuality. Britain and the Fall of France* (Farnborough, 1974). On the painful and still controversial British attack on the French fleet in July 1940, see Arthur J. Marder, *From the Dardanelles to Oran* (1974), and the recently published documents in Michael Simpson, ed., *The Somerville Papers* (1996); on the French side, see the careful discussion in Hervé Coutau-Bégarie and Claude Huan, *Mers-el-Kébir (1940). La rupture franco-britannique* (1994).

Wartime relations between France and Britain are dealt with in J-B. Duroselle, *L'abîme 1939–1945* (1982) and Sir Llewellyn Woodward's official history, *British Foreign Policy in the Second World War* (1962) – there is a six-volume edition for those in search of detail. R.T. Thomas, *Britain and Vichy. The Dilemma of Anglo-French Relations, 1940–42* (1979) is a valuable analysis; and A.B. Gaunson, *The Anglo-French Clash in Lebanon and Syria, 1940–45* (1987) is a balanced and careful account of a thorny subject. The complicated background to the Anglo-American landings in North Africa in November 1942 is elucidated in Arthur L. Funk, *The Politics of TORCH* (Lawrence, Kansas, 1974).

Relations between the British and the French Resistance are dealt with in detail (and with a keen eye to human interest) by M.R.D. Foot, *SOE in France. An Account of the Work of the British Special Operations Executive in France, 1940–1944* (1966). Hugh Verity, *We Landed by Moonlight. Secret RAF Landings in France, 1940–1944* (Wilmslow, 1995) tells a fascinating story, and includes a systematic list of all known RAF pick-up flights to France; the author himself flew many of the missions he describes. Hilary Footitt and John Simmonds, *France 1943–1945* (Leicester, 1988), a volume in 'The Politics of Liberation' series edited by Geoffrey Warner, is a careful review of the problems of civil affairs and British relations with de Gaulle and the Resistance. André Gillois, *Histoire secrète des Français à Londres de 1940 à 1944* (1973) is a readable, somewhat gossipy, account of the French in exile. Jean-Louis Crémieux-Brilhac's history of *France Libre* is due to be published in 1996. Antony Beevor and Artemis Cooper, *Paris after the Liberation* (1994) gives a lively, impressionistic picture of the time when the British rediscovered Paris.

The Vichy regime, its policies towards Britain, and the state of public opinion in France still form difficult subjects. Jean-Pierre Azéma and François Bédarida, eds, *Le régime de Vichy et les Français* (1990) publishes papers presented at a conference held in June 1990, and is full of illuminating detail and reflections. Pierre Laborie, *L'opinon française sous Vichy* (1990) is a valuable analysis of an obscure but vital subject. Henry Rousso, *Le syndrome de Vichy* (2nd edn, 1990) is an interesting assessment of how later French opinion has tried to come to terms with the Vichy episode, while François-Georges Dreyfus, *Histoire de Vichy* (1990) is a solid and up to date account of its subject. Herbert R. Lottman, *Pétain: Hero or Traitor?* (1985) is more subtle than its simplistic title might imply; Hervé Coutau-Begérie and Claude Huan, *Darlan* (1989) is a thorough and balanced biography. On Laval, see Geoffrey Warner, *Pierre Laval and the Eclipse of France* (1968) and Fred Kupferman, *Laval* (1987).

The war years form the best place to mention books about, and by, two of the towering figures in relations between Britain and France: Churchill and de Gaulle. Their influence, of course, continued well after the war, and in the case of de Gaulle was of decisive weight in the 1960s. Three volumes of Martin Gilbert's massive biography of *Winston S. Churchill* deal with the period under review here: *Finest Hour, 1939–1941* (1983); *Road to Victory, 1941–1945* (1986); *Never Despair, 1945–1965* (1988). Robert Blake and William Roger Louis, eds, *Churchill* (1993) is a collection of papers by many contributors, including an illuminating and entertaining essay on 'Churchill and France' by Douglas Johnson. Elisabeth Barker, *Churchill and Eden at War* (1978) is excellent on both statesmen, and also includes what remains the best brief account of relations between Britain and de Gaulle during the war. Churchill's own war memoirs, *The Second World War* (6 vols, 1948–54) include much on relations with France – see especially vol. II, *Their Finest Hour*, and vol. VI, *Triumph and Tragedy*. On de Gaulle, the commanding biography is Jean Lacouture, *De Gaulle*, vol. I, *Le rebelle, 1890–1944* (1984); vol. II, *Le politique, 1944–1959* (1985); vol. III, *Le souverain, 1959–1970* (1986). There is a translation, somewhat abridged: *De Gaulle: The Rebel, 1890–1944* (1990), and *De Gaulle: The Ruler, 1945–1970* (1992). Among biographies in English, Charles Williams, *The Last Great Frenchman. A Life of General de Gaulle* (1993) stands out for its insight and narrative skill; Bernard Ledwidge, *De Gaulle* (1982) includes valuable comments by an experienced diplomat. De Gaulle's memoirs, which must be approached as a carefully wrought work of art, have much to say about Britain and the British: *Mémoires de Guerre*, vol. I, *L'appel* (1954);

vol. II, *L'unité* (1956); vol. III, *Le salut* (1959); see also his later volumes on his time as President, *Mémoires d'espoir* (2 vols, one incomplete, 1970, 1971). There are translations: *War Memoirs* (3 vols, 1955, 1959, 1960); *Memoirs of Hope* (1971). François Kersaudy, *Churchill and de Gaulle* (1981) gives a detailed and lively account of an extraordinary relationship.

Several other individuals had much influence on relations between Britain and France during the war years, and often afterwards. On the British side, Eden was particularly important, mediating between Churchill and de Gaulle and with a strong sense of France's role in the world. See David Carlton, *Anthony Eden* (1981), which is often critical; and the more sympathetic account in Robert Rhodes James, *Anthony Eden* (1986); a revealing study by David Dutton is to appear shortly. Eden himself dealt with the war years in one of his volumes of memoirs: Lord Avon, *The Eden memoirs: The Reckoning* (1965). Duff Cooper was closely involved in Franco-British relations, first as Minister-Resident in Algiers, and then as Ambassador in Paris: see Lord Norwich, *Old Men Forget. The Autobiography of Duff Cooper* (1953), and John Charmley, *Duff Cooper. The Authorised Biography* (1986). Harold Macmillan's acquaintance with de Gaulle, later to be so important, began in wartime Algiers: see Harold Macmillan, *War Diaries. Politics and War in the Mediterranean, January 1943–May 1945* (1984), and Alistair Horne, *Macmillan*, vol. I, *1894–1956* (1988) (volume II is referred to later). There are two invaluable diaries by diplomats who were much concerned with the French: David Dilks, ed., *The Diaries of Sir Alexander Cadogan, 1938–1945* (1971); John Harvey, ed., *The War Diaries of Oliver Harvey* (1978).

On the French side, Jean Monnet had already been involved in Franco-British co-operation during the First World War, and resumed his role during the Second; his greatest significance was achieved as one of the architects of European integration. See Jean Monnet, *Mémoires* (1976), and the translation (by Richard Mayne, himself a historian of European integration), *Memoirs* (1978); also the biography by François Duchêne, *Jean Monnet. The First Statesman of Interdependence* (1994). René Massigli's memoirs, *Une comédie des erreurs* (1978) deal with the war years, and even more with the post-war period; they are a delight to read. Hervé Alphand, *L'étonnement d'être: Journal 1939–1973* (1977) covers much the same period, and is full of sharp and revealing comment.

THE POST-WAR PERIOD, 1945–57, AND
GENERAL ASPECTS

Directly on the subject of Franco-British relations, see the detailed study by John W. Young, *Britain, France and the Unity of Europe, 1945–51* (Leicester, 1984). There is a wide-ranging collection of essays, edited by Françoise de la Serre, Jacques Leruez and Helen Wallace, *Les politiques étrangères de la France et de la Grande-Bretagne depuis 1945* (1990); the writers pursue their discussion through into the 1980s. John Kent, *The Internationalisation of Colonialism. Britain, France and Black Africa, 1939–1956* (1992) is a detailed study of little-known attempts at co-operation between the two countries in Africa. On the European movement which came to divide France and Britain so deeply, there are many books. Particularly valuable are: Alan S. Milward, *The Reconstruction of Western Europe, 1945–51* (1984), and the same author's *The European Rescue of the Nation-State* (1992) – both books combine great detail with thought-provoking vigour. Brian Brivati and Harriet Jones, eds, *From Reconstruction to Integration: Britain and Europe since 1945* (Leicester, 1993) is a valuable collection of essays. William Nicoll and Trevor C. Salmon, *Understanding the New European Community* (Hemel Hempstead, 1990) is a good, straightforward guide to complicated matters, with useful tables and diagrams. Among French books on the same subject, Pierre Gerbet's *La construction de l'Europe* (1983) has already been mentioned, and remains a key work. Gérard Bossuat, *Les fondateurs de l'Europe* (1994) is a useful introduction, again with tables and diagrams.

On British policy, the key book on the post-war years is Alan Bullock, *Ernest Bevin*, vol. III, *Foreign Secretary, 1945–1951* (1983) – packed with detail, and drawing strength from the characters of both subject and author. Ritchie Ovendale, ed., *The Foreign Policy of the British Labour Governments, 1945–1951* (Leicester, 1984) is a collection of essays, including Frank Roberts on Bevin and Geoffrey Warner on western Europe. Saki Dockrill, *Britain's Policy for West German Rearmament, 1950–1955* (1991) discusses a subject which had considerable effects on Franco-British relations. Among first-hand accounts, Lord Avon, *The Eden Memoirs: Full Circle* (1960) has much material which is *not* about the Suez crisis, though that is the centre of the book. George Mallaby, *From My Level. Unwritten Minutes* (1965) is more enlightening and entertaining than its title might indicate; the author held, among other posts, that of Secretary-General of the Brussels Treaty Organisation, where he witnessed some sharp exchanges between Montgomery and de Lattre de Tassigny. Evelyn

Shuckburgh, *Descent to Suez. Diaries, 1951–56*, selected for publication by John Charmley (1986), is full of interest, and again not only about Suez. Lord Gladwyn, *The Memoirs of Lord Gladwyn* (1972) is urbane and illuminating, especially on the author's time as Ambassador in Paris.

On the French side, Pierre Gerbet, *Le relèvement, 1944–1949* (1991) is immensely detailed and informative; Gerbet was assisted by four other authors. Alfred Grosser, *Affaires extérieures. La politique de la France, 1944–1984* (1984) is a sweeping survey of its period. Frédéric Bozo, *La France et l'OTAN. De la guerre froide au nouvel ordre européen* (1990) traces a subject which was important for Franco–British relations from 1949 to 1990. Raymond Poidevin, *Robert Schuman: homme d'état, 1886–1963* (1986) is a scholarly and sympathetic biography. Vincent Auriol, *Mon septennat, 1947–1954: notes de journal présentées par Pierre Nora et Jacques Ożouf* (1970) is invaluable; those in search of further detail may refer to the full edition in seven volumes. Denis Lefèbvre, *Guy Mollet. Le mal aimé* (1992) explains a somewhat obscure figure who suddenly achieved prominence in Franco–British relations in 1956. Jean Chauvel, *Commentaire*, vol. II, *D'Alger à Berne, 1944–1952* (1972), and vol. III, *De Berne à Paris, 1952–1962* (1973) are useful – and sometimes very sharp – diplomatic memoirs. (The reader should also refer to the books about, or by, Jean Monnet, René Massigli and Hervé Alphand, noted above.) A valuable short work on what became a key element in French policy is Julius W. Friend, *The Linchpin. French-German Relations, 1950–1990* (New York, 1991). Hubert Bonin, *Histoire économique de la IV République* (1987) contrives to be both detailed and readable on a crucial subject.

The Suez crisis of 1956 has attracted an enormous literature in a short time; the following are a few of the most useful books for tracing Franco–British relations through this labyrinth. Keith Kyle, *Suez 1956* (1991) is an excellent, detailed narrative history. William Roger Louis and Roger Owen, eds, *Suez 1956. The Crisis and its Consequences* (1989), and Selwyn Ilan Troen and Moshe Shemesh, eds, *The Suez–Sinai Crisis, 1956* (1990) are scholarly collections of essays arising out of conferences; both contain invaluable contributions. David Carlton, *Britain and the Suez Crisis* (Oxford, 1988) is short, clear and to the point. W. Scott Lucas, *Divided We Stand. Britain, the US and the Suez Crisis* (1991) deals mainly with the subject declared in its title, but includes side-lights on relations between Britain and France. All these books draw on a wider range of sources than those available to Hugh Thomas at an earlier time; but Thomas's *The Suez Affair* (1966; 2nd edn, 1970) is still well worth reading.

French accounts of the Suez affair began with Merry and Serge Bromberger, *Les secrets de l'expédition de Suez* (1957), written by two well-informed journalists to put the case of the French Ministry of Defence. It remains valuable, and highly readable. Henri Azeau, *Le piège de Suez* (1964), also by a journalist, is solid in content and shrewd in its comments. Paul Gaujac, *Suez 1956* (1986) is a military history, with excellent charts and illustrations, and with much information on British as well as French military preparations for the expedition. A number of the French commanders have written valuable volumes of memoirs: André Beaufre, *L'expédition de Suez* (1967) is by one of the most intellectual of French generals; Paul Ely, *Mémoires*, vol. II, *Suez . . . le 13 mai* (1969) includes long extracts from notes taken by the author at the time; Jacques Massu and Henri le Mire, *La vérité sur Suez, 1956* (1978) is a work of collaboration between the fighting parachute commander and one of his staff. Abel Thomas, *Comment Israel fut sauvé. Les secrets de l'expédition de Suez* (1978) is by Bourgès-Maunoury's *chef de cabinet*, and presses to its extreme the view that the Suez campaign saved Israel from attack and probably extinction.

BRITAIN, FRANCE AND EUROPE, 1957–c. 1994

The first British application to join the EEC and de Gaulle's veto are dealt with in detail, with revealing extracts from Macmillan's diaries, in Alistair Horne, *Macmillan*, vol. II, *1957–1986* (1989). There is a first-rate contemporary account, full of shrewd and vigorous comment, in Nora Beloff, *The General Says No. Britain's Exclusion from Europe* (1963); and measured discussion by a powerful advocate of British entry in Lord Gladwyn, *De Gaulle's Europe; or Why the General Says No* (1969). Miriam Camps, *Britain and the European Community, 1955–63* (1964) was an early account by an academic writer, which remains valuable. On de Gaulle, see the books referred to in the section on the Second World War, and especially the biographies by Jean Lacouture and Charles Williams. Alain Peyrefitte, *C'était de Gaulle*, vol. I, *'La France redevient la France'* (1994) adds much detail – Peyrefitte set himself to be de Gaulle's Boswell, and records much fascinating conversation. J. Newhouse, *De Gaulle and the Anglo-Saxons* (New York, 1970) is a trans-Atlantic view, with much emphasis on the issue of nuclear weapons. Pierre Maillard, *De Gaulle et l'Allemagne. Le rêve inachevé* (1990) is a fascinating discussion, ranging from de Gaulle's experiences in German prisoner-of-war camps to his careful building of his relationship with Adenauer. The author was diplomatic adviser to de Gaulle in the crucial years, 1959–64, and helped the General to prepare his speeches to be delivered in German.

On the later British applications to join the EEC, see Ben Pimlott, *Harold Wilson* (1992); Philip Ziegler, *Harold Wilson* (1993) – the authorised biography; John Campbell, *Edward Heath: a biography* (1993); and Uwe Kitzinger, *Diplomacy and Persuasion: How Britain joined the Common Market* (1973).

On French personalities and policies in the period from c. 1975 to the early 1990s, two volumes of memoirs make good starting-points. Maurice Couve de Murville, *Une politique étrangère, 1958–69* (1971) gives a good impression of the author's firm, precise handling of French policy under the direction of General de Gaulle. Michel Jobert, *Mémoires d'avenir* (1974) goes into the Pompidou era. Charles Hargrove, *Valéry Giscard d'Estaing vu par un Anglais* (1981) is a perceptive book by a long-serving correspondent of *The Times* in Paris. Samy Cohen and Marie-Claude Smouts, eds, *La politique extérieure de Valéry Giscard d'Estaing* (1985) is a valuable collection of papers, originally given at a conference attended by both academics and participants in the events under discussion; it is significant that relations with Germany receive a chapter, but relations with Britain do not. On the Mitterrand Presidency, Jacques Attali, *Verbatim*, vol. I, *Chronique des années 1981–1986* (1993), vol. II, *1986–1988* (1995), and vol. III, *1988–1991* (1995) contain fascinating material – the author worked for much of the time in the next room to the President, and accompanied him on most of his travels, keeping a record of innumerable conversations. There is also much information in a book by two well-informed journalists, P. Favier and M. Martin-Rolland, *La décennie Mitterrand*, vol. I, *Les ruptures, 1981–1984* (1990). Jean-Marcel Jeanneney, ed., *L'économie française depuis 1967* (1989) includes much material on France and the EEC. P. McCarthy, ed., *France–Germany, 1983–1993. The Struggle to Co-operate* (1993) is a collection of papers on Franco-German relations; Julius W. Friend's *The Linchpin. Franco-German Relations, 1950–1990*, mentioned above, remains valuable on this period.

On the British side, Margaret Thatcher's memoirs, *The Downing Street Years* (1993) contain much of interest on relations with France. Christopher Johnson, *The Economy under Mrs Thatcher, 1979–1990* (1991) is a clear and judicious analysis, offering points of comparison with France. Studies across the Channel, where the 'Thatcher phenomenon' attracted a good deal of interest, include Jacques Leruez, *Le phénomène Thatcher* (Brussels, 1991), and Monica Charlot, ed., *L'effet*

Thatcher (1991). Two books by Nicholas Henderson are full of wisdom, wit and information: *Channels and Tunnels. Reflections on Britain and Abroad* (1987), and *Mandarin. The Diaries of an Ambassador, 1969–1982* (1994). The author was Ambassador in Paris, and later chairman of the company which made the successful bid to build the Channel Tunnel.

On issues concerning Franco–British relations within the EEC/European Union, Françoise de la Serre, *La Grande-Bretagne et la Communauté européenne* (1987) and Stephen George, *An Awkward Partner: Britain in the European Community* (1990) are both valuable guides. Andrea Boltho, ed., *The European Economy: Growth and Crisis* (1982) comprises some very solid papers, and is particularly useful for comparisons between countries within the EEC. This book is invaluable for understanding the complexities of the Common Agricultural Policy, on which another excellent work is Jean Chombart de Lauwe, *L'aventure agricole de la France de 1945 à nos jours* (1979). Alfred Grosser, ed., *Les politiques extérieures européennes dans la crise* (1976) deals with responses to the 'oil shock' of 1973. Peter Ludlow, *The Making of the European Monetary System* (1982) is a clear guide to a complicated subject whose ramifications are still very much with us.

Index